Children and Global Conflict

More than one billion people under the age of eighteen live in territories affected by armed conflict. Despite this, scholars and practitioners often lack a comprehensive knowledge of how children both struggle within and shape conflict zones. *Children and Global Conflict* provides this understanding with a view to enhancing the prospects of conflict resolution and peace building.

This book presents key ideas and issues relating to children's experiences of war, international relations and international law. The authors explore the political, conceptual and moral debates around children in these contexts and offer examples and solutions based on case studies of child soldiers from Vietnam, child forced migrants in Australia, young peace builders in post-conflict zones, youth in the international justice system, and child advocates across South Asia and the Middle East.

KIM HUYNH is Lecturer in Politics and International Relations at the Australian National University, Canberra. He teaches courses in refugee politics, political philosophy and international relations. He is author of *Where the Sea Takes Us* (2008) and *Vietnam as if* (2015), and co-editor with Jim George of *The Culture Wars: Australian and American Politics in the 21st Century* (2009).

BINA D'COSTA is a Fellow at the Peace, Conflict and War Studies Programme of the School of International, Political and Strategic Studies, the Australian National University and a Visiting Fellow at the Programme on Gender and Global Change, the Graduate Institute, Geneva. Her publications include *Nationbuilding: Gender and War Crimes in South Asia* (2011), *Gender and Global Politics in the Asia-Pacific* (2009) co-edited with Katrina Lee-Koo, and *Children and Violence: Politics of Conflict in South Asia* (2015).

KATRINA LEE-KOO is a Senior Lecturer in International Relations at Monash University. She teaches and researches in the areas of security studies and the gender/identity politics of conflict and post-conflict zones. She is co-editor of *Gender and Global Politics in the Asia-Pacific* (2009) with Bina D'Costa and co-author (with Anthony Burke and Matt McDonald) of *The Ethics of Global Security* (2014).

Children and Global Conflict

KIM HUYNH, BINA D'COSTA AND KATRINA
LEE-KOO

CAMBRIDGE
UNIVERSITY PRESS

CAMBRIDGE
UNIVERSITY PRESS

University Printing House, Cambridge CB2 8BS, United Kingdom

Cambridge University Press is part of the University of Cambridge.

It furthers the University's mission by disseminating knowledge in the pursuit of education, learning and research at the highest international levels of excellence.

www.cambridge.org
Information on this title: www.cambridge.org/9781107626980

© Kim Huynh, Bina D'Costa and Katrina Lee-Koo 2015

First published 2015

A catalogue record for this publication is available from the British Library

ISBN 978-1-107-03884-4 Hardback
ISBN 978-1-107-62698-0 Paperback

For our children – Xavier, William, Piyali and Aneesh

Contents

Contents   ix

Abbreviations

AIHRC	Afghanistan Independent Human Rights Commission
API and APII	Additional Protocols I and II to the Geneva Conventions of 1949
APMBC	Anti-Personnel Mine Ban Convention 1999
CAVR	Commission for Reception, Truth and Reconciliation (East Timor)
CCM	Convention on Cluster Munitions 2010
CEDAW	Convention to Eliminate all forms of Discrimination Against Women 1981
CRIN	Child Rights International Network
CRPD	Convention on the Rights of Persons with Disabilities 2008
CZOP	children as zones of peace
DRV	Democratic Republic of Congo
HRC	Human Rights Committee
IASFM	International Association for the Study of Forced Migration
ICC	International Criminal Court
ICRC	International Committee of the Red Cross
ICTR	International Criminal Tribunal for Rwanda
ICTY	International Criminal Tribunal for the former Yugoslavia
IDPs	internally displaced persons
IHL	international humanitarian law
ILO	International Labour Organization
IMA	Illegal Maritime Arrival
IR	international relations
ISAF	International Security Assistance Forces
LRA	Lord's Resistance Army (Uganda)
LTTE	Liberation Tigers of Tamil Eelam

MDGs	Millennium Development Goals
NGO	non-governmental organisation
NSSC	New Social Studies of Childhood
OSRSG-CaAC	Office of the Special Representative of the Secretary-General for Children and Armed Conflict
PEL	Practice of Everyday Life
R2P	Responsibility to Protect
RPF	Rwandan Patriotic Front
RUF	Revolutionary United Front of Sierra Leone
UNAMA	United Nations Assistance Mission in Afghanistan
UNCRC	United Nations Convention on the Rights of the Child 1989
UNGA	UN General Assembly
UNICEF	United Nations Children Fund
UNRWA	UN Relief and Works Agency
UNTAET	UN Transitional Authority in East Timor
UNDP	United Nations Development Programme
UNESCO	United Nations Education, Science and Cultural Organisation
UNHCR	United Nations High Commissioner for Refugees
UDHR	Universal Declaration of Human Rights

Introduction: why children matter to global conflict

BINA D'COSTA, KIM HUYNH AND KATRINA
LEE-KOO

Just over 1 billion children under the age of eighteen live in countries or territories affected by armed conflict; that is, almost every second child, or one-sixth of the total world population.[1] Of these, approximately 300 million are under the age of five.[2] In 2012, an estimated 17.9 million children were among displaced and vulnerable populations, of which there were around 5 million refugee children and 9 million internally displaced children.[3] In terms of sheer numbers and need, children clearly matter a great deal to global politics.

In recognition of this, the United Nations (UN) declared 2001–2010 to be the International Decade for a Culture of Peace and Non-Violence for the Children of the World. Given that the numbers of war-affected and displaced children remained largely constant over this period, it is worth

---

[1] A similar number of children live in poverty with there no doubt being a significant overlap in these populations. UNICEF, 'Children Living in Poverty'. Available at www.unicef.org/sowc05/english/poverty.html; UNICEF, *Machel Study 10-Year Strategic Review: Children and Conflict in a Changing World* (New York, NY: UNICEF, 2009). Available at www.unicef.org/publications/files/Machel_Study_10_Year_Strategic_Review_EN_030909.pdf.

[2] UNICEF, *Machel Study 10-Year Strategic Review* (2009), 10.

[3] These figures do not include Palestinian refugee children who are registered by the UN Relief and Works Agency for Palestinian refugees and do not necessarily fall under the 1951 UN Refugee Convention definition of a refugee. While there is a lack of comprehensive and reliable data with respect to Palestinian refugee children, one NGO estimates that close to half the 4.9 million Palestinian refugees registered with the UN Relief and Works Agency (UNRWA) are under the age of eighteen. UNHCR, 'Global Trends 2012: Displacement: The New 21st Century Global Challenge', 5. Available at http://unhcr.org/globaltrendsjune2013/; Badil Resource Center, 'Palestinian Refugee Children: International Protection and Durable Solutions', Information and Discussion Brief, 10 (January 2007), 5. Available at www.childmigration.net/Badil_07; Manara Network for Child Rights, 'Mapping Child Protection Systems in Place for Palestinian Refugee Children in the Middle East', (August 2011), 21. Available at http://mena.savethechildren.se/PageFiles/2131/Mapping%20Protection%20Systems%20August%202011.pdf.

looking back and asking some fundamental questions about what might be done to assist children in conflict zones. Are children any more or less deserving of peace than adults? Are they instinctively peaceful? Do they only become violent when raised improperly or within a conflict-ridden environment? Should campaigns for peace and non-violence incorporate children as a means of sustaining that mission across generations? How do we, as adults, scholars and policymakers meaningfully talk about and make representations for 'the children of the world'?

These types of questions go to the core of *Children and Global Conflict*. Put succinctly, this book is concerned with the confluence of children, armed conflict, and the international responses to both. It illustrates how children can represent both the reason for waging war and the reason to move towards peace. The first half of the book focuses on the philosophical, theoretical and legal debates over how to conceptualise war-affected children. The second half applies these ideas to major issues relating to children and global conflict; namely, child soldiers, forced migration, peace building, justice and advocacy. The book considers the impact of these issues on children and how they in turn shape these issues in their own interests, according to their own principles, and for the sake of their own communities.

The central argument of *Children and Global Conflict* is that children are customarily viewed by international actors as victims whose lives have been shattered by war; when they are acknowledged as active participants, they are primarily deemed wayward and dangerous. Along with being narrow and simplistic, this perspective does little to address the marginalisation and disempowerment of children, or to prevent the spread of conflict. While many children are undoubtedly traumatised by violence and combat, they also commonly endure hardship and resist persecution and external persuasion. Conflict-affected children often care for themselves, each other and for adults. They find ways to survive amid deprivation, create their own worlds when surrounded by destruction, and maintain a sense of identity in the face of indoctrination. In the aftermath of war and discord, they can serve as exemplars of peace and visionaries of post-conflict societies. Increasingly, it is becoming apparent that children have much to teach us. They should thus be recognised as actors who contribute in positive, less than positive, sometimes unique and enlightening ways to conflict, peace and security. Like everyone else, they should not be silenced or ignored.

Children and Global Conflict demonstrates the relevance of children to the disciplinary study of international relations (IR), and provides IR with an analytical framework that incorporates children's experiences. More specifically, it accounts for the marginalisation and at times complete absence of children within mainstream IR thinking and critically engages the assumptions made about them in the practice of global politics. This is done primarily through an assessment of how children are regarded in relevant fields of IR such as conflict analysis, IR theory, peace studies, security studies and international law. Beyond that, it offers readers an analytical-political framework that not only makes children visible in IR, but also enhances the discipline's capacity to understand conflict and its resolution. This framework incorporates the following objectives:

1. It examines the variation of children's experiences and notions of childhood in conflict zones across regions, cultures and time, while distilling common elements of those different experiences and notions.
2. It explores the complex interplay between the creative agency of children and their distinct vulnerabilities in the face of violence.
3. It promotes approaches to children's rights and security in global politics that are both protective and empowering.
4. It advances a meaningful place for children in the adult-centric study of IR and the practice of global politics.

The opening chapter of this book maps the conceptual terrain of its three core concerns: children, armed conflict and the engagement of international actors with conflict-affected children. In so doing, it demonstrates how childhood is socially constructed and challenges dominant understandings of children as politically passive or inconsequential. The chapter then examines children's experiences in armed conflict and how they are uniquely affected by it. In exploring the international community's responses to this issue, the chapter analyses each of the 'six grave violations against children during armed conflict' that are the current focus of the UN Security Council. It critically reflects upon how these 'six grave violations' reinforce an orthodox conceptualisation of children and conflict, while advancing a narrow and potentially detrimental liberal humanitarian agenda. It is increasingly recognised that children are agents in both their own and international affairs. Chapter 2 on

'Children and agency' considers the debates over protection and responsibility that arise from this recognition and which are particularly important in conflict zones. If children are autonomous and competent are they any different from adults? When are they victims and when are they villains? How do we assess and deal with children who are both? Responses to these questions amass around two conflicting positions. The caretaker position asserts that children are vulnerable, innocent, dependent and irrational; because of these deficiencies, they should as far as possible be shielded from public affairs, moral corruption and violence. On the other hand, free-rangers view children as beings in their own right, with their own identities and values. To declare that there is a universal notion of childhood is, according to free-rangers, to subjugate and silence the children and societies who fail to abide by that notion. This chapter examines these positions, touching upon how they are manifested in philosophy, literature, politics and law, while always returning to the question: 'What place should children have, if any, in global conflict?' It asserts that de Certeau's notion of the Practice of Everyday Life (PEL) can help to reconcile the caretaker and free-ranger positions by providing an appreciation of children's creative and resilient qualities without overriding the need to protect and nurture them.

The discipline of IR is centrally concerned with the causes and conduct of war, the prospects of peace, and the conditions of security. Yet with few exceptions, this discipline has ignored the one billion children who are affected by armed conflict. Chapter 3 asks why IR has such a blind spot. To this end, it focuses upon the three major IR schools of thought: realism, liberalism and critical approaches to IR. Drawing from Chapter 2's discussion of caretakers and free-rangers, this chapter argues that realism and liberalism, which together constitute the orthodox way of thinking and acting in IR, take an often implicit caretaker view of the role of children in political spaces. Specifically, children are assumed to be protected within the domestic sphere of the home, family and community, and are not equipped to influence international affairs. These traditions do not ignore the fact that children are caught up in conflict zones, but conceive of them as docile victims in an environment that they have not made and cannot remake. This gives rise to only a protection agenda, particularly within liberal discourses on children and conflict. Critical approaches, however, are more aligned with the free-ranger approach, which acknowledges the agency of individual children and the potential role that they might play in shaping conflict, as well as being shaped by it. In this sense, this chapter argues for a need to balance the protection agenda with one that includes a consideration of the capacity for some children to be meaningful participants in conflict and its resolution.

Chapter 4 on 'The rights of the child' argues that the protection offered to war-affected children by the international legal framework is limited. This is because it is based on an outlook and agenda that is far removed from the complex processes that shape, rupture and reshape global conflict. The first section of this chapter outlines the prevailing liberal humanitarian outlook and how it is implemented to protect children's rights in conflict zones. It then goes on to detail some of the key tensions in international law over children's rights and the social and cultural meaning of childhood, tensions which are also reflected in academic disciplinary divides. This chapter considers the extent to which the global language of children's rights has permeated down through local and state-based settings to communities and families that are affected and transformed by armed conflict. It draws upon and re-examines the history of children's rights in international platforms, paying particular attention to the United Nations Convention on the Rights of the Child (UNCRC) and its specific provisions relating to armed conflict.

There is a voluminous amount of material on the problem of child soldiers. Chapter 5 distils and organises this literature using the caretaker and free-ranger positions introduced in Chapters 2 and 3. In the process of reconciling these two positions, the chapter develops an indirect approach to solving problems relating to child soldiers that concentrates not so much on demobilising individuals and demilitarising societies, but rather on improving the socio-economic and security milieu that are conducive to the use of child soldiers. This pre-emptive approach minimises the dangers of colonising interventions on behalf of children and can also facilitate deeper cultural engagement between advocates and child soldier societies. The chapter offers, as a case study of such engagement, a series of inter-connected stories about Vietnamese child soldiers – from ancient legends to modern heroes – and includes a biographical exploration of the author's father, who at the age of twelve trained to become a Viet Minh revolutionary.

Chapter 6 examines the twenty-first century crisis of forced migration and the critical role that children play within it. It delves into the global dynamics of forced migration, using explanations from Giorgio Agamben and Didier Fassin as to why liberal democracies demonise and dehumanise unauthorised arrivals, especially children. Despite this, as exemplified in Anne McNevin's work, many child forced migrants can retain and fashion a degree of political autonomy even in contexts where they are highly constricted, and the outcomes of their actions are deeply ambiguous. Children are thus able to navigate through the complex and often harrowing political currents that push, pull and enable forced migrants to move around the world and which make them so prominent in the media. The final section of Chapter 6 portrays the bio-political contest in Australia over the suffering and resistance of irregular migrant children and how it serves as the cornerstone of an intense struggle over what it means to be a liberal democracy in the contemporary world.

Chapter 7 explores the relationship between children and peace building, arguing that some children have demonstrated their capacity to be everyday peace builders. Whether it is informal everyday acts such as going to school, or formal organised activities such as participating in peace forums, children actively contribute to cultures of peace within their societies. Yet, the dominant practices of liberal peace building often focus upon top-down and institutionalised approaches, which fail to harness and foster children's contributions to peace. This chapter thus argues for a reconfiguration of the international posture and position towards children in post-conflict zones, from one primarily of advocate and protector to one that simultaneously promotes participation. It examines some of the recent efforts by international organisations and scholars to invest in children as peace builders, which serve as a reminder that any hope for sustainable and inter-generational peace requires investment in – and the commitment of – children.

A growing body of international literature calls for the need to come to terms with histories of violence in order to create a peaceful future. Chapter 8 on 'Children and justice' acknowledges this need while noting that there is significant disagreement about how to deal with the past and exactly what kind of healing is necessary for conflict-ridden nations and their children. This chapter asserts that there is a large gap in transitional justice scholarship when it comes to children's experiences and their varying roles as victims, survivors, perpetrators and judges. It considers both the justice-oriented mechanisms for children and the children-oriented mechanisms for justice, and how they can contribute to the rehabilitation of traumatised individuals and their societies with a view to ending cycles of violence.

The final chapter on 'advocacy, activism and resistance' turns to the matter of norm-setting and agenda-framing on behalf of children in conflict zones. In particular, it follows the progression from the 1996 Machel Report on children in armed conflict to the UNCRC's Optional Protocols (2000) and the UN Security Council Resolutions 1261 (1999) (the first resolution to recognise children in armed conflict) and 1314 (2000) (which set out measures to protect children during and after conflict). This chapter traces the path from advocacy to law, and contemplates how this process might be extended and implemented for the benefit of children in global conflict. At the same time it addresses three questions: What factors mobilise global and local movements to respond to children's experiences in conflict zones? Secondly, what civil society initiatives protect children from abuse and exploitation? And thirdly, what political and policy tensions exist within the global and local advocacy discourse?

Children and Global Conflict articulates our desire to advance the scholarly understanding of children in conflict zones. We do so in order to advocate for their wellbeing, security and empowerment, and to promote sustainable peace for children and adults alike.

Being a child is often about living within categories and expectations based on age and development. Much of what is fun and vital about childhood involves playfully challenging and redefining those categories and expectations. In this vein, this introduction closes by challenging and redefining the traditional distinction between the subjectivity of the preface and the objectivity of the introduction; that is, by outlining why *Children and Global Conflict* matters to us, the authors. It matters because we three are the best of friends and because this book is born out of that camaraderie and our time together as postgraduate students at the Australian National University. More importantly, it embodies the commitment to one another that we have fostered as we have journeyed through the final years of our youth – defined in the broadest sense – and our experiences of work, teaching, learning, weddings, promotions, awards, relocations, childbirths and homecomings. Each chapter was written by one of us, but also reflects the efforts, insights and encouragement of the other two. We are grateful for the expertise and generosity of our colleagues Anne McNevin, Donna Seto, Georgia Swan and Andrew Watts. This book has taken a little longer than was intended. But as much as we could force and shape it, it has come together in its own time and is better for it. Perhaps the same can be said of our children.

1 | Children and armed conflict: mapping the terrain

KATRINA LEE-KOO

Introduction

Children live in the world's most violent places. Children do not start wars, yet armed conflict affects and devastates their lives in many ways. Armed conflict can lead to disruption of their schooling and everyday practices; the loss of family members; forced displacement; poverty and health concerns; and brings physical, structural and psychological violence into their lives. There is no doubt that conflict victimises children and hinders their futures. Yet children have demonstrated the capacity not only to be shaped by conflict, but also to shape conflict in ways that are both predictable and surprising. In short, children have complex and distinctive relationships with conflict. These relationships are produced by the nature of the conflict around them, the investment that stakeholders in conflict make to their protection, and the capacities and decisions of children themselves.

This opening chapter examines the relationship between children and armed conflict by focusing upon the three core concerns of this book: children, armed conflict and the responses of international actors. It begins by mapping the conceptual terrain of these three concerns, highlighting the debates that arise in response to key questions regarding what it means to be a child, how armed conflict shapes children's experiences, and what responsibilities the international community has to child protection. Based upon recent research by the global child advocacy network, the chapter then turns to an empirically based overview of some of the impacts of conflict on children. It does so via 'the six grave violations against children during armed conflict' that are the focus of the UN Security Council. It then critically engages these six grave violations in order to reflect upon how they construct and reinforce conceptualisations of children, conflict and the international community's responses towards them. Furthermore, in demonstrating the complex relationship that exists between these three themes, this chapter highlights the role that children themselves play in shaping conflict and their own experiences of it.

The social construction of childhood

The 1989 UNCRC has been ratified by 194 states, and therefore provides the most broadly accepted definition of childhood. It defines a child as 'every human being below the age of eighteen years unless under the law applicable to the child, majority is attained earlier.'[1] While the idea that a child is any person under the age of eighteen is widely accepted, it is nonetheless important to recognise that it is a social construction. It is not based upon universal biological certainty, but rather is developed through distinct cultural and social values and practices. It is based upon the notion that a child is a person who has yet to develop fully the fundamental features – be they physical, intellectual or social – that are necessary for achieving independent, active and responsible input into a community.[2] Thus, the process by which children develop into adults is an interplay between biological traits and social stimuli.[3] The end of a person's eighteenth year therefore provides a convenient, yet somewhat arbitrary, marker for the expectation that that person should exhibit the physical, intellectual and emotional maturity to fulfil the social expectations of adulthood.

The UNCRC's reference to the age of majority demonstrates an understanding that childhood has developed in ways that are socially and culturally specific to a society. The age of majority is determined by what a society thinks the responsibilities and expectations of a child should be when compared to an adult. This can be determined by historical practice, cultural norms, social attitudes, religious values, legal dictates or the needs of a society. For instance, western liberal democracies generally agree that young children should be denied the right to consume alcohol, drive automobiles, marry, have sexual intercourse or watch violent films. However, even though these values are reasonably consistent, there are legal inconsistencies in their application. For instance, age restrictions on drivers' licences

---

[1] UNCRC Article 1.
[2] See Tamar Schapiro, 'What is a Child?', *Ethics* 109(4) (July 1999), 716.
[3] Jason Hart and Bex Tyrer, 'Research with Children Living in Situations of Armed Conflict: Concepts, Ethics and Methods', Refugees Studies Centre Working Paper No. 30 (May 2006), 8.

may vary between countries and even between states in the same country. Furthermore, the parameters for these legalities are subject to changing social values across generations.

While societies may legally prohibit children from participating in adult activities, children are also legally free from the obligations and rights attending adult citizenship. These may include being financially independent, paying taxes, voting, being eligible to stand for election to public office, enlisting in the armed services, and being obliged to undertake national service and military conscription. In liberal democracies in particular, this reflects a broader social value that children should be excluded from political participation in their community because they are yet to acquire the experience, judgement and skills to do so responsibly. Children are therefore conceptualised as pre-political; that is, they are yet to develop an individual political consciousness and the capacity to bear the burdens that attend it.

These common views of childhood, evident in the UNCRC and many liberal states, are dominated by concerns with the legality, rights and freedoms of individual children according to age. Given this focus, it is important to recognise that this conceptualisation of childhood is the product of a liberal philosophical and historical tradition.[4] In this sense, the reference to rights and legal principles is reflective of the dominance of these values in liberal states, but historically has not been universal. There is, therefore, a tension between what are largely western and liberal notions of childhood, and those that are neither western nor liberal. Brocklehurst argues that many societies conceptualise children primarily through a social rather than a legal lens; see children's identities as community-based rather than individually based; and that there exists a range of competing views on the rights, obligations and duties that children should have in regard to their communities. She notes that in many societies children's lives are full of obligations to their family and their community, which might manifest in the form of household labour or caring responsibilities to younger siblings, elderly or infirm relatives. It might also be present in the sense of a familial respect or obligation to family.[5] Therefore the transition to adulthood might not be so stark as to denote the formal

---

[4] See Vanessa Pupavac, 'Misanthropy Without Borders: The International Children's Rights Regime', *Disasters* 25(2) (2001), 95–112.

[5] Helen Brocklehurst, *Who's Afraid of Children? Children, Conflict and International Relations* (Hampshire: Ashgate, 2006), 11.

access of rights and responsibilities at a particular age, but rather is seen as a gradual transformation, the finality of which might be marked by social and biological events such as puberty, menstruation for girls, cultural initiation rites, or marriage. These might not be defined by age or codified by legal rights and responsibilities, and may vary for each individual child within a community.

The influences of liberal and non-liberal values are not the only tensions that need to be recognised when considering divergent conceptualisations of childhood. There are a number of cross-cutting distinctions which destabilise both conceptualisations. For example, socio-economic formations of class may constitute an important factor in constructing childhood. In liberal and non-liberal societies alike, issues of class can determine the opportunities children have to develop within broadly accepted states of childhood according to the norms of those societies. The socio-economic position of a child and his/her family may have a major impact upon a child's access to education, the age at which they marry or undertake employment, their participation in conflict, and, in cases of extreme poverty, their physical development. For example, the international community currently insists that formal school education is a necessary feature of childhood. This was reflected in the UN's Millennium Development Goal (MDG) Number Two, announced in 2000, which sought to 'achieve universal primary education' by 2015.[6] However, as the UN's research on childhood education demonstrates, the capacity for a family or community to provide children with access to education can differ starkly according to income, location, family priorities and social values.[7] Children without extensive or any formal education may therefore transition into adulthood earlier than those with access to education, as the former are more likely to have entered full-time employment or marriage earlier. Another cross-cutting issue in conceptualising childhood is gender. Gender plays an important role in shaping understandings of childhood. The level of gender equality in a society shapes attitudes towards girls' education and participation in the workforce, the age at which they are deemed marriageable, and the

---

[6] See UN, 'Millennium Development Goals', 2000. Available at www.un.org/millenniumgoals/education.shtml.

[7] UN, 'The Millennium Development Goals Report (2010)', 16–20. Available at www.un.org/millenniumgoals/pdf/MDG%20Report%202010%20En%20r15%20-low%20res%2020100615%20-.pdf#page=18.

point at which they are thought to be mature and independent. All of these are social markers of adulthood. Social constructions of masculinity similarly create adult expectations of boys at different ages to girls. In patriarchal societies boys may be expected to become heads of households and primary breadwinners after the deaths of their fathers, may be forced into the workforce earlier, or given more freedoms than girls at an earlier age.

Furthermore, it is worth recognising the importance of age when considering children's roles in society. Arguably, at no other stage in a person's life does ten years make such a stark difference than in childhood. The competencies of a three-year-old are significantly different from those of a thirteen-year-old. For instance, English language terms such as baby, toddler, child, teenager, adolescent, youth, and young adult denote different stages of childhood development and different capacities and attributes of children. Thus, while a child may be anyone under the age of eighteen, it is important to recognise that there exist multiple social and biological constructs *within* childhood. For this reason, some scholars prefer the term 'youth' to 'child', recognising the complexities and emerging grey areas that exist with regard to children's agency and political participation at the older end of the childhood spectrum.[8] The United Nations Education, Science and Cultural Organisation (UNESCO) defines youth as being those aged between fifteen and twenty-five,[9] while the 2006 African Union's *African Youth Charter* extends the age limit to thirty-five.[10] The *African Youth Charter* explicitly acknowledges the obligations and expectations for 'the constructive involvement of Youth in the development agenda of Africa and their effective participation in the debates and decision-making processes in the development of the continent'.[11] Consequently, debates about childhood in relation to evolving capacities are heavily contingent upon age.

---

[8] See Siobhan McEvoy-Levy (ed.), *Trouble Makers or Peace Makers? Youth and post-Accord Peacebuilding* (Notre Dame, IN: University of Notre Dame Press, 2006).

[9] UNESCO, 'What Do We Mean by Youth?'. Available at www.unesco.org/new/en/social-and-human-sciences/themes/youth/youth-definition/.

[10] African Union Commission, 'African Youth Charter (African Union Commission, 2006)', 11. Available at http://esaro.unfpa.org/webdav/site/africa/users/africa_admin/public/CHARTER_English.pdf.

[11] Ibid., 2.

Finally, each child's individual identity and experience helps to shape personalised views of childhood. Children's individual identity and their familial and social settings impact the rate at which children develop the skill set or qualities that a society associates with adulthood. Biological development – such as height, the onset of puberty or the presence of disability – natural intelligence, personal confidence, the presence of family support, and the social stimuli around children can all influence the extent to which their society accepts them as adults. It can also be determined by the skills they master and the age at which they master them. These skills might include the capacity for sound judgement and rational thinking, consideration of others, and understanding of the consequences of one's actions. Children who care for ill parents or younger siblings may develop the skills of patience, care, sacrifice, responsibility and sound judgement at an age much younger than other children. They may also learn the practical skills associated with being the sole or main breadwinner in a family. Therefore a child who lives in a conflict zone or with social disadvantage may, at the age of eighteen, have acquired an entirely different set of skills, emotional and intellectual resources, and abilities than a child who has had a politically stable and financially secure upbringing with full access to formal education.

To understand the interplay of these legal, social and biological issues only begins to scratch the surface of the complexities involved in conceptualising childhood and determining who is or is not a child. It also highlights the problems associated with enforcing a universal definition of childhood as every human being below the age of eighteen years. When considered in the context of conflict zones, the distinction between a child and an adult is immediately blurred. As this book demonstrates, some children in conflict zones are performing the roles of adults: as armed combatants, heads of households, paid workers, carers for relatives, peace makers and community builders. Children also demonstrate political commitments in conflict, whether it be strategies for survival or more explicit active investments in belligerency. The capacity for children to do these things in conflict zones is also heavily influenced by age. In conflict zones the stages of childhood shape the changing roles and political competencies that young people have in relation to the conflict around them. It also influences the extent to which they have developed capacities to engage with the international community. For instance, older children may be able to make useful contributions to peace building discussions, while younger children may require different forms of protection. Again, this highlights the problems associated with universal definitions of children as 'every human being below the age of eighteen years'. This is not to say, however, that children – or even older children – should be treated as adults. Children should have rights unique to their status as children. For the reasons discussed in the remainder of this chapter, children are a category of human beings distinct from adults. They experience conflict in ways that are different from those of adults; they can have different needs for protection and recovery; and they have different investments in sustainable peace. Furthermore, they can also shape conflict and contribute to peace in ways that are unique from those of adults.

Conceptually, these debates create a bind. The answer to the question 'what and who is a child?' is clearly influenced by the social, legal and cultural values and norms of the community and nation-state in which the child is raised. It is also shaped by the geographical location, gender, socio-economic status, experience, abilities, appearance and age of the child. Clearly these values may not always subscribe to those of the liberal international community. On the one hand, the liberal inspired universal, legal and, ultimately, arbitrary age-contingent conceptualisation of childhood excludes many societies' views of childhood. It denies children's political consciousness and their agency, and it marginalises the diversity of lived experiences of many children, particularly in conflict zones. It sees children as ideally being apolitical, sheltered and separate from the political realm, but also, in the case of children in conflict zones, it regards them as only ever victims of adult political action. On the other hand, a conceptualisation of childhood that is entirely culturally contingent also has problems. It may be locally designed but nonetheless oppressive, discriminatory or violent, particularly when children are not perceived as active participants in their society. Furthermore, such definitions may exclude children from global protection and rights, and create boundaries for global child welfare actors.

For the purposes of this book, the UNCRC definition of a child will be used. However, it is nonetheless necessary to qualify and scrutinise the often simple meanings associated with that definition. We do this by recognising that childhood is not one state of being but many: it is a dynamic and fluid period of human development that is constantly changing and which brings with it new and evolving capacities. Secondly, this book regards childhood as a socially constructed concept. Thus, understandings of childhood vary across societies and cultural traditions, and multiple constructions of childhood are recognised as potentially legitimate, with the obvious exception of those that engage in violence against children. Furthermore, this book uses a child-centric conceptualisation of childhood that centralises children's views, voices and experiences in the debate of what it means to be a child. In turn, this creates an empirical focus on children – examining their experiences, capacities and potential in conflict zones. This allows us to re-open questions concerning children's status as political beings and political actors amidst conflict. It encourages curiosity about the lives and thoughts of children in conflict,[12] and produces an analysis that is wilfully complicated by the multiple subjectivities of children. In short, when referring to children in this book, the utility of pre-existing global legal infrastructure, which describes a child as being under the age of eighteen, is accepted but it is nonetheless worthwhile challenging the entrenched social constructions of what it means to be a child.

The construction of contemporary conflict zones

Like childhood, definitions and conceptualisations of armed conflict zones can vary according to context and perspective. Armed conflict can be broadly understood as involving widespread political and militarised violence. However, the specifics of what defines armed conflict are debated. Elements such as the role of the recognised government, the number of combatants and civilians killed, the mode of political violence used, and the stated goals of the belligerent parties can shape definitions of conflict. For instance, the Uppsala Conflict Database defines armed conflict as 'a contested incompatibility which concerns government and/or territory where the use of armed forces between two parties, of which at least one is the government of a state, results in at least 25 battle-related deaths'.[13] Project Ploughshares uses a

---

[12] This borrows from the methodology outlined in Cynthia Enloe, *The Curious Feminist: Searching for Women in a New Age of Empire* (University of California Press, 2004).

[13] Peter Wallensteen and Margareta Sollenberg, 'Armed Conflict 1989–2000', *Journal of Peace Research* 38(5) (2003), 629–44.

similar definition of armed conflict, however it raises the number of necessary battle deaths to 1,000. It defines armed conflict 'as a political conflict in which armed combat involves the armed forces of at least one state (or one or more armed factions seeking to gain control of all or part of the state)'.[14] Alternatively, the Heidelberg Institute for International Conflict Research provides a wider scope for conflict analysis. It does not require a state group to be among the belligerents, and determines the nature of conflict according to five levels of the intensity of violence that range from latent non-violent conflict through to organised warfare with high levels of violence.[15] Within these definitions there is a range of conflict typologies. The Heidelberg Institute distinguishes between conflicts for territory, secession, decolonisation, autonomy, ideology, national power, international power, regional predominance, and resources.[16] Project Ploughshares groups conflict into: those vying for state control, for example, revolutionary, decolonisation or identity-based conflicts; those seeking state formation, such as secession or regional autonomy; and those coalescing around state failure.[17] The International Institute for Strategic Studies categorises armed conflict into three groups: international armed border and territorial conflict, internal armed conflict, and terrorism.[18]

The labels that are given to conflict are often politically contested by belligerent parties – what may be a war of liberation to some might be labelled an insurgency by others. Thus, like childhood, conceptualisations of conflict are produced through political and social values. And this social construction of conflict matters, not least of all to children's lives. It matters because children are directly impacted by the consequences of how conflicts are understood and responded to by the international community; it also matters because children are often implicated in the social constructions of conflict. In the first instance, the social and political language used to describe a given conflict will shape the international response. For example, the

---

[14] Project Ploughshares, 'Defining Armed Conflict'. Available at http://plough shares.ca/programs/armed-conflict/defining-armed-conflict/.

[15] Heidelberg Institute for International Conflict Research, 'Conflict Barometer 2010', 88. Available at www.hiik.de/en/konfliktbarometer/pdf/ConflictBaro meter_2010.pdf.

[16] Ibid.   [17] Project Ploughshares, 'Defining Armed Conflict'.

[18] The International Institute for Strategic Studies, Armed Conflict Database. Available at http://acd.iiss.org.virtual.anu.edu.au/armedconflict/MainPages/dsp_Page.asp?PageID=2.

classification of any conflict as genocide triggers international responsibilities under the 1948 Genocide Convention as well as potentially triggering a sense of moral responsibility that manifests as political pressure upon states to act. The possibility of international action – be it political, military or humanitarian – produced by these moral and legal responsibilities will shape the experiences of children affected by armed conflict. In the second instance, ideas about children are often deployed to construct an understanding of conflict. This has been evident in post-2001 Afghanistan where the abuse and neglect of children, alongside women, has become an important narrative theme underpinning the need for an international militarised humanitarian response.[19] With this in mind, this book accepts a broad definition of armed conflict as any political and militarised violence that involves two or more belligerent parties. However, it is necessary to remain attuned to the political investments associated with the social construction of knowledge claims regarding conflict and the representations of children's experiences within it. Furthermore, this research is careful to identify the elements of conflict that directly target children or profoundly shape children's experiences. The interplay of these three concepts – children, conflict and the response of the international community – is at the centre of this book. Each chapter challenges passive and static conceptualisations of childhood, explores the impact that conflict has upon children, and seeks to create a balance between the obligation to protect children from conflict and recognition of their agency within it. With these foundations in mind, the remainder of this chapter is dedicated to demonstrating this interplay through an examination of armed conflict's impact upon children and the UN response to it.

The experiences of children affected by armed conflict

Children are physically, socially and psychologically affected by armed conflict. The physical effects can be both immediate and long-term and include not just the effects of weapons and physical abuse, but also the effects of the social disruption caused by war. For

---

[19] See Katrina Lee-Koo, 'Not Suitable for Children: The Politicisation of Conflict-affected Children in Post-2001 Afghanistan', *Australian Journal of International Affairs*, 67(3) (August 2013), 475–90.

instance, shortages of food and medical supplies, and the environmental pollution that attends conflicts, can be detrimental to children's physical wellbeing and susceptibility to mortality. This is demonstrated, for example, by the long-term effects that the conflict in the Democratic Republic of Congo (DCR) has had upon children's physical health and survival. While the Second Congo War ended in 2003, the International Rescue Committee reported that the rates of death in the country in 2007 were still as high as they had been during the conflict, with close to half of the dead being children under five years of age.[20] These deaths were largely due to famine and disease caused directly by the war. Similarly, the use of Agent Orange and other chemical defoliants has had a major impact upon the physical wellbeing of children who lived during, or were born after, the Second Indochina War in Vietnam. It has been estimated that 500,000 Vietnamese children have been born with birth defects as a result of their parents' exposure to defoliants.[21] Thus the physical effects of armed combat on children are much more extensive than direct exposure to combat.

The social effects of conflict on children include the disruption that conflict has upon their everyday lives. This involves obstruction to their capacity to function as – and be treated as – children within their social context. This might involve disruption to their education, disruption to their family if parents or siblings leave or die because of conflict, disruption to their familial and social contexts brought about by internal or external displacement or family separation, forced or voluntary recruitment, and the undertaking of extra-ordinary responsibilities such as paid work or care, that are a direct result of the surrounding conflict. As with the physical effects, the social impact of war can extend long after the conflict is over. For instance, conflict generates a dramatic increase in the number of children who become heads of household due to the death of one or both parents.[22] Similarly, the rate of child marriage often dramatically increases after conflict as

---

[20] International Rescue Committee, Mortality in the Democratic Republic of Congo: An Ongoing Crisis (2008). Available at www.rescue.org/sites/default/files/migrated/resources/2007/2006-7_congomortalitysurvey.pdf.

[21] Geoffrey York and Hayley Mick, '"Last Ghost" of the Vietnam War', *The Global and Mail* (31 March 2009).

[22] UNICEF, *Machel Study 10-Year Strategic Review* (2009) 20.

war-affected populations seek renewal.[23] These impacts may be contributing factors to the under-education of a generation of children affected by conflict. While this is a tangible social effect of conflict, there are also less tangible effects, such as the disruption to children's ability to develop enduring social relationships. As Boyden and de Berry observe, trust can be a commodity in short supply in conflict zones, and difficult to develop after conflict.[24] Yet to some extent trust is essential to breaking cycles of violence that may occur over many generations and to beginning the processes of establishing sustainable peace.[25]

Finally, the psychological impacts of war upon children are broad-ranging. Children are witness to, experience, learn about and occasionally perpetrate horrific acts during conflict. Their experiences can result in mental health concerns such as anxiety and depression, behavioural and learning difficulties, and emotional distress resulting in physical manifestations such as headaches and abdominal pain.[26] Wessells argues that 'the chronic stresses associated with armed conflict may lead to problems such as aggression, depression, truncated moral development, changed attitudes and beliefs, and diminished hope for the future'.[27] The extent of this has been demonstrated in post-2003 Iraq. A 2007 report by the Association of Iraqi Psychologists claimed that the conflict had affected millions of Iraqi children who would grow up deeply traumatised. Furthermore, the Association argued that the lack of doctors in Iraq, together with the social stigma attached to psychological and psychiatric care, means that many of these children will go untreated.[28]

A significant portion of the literature that attempts to document these physical, social and psychological effects of conflict on children

---

[23] World Vision, 'Untying the Knot: Exploring Early Marriage in Fragile States', March 2013. Available at www.worldvision.org/resources.nsf/main/press-reports/$file/Untying-the-Knot_report.pdf.

[24] Jo Boyden and Joanna de Berry, 'Introduction', in Jo Boyden and Joanna de Berry (eds.), *Children and Youth on the Front Line: Ethnography, Armed Conflict and Displacement* (New York, NY: Berghahn Books, 2004), xiv.

[25] Michael G. Wessells, 'Children, Armed Conflict, and Peace', *Journal of Peace Research* 35(5) (1998), 635–46.

[26] UNICEF, *Machel Study 10-Year Strategic Review* (2009) 22.

[27] Wessells, 'Children, Armed Conflict, and Peace', 641.

[28] Michael Howard, 'Children of War: The Generation Traumatised by Violence in Iraq', *Guardian Weekly* (6 February 2007). Available at www.guardian.co.uk/world/2007/feb/06/iraq.topstories3.

has emerged from the field research conducted by global civil society. In particular, an evolving children and armed conflict advocacy network that consists of non-governmental and international organisations has been responsible for presenting research and setting the global advocacy agenda on this issue.[29] The Office of the Special Representative of the Secretary-General for Children and Armed Conflict (OSRSG-CaAC), established in 1997, and the United Nations Children Fund (UNICEF) founded in 1946, are the two UN bodies mandated with children's rights concerns, both in conflict and more broadly. They work with key child advocacy non-governmental organisations (NGOs) to set the tone and the agenda of child protection in contemporary conflict zones, through Security Council resolutions, funding mechanisms and the publication of reports and documents. Their key achievements include the ground-breaking 1996 UNICEF Machel Report on the 'Impact of Armed Conflict on Children'[30] and its 2009 review 'Children and Conflict in a Changing World'.[31] While these reports document the range of issues impacting children in contemporary conflict, the OSRSG-CaAC, based on UN Security Council Resolutions 1539 (2004), 1216 (2005), 1882 (2009), 1998 (2011), 2068 (2012) and 2143 (2014) has chosen to focus upon six grave violations against children during armed conflict.[32] These specific violations against children are far from an exhaustive list and were chosen because of 'their ability to be monitored and quantified, their egregious nature and severity of their consequences upon the lives of children'.[33] These six violations are the killing and maiming of children in conflict zones, the recruitment or use of children by armed groups or forces, attacks against schools or hospitals, rape and other forms of sexual violence, abduction, and denial of humanitarian access.

The first of the six grave concerns outlined by the UN is the targeting of civilian children for killing or maiming. This is defined as 'any action

---

[29] R. Charli Carpenter, 'Setting the Advocacy Agenda: Theorizing Issue Emergence and Non-emergence in Transnational Advocacy Networks', *International Studies Quarterly* 51(1) (2007), 99–120.

[30] Machel, Graça, 'Impact of Armed Conflict on Children', UNICEF (1996). Available at www.unicef.org/graca.

[31] UNICEF, *Machel Study 10-Year Strategic Review* (2009).

[32] OSRSG-CaAC, 'The Six Grave Violations Against Children During Armed Conflict: The Legal Foundation', Working Paper No. 1, (October 2009), 3. Available at www.un.org/children/conflict/english/legalfoundation.htm.

[33] Ibid., 3.

that results in the death or serious injury – such as scarring, disfigurement or mutilation – of one or more children'.[34] This can include the deliberate targeting of children for violence for the purposes of instilling fear, forcing removal from an area, or creating terror in a group or community. It also involves using children for suicide attacks, and the incidental killing or maiming of children through their being incorrectly targeted, caught in the crossfire, or the victims of anti-personnel land mines or unexploded remnants of war. This accords with the foundational principles of civilian protection in conflict; the International Court of Justice describes the protection of civilians from direct targeting as one of the 'cardinal principles of international humanitarian law' and one of the 'intransgressible principles of international customary law'.[35]

Analysis suggests that children are deliberately targeted for violence during armed conflict. The new wars landscape, described in Chapter 3, illustrates the political and strategic value in targeting children. For instance, targeting children is a powerful psychological weapon that can be employed to intimidate individuals and communities. In the ongoing insurgency conflicts in Burma, which began soon after its 1948 independence, it has been reported that children have been killed and injured by 'the Myanmar Armed Forces [who] have shelled villages to encourage forced relocation or to depopulate areas'.[36] The direct targeting of children is also a pre-emptive strike against future armies. Brocklehurst points out that during the Rwandan civil war in the early to mid-1990s, male Tutsi children were deliberately targeted by Hutu militia as part of a strategy to eradicate future resistance.[37] The genocide in Srebrenica in July 1995 saw civilian male children targeted for execution by invading Serbian forces, in part because of a belief in their future capacity as combatants.[38] Similarly, male children are targeted because of the common expectation of their political activism. In the post-2001

[34] UNICEF, *Machel Study 10-Year Strategic Review* (2009) 21.
[35] Quoted in OSRSG-CaAC, 'The Six Grave Violations Against Children During Armed Conflict', 5.
[36] Watchlist on Children and Armed Conflict, 'No More Denial: Children Affected by Armed Conflict in Myanmar (Burma)', (May 2009), 16. Available at www.watchlist.org/reports/pdf/myanmar/myanmar_english_full.pdf.
[37] Brocklehurst, *Who's Afraid of Children?*, 39.
[38] R. Charli Carpenter, *'Innocent Women and Children': Gender, Norms and the Protection of Civilians* (Hampshire: Ashgate, 2006).

conflict in Afghanistan, the UN reported that anti-government forces executed children on suspicion that they had been spying for international military forces.[39]

Children are also killed and maimed as a result of their use as suicide attackers. The UN has documented cases of this in the Occupied Palestinian Territories[40] and the Taliban's use of children in this manner in Afghanistan.[41] Children are thought to be useful suicide attackers because of their malleability, their presumed innocence and consequent ability to launch surprise attacks, and the terror value involved in using children. In December 2008, a thirteen-year-old boy pushed a wheelbarrow bomb into a British Army patrol in Helmand Province, Afghanistan, killing four soldiers.[42] Strategically, this method of attack in Afghanistan served numerous goals: it disrupted the 'hearts and minds' project being waged by the International Security Assistance Forces (ISAF); it created confusion regarding the programme of civilian protection; and, as a psychological weapon, it impacted members of the local and international community. The conflict in Afghanistan has also generated high levels of child mortality due to so-called collateral damage. The UN reported that 1,302 children were killed or injured due to conflict-related violence in 2012[43] and 1,756 children were killed or injured in 2013.[44] This was a result of air strikes and ground attacks by international forces, as well as pro- and anti-government forces, and reflects a casualty rate that has remained consistent throughout the first decade of the conflict. The current conflict in Syria, which began in 2011, saw dramatic child mortality rates in its first three years. In 2014, Leila Zerrougui, the UN Special Representative, described Syria as 'one of the most dangerous places to be a child', with 10,000 children having died

---

[39] UN Security Council, 'Report of the Secretary-General on Children and Armed Conflict in Afghanistan', Document No. S/2011/55 (3 February 2011), 8.

[40] UNICEF, *Machel Study 10-Year Strategic Review* (2009) 21.

[41] UN Security Council, 'Report of the Secretary-General on Children and Armed Conflict in Afghanistan', 5.

[42] Gaby Hinsliff, 'Can We Be Sure Afghan Child Suicide Bomber Knew What He Was Doing?', Guardian.co.uk, (14 December 2008). Available at www.guardian.co.uk/world/blog/2008/dec/14/afghanistan-military.

[43] UNAMA, 'Afghanistan Annual Report: Protection of Civilians in Armed Conflict'. UN Kabul (2013), 54. Available at http://unama.unmissions.org/Portals/UNAMA/human%20rights/Feb_8_2014_PoC-report_2013-Full-report-ENG.pdf.

[44] Ibid., 11.

during the conflict.[45] Such statistics reinforce the importance of this issue as a primary concern in the children and armed conflict agenda. The issue of the recruitment of children into militarised groups for combat or combat-related activities (commonly referred to as child soldiering) is the second grave violation against children, and will be considered in Chapter 5.

The third grave violation is attacks against schools or hospitals. This is deliberate targeting with the goal of partial or full destruction of these facilities, their occupation by militarised groups, or the deliberate targeting of those associated with these facilities. Schools and hospitals are targeted because they are powerful symbols of the community and also because their destruction has the strategic value of causing widespread disruption to civilian life. Furthermore, they may represent a particular group's vision of social order, or a particular regime that is contested, especially in terrorist or anti-government campaigns. Attacks upon state-run institutions as insurgency targets fulfil a broader goal of social and political disruption and function as a reminder of contested state sovereignty. Children are inevitably caught up in such attacks. For instance, the UN Assistance Mission in Afghanistan has documented the sustained nature of threats and attacks against schools and hospitals, particularly those funded and built by the Karzai Government in collaboration with ISAF.[46] In Afghanistan, the attacks against schools are also symbolic in the sense that they intersect with the broader prosecution of a gendered war. It was reported in 2010 that while only 19 per cent of schools in Afghanistan are designated for girls, attacks upon girls' schools constituted 40 per cent of all school attacks. In some cases these were accompanied by targeted assaults against students, including throwing acid and poisoning by gas.[47] Schools are also targeted in Afghanistan because they have been used

---

[45] Leila Zerrougui, 'Syria Has Become One of the Most Dangerous Places to be a Child', OSRSG-CaAC (12 March 2014). Available at http://childrenandarmed conflict.un.org/statement/syria-has-become-one-of-the-most-dangerous-places-to-be-a-child/.

[46] UNAMA, 'Afghanistan Mid-Year Report 2010: Protection of Civilians in Armed Conflict'. UN Kabul, 2010, 11. Available at http://unama.unmissions.org/Portals/UNAMA/Publication/August102010_MID-YEAR%2020 10_Protection%20of%20Civilians%20in%20Armed%20Conflict.pdf.

[47] Watchlist on Children and Armed Conflict, 'Setting the Right Priorities: Protecting Children Affected by Armed Conflict in Afghanistan' (June 2001), 25.

as polling stations. The August 2009 parliamentary elections saw a massive increase in attacks upon schools, with the number of attacks reaching 249, compared with forty-eight in July, and thirty-eight in September.[48] In a 2010 mission report on Afghanistan, the Special Representative of the Secretary-General for Children and Armed Conflict reported that local communities in Afghanistan had failed to develop a strong commitment to, or investment in, newly built schools and that this indicated an unwillingness to protect or defend them.[49] This, coupled with a failure on the part of the international community to cross-reference policy on the staging of elections with the protection of children's rights, has resulted in the widespread presence of this particular form of violation. In an attempt to address this violation, in May 2014 the UN Special Representative released a guidance note entitled 'Protect Schools and Hospitals: End Attacks on Education and Healthcare', which is designed to assist in the implementation of UN Security Council Resolution 1998 (2011). This document seeks to strengthen the response to this violation by facilitating monitoring and reporting structures, promoting advocacy and dialogue, and increasing global advocacy partnerships.[50]

The use of rape and other forms of sexual violence against children as a strategy of war demonstrates the gendered nature of children's experiences in conflict zones. Like civilian war-rape and sexual violence against adults, the use or threat of such violence against children serves a number of strategic and military objectives. It can create compliance within a civilian community to facilitate the capture of resources or territory, it can drive a community from their homeland, or it can be used as a psychological attack against a group of people or a nation. Its specific use against children has been integral in the recruitment of children into armed groups,[51] and as a source of

---

[48] OSRSG-CaAC, 'Mission Report: Visit of the Special Representative for Children and Armed Conflict to Afghanistan' (20–26 February 2010), 10. Available at http://unama.unmissions.org/Portals/UNAMA/Publication/may22010_Public ationSRSG_CAAC_Afghanistan_mission_report.pdf.

[49] Ibid.

[50] OSRSG-CaAC, 'Protect Schools and Hospitals: Guidance Note on Security Council Resolution 1998' (New York, NY: United Nations, May 2014). Available at https://childrenandarmedconflict.un.org/publications/Attackson SchoolsHospitals.pdf.

[51] Janie L. Leatherman, *Sexual Violence and Armed Conflict* (Cambridge: Polity, 2011), 53.

financial gain through the trafficking of children out of conflict zones
for the purposes of sexual slavery. This fourth grave violation also
includes sexual violence in the form of forced prostitution, whereby
children trade sex with militarised or international personnel for food
or protection,[52] and criminal acts committed against children amidst
the fog of conflict, often with impunity. Sexual violence against
children in conflict can be a difficult issue to investigate due to the
lack of detailed information resulting from widespread under-
reporting of attacks; the social stigma often attached to sexual
violence; ongoing insecurity and vulnerability and limited access to
health, justice or reporting services in conflict zones. Sexual
violence – in its practice and the ways in which it is understood and
responded to – includes a strongly gendered element. It is important to
recognise that sexual violence targets both boys and girls in particularly
gendered ways. For instance, the OSRSG-CaAC notes that the practice
of BacchaBaazi (dancing boys) in Afghanistan targets boys for sexual
slavery and child prostitution.[53] Social constructions of gender in local
contexts therefore inform both the practice of sexual violence against
girls and boys and shape the capacity that they have to report, receive
protection and attain justice for such violations.

Rape and sexual violence against children and adults attend every
conflict. For example, the Darfur conflict (2003–2010) in the eastern
region of Sudan involved numerous documented cases of gender-based
sexual violence against children. Amnesty International, Human
Rights Watch, Physicians for Human Rights, the Watchlist on
Children and Armed Conflict, Medecins Sans Frontieres and the UN
have all published detailed reports on the use of sexual violence as a
weapon of war in Sudan.[54] Collectively, these reports outline the

---

[52] Save the Children, 'No One to Turn To: The Under-reporting of Child Sexual
Exploitation and Abuse by Aid Workers and Peacekeepers', (2008). Available at
www.un.org/en/pseataskforce/docs/no_one_to_turn_under_reporting_of_
child_sea_by_aid_workers.pdf.

[53] OSRSG-CaAC, 'Sexual Violence', 2013. Available at http://childrenandarmed
conflict.un.org/effects-of-conflict/the-most-grave-violations/sexual-violence/.

[54] See Physicians for Human Rights, 'The Use of Rape as a Weapon of War in
Darfur, Sudan', October 2004. Available at http://physiciansforhumanrights.
org/library/reports/darfur-use-of-rape-as-weapon-2004.html; Amnesty
International, 'Sudan: Rape as a Weapon of War: Sexual Violence and its
Consequences', September 2004. Available at www.amnesty.org/en/library/
asset/AFR54/076/2004/en/f86a52a0-d5b4-11dd-bb24-1fb85fe8fa05/
afr540762004en.html; Watchlist on Children and Armed Conflict, 'Sudan's

widespread prevalence of rape and its deployment as a weapon against 'women and girls [to] dehumanize, demoralize and generally humiliate them while seeking to control, terrorize and punish the non-Arab communities to which they belong'.[55] They document cases of public rape, multiple rape, gang rape and abduction of girls for sexual slavery. The UN reported in 2007 that '[i]n Darfur, rape is widespread and used as a weapon of war ... Increasingly, the trend in Darfur seems to indicate that younger girls are being specifically targeted for rape.'[56] This issue has increasingly gathered international attention. There is now a strong legal framework and precedent condemning war-rape and sexual violence as crimes of genocide and ethnic cleansing, as demonstrated in the International Criminal Tribunal for the former Yugoslavia (ICTY) and the International Criminal Tribunal for Rwanda (ICTR). With specific reference to children, both the Additional Protocol to the Geneva Convention and the UNCRC outline the need to protect children from sexual violence.

The fifth grave violation against children in conflict is their abduction. UNICEF describes abduction in conflict zones as ranging 'in purpose from recruitment by armed forces or groups, participation in hostilities to sexual exploitation or abuse, forced labour, hostage-taking, information gathering and indoctrination'.[57] One of the most notorious instances of child abduction for forced military recruitment occurred during the conflict in Uganda, where it is estimated that the number of abducted children reached 25,000.[58] The abduction of children for forced labour and military service has been prevalent in resource conflicts. In such instances children are often forced into particularly hazardous forms of labour. Between October 2008 and December 2009, the Watchlist on Children and Armed Conflict reported that the Lord's Resistance Army (LRA), based in Northern Uganda, engaged in cross-border abductions of children for forced

---

Children at a Crossroads: An Urgent Need for Protection', April 2007. Available at www.watchlist.org/reports/pdf/sudan_07_final.pdf; Medecins Sans Frontieres, 'The Crushing Burden of Rape: Sexual Violence in Darfur', March 2005. Available at www.doctorswithoutborders.org/publications/reports/2005/sudan03.pdf.

[55] Watchlist on Children and Armed Conflict, 'Sudan's Children at a Crossroads', 31.

[56] UN Security Council, 'Report of the Secretary-General on Children and Armed Conflict in the Sudan', Document No. S/2007/520 (29 August 2007), 7–8.

[57] UNICEF, *Machel Study 10-Year Strategic Review* (2009), 24.   [58] Ibid.

labour in the DRC, South Sudan and the Central African Republic.[59] The appearance of abducted children in militia-controlled diamond and mineral mines throughout central Africa in recent years has been well documented. Similarly, in Colombia, as a result of the displacement and lack of governance brought about by the decades of low-intensity conflict that has been waged since 1964 between the government forces and guerrilla groups, children have become increasingly vulnerable to abduction and exploitation by militant as well as criminal organisations. At the turn of the century it was estimated that Colombia was one of the three largest sources of trafficking in the western hemisphere.[60] Colombian children are also abducted for ransom, their release funding a shadow guerrilla economy that fuels the ongoing conflict.[61]

The final grave violation is the denial of humanitarian access for the provision of aid, which UNICEF describes as 'blocking the free passage or timely delivery of humanitarian assistance to persons in need, including children'.[62] The inaccessibility of conflict zones by international actors limits their capacity to ensure the safe delivery of humanitarian assistance to children. For instance, the UN reported in 2011 that Mogadishu has been virtually inaccessible to the international community since 2008 due to the ongoing conflict in Somalia between government forces and militarised insurgent groups. The UN reported that throughout 2009, some 1.8 million children relied on humanitarian assistance including food supplies, clean water and medical assistance.[63] However, militarised attacks along major humanitarian access routes, the violent targeting of humanitarian aid workers, and the general deterioration of the security situation, have severely limited access for aid organisations.[64] UNICEF reports that almost 640,000 children under the age of five suffer from chronic

---

[59] UN Security Council, 'Report of the Secretary-General on Children and Armed Conflict in the Democratic Republic of the Congo', Document No. S/2010/369 (9 July 2010), 8–9.

[60] Watchlist on Children and Armed Conflict, 'Colombia's War on Children', February 2004, 20.

[61] Andrew Gumbel, 'Colombian Kidnappers "Targeting Children"', *The Independent*, 1 February 2003.

[62] UNICEF, *Machel Study 10-Year Strategic Review* (2009), 24.

[63] UN Security Council, 'Report of the Secretary-General on Children and Armed Conflict in Somalia', Document No. S/2010/577 (9 November 2010), 5.

[64] Ibid., 14–15.

food insecurity. In civilian attempts to flee violence, drought and floods, 'children continue to be acutely affected by displacement, exhaustion, separation and emotional trauma, and deprived of access to basic services and protection'.[65] The isolation of civilian populations from outside assistance is often a deliberate strategy of conflict that attacks the capacity of civilians to resist armed groups, or punishes them for perceived political wrongdoing.

The importance of these six grave violations to the broader agenda of children in conflict zones is immediately apparent. These are issues which are abhorrent, widespread and in clear violation of well-understood international laws and norms. However, it is important to recognise that each of these violations brings with it a set of preconceived ontological ideals about the three key issues discussed in the first half of this chapter: childhood, conflict and the role of the international community to mediate the two. Such abuses represent children as victims of conflict, rather than actors or agents. They present children as being caught up in the wake of conflict, but nonetheless remaining apart from the politics that generate and sustain conflict. While this is often true, it is not universally the case. The research presented above makes it clear that children are affected by conflict in adverse ways. But, as demonstrated in later chapters, they also have the capacity to affect conflict, sometimes in positive ways, as peace brokers and peace builders, as community and family guardians, and in affecting their capacity to survive. Children's role as victims of conflict needs to be tempered by an understanding of their context and the ways in which they resist victimhood. The PEL outlined in Chapter 2 and the role of children in peace building in Chapter 7 offer such examples of children's capacities to shape conflict, even if it is only through shaping the lives around them. In recognising the complexities of children's lives in conflict zones, analyses should resist presenting children as docile and often mute entities incapable of imagining a life outside conflict, in automatic need of rescue by an international project designed by strangers.

It is also important to question the political framing of the six grave violations within the current practices of global politics. These six grave violations have been chosen by the UN because of their easy recognition within traditional methodologies of knowledge accumulation. In the

---

[65] Ibid., 6.

first instance, this refers to the use of quantifiable indicators such as statistics as a way of apprehending the problems at hand. As noted above, the UN selects these issues because of 'their ability to be monitored and quantified'.[66] The dominance of such indicators in designing the agenda of impact and successes of international organisations and in assessing the impact and successes of social justice and reform strategies is becoming increasingly widespread in the global civil society sector.[67] Critical of this potential over-emphasis, Sally Engle Merry argues that 'the deployment of statistical measures tends to replace political debate with technical expertise'.[68] The most extreme consequence of this is that issues are made visible, prioritised, researched and funded according to the ease with which they can be quantified. However, while quantitative approaches provide useful insight into key issues, it is also important to acknowledge their limitations. For instance, it is difficult to quantify some political problems facing children in conflict. Personalised conflict-related violence, such as sexual or domestic abuse, is notoriously under-reported in conflict zones. This may be due to a range of political, social and judicial constraints within particular zones. It is important, therefore, to reflect critically upon the accumulation of quantitative data, the assumptions being made by those who accumulate data, and the politics surrounding the policy, resourcing and intellectual purposes to which that information is put. This trend towards quantification must be restrained with a view to methodological pluralism; that is, a mix between quantitative data and an understanding of the extent to which that information can be disrupted by the political, social, cultural and historical contexts from which it is extracted. In short, the politics and political context matter – a deep understanding of *why* violations occurs in particular contexts and *how* they might be addressed is essential to any long-term effort to address them.

Furthermore, the six grave violations have been prioritised due to their strong standing in international law. While this has a pragmatic element to it in terms of enhancing the international community's capacity to address these issues, it nonetheless prioritises these

---

[66] OSRSG-CaAC, 'The Six Grave Violations Against Children During Armed Conflict', 3.

[67] Sally Engle Merry, 'Measuring the World: Indicators, Human Rights, and Global Governance', *Current Anthropology* 52(3) (April 2011), 83.

[68] Ibid., 2.

violations over others that may not be as legally clear-cut, immediately visible or politically palatable. Obviously, the six grave violations are both grave and significant, but a consideration of them does reveal prior political and legal biases. For instance, Charli Carpenter notes that the issue of children born of wartime rape is virtually absent from the international agenda.[69] Most of these children are born to a civilian mother and an enemy combatant father; their identities are complicated by the fact that they are the product of what has been declared a crime against humanity. Thus, the rights and wellbeing of children born of wartime rape are often wilfully neglected by a traumatised mother, community and nation who see the child as being a further reminder of enemy violence.[70] There are no clear pathways through these politically and morally sensitive issues. It is perhaps for this reason that they barely rate a mention in documents such as the 2009 UNICEF *Children and Conflict in a Changing World*, even though the numbers of children born of wartime violence are thought to rival, if not exceed, those of child soldiers.[71]

Similarly, there are a number of other issues facing children in contemporary conflict zones that are not covered by the six grave violations. These include the detention of children, health and mental health issues, the impact of physical disability, the displacement of children, forced labour, the needs of unaccompanied or separated children, and a range of other concerns. While these areas are addressed by the international community, their priorities and resources are superseded by the promotion of the six grave violations. Furthermore, this agenda largely ignores the effects that conflict has upon children who do not live in conflict zones. This includes the effect that conflict might have on military families in conflict-waging states such as the United States or the United Kingdom. For example, the overall number of reports of violence within military families in the United States has steadily increased since 2008.[72] It also includes the effects that the use of chemical or biological weapons have on the

---

[69] See Charli Carpenter, 'Setting the Advocacy Agenda'.

[70] See Donna Seto, *No Place for a War Baby: The Global Politics of Children Born of Wartime Sexual Violence* (London: Ashgate, 2013).

[71] Ibid., 15.

[72] Nancy Montgomery, 'Reports of Family Violence, Abuse, within Military Rise', Stars and Stripes (10 July 2011). Available at www.stripes.com/reports-of-family-violence-abuse-within-military-rise-1.148815.

capacity of veterans to have healthy children. After the first Gulf War, for instance, US veterans reported that exposure to depleted uranium and to medication issued to protect against chemical warfare had been responsible for birth defects in their children.[73] While these children may not have seen a conflict zone, they have been physically, socially and psychologically affected by conflict. It is important to consider the impact of the agenda-setting priorities regarding such issues. Ultimately the criteria that determine what issues are most important will be contestable. However, what is important is to understand the capacity of existing programmes to prioritise and marginalise certain issues, and, as a consequence, certain children.

Conclusion

The above discussion demonstrates that the abuse of children in conflict is widespread. It is not confined to a conflict type, to a historical period, to the identity of the belligerents involved, or to a specific geographical area. However, while it is rife, there are also analytical distinctions that assist in better understanding how and why children are vulnerable to violence in conflict. The first is to dispel the claim that children occupy a private or domestic sphere which exists apart from conflict. The cases discussed above demonstrate that children are not always hapless victims. They are also frequently soldiers, intelligence sources, resource-holders, symbols of innocence and future prospects, and – consequently – specific victims of violence. They are often expressly targeted in conflict *because* they are children. Thus, in terms of the strategies, tactics and weapons of war, children can play a central role. Children themselves may not have chosen it, but they are invested in conflict because conflict is invariably invested in them. As a result, any analysis of the effects of conflict on children cannot be separated from the surrounding conflict, and vice versa.

The second point that must be kept in mind is that any analysis of conflict's impact upon children must consider the conflict type. This enables greater analytical clarity in understanding the nature of the

---

[73] See 'Study: Gulf War Vets' Children Have Higher Birth Defect Rates', USA Today, 3 June 2003. Available at www.usatoday.com/news/health/2003–06-03-vets-birth-defects_x.htm.

violence, the agency of children, and the options available for addressing the issue. For instance, resource wars usually require labour for resource extraction and transport. Children are seen as useful miners because of their size, their agility and their compliance. Consequently, children in these wars become vulnerable to abduction and forced labour. UNICEF notes that during the Angolan civil war, UNITA (National Union for the Total Independence of Angola) rebels abducted large numbers of children to work and soldier in diamond mines.[74] Similarly, violent conflicts that are genocidal in nature deliberately target children. The 1994 genocide in Rwanda saw the brutal targeting of Tutsi children for murder, amputation and sexual violence by Hutu militia groups, which themselves contained child perpetrators.[75] Thus, the political goals and military strategies of belligerents shape the ways by which children are embedded in conflict's orbit.

Finally, the identities and actions of children matter in terms of understanding and anticipating their experiences in conflict. In cases where children are deliberately targeted for violence, they are not targeted simply because they are children, but also because that identity intersects with a range of other identities. For instance, their specific age matters. Children are more likely to be recruited into armed groups if they are older; babies and toddlers are more vulnerable than other age groups to serious health risks that arise from a lack of access to healthcare. Similarly, gender plays a significant role in determining the experiences of children in conflict zones. For example, the experiences of recruited children can vary greatly depending upon their gender: boys are more likely to see active combat duties, while girls are more likely to be kept as cooks and as sex slaves.[76] A child's location can be important: in the conflict in Afghanistan children are more likely to be able to access humanitarian aid if they live in Kabul; however, access in areas of dense fighting is far more limited. Ethnicity, race and religion can determine a child's experience in conflict. In some cases children may be targeted primarily because of their ethnic identity rather than their status as children. Finally, their capacity to be

---

[74] UNICEF, *Machel Study 10-Year Strategic Review* (2009), 12.

[75] Human Rights Watch, 'Lasting Wounds: Consequences of Genocide and War for Rwanda's Children' (March 2003). Available at www.hrw.org/en/reports/2003/04/03/lasting-wounds.

[76] Mary-Jane Fox, 'Girl Soldiers: Human Security and Gendered Insecurity', *Security Dialogue* 35(4) (2004), 465–79.

protected by members of their family, the local or international community can determine their vulnerability. Children who do not have strong and clear recourse to protection are far more likely to come into direct contact with conflict. Brett and Specht point out that children may make rational decisions to join armed groups because, ironically, they imagine that they will be safer in a group environment that is powerful, and which can feed and protect them.[77] Thus, the individual identities of children shape the extent to which conflict affects them and their capacities for resistance and survival.

Children, like all civilians, are victims of conflict. There is no escaping this fundamental claim. However, their relationship to conflict is far more complex than the label 'victim' suggests. The effects of armed conflict upon children cannot be separated from this broader local and global political context. An analysis which considers the inter-relational context, extent and effect of the worlds in which children live has a better chance of providing an accurate account, not just of how conflict affects children, but why it does, what its consequences will be, and what the most appropriate path of protection, recovery and future prevention is. Children themselves can play an important role in this process; after all, they play multiple roles in conflict. Children can and do move deftly between their status as civilian and combatant, perpetrator and peace maker, protector and protected. Thus, even as victims of conflict, some children have demonstrated the capacity of active empowerment, even if it is simply through their role as survivors of conflict. It is to this question of children and agency in conflict that this book now turns.

[77] Rachel Brett and Irma Specht, *Young Soldiers: Why They Choose to Fight* (Boulder, CO: Lynne Rienner, 2004).

2 | Children and agency: caretakers, free-rangers and everyday life

KIM HUYNH

Introduction

'I've been waiting ages to find out what's going on behind those piercing little eyes.' You shrugged. 'Snakes and snails and puppy dog tails.'

See? Kevin was (and remains) a mystery to me. You had that insouciant boy-thing going and blithely assumed that you had been there yourself and there was nothing to find out. And you and I may have differed on so profound a level as the nature of human character. You regarded a child as a partial creature, a simpler form of life, which evolved into the complexity of adulthood in open view. But from the instant he was laid on my breast I perceived Kevin Khatchadourian as pre-extant, with a vast, fluctuating interior life whose subtlety and intensity would if anything diminish with age. Most of all, he seemed hidden from me, while your experience was one of sunny, leisurely access.[1]

This fictional dialogue between the parents of a juvenile murderer expresses two important perspectives relating to the issues of how much agency children have and how much power adults can exert over them. Kevin's father sees his son as delicate yet malleable. For him, the weakness of the child evokes the power and duty of care that comes with being grown up. This is an essentially sanguine perspective because the child's incompleteness embodies the family's – and indeed humanity's – boundless potential for replenishment and growth. Kevin's mother, on the other hand, sees her son as more capable of shaping himself and others than her husband would like to believe. For her, children are complex and perhaps even unknowable. She is thus inclined to maintain some distance from them. However, Kevin's profound inaccessibility undercuts his mother's authority and maternal instinct; she is unable to steer him away from the world's worst evils or prevent him from becoming one.

[1] Lionel Shriver, *We Need to Talk About Kevin* (Melbourne: Text Publishing, 2003), 137.

Whereas the opening chapter of this book focused on the effects of conflict and political violence on children, this chapter examines the potential impact of children on conflict and politics. It examines the contexts and ways in which children are social actors. The chapter engages with work from across the social sciences and draws upon a broad range of examples from popular literature, war zones, everyday life and international law. It provides a framework which can be used to understand and assess debates relating to children and specific disciplines – such as IR – or issues, such as child soldiers, forced migration, and peace building. This conceptual framework is based around two diametrically opposed positions.

The 'caretaker' position – to which Kevin's father is aligned – asserts that all children are vulnerable, innocent, dependent and irrational. Because of these deficiencies, they should be shielded from public affairs, moral corruption and severe violence. Caretakers believe that by nurturing younger generations and gradually conferring to them rights as they become more competent, older generations pass on 'the best of all possible worlds'.[2] The caretaker view underpins many of the legal instruments and humanitarian efforts relating to children in the twentieth and twenty-first centuries and maintains that children have no place in conflict zones. Kevin's mother's insights and predicament reflect the now dominant understanding in the social sciences – with an important exception being IR – of children as sovereign beings. This 'free-ranger' position asserts that the concept of childhood changes across time and place. To declare that there is a universal notion of childhood is to subjugate and silence the children and societies who fail to abide by that notion. Free-rangers view children as beings in their own right, with their own identity and values. It is therefore both practical and principled to recognise them as social agents who can speak for themselves and contribute to society.

Michel de Certeau's foray into the PEL offers some common ground upon which caretakers and free-rangers might meet. He maintains that even within milieus that are not of their making, people operate in ways that preserve and exert their individuality. This tactical form of resistance can fruitfully coexist with a degree of caretaker paternalism. It also provides a lens with which to envisage how children's everyday activities, such as make-believe, play and

---

[2] With acknowledgements to Leibniz and Voltaire's enlightened optimism.

disobedience, can help them and adults cope in the midst of violence and oppression.

Caretakers: why children should be neither seen nor heard

Events such as the 2004 hostage-taking and subsequent massacre of almost 200 school children in Beslan in the northern Caucasus and the mass abduction of over 200 Nigerian school girls by the Boko Haram militants in 2014 evoke in many of us outrage and a deep sense of loss. Putting the political intricacies aside, such tragedies seem to show that children have no place in politics and conflict. Moreover, those who drag them into such adult affairs have committed an egregious act against not only the children, but also their societies or even the future of humanity which all children represent. Hence, the offers of international assistance to rescue the Nigerian schoolgirls and the global campaign to 'Bring Back Our Girls'. These sentiments and actions dovetail with a framework of thought that Archard refers to as the 'caretaker thesis'.[3] Caretakers stridently support the idea that each individual should be free to determine her or his own future. However, because children are not yet capable of making free and sound decisions, self-determination is too important to be left in their hands.[4] By this account, children can be likened to slender saplings: while attentive caretaking does not guarantee their vigour and longevity, left unattended they will surely grow crookedly or wither.

Caretaker paternalism is based on a conception of the child as 'a stage before and below adulthood'.[5] Children are deficient vis-à-vis adults in four interrelated ways. They are vulnerable – lacking in strength and resilience; innocent or unworldly – lacking in experience; dependent – lacking in free will; and irrational – lacking in coherent thought. These deficiencies are worth considering in detail as they underpin a wide range of laws and institutions which aim to separate the child's world from the adult one in which violence, exploitation and vice are all too prevalent.

According to the caretaker, children are physically, psychologically and emotionally vulnerable. This is a biological fact that is totally

[3] David Archard, *Children: Rights and Childhood*, 2nd edn (New York, NY: Routledge, 2004), 58.
[4] Ibid., 67.   [5] Ibid., 43.

independent of time, geography and social class.[6] Whereas hardship can scar grownups, it shapes and defines the nascent character of children. Exposing children to conflict is therefore wrong because it not only damages them but also determines the adults who they become.[7] In popular parlance 'women and children' are bundled together in such a way as to underline their mutual fragility and the injustice of their suffering.[8] Many women have sought to distance themselves from such associations in the belief that with patriarchal protection comes disempowerment. Modern caretakers may well support this position for women, but not for children, whose vulnerabilities are manifest and wide-ranging. Moreover, their disempowerment is justified because it is provisional, inspired by caretaker altruism and universally applicable. The dire need to protect the defenceless child is portrayed in a famous scene from Albert Camus' *The Plague*. After the infected city is sealed off from the world, Dr Rieux and Father Paneloux witness the drawn-out and excruciating death of a 'half-formed boy' with puny limbs covered in boils. The child writhes and screams, but ultimately puts up no resistance. For Dr Rieux, the boy's death underlines the absurdity of human existence. His emaciated body appears to be a 'grotesque parody of crucifixion'. Paneloux sees the child's suffering as a test for Christians and their faith in God. Both agree that the agonising loss of the nameless child represents a terrible and foreboding wrong, serving as a fulcrum point between hope and despair. Together they cry out, 'How can we let this happen to a child?' Similar cries followed the imprisonment and beating of fifteen Syrian boys who in 2011 graffitied on their school wall a popular slogan asserting that 'The people want to topple the regime.' Such acts of rebellion and repression were so common in the region that personal ID was required to buy spray cans. However, it was the ill-treatment of these vulnerable children that sparked the subsequent Syrian uprising.

[6] Harry Hendrick, 'Constructions and Reconstructions of British Childhood', in Allison James and Alan Prout (eds.), *Constructing and Reconstructing Childhood: Contemporary Issues in the Sociological Study of Childhood*, 2nd edn (New York, NY: Routledge, 1997), 51.

[7] Kristin Barstad, 'Preventing the Recruitment of Child Soldiers: The ICRC Approach', *Refugee Survey Quarterly* 27 (2008), 142–9.

[8] Cynthia Enloe, 'Women and Children: Making Feminist Sense of the Persian Gulf War', *The Village Voice* (September 1990), 25.

The second ground for denying agency to children relates to their innocence. A lack of worldly experience means that children cannot make well-informed decisions and therefore should not be held responsible for their actions in the same way as adults. This appeal to innocence can mitigate responsibility for everything from social faux pas to crimes against humanity. It follows, however, that if a child's responsibility should be curtailed, then so too should her or his autonomy. Where there is an imbalance favouring the latter we find a child who thinks she or he can act without due consideration of the consequences. But innocence is not merely an excuse; it is also a quality that must be protected for the good of the child and the community – this is the basis for many legal restrictions and classifications. In Renaissance art the affiliation between children and moral purity is illustrated by the use of putti, cherubim and angels. William Golding's classic novel, *Lord of the Flies*, tells of the dangers of leaving children unsupervised, exposing them to the state of nature and allowing them to grow up too fast.

The argument that children are intrinsically dependent on others and therefore should not make decisions about themselves and the world is enunciated by the eighteenth century philosopher and figurehead of the western Enlightenment, Immanuel Kant. At first glance, this idea conflicts with Kant's insistence that we acknowledge people as 'ends in themselves'; that is, as autonomous agents who should cast their vote on matters of significance to them.[9] Treating others as mere means to further our own interests, altruistic or otherwise, is by his thinking immoral, illogical and antithetical to human progress. However, Kant can be read as making an exception to this categorical imperative when it comes to children, one that aligns him closely with caretakers. For Kant, children are 'passive citizens' in contrast to true adults who are 'active citizens'.[10] The former are not entitled to the same recognition and agency as the latter because they are dependent, most commonly on their parents who shape and sustain them. In this vein, moral philosopher Tamar Schapiro asserts that childhood is a 'predicament': the child is not yet in a position 'to speak in her own voice because there is no voice which counts as hers'.[11]

Kant made a similar case with respect to women, who could not conceivably cast a vote free of the authority of their husbands.

---

[9] This idea is introduced in his 1785 *Groundwork of the Metaphysics of Morals*.
[10] Schapiro, 'What is a Child?', 719.   [11] Ibid., 729.

Equally, people in 'pre-political' societies were passive because they were beholden to archaic bonds and hierarchies.[12] Like many Enlightenment and evolutionary thinkers, Kant likened the development of a person from embryo to adult with the development of a people or race from barbarism to civility.[13] But even if the philosopher was not as liberal as we – or even he – would like to think, he was no conservative. He did not believe people should simply know their place and stay there. On the contrary, Kantian paternalism demands that active citizens take into account the long-term and open futures of passive citizens when legislating on their behalf. This notion of holding agency 'in trust' illustrates the conflicting responsibilities that all conscientious caretakers must negotiate. They must have a firm grasp of a child's immediate needs, without constricting the choices and opportunities that might allow her or him to flourish. Thus, because passive children are active adults in the making, they cannot be treated as 'members of a permanent underclass'.[14] So while children are not accorded a full array of political rights, their basic human rights are firmly intact and ideally protected by those who they are dependent upon. These rights allow them to take on a more active and effective role in society when they reach maturity. Before turning to the sorts of child rights that are critical to caretakers, it is necessary initially to examine the final basis for denying them full autonomy: their irrationality.

For caretakers, children are not just beholden to others, but also to their ignorance and unchecked urges. Adults, on the other hand, are able to form coherent and objective conceptions about themselves and the world. This ability to reason is developed over time through life experience, education and reflection. Reason is not only an accurate way of thinking, but also virtuous because it facilitates consensus without resorting to force, and subjects base appetites to self-control. Since children have not had the opportunity to cultivate this capacity they are impressionable, egocentric, fickle and incapable of planning for the future – they are, in effect, childish. The seventeenth-century liberal philosopher John Locke bluntly asserted in an essay on education that children are 'white paper, void of all characters,

---

[12] Ibid., 717–19.   [13] Archard, *Children: Rights and Childhood*, 46.
[14] Schapiro, 'What is a Child?', 719.

without any ideas'.[15] Jean Piaget placed children in a similar starting position in devising his model for human development, which became the dominant paradigm for much of the twentieth century and arguably remains so in international policy circles.[16] Piaget believed that human maturation was a punctuated journey from a basic sensory understanding of cause and effect to full cognitive maturity. The endpoint of this process, the formal operations stage, is defined by hypothetical and abstract thinking; that is, the ability to survey a range of theoretical options systematically with a view to determining the one that best suits the situation at hand. The universality of Piaget's model along with some of his methods have been widely criticised. In particular, after finding that children under six did not understand that a volume of liquid is conserved when it is poured into different containers, he concluded that they had an underdeveloped understanding of the world. His critics argue that when measured against adults, children will always come up short. Nonetheless, Piaget's focus on the capacity to reason as the defining difference between children and adults remains powerful, particularly among caretakers.

The caretaker conception of childhood is reflected in major twentieth-century international legal initiatives which stress the need to distance children from conflict zones and protect them from all forms of harm. Most notably, the Save the Children International Union (SCIU) rose to prominence after World War I with an agenda of rescuing children 'body and soul' from the horrors that humanity sought to impose upon them.[17] The SCIU drafted the Declaration of the Rights of the Child, which was adopted by the General Assembly of the League of Nations in 1924. As discussed in more detail in Chapter 4, it marked the entry point of the child into international affairs, stipulating a set of liberal humanitarian principles that go to the core of the caretaker ethos.[18]

---

[15] Cited in Archard, *Children: Rights and Childhood*, 11.

[16] Piaget's key books in this regard are *The Language and Thought of the Child* (trans. Marjorie Gabain) (London: Routledge & Kegan Paul, 1932), and *The Child's Conception of the World* (trans. Joan and Andrew Tomlinson) (London: Routledge & Kegan Paul, 1929).

[17] Lara Bolzman, 'The Advent of Child Rights on the International Scene and the Role of the Save the Children International Union 1920–1940', *Refugee Survey Quarterly* 27(4) (2009), 31.

[18] The Declaration can be found online at www.un-documents.net/gdrc1924.htm.

According to the Declaration, children are helpless victims who must be saved from 'every form of exploitation' and nurtured so that they might as adults devote their talents to the service of humankind. Indeed, the SCIU was convinced that prioritising the welfare of children and ensuring that they are the 'first to receive relief in times of stress' was vital to saving the world. The Declaration thus focused on 'welfare rights', which guarantee food, health and shelter, as distinguished from 'agency rights', which enshrine choice and participation.[19] Of course, a basic level of welfare is essential for anyone to exert agency. However, caretakers believe that because children do not know what is good for them, adults must be entrusted both to look after their wellbeing and to speak on their behalf. So while caring for hungry and sick children are primary objectives of the 1924 Declaration, it empowers adult feeders and nursers – parents, families, communities and states – as decision-makers.

Caretaker thinking and values also underpin key elements of the more recent and widely accepted children's rights treaty, the 1989 UNCRC, which signifies the emergence of the concept of the 'the world's children'.[20] The Convention conveys a degree of paternalism from the outset, emphasising children's welfare over their autonomy. The preamble of the UNCRC declares that the family is the 'fundamental group of society' and the opening articles stress the responsibility of states parties to serve and promote the 'best interests of the child'. However, the UNCRC is not as stridently caretaker in orientation as the 1924 Declaration. Other parts of the Convention allow a presence for children in the political sphere. Articles 14 and 15 specify rights to freedom of thought, conscience and religion, along with freedom of association. Crucially, Article 12 asserts that a child's voice should be 'given due weight in accordance with the age and maturity' in all matters affecting her or him. In this way, the UNCRC promotes an 'apprenticeship' perspective of rights

---

[19] Harry Brighouse, 'What Rights (If Any) Do Children Have?', in David Archard and Colin Macleod (eds.), *The Moral and Political Status of Children* (Oxford: Oxford University Press, 2002), 38. Brighouse draws from Amartya Sen's idea of welfare rights as wellbeing rights.

[20] Allison James and Alan Prout (eds.), *Constructing and Reconstructing Childhood: Contemporary Issues in the Sociological Study of Childhood*, 2nd edn (New York, NY: Routledge, 1997), 1.

and responsibilities in which agency is gradually bestowed upon children as they develop.[21]

While all caretakers support the measured introduction of children into the public sphere, not all of them agree with the process outlined in the 1989 Convention. For instance, Brighouse maintains that it is contradictory and hazardous to entrust children with the right to their own culture (Article 30) and religion (Article 14).[22] Children, he argues, are necessarily dependent upon their guardians to inform them of and induct them into a belief system. Indeed, the preamble of the UNCRC stresses the central role of the family and communities in the 'harmonious development of the child'. Moreover, for Brighouse, children should not be free to express themselves unless they can be held responsible for their views. By granting this freedom and in turn imposing this responsibility via Article 12, the Convention potentially restricts children from experimenting with different perspectives. Such experimentation, he asserts, is essential to the development of rational thinking. Despite critiques of the particular agency rights enshrined by the UNCRC, their very existence reflects a change in thinking about children which maintains that we cannot effectively address a child's welfare without paying close attention to what she or he thinks, believes and says. This linking of welfare to agency is a core feature of the free-ranger school of thought, which insists that children are far more resilient and able than caretakers would like to believe.

Free-rangers: why children are autonomous

In 2008, Lenore Skenazy allowed her nine-year-old son to take the New York subway home, alone. Skenazy recounted the experience in an opinion piece soon afterwards in which she argued that 'keeping kids under lock and key and helmet and cell phone and nanny and surveillance' is debilitating to both adults and children.[23] With

---

[21] Michael Wyness, Lisa Harrison and Ian Buchanan, 'Childhood, Politics and Ambiguity: Towards an Agenda for Children's Political Inclusion', *Sociology* 38(1) (2004), 90.

[22] Brighouse, 'What Rights (If Any) Do Children Have?', 50–1.

[23] Lenore Skenazy, 'Why I Let My 9-Year-Old Ride the Subway Alone', The New York Sun, 1 April 2008. Available at www.nysun.com/opinion/why-i-let-my-9-year-old-ride-subway-alone/73976/. Concerns about stifling children are not restricted to America or the West. There is, for example, a push among some urban Chinese parents to create space for 'children's unique natures and distinct

respect to her own child riding the subway, she was a little concerned at first, but felt vindicated by his return home 'ecstatic with independence'.[24] Skenazy's experiment generated fierce debate across the nation and overseas. Detractors accused her of child abuse and she was dubbed 'America's worst Mom'. But Skenazy also had a great many supporters and through a blog and book kick-started a worldwide movement for free-range kids.[25]

Three core convictions of this popular movement are shared by the New Social Studies of Childhood (NSSC) scholars, who aim to place children at the centre of their research. NSSC ideas have dethroned the functional and developmental thinking of caretakers, and now dominate childhood studies. They are also influential in the so-called helping professions such as social work, education and psychology.[26] Both scholarly and non-scholarly free-rangers question the universality of the caretaker model of childhood. They also challenge the ethics and efficacy of caretaker paternalism, asserting that it represses children and embeds incompetence. Finally, free-rangers maintain that children can and do create their own meaningful worlds, even in conflict zones, and that in doing so they can teach adults a thing or two about their worlds.

According to free-rangers it is not children who are malleable, but rather our notions of childhood.[27] Whereas caretakers believe that there is one path from immaturity to maturity, free-rangers favour plurality, presume complexity and celebrate difference.[28] Free-rangers seek to question fundamental conceptions of childhood, adulthood and growing up. To this end, the voluminous psychological and scientific

development requirements' that grows out of a vision of them as 'self-making, self-governing subjects' rather than as being made by their parents, families and studious endeavours; Orna Naftali, 'Recovering Childhood: Play, Pedagogy, and the Rise of Psychological Knowledge in Contemporary Urban China', *Modern China* 36(6) (2010), 591.

[24] Skenazy, 'Why I Let My 9-Year-Old Ride the Subway Alone'.

[25] Lenore Skenazy, *Free-Range Kids: Giving our Children the Freedom We Had Without Going Nuts With Worry*, (San Fransisco, CA: Jossey-Bass, 2009).

[26] David M. Rosen, *Armies of the Young: Child Soldiers in War and Terrorism* (New Brunswick: Rutgers University Press, 2005), 133.

[27] For a comprehensive discussion of how childhood is constructed through cultural politics see Allison James and Adrian James, *Constructing Childhood: Theory, Policy and Social Practice* (New York, NY: Palgrave Macmillan, 2004).

[28] Adrian L. James, 'Competition or Integration? The Next Step in Childhood Studies?', *Childhood* 17(4) (November 2010), 487.

research upon which caretaker models of development are based are, according to free-rangers, 'technologies of knowledge' that ultimately conceal the socially constructed nature of childhood.[29] This is not to say that children do not exist as physical entities or that their limitations are fabricated. Rather, free-rangers argue that 'what a society expects of children, the way that they are perceived, what is seen as good or bad for them and what they are competent or incompetent to perform depends upon the particular concept of childhood that society has constructed'.[30] It follows that there is an array of childhoods spanning class, locality and culture, none of which is totally superior to the other. For example, contemporary Europeans tend to think of the new-born child as a largely blank slate, while the widespread view in sub-Saharan Africa is that 'infants remember the world they came from and indeed that, to stay in this world or even in a way to become human, they have to forget this other life'.[31] While caretakers mark the end of childhood by age, free-rangers stress that many people adopt social markers for transition to adulthood, such as marriage, procreation and the death of parents along with rituals and rites of passage.[32] Furthermore, Skenazy points out that while some western parents are expected to keep constant watch over their children, in many parts of the world seven-year-olds take care of five-year-olds, and often the five-year-olds take care of the three-year-olds.[33] Bessell provides an example of how Indonesian child labourers

[29] Alan Prout and Allison James, 'A New Paradigm for the Sociology of Childhood? Provenance, Promise and Problems', in Allison James and Alan Prout (eds.), *Constructing and Reconstructing Childhood: Contemporary Issues in the Sociological Study of Childhood*, 2nd edn (New York, NY: Routledge, 1997), 9.

[30] Michael King, 'The Sociology of Childhood as Scientific Communication: Observations From a Social Systems Perspective', *Childhood* 14(2) (May 2007), 195. See also Erica Burman, 'Local, Global or Globalized?: Child Development and International Child', *Childhood* 3(1) (1996), 45–66.

[31] Cited in Karen Wells, *Childhood in a Global Perspective* (Cambridge: Polity Press, 2009), 2–3.

[32] Ah-Jung Lee, 'Understanding and Addressing the Phenomenon of "Child Soldiers": The Gap between the Global Humanitarian Discourse and the Local Understandings and Experiences of Young People's Military Recruitment', Working paper 52, Refugee Studies Centre (January 2009), 14. Available at www.rsc.ox.ac.uk/publications/working-papers-folder_contents/RSCworking paper52.pdf.

[33] Skenazy, *Free-Range Kids*, 8. The variability in terms of how childhood is understood is illustrated by the fact that in Peru a significant group of six to fourteen-year-olds are heads of households and principal breadwinners. And over 6 per cent of children in Bangalore, India are the sole working members of

are not so much dependent upon their families, but rather are interdependent.[34] Free-rangers may well acknowledge and support the idea of different notions of childhood intermingling in a globalised world, but they are stridently opposed to one model exerting itself over others, whether that be through corporate advertising, public policy, psychological diagnosis or international law.[35]

Radically different ideas regarding childhood are also evident across time: the most influential account of this is presented in Phillippe Ariès' *Centuries of Childhood*.[36] An accomplished and provocative historian, Ariès is best known for his assertion that 'in medieval society, the idea of childhood did not exist'.[37] This does not mean that pre-modern adults totally disregarded children. Rather, Ariès argued that western societies now have an acute awareness of a stage in a young person's development during which time she or he should be quarantined from the world of adults. Medieval people lacked this awareness, so that parents were relatively indifferent to infants and, moreover, after the age of about seven children were treated as miniature adults. Ariès based his claim on a range of evidence including historic paintings in which children and adults were dressed alike, the commonality of games between young and old, and diaries attesting to the absence of any need to shield the young Louis XIII from sexual discussions and deeds. All of this suggested that children and adults once existed in the same world. These worlds started to part during the western Enlightenment era and by the twentieth century were entirely detached. By and large this was caused by a marked decrease in child mortality rates, which meant that modern parents could rationally invest time, energy and capital in their children in the confidence that they would survive childhood. Another key milestone in this separation was the emergence of institutionalised schooling during the Industrial

---

their families: Jo Boyden, 'Childhood and the Policy Makers: A Comparative Perspective on the Globalization of Childhood', in Allison James and Alan Prout (eds.), *Constructing and Reconstructing Childhood: Contemporary Issues in the Sociological Study of Childhood*, 2nd edn (New York, NY: Routledge, 1997), 198.

[34] Sharon Bessell, 'Indonesian Children's Views and Experiences of Work and Poverty', *Social Policy and Society* 8(4) (2009), 538.

[35] Erica Burman, 'Local, Global or Globalized?', 45–66.

[36] Philippe Ariès (trans. R. Baldick), *Centuries of Childhood* (London: Jonathan Cape, 1962).

[37] Ariès, *Centuries of Childhood*, 125.

Revolution, which established childhood as the essential and only time for learning. According to Ariès, then, social conditions crafted our understanding of a child's needs and sensibilities, not vice versa. Ariès' narrow focus on the upper classes has led many to question the reach of his evidence and argument. Along with others, Archard argues that previous societies did not fail to regard children as different from adults; they 'merely thought about the difference in different ways'.[38] Nonetheless, free-rangers are indebted to Ariès in an epistemological sense; that is, for his assertion that childhood is socially constructed. Where they disagree with him most fervently is in normative and political terms; for while Ariès lauded the modern caretaker notion of childhood as principled and effective, free-rangers are far more sceptical if not scathing of it.

Free-rangers believe that institutions such as childhood do not take shape in a benign fashion but rather in accordance with power agendas. And because caretakers are insufficiently aware of their own agendas, they are prone to reinforce the most dominant and sometimes pernicious ones. Specifically, the objective judgement and altruistic aims of caretakers often mask a compulsion for control. This compulsion pervades the caretaker notion of children as vulnerable, innocent, dependent and irrational. Free-rangers do not believe that children are the physical equals of adults or that they are competent in every way. Rather, they seek to expose an ideological project that elevates adult interests by stressing children's vulnerability and incompetence while ignoring their resilience and capabilities.[39] Watson observes that childhood is not just a social construct, it is a 'social stereotype' that engenders economic exploitation, physical coercion and symbolic power.[40] This stereotype has become so pronounced and pervasive that, for Skenazy, childhood can be likened to a disability that prevents people from preparing their own lunch, climbing a tree, walking a couple of blocks or making decisions: '10 is the new 2', she proclaims: 'we're infantilizing our kids into

---

[38] Archard, *Children: Rights and Childhood*, 34.

[39] The debates over to what extent and in what ways children are resilient are covered in Ch. 3 of E. Cairns (ed.), Children and Political Violence (Understanding Children's Worlds) (Oxford: Blackwell, 1996).

[40] Alison Watson, 'Children's Rights and the Politics of Childhood', in Patrick Hayden (ed.), *The Ashgate Research Companion to Ethics and International Relations* (Farnham: Ashgate, 2009), 251.

incompetence'.[41] There is a correlation here with portrayals of women as vulnerable, frail, meek and helpless, or as 'the fairer sex'. Similarly, adults, 'want children to be helpless so that we can help them' and we need them to be dependent and irrational so that we can hold on to idealised visions of ourselves as figures of rational authority.[42] It follows that seemingly innocuous or even complimentary adjectives used to describe children, such as 'cute', promote an adult-centric agenda.[43] For free-rangers, then, children are one of the major subjugated groups in the western-dominated world, along with women, the working class, coloured people, homosexuals and the global poor. The 'caretaker's burden' to nurture them, just like the 'white man's burden' to instruct the coloured people of the world, merely justifies oppression.

Free-rangers also view caretaker conceptions of childhood as a state of innocence as factually flawed. Most people, assert free-rangers, simply do not experience childhood as a time of carefree play, 'an asexual and peaceful existence within the protective bosom of the family'.[44] More importantly, attempts to realise this romantic vision have adverse consequences. Innocent children, like vulnerable ones, may well be protected from the world, but in the process they are denied any knowledge of it. As a consequence they are isolated from others, denied a voice in their own affairs and even control over their own bodies. This emphasis on preserving innocence thus creates children who are ignorant and inept. Moreover, the 'fetishistic glorification' of childhood innocence means that individuals who do not fit into the caretaker mould are not only marginalised, but

---

[41] Nancy Gibbs, 'The Growing Backlash against Overparenting', *Time* (20 November 2009). Available at http://content.time.com/time/magazine/article/ 0,9171,1940697,00.htm. Skenazy is not the first to observe how societies that over-nurture children also tend to constrain them. Scheper-Hughes, for instance, asserted in 1987 that 'the instrumental value of children has been largely replaced by their expressive value. Children have become relatively worthless (economically) to their parents, but priceless in terms of their psychological worth': Nancy Scheper-Hughes, *Child Survival: Anthropological Perspectives on the Treatment and Maltreatment of Children* (Dordrecht: D. Reidel, 1987), 12.

[42] Archard, *Children: Rights and Childhood*, 63.   [43] Ibid.

[44] Jenny Kitzinger, 'Who are you Kidding? Children, Power, and the Struggle against Sexual Abuse', in Allison James and Alan Prout, *Constructing and Reconstructing Childhood: Contemporary Issues in the Sociological Study of Childhood* (New York, NY: Routledge, 1997), 160.

demonised.[45] This is because the caretaker ideal of childhood is, according to free-ranger critics, acutely bipolar, so that premature knowledge of elements of the adult world, such as conflict, violence or sex, is enough to turn the purest angel into a wicked devil.[46] This irrevocable shift is observable in the moral panic that accompanies cases of minors who commit horrific crimes, such as the 1993 abduction and killing in the UK of two-year-old James Bulger by two ten-year-old boys. Thus, despite their appeals to liberal progress and universal rights, caretakers arguably reinforce practices from the 'Age of Quarantine' when wayward children were deemed to have reverted to a naturally fallen or depraved state that could only be rectified through isolation and the severest forms of corporal punishment.[47]

The key point for free-rangers is that while childhood is an oppressive adult-centric construction, children themselves can and do exert agency. Agency relates to the capacity to exert and interpret power to produce an intended effect, even in situations that are created and regulated by others.[48] Alan Prout argues that NSSC scholars have clearly established that 'while children's lives are constrained and influenced by sociocultural contexts and by the adults surrounding them', they nevertheless create and recreate 'their own social worlds'.[49] Similarly, William Corsaro argues that children borrow and adapt from adult worlds to fashion their own unique childhood cultures. Corsaro 'goes native', entering into these

---

[45] Ibid.

[46] Lorraine Macmillan, 'The Child Soldier in North-South Relations', *International Political Sociology* 3(1) (2009), 36–52, 38. Macmillan refers to the contrasting logics of innocence and evil that govern childhood: Bob Franklin, *The New Handbook of Children's Rights: Comparative Policy and Practice* (New York, NY: Taylor & Francis, 2001), 16. Franklin asserts that children are increasingly portrayed as either 'victims' or 'villains'.

[47] John Keane, 'Children and Civil Society', Presentation for *Neglecting Children and Youth: Democracies at Risk*, a seminar held at The University of Sydney, 5 November 2008.

[48] This definition of agency is derived from Rosen, *Armies of the Young*, 133; and Julia Meredith Hess and Dianna Shandy, 'Kids at the Crossroads: Global Childhood and the State', *Anthropological Quarterly* 81(4) (October 2008), 765–76, 770.

[49] Alan Prout, 'Researching Children as Social Actors: An Introduction to the Children 5–16 Programme', *Children and Society* 16(2) (2002), 67–76. Cited in Kathryn Backett-Milburn et al., 'Challenging Childhoods: Young People's Accounts of "Getting By" in Families with Substance Use Problems', *Childhood* 15(4) (1 November 2008), 462.

childhood cultures as an ethnologist does a foreign society, all the while maintaining that 'kids are deserving of study as kids'.[50] Kitzinger's research into sexually abused children is important in this context because it demonstrates that, contrary to popular depictions, children in even the most repressive situations are not passive victims. They fight, hide, negotiate, repel and deceive their abusers in a myriad of ways. And when this does not work they can psychologically withdraw, so that lifelessness and passivity are themselves forms of agency and resistance. As one of Kitzinger's interviewees recounted, 'When he touched me I used to be really stiff, obviously I'd let him do it, but that didn't mean I had to take any type of part in it. I just felt like a doll.'[51] The point stressed by Macmillan in the context of girl soldiers is that, while children may well suffer and be degraded, they should not be understood as objects but rather 'agents operating under very unequal relations of power'.[52] In this vein, free-rangers would acknowledge that it was the imprisonment of children that sparked the Syrian uprising in 2011, but would focus not so much on the adult reaction to the brutalisation of innocent children but rather the children themselves who had the courage and vision to graffiti the school wall.

To stress that children are important actors in society is not to say that they act in adult ways or that the differences between children and adults are minimal.[53] There are, to be sure, children's rights movements promoting an end to all age-based restrictions on drug and media consumption along with participation in politics, the workforce and the military.[54] While not necessarily opposed to these abolitionist causes, free-rangers are also not ideologically aligned with them. This is because they seek to create more elastic and inclusive forms of childhood rather than abolish it altogether. Childhood should be seen as 'a process of maturation that has no point of complete separation from adulthood. "Adulthood" can include and retain childlike qualities, and correspondingly virtues or disadvantages of adulthood

---

[50] William Corsaro, *The Sociology of Childhood*, 3rd edn (London: Sage, 2011), 120.

[51] Kitzinger, 'Who are you kidding?', 165.

[52] Macmillan, 'The Child Soldier in North-South Relations', 42.

[53] This is asserted by free-ranger critics such as King, 'The Sociology of Childhood as Scientific Communication', 200.

[54] See, for example, Americans for a Society Free of Age Restrictions (ASFAR).

may also be found throughout childhood.'[55] Put another way, free-rangers do not want to make children the same as adults, but rather remove the barriers to them exploring and articulating their similarities and differences. In this regard, children can be understood as an ethnic group in a multicultural society: their civic freedoms are protected not just for their own sake, but so that their values and insights can be woven into the social fabric. Feminist parallels are also instructive because many free-rangers aim through their research and activism to empower children.[56] Borrowing from feminist terminology, free-rangers seek to develop through dialogue and empathy a 'child standpoint' or 'childpoint' that destabilises the 'paradigm of sovereign man'.[57] But it is important to note that movements such as multiculturalism and feminism serve as guidelines rather than blueprints for free-range reform; the point being that children should define the world in their own terms.

Alison Gopnik makes a valuable contribution to the free-ranger argument in this area by drawing upon recent psychological and neurological research to highlight the distinctive capabilities and qualities of infants.[58] Gopnik asserts that practically from birth, and certainly by the age of two, people are moral agents who can empathise with others and decide what is right and wrong.[59] Infants are also reasoning beings, but not in the way that caretakers expect them to be. Indeed, children and adult worldviews are often so dissimilar that

---

[55] Brocklehurst, *Who's Afraid of Children?*, 4–5.

[56] Wells, *Childhood in a Global Perspective*, 16.

[57] Berry Mayall, *Towards a Sociology for Childhood*, 1st edn (Buckingham: Open University Press, 2002), Ch. 12.

[58] Alison Gopnik, *The Philosophical Baby: What Children's Minds Tell Us about Truth, Love, and the Meaning of Life* (New York, NY: Farrar, Straus and Giroux, 2009).

[59] 'The Philosophical Baby – Alison Gopnik', *The Philosopher's Zone*, 29 January 2011. Available at www.abc.net.au/rn/philosopherszone/stories/2011/3121263. htm. Similarly, Hamlin has found that infants as young three to four months, who have had very limited cultural conditioning, make moral judgements. In particular, after they have watched puppet plays in which a character is either 'good' – in the sense that it pushes a protagonist up a hill – or 'bad' – in the sense that it pushes a protagonist down the hill, steals toys or slams boxes – 85 per cent of the time infants will choose the helpful puppet by way of grabbing, staring and/or sucking. Of itself this research does not show that we are predisposed to be good, but it does indicate that we make moral assessments from a very early age and prefer others, puppets and people, to be good: see J. Kiley Hamlin, 'A Developmental Perspective on the Moral Dyad', *Psychological Inquiry* 23(2) (2012), 166–7.

they are 'different forms of homo sapiens'.[60] By 'different', Gopnik infers that children in some ways are better than adults, more creative, smarter, more conscious and caring.[61] Whereas adults specialise in focusing in a Piagetian sort of way on a particular problem that has to be solved, infants are inclined to take in many things at once. Furthermore, children experience great difficulty thinking about how the world is without also envisaging numerous ways in which it might be otherwise. This aligns with what Gopnik suggests is a healthy scientific and creative mind-set in which nothing is taken for granted and whereby imaginative leaps become both possible and laudable.[62] 'Children are the vibrant, wandering butterflies who transform into caterpillars inching along the grown-up path.'[63] If this is correct, adults should not only have more regard for children's agency, but also consider how childish thinking and behaviour can enhance and even revolutionise our adult-centric world.

Not surprisingly, free-rangers favour agency rights over welfare rights. However, they are wary of the international children's rights regime, which they believe is animated by caretaker values.[64] Pupavac argues that the regime is preoccupied with deviancy or delinquency and that by imposing idealised versions of childhood upon other states it paves the way for neo-colonial incursions upon children generally, but particularly upon non-western children.[65] Burr's study of the implementation of the UNCRC in Vietnam after it was ratified in 1990 provides an insight into how the Convention, despite containing elements that support child participation and cultural difference, nonetheless operates in a paternalistic and Eurocentric fashion.[66] In her research on organisations assisting street children,

---

[60] Gopnik, *The Philosophical Baby*, 9.   [61] Ibid.

[62] See Alison Gopnik, Andrew. N. Meltzoff and Patricia K. Kuhl, *The Scientist in the Crib: Minds, Brains and How Children Learn* (New York, NY: HarperCollins 2000); A. Gopnik and H. Wellman, 'The Theory Theory', in L. Hirschfield and S. Gelman (eds.), *Mapping the Mind: Domain Specificity in Cognition and Culture* (New York, NY: Cambridge University Press, 1994), 257–93.

[63] Gopnik, *The Philosophical Baby*, 38.

[64] See James and James, *Constructing Childhood*, Ch. 4: 'The Universalization of Law?', 78–108.

[65] Vanessa Pupavac, 'The International Children's Rights Regime', in David Chandler (ed.), *Rethinking Human Rights: Critical Approaches to International Politics* (Basingstoke: Palgrave, 2002), 57–75.

[66] Rachel Burr, 'Global and Local Approaches to Children's Rights in Vietnam', *Childhood* 9(1) (February 2002), 49–61.

Burr was impressed by two aid agencies that accepted and respected the children's lifestyles and were eager to work within the Vietnamese social system. At the request of the street children, one of them funded an informal night school to teach motorbike repair skills. However, after assessing the scheme, UNICEF bureaucrats accused the agency of facilitating child labour and violating the children's right to schooling. This was despite the fact that the night school helped them to find paid work, which in turn led to further study or training. Burr concludes that the UNCRC was imposed in Vietnam without due regard for the social context and too often served western prejudices rather than Vietnamese children's interests.

David Rosen makes a similar argument with respect to some of the most vulnerable and afflicted children in international affairs – child soldiers. Rosen is deeply critical of what he calls the 'humanitarian' – or caretaker – concept of childhood and the associated campaign for welfare rights. He targets, for instance, UNICEF's 1997 Cape Town Principles and Best Practices, which define a child soldier as 'any person under 18 years of age who is part of any kind of regular or irregular armed force or armed group in any capacity' including cooks, porters, messengers and girls recruited for sex. This definition, argues Rosen, is not a noble attempt to keep as many children as far away from conflict as possible. Rather, the 'Straight 18' position is a proxy for a 'new political agenda' in which customary versions of childhood and conflict are sacrificed in favour of 'a single international standard'.[67] According to Rosen, caretakers justify their broad-brush and heavy-handed approach to child soldiers in a number of ways. First, they tend to criminalise war in general so that almost any involvement with it is seen to be abhorrent.[68] Secondly, they discriminate against 'new wars' in particular – that is, post-Cold War internecine conflicts in 'failed' or failing states – portraying them as chaotic and aberrant.[69] For example, the pivotal 1996 Machel Report into the Impact of Armed Conflict on Children bemoans the 'callousness of modern warfare' in postcolonial states

[67] David M. Rosen, 'Child Soldiers, International Humanitarian Law, and the Globalization of Childhood', *American Anthropologist* 109(2) (June 2007), 297.
[68] Ibid., 298.
[69] New wars and their relationship to children are explored in greater detail in Chapter 3 of this book.

and its 'abandonment of all standards'.[70] Thirdly, because of their unruliness and depravity, new wars are likely to entrap and exploit child soldiers. It follows that the use of child soldiers is automatically an international crime that calls out for international action.

This caretaker line of reasoning, Rosen contends, misrepresents warfare and children so as to promote a western interventionist agenda. More specifically, it exaggerates the differences between the new wars of the global south and the old and not-so-old wars of the global north. In so doing caretakers inflate their own civility while denigrating many resistance movements in non-western societies that depend on young soldiers.[71] To jettison this civilisational and generational bias is to realise that child soldiers are not passive and ignorant victims. They are not routinely forced to fight, abducted, drugged or lured into war by a false sense of 'power associated with carrying deadly weapons' as the Machel Report suggests.[72] Instead, according to Rosen, the 'vast majority' make rational decisions to enter into combat.[73] Drawing from case studies in Europe during World War II, Sierra Leone and Palestine, Rosen finds that child soldiers join armed groups in search of safety from deeply insecure environments, to address injustice, to ventilate frustration and to attain honour and wealth. Moreover, they are sometimes amongst the first and most belligerent combatants.[74] This sense of agency extends into battle, where children devise 'individual survival strategies, apply their own intelligence, strategize about situations, enter into relationships' and 'do anything that ordinary soldiers might do'.[75] Moreover, children's decisions to fight are commonly vindicated not only by immediate rewards – security, skills and kudos – but also by the empowerment that comes with ideological commitment, and the resilience that can grow out of facing violence and hardship.[76] So whereas Skenazy claims

---

[70] Cited in Rosen, 'Child Soldiers, International Humanitarian Law, and the Globalization of Childhood', 298.
[71] Ibid.   [72] Ibid., 299.   [73] Rosen, *Armies of the Young*, 16.
[74] Rosen, 'Child Soldiers, International Humanitarian Law, and the Globalization of Childhood', 299.
[75] Rosen, *Armies of the Young*, 134.
[76] Rosen, 'Child Soldiers, International Humanitarian Law, and the Globalization of Childhood', 299; Raija-Leena Punamaki, 'Can Ideological Commitment Protect Children's Psychosocial Well-Being in Situations of Political Violence?' *Child Development* 67(1) (1996), 66; Cairns, *Children and Political Violence*, 53–5.

a rightful seat for her son on the subway, Rosen reserves a spot for children on the battlefield.

Children and the practice of everyday life

While now firmly established in childhood studies, the free-ranger thesis has been criticised from both outside and inside the ranks of the NSSC. In a forceful reassertion of the caretaker thesis, King argues that it is absurd and reckless to suggest that children are another 'oppressed identity group who cannot be spoken for'; the key difference being that adults have all been children at some stage and are therefore qualified to speak on their behalf.[77] Moreover, unlike subjugated minorities, children invariably grow up, at which time their competency and social inclusion is all but guaranteed. While not necessarily agreeing with King, several NSSC scholars are conscious of the need to examine critically and even destabilise the free-ranger paradigm in the social sciences. This in part grows out of a recognition that the unquestioning dominance of a school of thought in any field can easily devolve into intellectual stagnation.[78] Kostelny argues that free-rangers have confronted the hysterical focus on children's vulnerability with such vigour that there is now concern that 'the pendulum will swing too far in the opposite direction'; that is, there now may well be too much of a focus on children's agency.[79] Caretakers, she suggests, might not have been so wrong after all. Indeed, Kostelny points to recent empirical evidence indicating that more attention needs to be paid to the ways in which children 'move in and out of relative autonomy and dependence'.[80]

[77] King, 'The Sociology of Childhood as Scientific Communication', 204.

[78] Allison James, 'Giving Voice to Children's Voices: Practices and Problems, Pitfalls and Potentials', *American Anthropologist* 109(2) (2007), 261–72; Robert M. Vanderbeck, 'Reaching Critical Mass? Theory, Politics, and the Culture of Debate in Children's Geographies', *Area*, 40(3) (2008), 393–400. Huijsmans refers to an emerging 'counter-movement', which is 'critical of the tendency in childhood studies to treat children's agency in a celebratory, uncritical, a-theoretical, non-relational, locally-bound and nonreflective manner': see Roy Huijsman, 'Child Migration and Questions of Agency', *Development and Change* 42(5) (2011), 1308.

[79] Kathleen Kostelny and James Garbarino, 'Coping with the Consequences of Living in Danger: The Case of Palestinian Children and Youth', *International Journal of Behavioral Development* 17(4) (December 1994), 595–611.

[80] M. Kesby, F. Gwanzura-Ottemoller and M. Chizororo, 'Theorising *Other*, Other Childhoods: Issues Emerging from Work on HIV in Urban and Rural

Questions also remain over the practical application of free-ranger theory. Vanderbeck reflects that this field has had 'precious little to say' about many 'big contemporary issues' and that some of these silences reflect a hesitancy to confront the implications of how it conceptualises children's agency.[81] What does recognising children as competent social actors mean for legislators, judges, social workers and advocates? Can children be relied upon to make laws not only for themselves but also for adults? Should a child who only knows abuse be held accountable for abusing others? How should society deal with child soldiers or suicide bombers who have been abducted or deeply indoctrinated? Similarly, the free-ranger thesis is hard to explain and sell to the public at large. This is because by emphasising multiplicity and complexity, free-rangers sacrifice the unifying power of the singular and simple.[82] For example, during Chinese President Hu Jintao's visit to the United States in 2011, President Obama asserted that despite some very real disagreements over human rights, economic policy and foreign affairs, Americans and Chinese could come together by focusing on their shared core values, the most important being, 'the desire to give our children a better life'.[83] For free-rangers such a declaration masks an attempt to impose a western worldview on the Chinese and to speak over children. This interpretation might be to some extent valid, but it is far from sufficient when it comes to negotiating complex social and political realities.

Free-rangers would thus benefit from engaging more with caretakers and – where possible – moving beyond the dichotomy altogether. Their aim should be to better identify not only instances of children's agency, but also the conditions and extent to which they need protection. Staying true to the free-ranger ethos, their objective should be to guide rather than dictate, and their prescriptions should have

---

Zimbabwe', *Children's Geographies* 4(2) (2006), 185–202; A. T. Kjørholt, *Childhood as a Social and Symbolic Space: Discourses on Children as Social Participants in Society* (Trondheim: Norwegian Centre for Child Research, 2004). Cited in Tatek Abebe and Anne Trine Kjørholt, 'Social Actors and Victims of Exploitation', *Childhood* 16(2) (May 2009), 191–2.

[81] Vanderbeck, 'Reaching Critical Mass?', 297.

[82] James, 'Competition or Integration?', 488; James and James, *Constructing Childhood*, 48.

[83] 'Obama and Chinese President Hu Jintao exchange toasts at state dinner', *The Washington Post*, 19 January 2011. Available at http://blogs.wsj.com/chinar ealtime/2011/01/20/hus-white-house-dinner-the-toasts/.

overarching utility without overreaching their purview. To this end, the work of Michel de Certeau can be fruitfully adapted to childhood studies, as it offers insights into 'big contemporary issues' such as how children and adults can get by in conflict zones.

Michel de Certeau (1925–1986) was a French postmodernist and public intellectual whose ideas have influenced many historians, philosophers and psychologists. In terms of style and ideology, de Certeau is more closely aligned to the free-ranger camp, but the fact that he was also a Jesuit priest suggests that he is not easily pigeonholed. De Certeau is most well known for his study of the PEL.[84] By this he means 'the ways in which users – commonly assumed to be passive and guided by established rules – operate'.[85] 'Users' are everyday people whose operations include cooking, reading, cleaning, speaking to one another, shopping and, most famously, walking in the city. These activities are viewed as insignificant in historical and political terms. The people who undertake them are often regarded as mere 'consumers' who passively accept and live within the cultural and material structures put in place by 'producers' – states, corporations, powerful individuals and organisations. De Certeau refutes this distinction, asserting that through the PEL people articulate meaningful and distinctive forms of agency. Four points must be made by way of elaboration.

First, the PEL is tactical in nature as opposed to strategic. In this famous distinction, de Certeau points out that strategies aim to shape the terrain of power. So 'a business, a state, a city, a scientific institution' acts in strategic ways by managing 'customers, citizens or objects of study' and the contexts in which they operate. However, strategic action is not the reserve of powerful organisations, the status quo, or adults. Everyone who performs on – or seeks to perform on – a public stage is a strategic actor.[86] This includes, for instance, the pint-sized insurgent, Gavorche, who valiantly sacrifices himself for the Revolution in Victor Hugo's *Les Misérables*. By crossing into the politico-military realm, child soldiers are also strategic actors

---

[84] Michel de Certeau (trans. Steven Rendall), *The Practice of Everyday Life*, 1st edn (Berkeley, CA: University of California Press, 1984).

[85] Ibid., xi.

[86] I touch here upon the related work of James C. Scott, *Domination and the Arts of Resistance: Hidden Transcripts* (New Haven, CT: Yale University Press, 1990).

although, as will be discussed below, they can simultaneously operate in a tactical fashion.

On the other hand, 'the place of the tactic belongs to the other'; that is, tactical activities are conducted within a predefined terrain that is tolerable even if it is not favourable to subordinate figures. Everyday people, asserts de Certeau, do not commonly seek to remodel prevailing cultures, ideologies or values, and often cannot even imagine such a prospect. They exist within 'a system too vast to be their own, too tightly woven for them to escape from it'.[87] Consequently, they try to get by in the most efficacious way possible. But this does not mean that they are inert or inconsequential. They can and often do reinterpret – without reforming or revolutionising – social structures so as to operate in 'a different register', one that deviates from the goals of their strategic masters. De Certeau refers to this ability to manipulate pre-fabricated power for heterodox purposes as 'poaching' and labels makeshift mash-up compilations of power as forms of 'bricolage'.

Secondly, the PEL is a form of resistance. Obviously, it is not a public organised and collective uprising – which by definition is strategic. Instead, the PEL can be likened to the resistance in an electrical circuit.[88] A resistor dissipates rather than repels power so that the circuit does not malfunction or explode, but instead operates more smoothly. The PEL is not aberrant or unusual behaviour, but rather constitutes activities that would be carried out even in the absence of stultifying power. The significance is not the act itself: it is in the manner in which it is conducted under strain. For this reason, those who are resisting do not need to be conscious that they are resisting. In his most cited example, de Certeau discusses 'walking in the city' as an effective way of evading the grids and plans that have been imposed by politicians, architects and businesses on metropolises all over the world. Walking, he asserts, is idiosyncratic. It facilitates daydreaming and the taking of detours, and allows us to bump into others. We may well still arrive at work on time, but we do so in a less compliant manner.

Thirdly, the PEL is inherently creative, incorporating what de Certeau refers to as 'microinventions'. This means that even in the most repressive milieus everyday people, by going about their

[87] Catherine Driscoll, 'The Moving Ground: Locating Everyday Life', *The South Atlantic Quarterly* 100(2) (2001), 386.
[88] Ben Highmore, *Everyday Life and Cultural Theory: An Introduction*, 1st edn (New York, NY: Routledge, 2001), 153.

everyday lives, can preserve their inner selves, make meaning of the world and maintain connections with one another. Much of what we take for granted, argues de Certeau, is profoundly important to our humanity. In Orwell's *1984*, for instance, Winston's radical deviance from Big Brother begins with the simplest of acts: he writes in a diary, walks in the forest, treasures a trinket and remembers a ditty. Similarly, one of the great witnesses of the Nazi work camps, Primo Levi, counts as a 'moment of reprieve' the opportunity to excavate from his memory and translate for another inmate 'the Canto of Ulysses' from Dante's *Inferno*.[89] Levi becomes so enthralled by the task that he insists he would have exchanged a day's soup to remember and recite another line or two. Simply recalling a poem and expressing himself to another was 'like the blast of a trumpet, like the voice of God'. For a moment, says Primo Levi, 'I forget who I am and where I am.'[90]

Finally, the PEL is at once visible and hidden. Its quotidian character means that it can take place both on enemy terrain and in the enemy's 'field of vision' and yet remain largely ignored. De Certeau cites as examples instances of *la perruque* (literally 'the wig'): 'the worker's own work disguised as work for his or her employer'.[91] This includes secretaries writing love letters on 'company time' or cabinetmakers 'borrowing' a lathe to make a piece of furniture for their living room. Returning to *1984*, Winston's lover Julia, a 'revolutionary from the waist down', is adept at playing up to power; by avidly following the little everyday rules she is able to break the largest rules:

I'm good at games. I was a troop-leader in the Spies. I do voluntary work three evenings a week for the Junior Anti-Sex League. Hours and hours I've spent pasting their bloody rot all over London. I always carry one end of a banner in the processions. I always look cheerful and I never shirk anything. Always yell with the crowd, that's what I say. It's the only way to be safe.[92]

De Certeau views such behaviour as inborn and instinctive, linking it to the 'age-old ruses of fishes, plants and insects that disguise or transform themselves in order to survive'.[93] The PEL is thus a form of camouflage that allows us to fight another day. It is a 'science of singularity', bringing

---

[89] Primo Levi (trans. Stuart Woolf), *If this is a Man and the Truce* (New York, NY: Abacus, 1988), 118–21.
[90] Ibid., 119.   [91] de Certeau, *The Practice of Everyday Life*, 30.
[92] George Orwell, *1984*. Available at http://gutenberg.net.au/ebooks01/0100021.txt.
[93] de Certeau, *The Practice of Everyday Life*, xx.

together animals and humans, the powerful and the powerless, and children and adults.[94] All of us, de Certeau believes, are united in our uniqueness and aversion to control. But ultimately the existence and exercise of PEL is, for the Jesuit postmodernist, a matter of faith and not science; it is a gift from God who wants us to make our own worlds and thereby live in his image.[95]

If tactical behaviour is innate and instinctive, then signs should be evident in individual humans from their earliest age. For this reason examples of the PEL from children's worlds would bolster de Certeau's conceptual framework, which, because it ultimately relies on faith, is sometimes shaky.[96] But the PEL also strengthens childhood studies in developing its understanding of the tactical side of children's worlds and their activities as users and consumers. Moreover, de Certeau's work offers a pathway towards reconciling the tension between caretakers and free-rangers over the question of agency. It acknowledges both the inability of children to define their own surroundings while also celebrating their inherent autonomy. Importantly, de Certeau's conception of autonomy in everyday life is not so rigid or sacred that it precludes altruistic and paternalistic intervention. This is because dissipating forms of resistance and evasive camouflage may well be necessary and laudable when it comes to individual survival, but at a collective level they can be critiqued for tending to preserve an iniquitous status quo.

There is reason to believe that children in conflict zones are tactical actors par excellence. Utas, for instance, conflates victimhood and agency to describe the 'victimcy' of child soldiers who deliberately live down to the victim stereotypes of aid workers, journalists and academics in order to accumulate material advantages.[97] All of this

---

[94] Driscoll, 'The Moving Ground', 388.

[95] Highmore, *Everyday Life and Cultural Theory*, 170.

[96] de Certeau offers one example of tactical behaviour relating to children: 'the child still scrawls and daubs on his schoolbooks; even if he is punished for this crime, he has made a space for himself and signs his existence as an author on it': de Certeau, *The Practice of Everyday Life*, 31. See also for a brief discussion of children's tactics Charles Watters, *Refugee Children: Towards the Next Horizon* (New York, NY: Routledge, 2000), 122.

[97] Mats Utas, 'West-African Warscapes: Victimcy, Girlfriending, Soldiering: Tactic Agency in a Young Woman's Social Navigation of the Liberian War Zone', *Anthropological Quarterly* 78(2) (Spring 2005), 409; Mats Utas, 'Victimcy as Social Navigation: From the Toolbox of Liberian Child Soldiers', in

without truly regretting what they have done or revising who they are. Utas regards gun-wielding Liberian child soldiers who danced in front of journalists as being acutely conscious that the western media expected them to be damaged, dangerous and in need of help: 'young children were more or less playing war in front of the cameras; it had the effect of a slightly choreographed dance'.[98] He goes on to argue that victimcy as a form of camouflage is also useful after a conflict has subsided for child soldiers to play up their victim status to their own families and communities as a means of dissipating guilt, deflecting condemnation and facilitating reintegration.[99] Honwana specifically draws upon de Certeau in her examination of the 'tactical agency' of young combatants in Mozambique and Angola. These youth exist, she argues, in a strategic terrain that they often cannot shape or overturn. Nonetheless, their tactical agency is expressed in their capacity to 'get by', to 'cope with the concrete, immediate conditions of their lives in order to maximize the circumstances created by their military and violent environment'.[100]

Thus the impishness, dilly-dallying, magical thinking and playfulness that we commonly associate in a pejorative sense with childishness may well constitute effective forms of agency and resistance in times of violence and oppression. Two examples from the world of film are instructive here. The first is from Guillermo del Toro's highly regarded 2006 film, *Pan's Labyrinth*. It tells the story of young Ofelia, who copes with the acute perils of 1944 Spain and her Falangist stepfather, Captain Vidal, by interweaving her real world with a fantasy one.[101]

Alpaslan Özerdem and Sukanya Podder (eds.), *Child Soldiers: From Recruitment to Reintegration* (Houndmills: Palgrave Macmillan, 2011) 215.

[98] Utas, 'Victimcy as Social Navigation', 216.

[99] Ibid., 221. See also Susan Shepler, 'The Rites of the Child: Global Discourses of Youth and Reintegrating Child Soldiers in Sierra Leone', *Journal of Human Rights* 4 (2005), 199.

[100] Alcinda Honwana, 'Innocent and Guilty: Child-Soldiers as Interstitial and Tactical Agents', in Alcinda Honwana and Filip de Boeck (eds.), *Makers and Breakers: Children and Youth in Postcolonial Africa* (Oxford: James Currey, 2005), 49. See also Alcinda Honwana, 'Negotiating Postwar Identities: Child Soldiers in Mozambique and Angola', in George Bond and Nigel Gibson (eds.), *Contested Terrains and Constructed Categories* (Boulder, CO: Westview Press, 2002) 277–98.

[101] *Pan's Labyrinth* accords with other Spanish language films such as *The Spirit of the Beehive* (1976), *Butterfly's Tongue* (1999) and *Black Bread* (2010), which are also told through the perspective of children and, in so doing, highlight fundamentally tragic and senseless aspects of civil war.

Secondly, in his autobiography, the talented and infamous director Roman Polanski tells of how as a ten-year-old child he escaped from the Warsaw ghetto after his parents were deported to concentration camps.[102] He spent much of the war hidden in the countryside, toiling in the fields, despised by his minders and compelled to be Catholic. Yet amidst the deep trauma and despair, Polanski found a flight of escape. Using leftover bits of candle and tin he manufactured his very first camera and, by manipulating the shadow and light, gave life to his fantasies. His indomitable imagination and flair propelled him to stardom as an actor and academy award-winning director. The fact that as an adult Polanski fled from the United States after being charged with raping a thirteen-year-old girl suggests that the sort of tactical and evasive actions that may be necessary for the powerless can be dangerous where they persist in the hands of the powerful.

Emmanuel Jal's memoir, *War Child*, also contains some illustrative acts of childhood everyday resistance.[103] Jal tells of how from an early age he was taught to hate the Arabs, who had colonised and repressed his people in South Sudan. The jallabas beat his mother on the way to church, stole their resources, and kept his people poor so that they could grow rich. Raids on Jal's village instilled in him the conviction that 'the jallabas were to blame for all I had seen; they were the reason my family had been tossed on to the wind as our world disappeared'.[104] But this hatred did not consume the young boy, in part because of his ongoing ability to play. 'The moment the battle was behind us, we would start playing again and laugh as we remembered how funny people looked as they ran. It was only at night that you couldn't forget, but in the day we would always find a game to play in the dust or a joke to tell.'[105]

After joining the South Sudanese resistance, Jal was systematically instructed to hate the enemy. At the same time he was indoctrinated to relinquish all of his pre-existing loyalties to friends and family so that 'the gun is your mother and father now'.[106] While these techniques had a profound impact upon Jal, he was never completely remade or dehumanised. The boy managed to preserve a moral core which reminded him that the atrocities committed by his own side were

---

[102] Roman Polanski, *Roman* (London: Heinemann, 1984), 18.
[103] Emmanuel Jal and Megan Lloyd Davies, *War Child: A Child Soldier's Story*, 1st edn (New York, NY: St. Martin's Griffin, 2010).
[104] Ibid., 32.   [105] Ibid., 33.   [106] Ibid., 80.

unjustifiable. And when his boot camp officer, the *talemgi*, ordered Jal and his friend Malual to whip one another so as to break their unsanctioned bond, the boys feigned compliance by pretending to holler with pain as they slowed the whip down at the last instant. They were playing, recounts Jal, a 'game … right under the nose of the talemgi. I smiled to myself as I lay down in the dust. I would cry and scream even as the whip landed softly on my arse.'[107]

Caretakers tend to view make-believe and play as a way for children to try out roles that they may adopt as adults.[108] They assert that political violence disrupts or corrupts the development process, creating adults who are highly aggressive or morally deviant. However, there is also evidence to suggest that conflict may 'stimulate children's play' and that play and make-believe can help children to make sense of and interpret their experiences.[109] Viewed from de Certeau's perspective, play is important in and of itself as a form of relief and escape. And extending this point to incorporate Gopnik's arguments about the value of children's reasoning, a youthful imagination and insistence on making the world anew could be a valuable resource in peace keeping, demobilisation, reconciliation and reintegration efforts.[110] These examples point to the great scope and potential value of exploring the childhood PEL in conflict zones.

Conclusion

The differences between caretakers and free-rangers are not about to be resolved. This is in part because they reflect much deeper antagonism between positivist and post-positivist approaches to knowledge. Nor are these differences necessarily all that bad. Indeed, in many ways they suit their particular contexts and functions. Caretakers need to make concrete and passionate claims about vulnerable children so that they can amass resources to help them. On the other hand, free-rangers need to emphasise the variability of childhood so as to ensure that children

---

[107] Ibid., 156.   [108] See Schapiro, 'What is a Child?', 732.

[109] Cairns, *Children and Political Violence*, 83–5.

[110] Reflecting upon the universality of children's games, Primo Levi observed, 'the fact remains that political frontiers are impervious to our verbal cultures, while the substantially non-verbal civilisation of play crosses them with the happy freedom of the wind and the clouds'. Primo Levi (trans. Raymond Rosenthal), *Other People's Trades* (London: Michael Joseph, 1989), 169.

are properly regarded as human beings and not just 'human becomings'.[111]

This chapter, then, has not proposed a resolution to this debate, but rather sets the parameters for a more constructive one. This can be achieved through enhanced self-awareness of whether and when we are animated by a caretaker or a free-ranger ethos. While there are good reasons to be devoted to a single camp for a particular issue, the caretaker and free-ranger positions are ultimately ideal types that are better applied in moderation and with due attention to circumstance. De Certeau's notion of the PEL can assist in this process, particularly when it comes to conflict zones. It acknowledges the pervasiveness of strategic power without denying the resilience and significance of tactical agency as practised by children. It can help us to appreciate children's creative and edifying qualities, even as we protect and nurture them.

The caretaker/free-ranger dynamic pervades many of the arguments and debates throughout this book. As Chapter 1 illustrates, children are often embroiled in global politics as apparently helpless victims, but they are also key participants. Chapter 4 examines how the international laws, institutions and organisations committed to the service of children have promoted the need to nurture children while also recognising them as autonomous individuals capable of both good and harm. The question of agency also underpins arguments about the vulnerability and responsibility of children as soldiers (Chapter 5), forced migrants (Chapter 6) and peace builders (Chapter 7). The next chapter turns to an exploration of the place of children in IR theory. To a greater extent than other fields in the social sciences, IR has been dominated by a caretaker ethos in which children have very limited political status. However, free-ranger thinking flavours recent critical scholarship, which seeks to break through the established horizons of global politics to include new actors and contexts traditionally considered to be illegitimate or inconsequential.

---

[111] Jens Qvortrup et al. (eds.), *Childhood Matters: Social Theory, Practice and Politics* (Aldershot: Avebury, 1994), xi.

3 | Children and IR: creating spaces for children

KATRINA LEE-KOO

Introduction

Armed conflict is one of the central considerations of the discipline of IR. Yet, IR has demonstrated no curiosity concerning the impact of conflict on children, or, alternatively, children's impact on conflict.[1] This is in spite of the fact that, as noted in the Introduction, UNICEF calculates that around one billion children currently live in conflict zones.[2] IR, which has remained largely silent on this issue, is therefore an outlier with respect to other social science disciplines such as sociology, anthropology, philosophy and social work, all of which have made significant contributions to the contemporary understanding of children in conflict zones. Watson notes that the discipline of IR is unique within the social sciences for its neglect of children. She writes that 'no international relations theory currently makes any specific reference to children as actors'.[3]

This chapter investigates the relationship between children and the disciplinary study of IR in relation to the discipline's core concerns of conflict, peace and security. To this end, it focuses upon three theoretical traditions: realism, liberalism and critical approaches to IR. It considers the theoretical contribution of these traditions within contemporary conflict and the prevalence of so-called 'new wars', whose non-traditional features challenge conventional understandings of war as a clearly defined state-against-state enterprise. While this is only a snapshot of the rich and complex theoretical tradition in IR's study of conflict, it nonetheless provides an analysis of a dominant orthodox tradition and powerful contemporary critique. Realism's analysis of

---

[1] With the notable exceptions of the work of Alison Watson, 'Children and International Relations: A New Site of Knowledge?', *Review of International Studies* 32(2) (2006), 237–50 and Brocklehurst, *Who's Afraid of Children?*.
[2] UNICEF, *Machel Study 10-Year Strategic Review* (2009).
[3] Watson, 'Children and International Relations', 244.

conflict, contemporary ideas of the liberal peace and critical approaches to IR's re-visioning of conflict analysis currently dominate IR debates with regard to conflict. While these approaches have made important contributions to the study of conflict analysis, it is worth noting that none of these traditions have explicitly developed either a significant body of work or dedicated theorising on the role that children play in conflict zones. However, despite this explicit silence, implicit theorising on the relationship that children have with conflict can be detected in each approach. Realism and liberalism, which together constitutes the orthodox tradition in IR, takes an often implicit caretaker view of the role of children in political space. In this sense, children are assumed to be protected within the domestic sphere of the home, family and community, and are neither able nor equipped to affect international affairs. These traditions are not ignorant of the extent to which children are caught up in conflict zones, but conceptualise their role as victims of an external environment not of their making or capacity to influence. Consequently, children are of peripheral interest in the study of conflict and theorists delegate the responsibility for their protection and consideration to domestic actors.

Critical approaches to IR offer a contemporary challenge to this tradition. Such thinking on the construction of identity and knowledge and the fluid operation of non-conventional forms of power loosely align critical IR with elements of the free-ranger approach developed in the previous chapter. In this sense, critical IR approaches suggest that children may not only possess agency within conflict, but also the capacity, however limited, to affect the trajectories of conflict and peace. Furthermore, the focus of critical approaches on 'bottom-up' analyses encourages a consideration of the experiences of children and other civilians in any global project of conflict, peace or security. Consequently, critical approaches have the potential to envisage children as both legitimate actors and knowledge bearers in IR.

The realist way of conflict

The study of conflict within the discipline of IR has been dominated by the realist tradition.[4] This tradition is complex and replete with internal

---

[4] Peter Hough, *Understanding Global Security* (London: Routledge, 2004), 22.

debates and inconsistencies;[5] however, its core tenets remain steadfast in its consideration of conflict. In its classical, neo-realist defensive and offensive formats, the realist tradition identifies conflict as a central and enduring feature of an immutable and anarchical international system.[6] In the absence of a global sovereign, states protect themselves and their interests through the accumulation and assertion of power. Consequently, the capacity of states to project power into the external environment is more relevant to the likelihood and outcome of conflict than the domestic dynamics of each individual state. For Mearsheimer, this means that 'realists tend not to draw sharp distinctions between "good" and "bad" states, because all great powers act according to the same logic regardless of their culture, political system, or who runs the government'.[7] The possibilities of conflict are therefore determined by objective conditions rather than by the subjective political values of nations or citizens. Whether that conflict is the product of flawed human nature – as argued by classical realists – or by the anarchical structure of the international system – as argued by neo-realists – the pursuit of power carries the inherent possibility for war. For realists then, the potential for conflict is always on the horizon, as conflict is a product of the machinations of state activities driven by competition for power in an international anarchical system for the purposes of self-preservation and security.

The realist account of conflict constitutes a powerful tradition in IR. For centuries it has offered analysts and practitioners a compelling explanation for the occurrence of conflict in the international system, and has provided guidance for the deployment of power in the search for the continued viability of sovereign states. While it has been the subject of much critique, it nonetheless retains a strong contemporary influence.[8] Its dominance is a product of its enduring capacity to focus upon, and to some extent resolve, the pressing issues of conflict and state behaviour in the international system. Yet what it has less adequately

---

[5] See Jim George, *Discourses of Global Politics: A Critical (Re)Introduction to International Relations* (Boulder, CO: Lynne Rienner, 1994), 91–107.

[6] John J. Mearsheimer, *The Tragedy of Great Power Politics* (New York, NY: Norton, 2001), 17.

[7] Ibid., 17–18.

[8] Sean M. Lynn-Jones, 'Realism and Security Studies', in Craig A. Snyder (ed.), *Contemporary Security and Strategy* (New York, NY: Palgrave, 2008), 14–33.

theorised is the social and individual consequences of its theorising, namely the effects of conflict and state behaviour on those caught up in conflict zones. The question therefore becomes: can a tradition which focuses primarily upon the external behaviour of states make any contribution to the wellbeing of children affected by armed conflict? For realists, the answer to this question is 'yes'. While realism does not provide explicit analysis of children in conflict zones, there remains an implicit expectation that only a strong state can protect its children and enable the provisioning of children's wellbeing. For realists, a state that can demonstrate power externally can simultaneously provide security internally. Though Machiavelli's enduring contribution to realist thought has been to assert that states and their leaders distance themselves from what we might now consider to be standard values of humanitarianism, it would be wrong to suggest that realism does not have a moral standard which would, by default, include a state's protection of its children. Therefore, states do not accumulate power as an end in itself, but rather they accumulate power in order to deploy that power in ways that enable the security of their citizens. For many who live in the global north and western, liberal states, this has been a common experience. Realists will point to a long tradition that equates a state capable of defending its interests and staving off attack with a state capable of feeding, clothing, educating, housing and caring for its children. Whether a state chooses to deploy its resources in such a way is, however, not guaranteed. Meanwhile, a weak, threatened and conflict-ridden state can neither defend itself nor its citizens. However, this survivalist aspect of realism, and its subsequent inability to address complex insecurity in the global south, has attracted substantial criticism.

As part of a broader critique of realism, Ken Booth has argued that the realist assumption that the state's ultimate *raison d'état* is the protection of its own citizens is fundamentally flawed. Instead, he suggests that the vast and ongoing insecurities endured by many in today's world provide compelling evidence that 'realism fails the test of practice'.[9] He argues that the assumption of a state's good intentions towards its own citizens is founded upon a generalised modern Eurocentric experience. This, consequently, does not reflect the

---

[9] Ken Booth, 'Critical Explorations', in Ken Booth (ed.), *Critical Security Studies and World Politics* (Boulder, CO: Lynne Rienner, 2005), 7.

experiences of a majority of the world's population. Furthermore, it is not something that can be consistently claimed within liberal states. For realism's critics then, the study of IR needs to go back to the drawing board; it needs to investigate all of realism's foundational assumptions. While these critiques are wide-ranging, many of them are relevant to the issue of children in conflict zones. They may help explain why realism, at best, can only theorise the experiences of children in conflict insofar as it implicitly assumes that children will be protected by a strong caretaker state, or else be conflict's victims. Realism's limitations in this regard may be found in three areas of its theorising.

Firstly, the historical tendency of realism is to assume that all human beings will and always have behaved predictably. For instance, classical realist Hans J. Morgenthau writes in his first principle of political realism that '[h]uman nature, in which the laws of politics have their roots, has not changed since the classical philosophies of China, India, and Greece endeavoured to discover these laws'.[10] While not all realists will agree with Morgenthau's contention that human nature is inherently evil[11] it is worth noting that all realists frame universal human nature in adult, male terms.[12] This presumption of male, adult rationality in human experience demonstrates little curiosity regarding the experiences and actions of children in global politics. In fact, the realist tradition generally disregards diverse human identities in preference to the cover-all claim that conflict's agents will behave in this rational, self-interested manner. As a consequence, children are simply written out of analyses of conflict. Cairns observes: 'one gets the impression that the world of political violence is largely a world of adults, indeed a world of adult men'.[13] IR's account of human nature precludes consideration of children as political beings with unique experiences of global life. This in turn develops into a lack of consideration of children as political actors. Consequently, the rational actor model does not usefully illuminate the experiences of children and, instead, the assumption of its universality

---

[10] Hans J. Morgenthau, *Politics Among Nations: The Struggle for Peace and Power*, 4th edn (New York, NY: Alfred A. Knopf, 1967), 4.

[11] See, for example, Kenneth Waltz, *Man, the State and War* (New York, NY: Columbia University Press, 1954), 16–41.

[12] See J. Ann Tickner, *Gender in International Relations: Feminist Perspectives on Achieving Global Security* (New York, NY: Columbia University Press, 1992), 34–35, 36–41.

[13] Cairns, *Children and Political Violence*, 1.

marginalises both children and attempts to legitimate, explain or address their experiences.

Secondly, the exclusion of children and non-state actors more broadly side-lines those actors committed to children's protection. While the realist tradition has never denied the activity of non-state actors in the international system,[14] this influence is significantly downplayed when compared with state activity. Consequently, under realist frameworks, little legitimacy is given to the capacity for the global child advocacy network to affect the trajectory of conflict or generate international norms surrounding child protection in conflict. For realists the impact of such regimes on state action would be, at most, minimal and voluntary. More recently, this has been challenged by constructivist approaches to the study of IR that explore the capacity of norms generated by members and movements within international society to influence the onset or outcome of conflicts.[15] Constructivists have demonstrated that non-state actors involved in the global child advocacy network have the capacity to generate or contribute to norms of child protection, which may in turn shape conflict.[16] For instance, while the controversial *Kony2012* campaign failed to end in the arrest of Ugandan LRA Leader Joseph Kony, it arguably succeeded in its goal to 'Make Kony Famous'. This in turn contributed to growing global awareness around child soldiers in Uganda, and generated high-level support for militarised or humanitarian action.[17] Similarly, the April 2014 kidnapping of 276 schoolgirls in northern Nigeria by the militant Muslim Boko Haram has generated much global attention. This included the decision by US President Barack Obama to send 'military, law enforcement and other agencies' to assist in locating the captured girls, as well as sanctions by the UN Security Council blacklisting the group as a terrorist organisation. In this sense, the global moral and social outrage

---

[14] See Morgenthau, *Politics Among Nations*, and Joseph S. Nye, *Peace in Parts: Integration and Conflict in Regional Organization* (Boston, MA: Little Brown and Company, 1971).

[15] Christian Reus-Smit, 'Constructivism', in Scott Burchill et al, *Theories of International Relations*, 4th edn (Hampshire: Palgrave, 2009), 220.

[16] See R. Charli Carpenter, '"Women, Children and Other Vulnerable Groups": Gender, Strategic Frames and the Protection of Civilians as a Transnational Issue', *International Studies Quarterly* 49(2) (2005), 295–334.

[17] See *Invisible Children*, 'Kony 2012 Online Video', (6 March 2012). Available at http://invisiblechildren.com/media/videos/program-media/kony-2012/.

generated by the schoolgirls' abduction has moved major states and international organisations into action in a way not anticipated by realist theory's division between local and global issues.

Thirdly, confounding this excision of children from the analysis of conflict is the so-called 'great divide' between the anarchical international realm and the ordered domestic spheres of politics.[18] According to the realist tradition, the domestic sphere is separate from state action in an international anarchical system. This separation enables a dual morality whereby the state may deploy its power immorally in the international system on the understanding that 'it is the existence of the state that creates the possibility for an ethical political community to exist domestically'.[19] Yet, this conceptualisation of the relationship between the domestic and international realms in global politics silences children twice over. In the first instance, the separation of domestic from international space places children as non-rational and passive entities *within* the state. The state is the designated caretaker which, as sovereign actor, severs the child from international space while simultaneously relieving the international actors from any responsibility towards children. This, of course, isolates those children who exist in states that commit violence against them. In the second instance, the public/private divide that exists within domestic space can also isolate children. For orthodox scholars the private sphere within the domestic state is a separate site devoid of political activism or knowledge. This is the primary location of children; the domestic home remains largely free of state intervention. In this space, parents/adults are supposed to protect children and act as their public sphere agents, just as the state is supposed to behave in the interests of its citizens on the international stage. Yet, this assumption is problematic. As demonstrated in Chapter 1, families are not always able, or willing, to protect their children from armed conflict, and the effects of armed conflict seamlessly cross the threshold of the home. Overall, this reveals the problems associated with making assumptions about the smooth operation of divisions between domestic and global life.

---

[18] Kenneth Waltz, *Theory of International Politics* (New York, NY: McGraw Hill, 1979), 88.

[19] Tim Dunne and Brian C. Schmidt, 'Realism', in John Baylis and Steve Smith (eds.), *The Globalization of World Politics: An Introduction to International Relations*, 3rd edn (Oxford: Oxford University Press, 2005), 163.

Furthermore, it suggests the need to problematise relationships between children and the home, the state and the international system, particularly in terms of conflict. Feminists particularly have demonstrated how the public/private divide situates women – and children – at the powerless end of a set of binary relationships – such as masculine/feminine, strong/weak, rational/emotional – which presupposes that conflict is isolated to, and managed by, the former for the protection of the latter.[20] In this sense, feminist critiques of the realist tradition are useful for explaining the absence of children as an analytical unit under traditional approaches to IR. Children are feminised and, as Elshtain notes, become 'the companions of women in the closet of political science'.[21] In their relationship with adults they are the emotional, irrational, docile entity in need of protection by moral others. However, while feminists have noted that women's exclusion from the realms of political action result in their being second-class citizens,[22] children are regarded as, at best, 'apprentice citizens'.[23] This reinforces conceptualisations of children as apolitical entities who sit apart from political action.

While these critiques reveal concerns about the foundations of realist theorising, it is important to recognise that like all theories, the realist tradition is not static. Since the end of the Cold War particularly, the realist tradition has adapted to confront a breadth of threats to state interests that emerged or became visible after the collapse of the bipolar state system.[24] However, the widening of the realist agenda does not equate to a rethinking of the discipline's foundations. Thus, while the realist agenda may have expanded to include threats to the state posed by such contemporary concerns as environmental change[25] and HIV/AIDS,[26] there has not been a simultaneous deepening of analysis to

---

[20] Jan Jindy Pettman, *Worlding Women* (St. Leonards: Allen and Unwin, 1996), 99–100.

[21] Jean Bethke Elshtain, *The Family in Political Thought* (Amhurst, MA: University of Massachusetts Press, 1982), 289.

[22] See Pettman, *Worlding Women*, 17–18.

[23] Charlotte Wagnsson, Maria Hellman and Arita Holmberg, 'The Centrality of Non-traditional Groups for Security in the Globalized Era: The Case of Children', *International Political Sociology* 4(1) (2010), 8.

[24] See Lynn-Jones, 'Realism and Security Studies', 14–33.

[25] Jessica Tuchman Mathews, 'Redefining Security', *Foreign Affairs* 68(2) (Spring 1989), 162–77.

[26] See Stefan Elbe, *Strategic Implications of HIV/AIDS* (Oxford: Oxford University Press, 2003).

enable rethinking of the 'threats to state and state interests' formula.[27] Consequently, widening of the agenda may result in children becoming visible within the framework of state practice in IR. However, that visibility comes in the form of children as threats – or at least challenges – to state interests. For example, children as soldiers, as terrorists, or as agents in criminal syndicates may be identified as contributing to the conditions for state instability. Similarly, children who have not been successfully reintegrated into post-conflict states may threaten the long-term viability of peace settlements and state/ nation rebuilding. This in turn may generate efforts to securitise some children, such as child soldiers or irregular child migrants, as threats to states.[28] The major concern of this from a child advocacy perspective is that the referent for analysis remains the state. The introduction of children onto the realist agenda is not done for the protection of children, but rather for the protection of the state from children. For instance, in his influential 1994 *Atlantic Monthly* article Robert Kaplan constructs West Africa as a new threat to the global north through provocative imagery involving children. He points to the menacing 'boys' in Sierra Leone, the 'corrugated metal shack teeming with children', and a scene where children with 'protruding bellies, seemed as numerous as ants'. To complete the anarchical scene, Kaplan notes that 'children defecate in streets filled with garbage and pigs'.[29] In such imaginaries, the sheer number of children, free of liberal education and civilising influences, are constructed as portending threats to the global system. Consequently, the analytical category of children within the realist frame oscillates between invisibility as an entity under the implicit protection of the state, and visibility as a threat to state interests and peace.

The liberal peace

The revival of the Kantian liberal peace project in recent decades has had a significant impact upon the global politics of conflict in the post-

---

[27] Booth, 'Critical Explorations', 14.

[28] See Chapters 5 and 6 in this book respectively for a discussion of these issues.

[29] Robert D. Kaplan, 'The Coming Anarchy', *Atlantic Monthly* (1 February 1994). Available at www.theatlantic.com/magazine/archive/1994/02/the-coming-anar chy/304670/; see also, Katrina Lee-Koo, 'Horror and Hope: (Re)Presenting Militarised Children in Global North-South Relations', *Third World Quarterly* 32(4) (May 2011), 725–42.

Cold War world.[30] Like realism, liberalism offers the study of IR a
powerful positivist view of the possibilities and limits of global politics.
Unlike realists, liberals see conflict as something that can be mediated
through the practice of international politics. Most recently, liberals
have revived the concept of liberal peace as a possibility for a stable
international system in the post-Cold War period.[31] According to
Thomas Paine in his 1791 *The Rights of Man*, war was a process to
'preserve the power and the employment of princes, statesmen,
soldiers, diplomats and armaments manufacturers, and to bind their
tyranny ever more firmly upon the necks of the people'. For modern-
day liberals, these ideas have translated into the argument that peace
would be more likely when the decisions to commit to war were taken
out of the hands of the elite, and placed in the hands of those most likely
to fight the wars. Doyle argues that 'when the citizens who bear the
burdens of war elect their governments, wars become impossible'.[32]
The liberal peace therefore envisions the prospect of peace among
liberal states and argues that the more widespread liberal values are,
the more likely peace is to occur. At its most fundamental level, the
liberal peace proposition is that liberalism provides the best
opportunities for individuals' rights to be promoted at one end, and
for the globalised international system to be stabilised at the other.

At its most simplistic, the liberal peace is premised upon the
argument that liberal democratic states do not go to war with each
other.[33] While this perhaps over-simplifies the case, it embodies a core
conviction that democracy breeds peace. However, liberal scholars are
also wary of overstating this claim. According to Doyle, 'liberalism
does leave a coherent legacy on foreign policy. They [liberal states] are
indeed peaceful, yet they are also prone to make war...'[34] For instance,
while the United States and Britain are unlikely to go to war against
each other, the twenty-first century has already offered multiple
examples of these two states working in coalition to initiate conflict
in a third, non-liberal state. With this in mind, Doyle argues that the
challenge for liberal leadership in global politics is both moral and

---

[30] See Michael Doyle, 'Liberalism and World Politics', *American Political Science
     Review* 80 (December 1986), 1151–69.
[31] Ibid.   [32] Ibid., 1151.
[33] Scott Burchill, 'Liberalism', in Scott Burchill, et al, *Theories of International
     Relations*, 4th edn (Hampshire: Palgrave, 2009), 61–2.
[34] Doyle, 'Liberalism and World Politics', 1151–2.

strategic, having to negotiate between 'preserving the legacy of the liberal peace without succumbing to the legacy of liberal imprudence'.[35] Yet, like realism, liberalism's investment in the politics of peace and conflict is subject to internal debate. Questions immediately emerge regarding how liberal peace should be encouraged on a global level, and about when the pursuit of liberal peace tips over into liberal imperialism. Particularly in the post-Cold War period, the rhetoric of liberal values has been applied to a range of military adventures, from the NATO bombing of Yugoslavia (1999) to the US-led interventions in Afghanistan (2001) and Iraq (2003) and the UN-authorised bombing of Libya (2011). In these cases, liberal principles were lauded as being both the reason – for instance, the protection of civilians' human rights – and the possible outcome – the establishment of a democratic state system in the conflict zone – for intervention. Liberal principles have also inspired documents such as the 2001 *Responsibility to Protect* (R2P), which reimagines sovereignty as an explicit responsibility – rather than a right – for states to protect their own citizens, thereby seeking to enhance the international community's capacity to respond to state-sponsored atrocities against its own people.[36] Unlike realism, which sees state responsibility to its citizens as implicit but largely unenforceable, the liberal peace seeks to patrol these boundaries of responsibility actively.

While notions of the liberal peace may be internally and externally debated, it presents a powerful set of principles which have had an important impact upon post-Cold War conflicts – particularly military interventions mounted by international coalitions – and policies towards conflict, such as R2P. Both the rhetoric and ideas driving policy in this regard enable liberals to theorise and speak explicitly on the rights of children in conflict zones, be it an internal civil conflict or an international intervention. This is enabled through a number of avenues. Firstly, liberalism's explicit concern with human rights is extended to include children. This is primarily through the 1989 UNCRC – discussed in depth in the next chapter, but also through a range of human rights instruments which both explicitly and implicitly cover children. For instance, in 2003 the Afghanistan government acceded to the second Optional Protocol of the UNCRC regarding

[35] Ibid., 1163.
[36] See Alex J. Bellamy, *Responsibility to Protect* (Cambridge: Polity Press, 2009).

children in armed conflict. While this has not addressed the problem of child recruitment in Afghanistan, it has at least provided a rhetorical commitment to do so, which affords a platform from which advocates can deploy resources to address the issue. Secondly, the promotion of democratic institutions may encourage accountability in terms of the state's responsibility to child protection. This includes governance structures designed to protect children from violence, as well as programmes that actively promote children's education, healthcare and wellbeing. Thirdly and in a similar vein, the support for the norm of the rule of law can work in the interests of war-affected children. Finally, the international community's increasing focus on conflict-affected civilians and their rights speaks directly to the rights of children in conflict zones and the responsibilities of the international community to facilitate their protection. For instance, Chapter 8 examines the growing trend of including crimes against children in post-conflict punitive and restorative justice programmes.

Yet a number of scholars have contested the short and long-term viability of liberal values in promoting the rights of children in conflict, particularly when they are imposed upon states that do not have a tradition of liberalism. The first major critique is that the liberal peace is too statist and institutionally focused, and therefore does not consider diverse human experiences. The claim that democratic institutions are the key to peace, critics argue, is too rigid for the complex and diverse social and cultural contexts in which liberal peace is being imposed. In this vein Watson argues that the liberal peace has not lived up to 'its lofty principles because, despite rhetoric to the contrary, it remains rooted in an institutional rather than "human" prescription'.[37] This fosters an inflexible, top-down or 'toolbox' model that has a limited capacity to adapt to the different and changing zones in which it is operating.

Interrelated with this is the second critique, which asserts that the liberal peace model promotes a set of universalised liberal values that does not reflect the diversity of children's experiences and contexts – as discussed in Chapters 1 and 2. In particular, it promotes the UNCRC as an integral part of the human rights regime. Despite its near-universal ratification, the UNCRC has generated a great deal of criticism for its

---

[37] Alison Watson, 'Can There Be a "Kindered" Peace?', *Ethics and International Affairs* 22(1) (2008), 35.

particularly western perspective of childhood.[38] This criticism argues that liberal documents such as the UNCRC offer no consideration of – or legitimacy to – alternative experiences of childhood that exist outside the developed and western worlds.[39] For some, its dominance has resulted in an inability among liberal proponents to 'listen to those whose generational, racial, sexual, and even moral language may differ from their own'.[40] Rather than accepting plurality in what should constitute children's rights, critics suggest that the liberal system posits the western experience as the ideal, and rejects other versions of childhood as less civilised, less developed and morally inferior.[41] This generates a familiar debate between those who see the imposition of western values as necessary and inevitably beneficial, and those who see it as cultural imperialism that is both oppressive and inappropriate.[42] Critics also read into the UNCRC's surrounding culture 'a moral condemnation of the south' for its failure to provide children with the western experience of childhood.[43]

The practice of embedding the children rights regime into the liberal peace process is also of concern to critics. The ways in which the international sector – usually a combination of states, military actors, NGOs and international organisations – responds specifically to the needs of children within conflict zones requires careful monitoring. There is a danger, particularly in zones where there is no strong grass-roots civil society, or where that society is not working co-operatively with international organisations, that children could be either neglected altogether, or separated from their local communities by the activities of international actors – a point explored in Chapter 9. Similarly, the discursive deployment of the children's rights regime as part of the broader liberal peace project also requires analysis. For instance, the architects of liberal peace can manipulate the negative experiences of children in conflict zones in their international discourse in ways that promote the moral efficacy of the liberal project.[44] In particular, the issue of the ill-treatment of children has been a strong

---

[38] Watson, 'Children and International Relations', 231; Pupavac, 'Misanthropy Without Borders', 101; Burman, 'Local, Global or Globalized?', 52.
[39] Burman, 'Local, Global or Globalized?', 47–8, 52.
[40] Watson, 'Can There Be a "Kindered" Peace?', 35.
[41] See Pupavac, 'Misanthropy Without Borders', 101–3.
[42] Burman, 'Local, Global, or Globalized?', 46.
[43] Pupavac, 'Misanthropy Without Borders', 102.
[44] See Lee-Koo, 'Horror and Hope'.

narrative theme that has been used to condemn non-liberal regimes and demonstrate their delinquency when juxtaposed to a broader liberal international order.[45] In this sense, children become a powerful metaphor for the strong undercurrent of rescue and paternalism that exists in the liberal peace discourse. Children are cast in the role of the infantile, irrational, lost state that requires the guiding hand of the international order if it is to be rehabilitated.[46]

Finally, the consequence for children of military intervention in the pursuit of liberal peace needs to be explored. When military intervention is embedded in the liberal project, it can engender short, medium and long-term negative effects on children. The post-2001 liberal project in Afghanistan provides evidence of this. More than a decade after the initial intervention, Afghanistan remains one of the worst places in the world to be a child.[47] While there have been a small number of developmental improvements for some children in select areas, the promised benefits of the liberal peace have not been widely or consistently experienced by children, while many aspects of their lives have deteriorated significantly.[48] Consequently, there is an entire generation of Afghan children whose childhood will be negatively marked by this liberal inspired intervention. These children have not had the opportunity to access the rights promised to them under the UNCRC, despite the fact that Afghanistan ratified the treaty in 1994. This provides some evidence of the rhetoric/reality gap in the liberal peace programme and its limited capacity to deliver promised rights and protection to children.[49]

The new wars

The problems confronting the liberal international community in today's conflict zones reflect to an extent changes in the manner and means of

---

[45] R. Charli Carpenter, '"A Fresh Crop of Human Misery": Representations of Bosnian "War Babies" in the Global Print Media, 1991–2006', *Millennium – Journal of International Studies* 38(1) (2009), 39.

[46] See Pupavac, 'Misanthropy Without Borders', 102–3.

[47] See OSRSG-CaAC, 'Mission Report: Visit of the Special Representative for Children and Armed Conflict to Afghanistan'.

[48] See Watchlist on Children and Armed Conflict, 'Setting the Right Priorities'.

[49] See Edward Newman, '"Liberal" Peacebuilding Debates', in Edward Newman, Roland Paris and Oliver P. Richmond (eds.), *New Perspectives on Liberal Peacebuilding* (Tokyo: United Nations University Press, 2009), 26–53.

war. From orthodox and critical quarters alike, the end of the Cold War is identified by IR scholars as a turning point in contemporary conflict and conflict analysis. The post-Cold War period fuelled theoretical challenges to the realist conceptualisation of war, empirical challenges to what constitutes conflict in the post-Cold War world, and a renewed call for the incorporation of humanitarian action and the protection of civilians into the global agenda. Commitment to some, or all, of these issues has led to a proliferation of debates about the nature of contemporary conflict and how the discipline of IR should research it. Within academia the study of global conflict has seen a focus on the transformation and proliferation of conflict typologies. These include analyses of, for example, high-technology 'spectacle wars',[50] resource wars,[51] terrorism,[52] and complex emergencies.[53] However, it is worth noting that few of these typologies directly consider the experiences of children as either combatants or civilians in conflict. Nonetheless, as will be illustrated below, the changing nature of conflict, and the challenges to how the discipline studies and maps ways to end conflict, do affect children. Therefore, it is important to look for spaces where children's experiences should be considered, and adopt methodological tools that ensure children's experiences are brought into focus.

Many of the debates on emerging conflict types in the post-Cold War period at least touch upon what Mary Kaldor has described as 'new wars.'[54] For instance, post-Cold War conflicts in the Sudan, the Balkans and Afghanistan, among others, demonstrate at least some of the characteristics of these new wars. For Kaldor, new wars are identified through a number of intersecting features. The first involves the deliberate targeting of civilians as a core purpose of conflict.[55] The terror, fear and forced compliance engendered through attacks against

---

[50] See James Der Derian, *Virtuous War: Mapping the Military-Industrial-Media-Entertainment Network*, 2nd edn (London: Routledge, 2009) and Jean Baudrillard, *The Gulf War Did Not Take Place* (Bloomington, IN: Indiana University Press, 1995).

[51] Michael Klare, *Resource Wars: The New Landscape of Global Conflict* (New York, NY: Henry Holt and Company, 2002).

[52] Richard Jackson, Marie Breen Smyth, and Jeroen Gunning (eds.), *Critical Terrorism Studies* (London: Routledge, 2009).

[53] David Keen, *Complex Emergencies* (Oxford: Polity Press, 2007).

[54] Mary Kaldor, *New and Old Wars: Organised Violence in a Global Era*, 2nd edn (Oxford: Polity Press, 2006).

[55] Karen Wells, *Childhood in a Global Perspective*,142.

civilian populations, it is argued, constitute a weapon wielded to effect political and military objectives, which may range from genocide to resource capture, to criminal activities. The second feature of new wars involves the proliferation of militant actors in conflict zones. This includes insurgents, resistance fighters and separatists, opposition forces, militias, rebels, tribal or religious factions, as well as local defence groups and paramilitary units, external armies, external coalition forces, private military companies and private security forces. Some have also added to this a number of non-militarised actors who work to achieve specific goals in a conflict zone. This might include humanitarian actors such as civilian aid, human rights or development contractors who may or may not be working alongside militarised personnel, external states or UN officials, and criminal networks such as human traffickers, weapons' merchants and goods smugglers.

Complicating matters further is the third key feature of new wars. This is the network of local/global inter-connections, which Kaldor suggests has become part of the new globalised security landscape.[56] The rapid movement of weapons, aid, financial support, people, politics and ideas into and out of conflict zones across global networks challenges contemporary analysis of conflict in a variety of ways. It becomes more difficult to identify protagonist and interest groups and to trace the movement of goods, people and money. Fourth, new wars scholars examine conflict-driven shadow economies that may emerge as a result of conflict, but can also serve to sustain conflict. Kaldor notes that the new wars dismantle existing state economies as conflict creates unemployment, internal and external migration, and the general disruption of day-to-day economic cycles. These are replaced with an informal economy that is nourished by violence and the veil that violence provides to capture resources and humanitarian aid.[57] This gives certain parties a vested interest in the continuation of the conflict which, in turn, makes conflict resolution difficult.

The new wars literature has generated much debate within academia. There is significant debate regarding whether these examples of contemporary conflict are in fact new, and whether it is possible to draw such distinct lines between these and the preceding 'old'

---

[56] Kaldor, *New and Old Wars*, 121.
[57] See Mark Duffield, *Global Governance and the New Wars: The Merging of Development and Security* (London: Zed Books, 2001).

wars.[58] Regardless of whether or not these elements are significantly different from those that preceded it, this literature makes important contributions to the analysis of contemporary conflict. It contests traditional claims that states alone drive conflict, and that states are the most relevant – or only – consideration for understanding the causes and consequences of conflict. Similarly, it contests traditional methodologies for studying conflict. Thus, the new wars literature encourages analysts to follow conflict across the historical divisions within politics between domestic/international, public/private, local/global and first world/third world contexts. Furthermore, it encourages scholars to see conflict as an intersection of political, military, ideological, criminal and economic goals. These are important starting points in including a consideration of children's roles in conflict.

The landscape of conflict that the new wars literature paints increasingly encroaches upon the space of children. Conflict as a personalised, civilian-targeted network of violence which invades domestic as well as public space clearly envelops the lives of children. The transposition of conflict from battle zones into civilian spaces brings conflict into children's homes, hospitals and schools. As outlined in Chapter 1, UNICEF has identified the widespread and deliberate targeting of children as the first of six 'grave violations against children' and documents its prolific practice in contemporary conflict zones.[59] The widespread targeting of children is a strategy of war that serves a range of military and political objectives. This includes instilling a climate of fear and compliance among adult civilian populations through the targeting of their children.[60] Children may also be directly targeted in order to destroy the 'armies of the future'. Boys in particular are targeted in campaigns to rid future generations of militarised resistance.[61] Yet, few of the academic analyses of new wars identify the unique politics associated with the targeting of children. While it is an element of the broader debate regarding the targeting of civilians in conflict, it is nonetheless one which has unique features and politics associated with it.

Children can also constitute non-traditional actors in conflict zones, and be affected by the actions of non-traditional actors. While there is a

---

[58] Patrick A. Mello, 'In Search of New Wars: The Debate about a Transformation of War', *European Journal of International Relations* 16(2) (2010), 305.
[59] UNICEF, *Machel Study 10-Year Strategic Review* (2009), 21.   [60] Ibid.
[61] Brocklehurst, *Who's Afraid of Children?*, 39.

growing literature on issues associated with child soldiering in new wars contexts[62] (see Chapter 5), children also become non-traditional actors through their roles as peace brokers, community negotiators, and leaders[63] (see Chapter 7). Furthermore, other non-traditional actors can shape the lives of children living in conflict zones. For instance, in 2008 Save the Children published a report examining the abuse of children in conflict zones by peace keepers, humanitarian workers and other globalised actors traditionally mandated with child protection.[64] Added to these 'legitimate' international actors are those criminal groups who prey upon children for trafficking, slavery, labour or military recruitment in and out of conflict zones. This demonstrates how children are invested in the globalisation of new wars. Children play a role as both victims and agents in each element of the new wars agenda. Thus, a more sophisticated understanding of the patterns of conflicts and the roles of conflicts' agents emerges when the experiences of children are considered.

Critical approaches to IR theory

With this conflict landscape in mind, this chapter now turns to the contribution that critical approaches to IR have made in considering children in conflict analysis. These approaches have gathered momentum as part of the so-called third debate in IR between positivists and post-positivists, which has seen post-positivists question the foundational claims of orthodox approaches to understanding key IR concerns.[65] While the central body of critical scholarship has yet to consider seriously the relationship between children and conflict, there is nonetheless an emerging body of work within IR using critical methods to explore this relationship.[66] This

---

[62] See, for example, Scott Gates and Simon Reich (eds.), *Child Soldiers in the Age of Fractured States* (Pittsburgh, PA: University of Pittsburgh Press, 2010).
[63] See Watson, 'Can There Be a "Kindered" Peace?', 35–42.
[64] Save the Children, 'No One to Turn To'.
[65] See the special issues on: 'Speaking the Language of Exile: Dissidence in International Studies', *International Studies Quarterly* 34(3) (Special edition, September 1990) and 'Critical International Theory after 25 Years', *Review of International Studies* 33(1) (Special edition, April 2007).
[66] See Brocklehurst, *Who's Afraid of Children?*; McEvoy-Levy, *Trouble Makers or Peace Makers?*; and Lesley Pruitt, *Youth Peacebuilding: Music, Gender, and Change* (New York, NY: SUNY Press, 2013).

builds upon Helen Brocklehurst's claim that '[t]he third debate in IR offers the most promising way into the child's world'.[67]

Like all theoretical traditions, critical approaches have many internal debates, but are broadly linked together through a subscription to the following: firstly, they seek to uncover 'the political nature of knowledge claims in international relations'; secondly, they 'attempt to place questions of community at the centre of the study of international relations'; and finally, they are committed to 'the idea that the study of international relations should be orientated by an emancipatory politics'.[68] Critical approaches to IR accept the complexity and indeed embrace the cacophony of international life, recognising and analysing the complex web of inter-connections, historical experiences, identities and knowledge claims that shape the contemporary world and understandings of it. In their study of war they therefore identify the new wars framework as one of a series that can offer a more complex vision of the multiple subjectivities involved in enabling, enduring and ending conflict. In short, critical approaches to IR seek to reorient their theorising away from a solitary focus on the operation of powerful states in the international system – and a top-down approach to thinking about IR – towards a bottom-up approach that can work for those who have limited power in the international system and have been historically excluded from orthodox IR's theorising. It is for these reasons that critical approaches attract, among others, feminist[69] and security studies theorists[70] who attempt to gain a better understanding of the breadth of armed conflict.

As a form of critique, critical approaches involve a number of interrelated commitments. Firstly, they reject claims to objective and universalised knowledge in the social world. They suggest that knowledge claims which have traditionally been thought to be immutable in IR are socially constructed. Their capacity to be continually reified and be considered true is ultimately the consequence of a knowledge/power relationship that exists within the

---

[67] Brocklehurst, *Who's Afraid of Children?*, 145.
[68] Richard Devetak, 'Critical Theory', in Scott Burchill et al. (eds.), *Theories of International Relations*, 4th edn (Hampshire: Palgrave, 2009), 160.
[69] See, for example, Linda Ahall and Laura Shepherd (eds), *Gender, Agency and Political Violence* (Basingstoke: Palgrave, 2012).
[70] See Ken Booth, *Theory of World Security* (Cambridge: Cambridge University Press, 2007) and Duffield, *Global Governance and the New Wars*.

similarly constructed international system.[71] Related to this, critical
scholars are also interested in how ideas, images and narratives about
international life and its constituent parts are politically deployed to
generate and sustain meaning about the world. Therefore critical
scholars are committed to deconstructing knowledge claims in order
to understand the genealogy of those claims and their capacity to
animate international life. Consequently, discourse and an
understanding of its relationship to knowledge and power are
important to this project. Analysis of the discursive practices of both
the discipline of IR and global politics can demonstrate the powerful
role that discourse plays in shaping political possibilities within the
world. This critique provides the framework through which critical
approaches seek to refocus IR's analysis of conflict. At its core, the goal
of this critique is to develop a social theory that endeavours to recognise
and address existing constraints upon the capacity for human
freedom.[72]

As stated earlier, the worldview employed by critical approaches to
IR shares a great deal in common with the free-ranger views of
childhood agency discussed in Chapter 2. In particular, both share
the belief that identities are socially constructed. As discussed in
Chapter 1, while childhood may involve stages of biological
development, our understandings of the identity and nature of a
child is socially constructed. Critical approaches are therefore
concerned with how certain constructions of identity come to
dominate IR, and who benefits from them. For instance, do those in
global positions of power benefit from the imposition of liberal values
of childhood in non-liberal states? An excavation of the knowledge
claims about childhood therefore requires critical scholarship to
consider existing state, cultural, religious and historical cleavages
and power relations. This leads to the argument that any
universalist claim to childhood identity – for example, the claim that
all children are passive in the face of conflict – is not so much true as it
is the product of power arrangements. Furthermore, critical scholars
demonstrate that such claims exclude those communities who
imagine childhood differently.[73]

[71] Richard K. Ashley, 'The Poverty of Neorealism', *International Organization*
       38(2) (Spring 1984), 248–54.
[72] Devetak, 'Critical Theory', 169.
[73] See Chapter 1 of this book for a further discussion of this point.

Critical approaches are not simply interested in the construction of childhood identity, but also how that construction is discursively represented, particularly in times of global crisis. Conceptualisations of childhood, for example, are deployed by belligerents to generate knowledge claims about children and conflict. For instance, the US-led coalition in Afghanistan consistently referred to the Taliban's ill-treatment of children. Upon assuming his role as Commander of ISAF in Afghanistan, General David Petraeus told the world: '[n]o tactic is beneath the insurgents; indeed, they use unwitting children to carry out attacks, they repeatedly kill innocent civilians, and they frequently seek to create situations that will result in injury to Afghan citizens'.[74] Petraeus' reference to the enemy's deliberate targeting of civilians and the abuse of children is an attempt both to demonise the enemy and reinforce the moral certitude of domestic audiences by reminding them that the campaign in Afghanistan has morally sound foundations. This was part of a broader strategy by members of the US political-military elite to discursively situate children at the moral dividing line of the conflict.[75] On the eve of the US-led invasion, for instance, First Lady Laura Bush told US audiences in a presidential radio address that 'one in every four children won't live past the age of five [in Afghanistan] because health care is not available'.[76] For critical scholars, it is important to note further that in the discursive placement of children in the Afghan conflict, Afghan children themselves are muted; others spoke *of* them and their experiences. This demonstrates how orthodox approaches employ the symbolic power of children in global politics without empowering children as actors.

This encourages a further element of the critical approach: curiosity about children's lives and experiences in conflict zones. This seeks to centralise children as the focus of analysis. Such curiosity enables three revisions of traditional conflict analysis: firstly, it legitimates children's experiences of conflict as relevant to IR and conflict analysis. This allows the relationship between a conflict's trajectory and children's experiences to be fully explored. Secondly, a critical approach

---

[74] David Petraeus, 'Full Text: Gen Petraeus speech' (4 July 2010). Available at www.bbc.co.uk/news/10501541.

[75] Lee-Koo, 'Not Suitable for Children'.

[76] Laura Bush, 'Radio Address by Mrs Bush, 17 November 2001'. Available at: www.presidency.ucsb.edu/ws/index.php?pid=24992#axzz1IhiWhs6z.

demonstrates and validates their individual subjectivities within conflict. This encourages recognition that different children experience conflict differently, based upon a range of intersecting identity markers. Such analysis highlights the poverty of claims such as 'all children are innocent/passive/victims of conflict'. In turn, this demonstrates the capacity that some children may have for agency within conflict. Finally, it allows children to become a significant analytical focus of conflict. This produces a child-centric lens which brings children's lives into focus in analysis of the causes, strategies and resolutions of conflict. Importantly, it also centralises children as the site for emancipatory enquiry. In this sense, it not only seeks to understand how various children experience conflict, but also seeks to support children to be free from conflict.

The question of emancipation, while complex and contested in its own right,[77] has the capacity to generate significant debate within IR when considered in relation to children. These debates would echo those within the free-ranger and PEL movements and revolve around the question: how might children be emancipated? As discussed in Chapter 2, this came to the fore when Lenore Skenazy allowed her nine-year-old son to ride home alone on the New York subway in 2008. While she may have lauded the independence and confidence it gave him, others found this an unreasonable risk for which the child was not prepared, or from which the parent was responsible for protecting the child. When transposed into an IR context, critical scholars must reflect upon what it means to emancipate children. Critical approaches reveal children's capacities to understand their own oppression, but does it also mean that children understand their own emancipation? To what extent are children materially different from adults who may be similarly weighed down under the oppression of civilian, racial or gender-based violence? Is it reasonable to expect that children should be emancipated, or is this suggestion imbibing children with a politics that they are simply not capable of undertaking responsibly, or should be wilfully protected from? If it is recognised that children can indeed demonstrate rational decision-making and

---

[77] See Mark Neufeld, 'Pitfalls of Emancipation and Discourses of Security: Reflections on Canada's "Security with a Human Face"', *International Relations* 18(1) (2004), 109–23 and Columba Peoples, 'Security After Emancipation? Critical Theory, Violence and Resistance', *Review of International Studies* 37(3) (2011), 1113–35.

agency in conflict zones to effect their own security and wellbeing, at what point does enabling children's emancipatory potential cease? Should children be allowed to enlist in armed forces, to work to support their families in conflict zones, be involved in peace building, give testimony at truth commissions and war tribunals if it can be demonstrated that this in some way promotes their security? These are difficult questions. However, when children become partners in their own emancipatory politics, analysis of the issues affecting children has the potential to be richer, and the policies designed to address them becomes more specific to their needs. As demonstrated in Chapter 7, children's input has the capacity to shape the sustainability of peace across generations. This promises an important step forward in conflict analysis.

Conclusion

There remains an active silence within the academic study of global conflict regarding the experiences of children in conflict zones. On the one hand, traditional approaches to thinking about conflict zones, such as the realist and liberal traditions, use theoretical frameworks that rely upon universalised notions of identity and broad assumptions as to the absence of children from the political and public spaces of conflict. The consequence of this for children is that they are only implicitly invested in statist programmes of conflict and peace building. The assumption is that as civilians and pre-citizens of a state they will be protected by the caretaker state or a paternal international community, but remain largely apart from the business of conflict. Children are not considered as individual agents or referents worthy of analysis. Their capacity to affect the trajectory or nature of conflict is often denied, and their experiences as victims of war are marginalised.

On the other hand, critical IR theories and literatures which possess the tools to expand, diversify, and critically engage the breadth and depth of contemporary conflict zones have, as yet, failed to engage in comprehensive analysis of the question of children, which spans the breadth of critical IR. The new wars literature relocates the study of conflict away from the state and instead presents conflict as a network of complex identities, relationships, goals, strategies and experiences; however, it seldom provides significant analysis of children. Borrowing in part from this network, critical theorising creates openings for an analytical focus on children in conflict zones; this opens up opportunities to establish a critically reflective analysis of children as actors, agents and symbols in conflict zones. However, it stills needs to build up a significant literature that addresses these issues, and a willingness to engage the experiences of children in conflict as part of conflict analysis. This literature will need to be involved not only with questions of children's experiences, agency and emancipation, but also with their role as rights-bearers, an issue to which the next chapter turns.

4 | The rights of the child: political history, practices and protection

BINA D'COSTA

Introduction

As demonstrated in Chapter 1, there are a range of direct and indirect threats to children and their rights in armed conflict. Accepting that it is 'law that creates and sustains the regulatory frameworks that define childhood and therefore also the social practices that encapsulate and systematise everyday interactions between adults and children',[1] a variety of national, regional and international legal standards and practices are integral to the rights of the child.[2]

In Chapter 1 it was argued that certain cultural and legal specificities have influenced the definition of childhood in the UNCRC, and Chapter 2 noted that de Certeau's PEL could be adopted in childhood scholarship to offer insights into developing responsible and responsive approaches to children's lives in highly stressful environments. This chapter draws on these two observations about childhood to consider various perspectives that have contributed to the legal basis of children's rights. The chapter examines how the development of international and national discourses on children's rights is relevant to children's specific rights in armed conflict situations. It argues that ideas regarding children's rights are culturally constructed and contested; that they emerged from historical and social crises and are the product of particular power relations. It is further argued that a combination of legislative and regulatory frameworks and innovative advocacy measures co-ordinated between international, regional and national levels is the way forward in ensuring the rights of the child.

---

[1] Adrian L. James and Allison James, 'Childhood: Toward a Theory of Continuity and Change', *Annals of the American Academy of Political and Social Science* 575(1) (2001), 34.

[2] For an analysis of the various discourses, see Anna Holzscheiter, *Children's Rights in International Politics: The Transformative Power of Discourse* (New York, NY: Palgrave Macmillian Press, 2010).

The first part of this chapter focuses on children's rights across cultural contexts. It examines a number of aspects in detail: the search for common ground and a common global language of children's rights that permeates the local/state-based settings and reaches communities and families; secondly, the manner in which children endure, despite deeply divisive social/cultural orders that are in many cases perpetually transformed due to armed conflict. Reviewing the history of children's rights in international forums it then argues that although debate regarding children's rights is ongoing, it was only in the second half of the twentieth century that it shifted from a language of 'salvation' to substantive protection of those rights.[3] Following this discussion is a detailed examination of the UNCRC. Finally, this chapter considers the specific provisions for those rights in armed conflict.

Children's rights across cultural contexts

Children's experiences during periods of conflict and post-conflict are diverse, reflecting their complex roles in society and in their political community.[4] Understanding these roles also involves critical analysis of where the child is situated in relation to her/his family, social networks and the state. However, there exist significant tensions between universal and local approaches to childhood. Whereas a global language implies that there is a shared acceptance of children's rights as a universally understood concept,[5] much of the scholarship on children's rights demonstrates that this is far from the reality. Some of the primary questions that have emerged concern the legitimacy of children as rights-bearers; the biases of western versus non-western concepts of children's rights; and the context of universal versus cultural relativism, specifically as it concerns the impact of religion on children's rights in the global south. Stephen Nmeregini Achilihu

---

[3] Michael D. Freeman, *The Rights and Wrongs of Children* (London: Frances Pinter, 1983), 18.

[4] The scholarship on nation building and nationalism suggests that four predominant and interrelated political communities are important in the formation of identity politics and conflicts. These are ethnic, religious, territorial and racial communities. Bina D'Costa, *Nationbuilding, Gender and War Crimes in South Asia* (London: Routledge, 2011) 27–30.

[5] Adele Jones, 'Child Asylum Seekers and Refugees: Rights and Responsibilities', *Journal of Social Work* 1(3) (2001), 257.

considers such issues by asking whether African children have rights in the context of a nation replete with a history of recurrent violent and protracted conflicts. Because half of the population is under eighteen in Angola (52 per cent), Ethiopia (53 per cent), Ghana (51 per cent), Liberia (50 per cent), Mozambique (51 per cent), Sierra Leone (50 per cent) and Uganda (56 per cent), he argues that restrictive decision-making could lead to serious disenfranchisement of a significant percentage of African society.[6]

Ratification of the UNCRC created new political opportunities in 1989; the UNCRC attempted to set aside the claims of cultural relativists by offering a global, shared understanding of the social and political identity of children, irrespective of culture, nationality, gender and race.[7] However, two critical challenges remain: the first is the west versus the 'rest' divide in conceptualising childhood. In 1993 an academic journal titled *Childhood* first appeared, probing global perspectives on issues such as children's rights, agency, labour and sexual exploitation. In her conceptualisation of an international social theory of childhood, Leena Alanen discussed the Anglo-centrism of the claims of the founding authors of the journal.[8] While Alanen wrote this a decade ago, one of the journal editors recently observed that a bulk of the contributions still derive from the United Kingdom, Scandinavian states, the United States, Australia and South Africa, and remained concerned with the underlying essentialism of the dominant social theory of childhood.[9]

Related to this is the second challenge that emerges from disciplinary divides in theorising children's lives: a number of approaches and forms of discourse raise critical questions with regard to children's rights, but also have biases and limitations. These include: the sociological approach to childhood; children's rights from a legal perspective; the anthropological understanding of cultural relativism; universalism, which extends beyond the realm of human rights and pervades legal discourse; and finally, politics and IR, with their focus on actors and

---

[6] Stephen Nmeregini Achilihu, *Do African Children Have Rights? A Comparative and Legal Analysis of the United Nations Convention on the Rights of the Child* (Florida: Universal Publishers, 2010).

[7] Olga Nieuwenhuys, 'Keep Asking: Why Childhood? Why Children? Why Global?', *Childhood* 17(3) (2010), 291–6.

[8] Leena Alanen, 'Review Essay: Visions of a Social Theory of Childhood', *Childhood* 7(4) (2000), 504.

[9] Nieuwenhuys, 'Keep Asking', 294.

structural processes. Both multi-disciplinary and inter-disciplinary linkages are often overlooked by scholars, who for various reasons do not draw upon work from other fields, resulting in disciplinary silos and encouraging essentialist understandings of childhood and children's rights. The multi-disciplinary debate within human rights discourse partly illustrates these tensions and complexities.

Jack Donnelly traces the history and idea of human rights in mainstream political theory to seventeenth-century Europe when they served as a response to the social disruptions and transformations of modernity.[10] John Locke's *Second Treatise on Government* published in 1688 offered a natural rights theory of life, liberty and estate that is consistent with later developments in human rights. However, in spite of the universalism entrenched in natural rights, Locke's theory was developed for the 'protection of the rights of propertied European males' and excluded women, 'savages', servants and wage labourers as legitimate rights-bearers.[11] It also failed to distinguish between adults and children, reflecting an implicit assumption that children, like women could not be legitimate rights-bearers because of their dependency on men. The struggle for human rights in the following centuries gradually expanded to the extent that human rights regimes uniformly recognise all human beings as rights-bearers. Human rights discourse rejects the practice of employing different identities such as race, religion, gender and property as grounds for exclusion of others for the enjoyment of rights. Classical western liberal notions of human rights emphasise the individual's political and civil rights, whereas in many non-western traditions, economic and social rights and duties prioritise a community's rights or group rights over individual rights. Economic and social rights and duties based on collectivist principles are also stressed by Marxist and socialist ideas.[12] In his influential work *Universal Human Rights: In Theory and Practice*, Donnelly articulates that rather than constituting an orthodox system of fundamental

---

[10] Jack Donnelly, 'The Social Construction of International Human Rights', in Tim Dunne and Nicholas J. Wheeler(eds.), *Human Rights in Global Politics* (Cambridge: Cambridge University Press, 1999), 82–3.

[11] Ibid.

[12] M. Glen Johnson, 'Human Rights in Divergent Conceptual Settings – How Do Ideas Influence Policy Choices?', in David Louis Cingranelli (ed.), *Human Rights Theory and Measurement* (London: Macmillan Press, 1988).

values, human rights 'are a set of social practices that regulate relations between, and help to constitute, citizens and states in "modern" societies'.[13] Stressing that his analysis is structural rather than cultural, Donnelly argues in the first instance that the theory and practice of human rights 'began in the West and have become a central, and in many ways a politically defining, part of contemporary Western societies'.[14] For him, specific cultural protections of moral and social rights might be worthy and protective of human dignity, but these do not constitute human rights. Secondly, non-western cultural and political traditions, such as those existing in pre-modern western societies, lacked not only the practice of human rights but also the concept underlying these traditions.[15] This is in contrast with scholars who have argued that the idea of human rights existed in Islamic societies and other forms of traditional communities.

As will be further illustrated, the heated debates about what exactly culture is and how it shapes the concept of rights have been sharply divided along both disciplinary lines and global north–south relations.[16] In his reflection on why culture matters for development and for the reduction of poverty, Arjun Appadurai argues that culture has often been perceived in relation to past habit, custom, heritage and tradition, whereas development is conceived as comprising future plans, hopes, goals and targets.[17] By providing a decentralised model of global cultural flows, Appadurai replaces the centre-periphery model in which the west dominates the 'rest'. He terms these global cultural flows as ethnoscapes, mediascapes, technoscapes, finanscapes and ideoscapes.[18] The global diffusion of cultural forms and processes

[13] Jack Donnelly, *Universal Human Rights: In Theory and Practice* (Ithaca, NY: Cornell University Press, 2003), 61.
[14] Ibid., 63.   [15] Ibid., 71.
[16] For critiques on this position see Abdullahi Ahmed An-Na'im, 'Problems and Prospects of Universal Cultural Legitimacy for Human Rights', in A. An-Na'im and F. Deng (eds.), *Human Rights in Africa: Cross-Cultural Perspectives* (Washington, DC: Brookings Institution, 1990), 331–67; William Twining, *Human Rights, Southern Voices* (Cambridge: Cambridge University Press, 2009).
[17] Arjun Appadurai, 'The Capacity to Aspire: Culture and the Terms of Recognition', in Vijayendra Rao and Michael Walton (eds.), *Culture and Public Action* (Stanford, CA: Stanford University Press, 2004). He also offers a critical self-reflection of his own discipline, anthropology, by noting that 'the future remains a stranger to most anthropological models of culture'. Ibid., 2.
[18] Ethnoscapes, according to Appudurai, are 'landscape[s] of persons who constitute the shifting world in which we live; tourists, immigrants, refugees, exiles,

has also been examined by Ulf Hannerz through four frames: forms of life, whereby culture is shaped through everyday life; the state, by which culture is transmitted from the state to its citizens; the market, whereby culture is commodified through its passage from producer to consumer; and movements, through which people are converted to various forms of belief.[19]

Donnelly, whose fields are political theory and IR, criticises the way anthropologists have understood culture and suggests that throughout the Cold War anthropologists have consistently failed to provide sophisticated critique of the role of culture in human rights discourse: 'ideas and social practices move no less readily than, say, noodles and gunpowder. If human rights are irrelevant in a particular place, it is not because of where they were invented or when they were introduced into that place. Culture is *not* destiny.'[20]

Appudurai, Donnelly and Hannerz began with comparable arguments pointing to the fluidity and inter-subjectivity of culture. The differences are clear, however, in the opposing arguments of universalism versus cultural relativism that divide scholars and practitioners alike in the politics of culture. The question remains, is it culture that is at issue?[21] Anthropologists opine that rather than

guestworkers and other moving groups and persons constitute an essential feature of the world and appear to affect the politics of (and between) nations to a hitherto unprecedented degree'. Mediascapes involve 'the distribution of the electronic capabilities to produce and disseminate information', and 'the images of the world created by these media'. Technoscapes refer to the 'global configuration ... of technology, and of the fact that technology, both high and low, both mechanical and informational, now moves at high speeds across various kinds of previously impervious boundaries'. Finanscapes refer to the flows in 'currency markets, national stock exchanges, and commodity speculations'. And finally, ideoscapes 'are often directly political and frequently have to do with the ideologies of states and the counter-ideologies of movements explicitly oriented to capturing state power or a piece of it'. Arjun Appadurai, 'Disjuncture and Difference in the Global Cultural Economy', in M. Featherstone (ed.), *Global Culture: Nationalism, Globalization and Modernity* (London: Sage, 1990), 295–310.

[19] Ulf Hannerz, *Transnational Connections: Culture, People, Places* (London: Routledge, 1996). See also Gordon Mathews, *Global Culture/Individual Identity: Searching for Home in the Cultural Supermarket* (New York, NY: Routledge, 2000).

[20] Ibid., 87–8.

[21] Jane K. Cowan, Marie-Benedicte Dembour and Richard A. Wilson (eds.), *Culture and Rights: Anthropological Perspectives* (Cambridge: Cambridge University Press, 2001), 6.

culture, it is law – with its grounding in a positivist view of truth – that essentialises social categories and identities.[22]

Some scholars argue that employing a pluralist approach and negotiating rights in specific circumstances is a more efficient way to resolve these tensions. For example, anthropologist Ellen Messer tags Donnelly as an anti-cultural relativist and argues that it is more useful to consider pluralist or evolutionary approaches to human rights. Tracing through four major sources of modern human rights – namely, western political liberalism, socialism and social welfare principles, cross-cultural rights traditions and finally the UN instruments – she advocates a pluralist approach. Messer suggests that anthropologists could help to clarify notions of rights in culture-specific contexts through their analyses of concepts of 'personhood at multiple social levels' that leave certain categories of individuals without protections, and also by 'creating effective human rights educational materials that can link sentiment to human rights reasoning'.[23]

Messer further notes that by identifying local, cultural and household notions and practices of obligation to feed and provide medical care for young children, anthropologists could help to clarify where the right to food exists and where additional protection is needed by children.[24] Local level research provides greater opportunity to elucidate the notion of rights and duties, and to understand the construction of inclusion and exclusion from protection as a member of the community. Political theorist Brooke Ackerly, for example, seeks to bridge the universalist and relativist debate by suggesting that universal human rights are immanent rather than transcendent, and that the foundation of universal human rights can be found in contestation over these rights at the local level.[25] Disciplinary analyses and debates have primarily focused on how human rights are to be understood and the extent to which children's human rights concern cultural norms and beliefs. Beyond academia, international actors are also divided in resolving some of the cultural contexts of human rights and children's rights.

[22] Ibid.
[23] Ellen Messer, 'Pluralist Approaches to Human Rights', *The Journal of Anthropological Research* 53(3) (1997), 309.
[24] Ibid.
[25] Brooke Ackerly, *Universal Human Rights in a World of Difference* (Cambridge: Cambridge University Press, 2008).

A history of children's rights: laying the moral foundations

While Plato viewed the family as a layer of individualism, Aristotle regarded the nature of family as personal and private, with children constituting an extension of their parents. He understood grown children as owing a debt to their parents based on shared pleasure, mutual usefulness and common virtue.[26] Thomas Aquinas recognised children as individuals separate from the family.[27] However, the sixteenth-century French philosopher Jean Bodin was arguably the first person to argue that a child needed protection within a family, reasoning that this environment was the training ground for citizenship. In this way, he linked the family and the state as mutually responsive to each other and bounded by citizenship. Other prominent western political philosophers also examined the inter-familial relationships between children and parents. Hobbes perceived children to be in the power of their parents, who could either protect them or destroy them; he observed that children tacitly understood this and, therefore, obeyed their parents.[28] John Locke argued that children must obey their parents, not so much because of their physical power, but because their parents controlled their inheritance rights.[29] Both Locke and Rousseau distinguished between the nurturing parent – the mother – and the teaching parent – the father.[30]

The idea of children's rights movements, at least in the west, can be traced back to 1852, when an article was published with the title: 'The Rights of Children',[31] and to Jules Vallès' 1879 novel *L'Enfant*.[32]

---

[26] This understanding of looking after parents by children, and the responsibilities of children was also debated during the drafting of the UNCRC, introduced by Senegal.

[27] See Katherine Archibald, 'The Concept of Social Hierarchy in the Writings of St. Thomas Aquinas', in John Dunn and Ian Harris (eds.), *Great Political Thinkers, Volume 4*, (Cheltenham: Edward Elgar Publications, 1997, orig. 1947), 116–92.

[28] Thomas Hobbes (edited by Michael Oakeshott), *Leviathan* (New York, NY: Collier, 1962, orig. 1651).

[29] Lee Ward, *John Locke and Modern Life*, (Cambridge: Cambridge University Press, 2010), 162–3.

[30] Jean-Jacques Rousseau, *Basic Political Writings* (trans. Donald A. Cress), (Indianapolis, IN: Hackett, 1987).

[31] Michael D. Freeman, 'The Limits of Children's Rights', in Michael D. Freeman and Philip Veerman (eds.), *The Ideologies of Children's Rights* (Dordrecht: Martinus Nijhoff, 1992).

[32] Michael D. Freeman, 'Children as Persons', in Michael Freeman (ed.), *Children's Rights: A Comparative Perspective* (Aldershot: Dartmouth, 1993).

However, instead of focusing on the child as an individual, Vallès and others during the nineteenth century were more concerned with saving the child.[33] The focus on modern systems, orphanages and juvenile courts was associated with nurturing childhood instead of self-determination (Chapter 2 looks in detail at this 'caretaker' perspective).[34] It was not until the end of the nineteenth century that Kate Douglas Wiggin and Janusz Korsczak's writings expressed ideas that could be perceived as recognition of children as individuals with rights, choices and freedom.

The first attempt to establish a normative framework of children's rights occurred in September 1924 when the Fifth Assembly of the League of Nations adopted the Declaration[35] of the Rights of the Child, also known as the Declaration of Geneva. It was drafted in Geneva by Eglantyne Jebb,[36] whose advocacy campaign responded to the trauma of World War I, establishing the SCIU in 1919. While the Declaration contained only five paragraphs, it covered a range of concerns such as food, healthcare, delinquency, shelter, emergency relief, work and exploitation. It also provided explicit connection between children's needs and their development.[37] Mark Ensalaco

---

[33] Early documentation of children's rights advocacy involving interventions by 'child savers' demonstrate that the historical experience of childhood in Europe and elsewhere has, in many cases, been brutal. In many cases children were abandoned, imprisoned with adults and were forced to work in factories. The factory reform movement in the United Kingdom got momentum when, in 1815, Robert Owen, a Welsh social reformer, factory owner and one of the founders of the co-operative movement started an appeal for overworked factory children. Children as young as six years old were working in Lancashire towns from thirteen to fourteen and a half hours daily. The appeal focused on detrimental health conditions for children. For details see, R. G. Kirby and A. E. Musson, *The Voices of the People: John Doherty, 1798–1854, Trade Unionist, Radical and Factory Reformer* (Manchester: Manchester University Press, 1975) 347–80.

[34] For details see Freeman, 'The Limits of Children's Rights' and Freeman, 'Children as Persons'.

[35] The term 'declaration' has been officially defined by the UN Secretariat as 'a formal and solemn instrument, suitable for rare occasions when principles of great and lasting significance are enunciated'. While these are not legally binding, a declaration 'may by custom become recognized as laying down rules binding upon states'. For details see, UN Doc. E/CN, 4/L.610, 1962.

[36] In the aftermath of the war Jebb was the President of the Save the Children Fund and the ICRC.

[37] Mark Ensalaco, 'The Right of the Child to Development', in Mark Ensalaco and Linda C. Majka (eds.), *Children's Human Rights: Progress and Challenges for Children Worldwide* (Oxford: Rowman and Littlefield, 2005), 9–30.

argues that the decades following this Declaration saw the rise of fascism, World War II, and the extinction of the League of Nations, all of which had catastrophic consequences for children's rights[38] and limited the Declaration's impact. However, Achilihu suggests that the Declaration was elitist: it focused on children's 'care and protection rights' to the exclusion of their civil and political rights; the word 'rights' was absent from the text; and the non-binding nature of the document also limited its influence.[39] Its prevailing intention was aspirational, merely inviting states to be guided 'by its principles in the work of child welfare'.[40]

The UN was established in 1945, and at the end of 1946 the UN International Children's Emergency Fund was established, which was renamed UNICEF in 1953. This specialised agency, which was created for the protection, development and wellbeing of children, recognised that the horror and trauma of World War II permanently affected many children and would influence the future of the world. The Universal Declaration of Human Rights (UDHR), adopted in December 1948, was the first major statement of human rights in the post-war era. Yet, similar to the Declaration of Geneva, it only contained brief reference to family and children. Article 16.3 states, 'the family is the natural and fundamental group unit of society and is entitled to protection by society and the State'.

The Declaration of the Rights of the Child (1959 Declaration) was adopted unanimously on 20 November 1959 by the General Assembly of the UN, and included the support of seventy-eight governments at that time. The document contained ten principles, but retained the limited status of a declaration. It did not encompass legally binding rights, but rather urged states to take note of these principles as universal and applicable to all children.[41] Despite using gendered language throughout the Declaration, Principle 1 was attentive to the development of norms in the post-war period and recognised emerging global risks. It stated that the rights it enunciated were applicable to all children, 'without distinction or discrimination on account of race,

---

[38] Ibid.   [39] Achilihu, *Do African Children Have Rights?*, 19–21.
[40] Douglas Hodgson, 'The Historical Development and Internationalisation of the Children's Rights Movement', *The Australian Journal of Family Law* 6 (1992), 252–78, 261.
[41] Jane Fortin, *Children's Rights and the Developing Law* (Cambridge: Cambridge University Press, 2003), 35.

colour, sex, language, religion, political or other opinion, national, or social origin, property, birth or other status, whether of himself or of his family'.[42] The Declaration introduced the concept of protection of the child against all forms of discrimination. Although the Declaration of Geneva (1924) did not mention education,[43] the 1959 Declaration included two references to education in Principles 5 and 7.

A pivotal contribution of the 1959 Declaration was its clear reaffirmation of the rights of the child prior to birth; these rights were present in the UDHR. The 1959 Declaration:

retains its full force as reaffirming and providing proof that, eleven years earlier in the Universal Declaration, an international consensus was reached recognising the need for human rights protection for the child before birth ... Universal recognition of the child before birth as a juridical personality entitled to a legal protection had been established and accepted in the very foundation instrument of modern international human rights law.[44]

While the 1959 Declaration now appears overly general and idealistic, including obsolete principles and containing vague and stereotyped perceptions of the roles and responsibilities of families and parents, its significance should not be understated. It attempted to codify children's 'overriding claims and entitlements'.[45] Ensalaco observes that by the time the 1959 Declaration was adopted, the evolution of universal standards – especially in the areas of education and work – was more visible.[46]

In addition to both the 1924 and 1959 declarations, the roles of international institutions were critical in developing the norm of protection, especially with regard to child labour. For example, the International Labour Organization (ILO) was established in 1919, following which global labour standards began to emerge. While the Declaration of Geneva states in paragraph 4 that 'the child must be put in a position to earn a livelihood and must be protected against every form of exploitation',[47] Principle 9 of the 1959 Declaration requires

---

[42] Declaration of the Rights of the Child. Available at www.unicef.org/lac/spbar bados/Legal/global/General/declaration_child1959.pdf.
[43] Rita Joseph, *Human Rights and the Unborn Child* (Leiden: Martinus Nijhoff Publishers, 2009), 3.
[44] Ibid.   [45] Fortin, *Children's Rights and the Developing Law*, 36.
[46] Ensalaco, 'The Right of the Child to Development', 11.
[47] Ensalaco writes, 'the juxtaposition of work and exploitation is not coincidental'. Ibid.,12.

child protection against neglect, cruelty, exploitation and trafficking without reference to the requirement to earn a living. It also advocates a minimum age for employment and a non-prejudicial guarantee of the physical, mental or moral development of the child. However, the 1959 Declaration does not offer any acknowledgement that, similar to adults, children are also entitled to first generation human rights[48] in the form of freedoms from state oppression. Except for reference to children's names and nationality, it contains no mention of civil and political rights.[49]

It was not until the early 1970s that authors such as John Holt and Richard Farson began publishing work that focused on children's liberation: their rights to work, to vote and to assert their sexual freedom.[50] During the Vietnam War protests, attacks on social institutions by liberationists included the influence of juvenile justice procedures in the United States through an expansion of the scope and application of children's rights. Holt advocated the right of children to use drugs. Some of these suggestions were considered extreme, and children's liberationist theory took another twenty years before it made any impact on public policy. In the meantime, however, the discourse of positive law contributed to the concept of protection, which began to emerge as the basis of children's rights. The section that follows turns away from debates over children's rights, which occurred largely within the west, to consider debates between the global north and south, which grew out of the postcolonial period and became prominent in the 1980s and 1990s.

Discursive practices of rights along the global north and south divide

In the three decades following World War II and the reconstruction of Europe, anti-colonial and national movements in Africa, Latin America and Asia culminated in the rise of new states. In the face of enormous reparations and loan repayments in the aftermath of World War II, the former colonial powers could no longer afford to maintain

---

[48] Those which deal with liberty and participation in political life such as freedom of speech, right to fair trial, freedom of religion and voting rights.
[49] Fortin, *Children's Rights and the Developing Law*, 37.
[50] John Holt, *Escape from Childhood* (Boston, MA: E. P. Dutton, 1974); Richard Farson, *Birthrights* (New York, NY: Penguin, 1978).

their colonies and wanted them to become independent as quickly as possible.[51] As a result, new states emerged on the global stage through a haphazard demarcation of borders – for instance, in Pakistan, India, Burma, Congo – and the smokescreen of apparently peaceful transition from colonial to indigenous leadership based on divided loyalties and local power politics, as occurred in Zimbabwe, Uganda, Sierra Leone, Sri Lanka and Burma. By the 1980s, different kinds of conflicts were brewing within and beyond these states. These were both intra-state and inter-state conflicts, involving neo-colonial and power-hungry rulers and interest groups who were equally repressive,[52] and who used anachronistic colonial legislation to exploit the population. These conflicts were ruthless, enduring, protracted and complex; they dangerously intensified political identities, such as those of ethnicity, race, language, religion and location. These conflicts also caused high numbers of civilian casualties, in which women and children were increasingly prominent. On the other hand, a number of factors contributed to deeply entrench the insecurities of people living in these worlds, including: intense militarisation of former colonised states, for example El Salvador, Guatemala, Nicaragua and Indonesia; the extreme poverty of developing states, many of which had authoritarian regimes, for example Argentina and Brazil; the formation of Israel amid a hostile Arab world; Cold War politics; and massive population displacement. In this context the paths of

---

[51] See various contributions to the postcolonial scholarship: Kwame Anthony Appiah, *In My Father's House: Africa in the Philosophy of Culture* (New York, NY: Oxford University Press, 1992); Sanjay Seth (ed.), *Postcolonial Theory and International Relations: A Critical Introduction* (London: Routledge, 2013); Sankaran Krishna, *Globalisation and Postcolonialism: Hegemony and Resistance in the Twenty-first Century* (Lanham, MD: Rowman and Littlefield, 2009); Ashis Nandy, *The Intimate Enemy: Loss and Recovery of Self Under Colonialism* (Delhi: Oxford University Press, 1983). Also see, Gary Teeple, 'Chapter 2', in Gary Teeple, *The Riddle of Human Rights*, (Toronto: University of Toronto Press, 2004).

[52] A. Curthoys, 'Whose Home? Expulsion, Exodus, and Exile in White Australian Historical Mythology', *Journal of Australian Studies* 61(1999), 1–19; Alexandra Xanthaki, *Indigenous Rights and United Nations Standards: Self-Determination, Culture and Land* (Cambridge: Cambridge University Press, 2004). Also see the excellent analysis of Lemkin's unpublished work in Dominik K. Schaller, 'Raphael Lemkin's View of European Colonial Rule in Africa: Between Condemnation and Admiration', *Journal of Genocide Research* 7(4) (2005) 531–8.

children's lives were ever more determined by overlapping identities – racial, linguistic, religious, regional and ethnic – and caught between local and global conflicts. The emergence of a children's rights-based approach must also be understood in this context.

The development studies discourse on rights describes this issue as an impasse in the global patron-client relationship. A paradoxical mistrust exists between the international donor community – the global patron – and the recipient states and institutions – the global client. Such competing international debates about development, security and protection have influenced how children's rights in situations of armed conflict have developed.

While the former colonial rulers in Europe and the significant Cold War powers of the United States and the Soviet Union have fuelled many conflicts in the global south, human rights practitioners, advocacy networks, and activists of these states campaigned for the universal applicability of children's rights. The international donor community as global patron has formed various consortiums that fund their clients, which are either states or NGOs in the global south. But the profound mistrust generated within the local environment because of various interlinked factors – global politics following centuries of colonial rule; Cold War securitisation; support of indigenous dictators and the use of military technology, weapons and intelligence for domestic human rights violations – could not so easily be resolved by these new kinds of patron-client relationship.

Human rights constitute the primary discourse where differences and tensions between these two worlds have become apparent. When the global north raises the question of human rights, leaders and activists of the global south alike point to the continuing rights violations of the northern states. In addition to this, southern leaders, such as Mahathir Mohammad of Malaysia and Lee Kuan Yew of Singapore, advocated for cultural relativism and Asian values over universality in the 1980s and 1990s. They further argued that the UDHR celebrated individual rights over community rights. In Asia, they argued, economic development and social rights are more important than civil and political rights. While the purpose of their stance was to justify existing repressive policies, the question remains, to what extent has the language of human rights, especially when it deals with children, become a global and shared language? The answers can be especially opaque when different societies and cultures place different values on their children.[53]

Following almost a decade of negotiation, the new international legal instrument on children's rights, the UNCRC, was drafted in 1988. It was clear that some of the cross-cultural factors discussed above were critical in setting the norms expounded by the UNCRC. The draft Convention was adopted in its entirety following the Second Reading held between 28 November and 9 December, 1988. There were twenty-two separate meetings held, where government delegations, inter-governmental organisations and NGOs representing various parts of the world debated differences arising from cultural, regional, religious and socio-economic perspectives.[54] There were five regional caucuses comprising: (i) the west – Western Europe, the United States, Canada, Australia and New Zealand, (ii) the east – the former Soviet Union and Socialist Eastern Europe, (iii) Africa, (iv) Asia and (v) Latin America. African nations were least represented at working group meetings. However, as David Johnson points out, a lack of financial resources might have discouraged African representatives from participating in meetings in Geneva.[55] If this was the case, the creation of new international norms such as the UNCRC was shaped from the outset by the dynamics of global inequality. The working groups debated a variety of issues, especially freedom of religion; inter-country adoption; rights of the unborn; traditional practices harmful to children; and the duties of children towards their parents. These UNCRC negotiations demonstrate that not only legal and political, but also cultural and religious, values have influenced international standards for protecting children's rights. The following section examines the UNCRC in detail with particular attention to how it interacts with other international legal instruments.

---

[53] Based on her fieldwork in Cambodia and Burma, Cecilia Jacob argues that both age and seniority constantly produce and reproduce social and gender orders. While these are not always fixed, even higher education and the social and economic status of the younger generation may not be considered as vital as the seniority of decision-makers in mediating local conflicts. Jacob suggests that children's security in Cambodia and Burma must be understood in this context of age hierarchy. Cecilia Jacob, *Child Security in Asia: The Impact of Armed Conflict in Cambodia and Myanmar* (London: Routledge, 2014).

[54] David Johnson, 'Cultural and Regional Pluralism in the Drafting of the UN Convention on the Rights of the Child', in Michael Freeman and Philip Veerman (eds.), *Ideologies of Children's Rights* (Dordrecht: Martinus Nijhoff, 1992).

[55] Ibid., 97.

The UNCRC

In 1976, the UN General Assembly (UNGA) declared 1979 the International Year of the Child in order to increase the visibility of children in development and human rights discourses. Earlier the chapter discussed the drafting sessions of the UNCRC. The UNGA adopted the UNCRC on 20 November 1989. The UNCRC was developed out of the 1948 UDHR and superseded the 1959 Declaration of the Rights of the Child. It entered into force on 2 September 1990 and has been ratified by 194 countries. It is a binding human rights instrument concerning persons below the age of eighteen. The general principles of the UNCRC encompass all actions affecting children and young people. The key substantive objective is to ensure the survival and development of children.[56] Although UNICEF and other child rights organisations consider that 'survival and development' is a general principle of the UNCRC, there is a different view that suggests that 'survival and development' encompass the overall substantive objectives of the UNCRC and is therefore different from the other three general UNCRC principles – best interests of the child, non-discrimination and participation – which provide an operational framework. Through directing implementation measures, these three general principles achieve the survival and development of children.[57] Figure 4.1 explains the UNCRC framework and general principles for implementing children's rights.[58]

The UNCRC is the most widely ratified treaty in the history of international law. The Convention was opened for signature in January 1990, and it became effective just eight months later on 2 September 1990, thirty days after the deposit of the required twentieth instrument of ratification.[59] Critics have suggested that the keen interest that states showed to sign the treaty had more to do with the perception that the UNCRC was a 'soft' treaty based on various values that are fundamental to cultures across the globe rather than a

---

[56] Karin Arts, 'General Introduction: A Child Rights-Based Approach to International Criminal Accountability', in Karin Arts and Vesselin Popovski (eds.), *International Criminal Accountability and the Rights of Children* (The Hague: Hague Academic Press, 2006), 3–16, 10.

[57] Ibid., 10.   [58] Ibid., 11.

[59] Alfred Glenn Mower, *The Convention on the Rights of the Child: International Law Support for Children* (Westport, CT: Greenwood Publishing Group, 1997), 14.

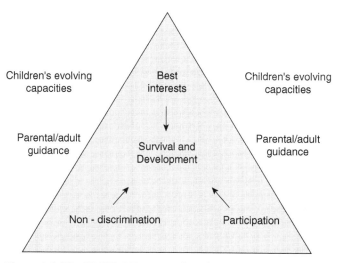

Figure 4.1 The UNCRC Framework and General Principles

genuine commitment to children's rights. A broad variety of rights is covered in the UNCRC. It contains fifty-four articles, of which forty are concerned with substantive rights and cover civil, political, economic and social concerns. It has been accepted by states more quickly and comprehensively than any other international convention. The United States, South Sudan and Somalia are the only UN-member states that have not ratified the UNCRC. As legal scholars in the United States have argued, the UNCRC creates a serious risk to children without parents because its key provisions limit adoption possibilities and the right of children to find a positive environment to grow up in. While it is clear that the Convention has deficiencies, by not ratifying it, the United States' ability to promote human rights in other countries has been compromised.[60]

The Convention is based on the principle that childhood requires special care and support; it therefore addresses a range of political, economic, civil, social, and cultural rights. The fifty-four articles are articulated in three parts. Part I deals with children's rights, and Parts II and III deal with administrative rules. Many states that signed and

---

[60] Elizabeth Bartholet, 'Ratification by the United States of the Convention on the Rights of the Child: Pros and Cons from a Child's Rights Perspective', *The Annals of the American Academy of Political and Social Sciences* (2011), 633–80.

ratified the UNCRC have either violated international standards of human rights or committed – and continue to commit – mass violations of children's rights.

For example, in 2012 Yemen executed a fifteen-year-old girl, Hind Al-Barti, in Sana'a. It was a clear violation of a binding UN treaty. Jean Zermatten, the Chairperson of the UN Committee on the Rights of the Child[61] – the body of independent experts that monitors implementation of the UNCRC by its states parties – delivered an official statement following the execution. Zermatten noted, '[s]he was executed in violation of Article 6 of the Convention on the Rights of the Child proclaiming the inherent right of every child to life; and of Article 37(a), which provides that neither capital punishment nor life imprisonment without possibility of release shall be imposed for offences committed by minors'.[62] According to a variety of sources, fourteen juveniles were executed in Yemen between 2006 and 2010. On 18 January 2012, a further juvenile offender was reportedly executed.

Although the United States has not ratified the UNCRC, it is a party to the Optional Protocols and submits periodical reports to the Committee. On 28 January 2013, the Committee on the Rights of the Child considered the second periodic report – under the Optional Protocol to the UNCRC – on the US detention and maltreatment of foreign child combatants.[63] It expressed concerns that: children were in detention facilities with only the International Committee of the Red Cross (ICRC) and the Afghan Independent Human Rights Commission

---

[61] The Committee also monitors implementation of two optional protocols to the Convention, on involvement of children in armed conflict and on sale of children, child prostitution and child pornography. All states parties are obliged to submit regular reports to the Committee on how the rights are being implemented. States must report initially two years after acceding to the Convention and then every five years. The Committee examines each report and addresses its concerns and recommendations to the state party in the form of concluding observations. For details see, www2.ohchr.org/english/bodies/UNCRC/.

[62] Press release, available online at UN Committee on the Rights of the Child. Available at www2.ohchr.org/english/bodies/UNCRC/index.htm. In total, twenty-one juvenile offenders, all under eighteen years at the time of the commission of the offences, have been condemned to death, with an additional 186 alleged juvenile cases reportedly still threatened with execution in Yemen.

[63] Optional Protocol on the Involvement of Children in Armed Conflict. Concluding observations on the second report of the United States of America, adopted by the Committee at its sixty-second session (14 January–5 February 2013), CRC/C/OPAC/USA/CO/2 28 January 2013.

being granted access; children were generally denied access to legal assistance; alleged child soldiers had been subjected to torture, ill-treatment and abusive interrogations and that in the case of convicted child terrorist Omar Khadr,[64] the judge barred the defence from presenting significant evidence of Khadr's ill-treatment while in custody; only children under the age of sixteen are separated from adults; and children transferred to Afghan custody would face torture and ill-treatment.[65] One of the recommendations by the Committee included ensuring that all children under the age of eighteen be handled by the juvenile justice system.[66]

Drawing upon natural law and legal positivism, Cohen argues that the UNCRC is an anomaly among human rights treaties, as the Convention was not preceded by rights claims based on natural law, and does not closely replicate the related 1959 Declaration.[67] It extensively expanded the elements of the 1959 Declaration, including the protection of children's rights and – for the first time – recognised children as legitimate rights-bearers.[68] In addition to the Convention's fifty-four articles, there are also two Optional Protocols that address armed conflict and the sale of children, setting out the responsibilities of governments, families and caregivers in supporting children; it also details the inherent rights of children as young citizens. Furthermore, the UNCRC emphasises the foundational function of the family and the principal role of parents and guardians in caring for children. Articles 5, 18 and 19 state that the basic institution in society required for the survival, protection and development of the child is the family. The UNCRC stipulates that the family has an important role to play in securing the right of the child to be registered with a name and a nationality, to know as far as

---

[64] Omar Ahmed Khadr, a Canadian citizen was one of the youngest captives to be held at Guantanamo Bay Detention Camp. He was also the first person since World War II to be prosecuted in a military commission for war crimes committed while still a minor. See www.defense.gov/news/AE%20200-B-D%20-%20Motion%20to%20Suppress%20Accused%27s%20statements%20%28 redacted%29%202nd.pdf.

[65] Ibid., Chapter VI on Protection, recovery and reintegration.

[66] This point will be considered further in Chapter 8 of this book.

[67] Cynthia Price Cohen, 'The Relevance of Theories of Natural Law and Legal Positivism', in Michael Freeman and Philip Veerman (eds.), *The Ideologies of Children's Rights* (Dordrecht: Martinus Nijhoff, 1992) 53–70, 54.

[68] Ibid.

possible his or her parentage and to preserve his or her identity (Articles 7 and 8).[69]

The Convention specifies that children are future persons in the making who are not to be seen as the property of the family or the parents, thereby emphasising inalienable rights of children unattached to family identity. Its articles also acknowledge the vulnerability of children, and the extant routine attitude of discounting or neglecting children's interests. Of the core international human rights treaties that incorporate interpretive bodies to monitor implementation, the Children's Convention is the only one that discusses humanitarian law explicitly (Article 38). Consequently, the UNCRC is the only human rights treaty body with substantial humanitarian law jurisprudence. The UNCRC has unique institutional potential to interpret humanitarian law – perhaps greater than that of the Human Rights Committee (HRC), whose constitutive treaty, the International Covenant on Civil and Political Rights does not refer explicitly to humanitarian law.[70]

Scholars have considered the Convention's limitations. At the domestic level, various reservations placed on it by the states have affected the way it can be implemented. For instance, Fortin opines that the articles demonstrate a strange mixture of idealism and practical realism;[71] while Article 12 takes a philosophical approach to ensuring respect for the child's view and the capacity for autonomy, Article 28 – concerning education – includes practical goals such as the 'reduction of drop out rates'.[72]

Feminist critics further argue that while the notion of choice is enshrined in the Convention, the only recognised inhibition to choice is the age and concomitant maturity of the child: no mention is made regarding power.[73] Secondly, the Convention is unclear as it contains

---

[69] Convention on the Rights of the Child. Available at www.ohchr.org/Documents/ ProfessionalInterest/crc.pdf.

[70] David Weissbrodt, Joseph C. Hansen and Nathaniel H. Nesbitt, 'The Role of the Committee on the Rights of the Child in Interpreting and Developing International Humanitarian Law', *Harvard Human Rights Journal* 24(1) (2011), 115–53.

[71] Fortin's argument here is primarily drawing on the UK government's position (The Children Act 1989 – it does not apply to Scotland and Northern Ireland). Fortin, *Children's Rights and the Developing Law*, 37

[72] Article 28(1)(e); also see Fortin, *Children's Rights and the Developing Law*, 37–8 for detailed analysis.

[73] Frances Olsen, 'Children's Rights: Some Feminist Approaches to the United Nations Convention on the Rights of the Child', in Philip Alston, Stephen Parker

conflicting and inconsistent rights. For example, the right of access to care conflicts with children's right to autonomy; the right to formal equality conflicts with the right to substantive equality; the right to security conflicts with the right to freedom of action; and children's rights generally conflict with the rights of others, especially mothers.[74] Finally, feminist critical legal approaches have raised the notion of false universalism and abstraction. Olsen observes:

White people think of themselves as white and without a race, just as men (and often women) consider gender to be an issue for women. The claim of unsituatatedness is made by and on behalf of those with power. To the extent the Convention deals with children as unspecified, unsituated people, it tends in fact to deal with white, male, and relatively privileged children.[75]

By reading the UNCRC together with other international instruments,[76] international law can provide for children's protection during conflicts. The gamut of these international conventions constitutes the basis for promoting and protecting children's rights, especially in situations of armed conflict. Just to give one example of how the UNCRC relates to another UN Convention, it is useful to turn to the 1951 Refugee Convention. Goodwin-Gill argues that neither the UNCRC nor the Refugee Convention provides any adequate basis for promoting durable solutions for children who are refugees.[77] While Article 22 of the UNCRC endorses the entitlement of refugee children to 'appropriate protection and humanitarian assistance', the Refugee Convention

and John Seymour (eds.), *Children, Rights and the Law* (Oxford: Oxford University Press, 1992, reprinted 1995), 192–220, 195.
[74] Ibid. [75] Ibid.
[76] These include the International Covenant on Civil and Political Rights (ICCPR) adoption in 1966 and entry into force in 1976; the International Covenant on Economic, Social and Cultural Rights (ICESCR), adoption in 1966 and entry into force in 1976; the Convention on the Elimination of All Forms of Racial Discrimination, adoption in 1965, entry into force in 1969; the Convention on the Elimination of Discrimination against Women (CEDAW), adoption in 1979, entry into force in 1981; the Convention against Torture and Other Cruel, Inhuman or Degrading Treatment or Punishment (CAT), adoption in 1984, entry into force in 1987; the Convention Relating to the Status of Refugees, adoption in 1951, entry into force in 1954; and the Convention on the Rights of Persons with Disabilities, adoption in 2006, entry into force in 2008.
[77] Guy S. Goodwin-Gill, 'Protecting the Human Rights of Refugee Children: Some Legal and Institutional Possibilities', in Jaap Doek, Hans van Loon and Paul Vlaardingerbroek (eds.), *Children on the Move: How to Implement their Right to Family Life* (The Hague: Martinus Nijhoff Publishers, 1996), 97–111.

merely 'recommends' that national governments ensure family unity and protection and provide for access to primary education. For refugees, durable solutions mean voluntary repatriation, local reintegration or third country settlement. In addition, for refugee children durable solutions mean not future, but immediate responses to contribute to the full development of the child.[78] As argued in Chapter 8, the role of the United Nations High Commissioner for Refugees (UNHCR) is critical in carrying out the provisions of the UNCRC as they relate to the Refugee Convention. Through the collaborative efforts of the ICRC, UNHCR and UNICEF, a clear pattern of international policy and practice with respect to the care of unaccompanied children in situations of armed conflict is emerging. For unaccompanied refugee children the most important activities that should be undertaken based on Article 22 of the UNCRC, in conjunction with Article 9 and 10 are: (1) tracing family members, parents and others; and (2) reunification with the family. Both activities require commitments by state authorities to both the UNCRC and the Refugee Convention.

The following section of this chapter describes children's protection under International Humanitarian Law (IHL), and international law's prohibition of children's involvement in forced labour and armed conflict. The section analyses the key international legal instruments and discusses relevant provisions protecting children in situations of armed conflict.

International law and the protection of children in armed conflict

'To kill the big rats, you have to kill the little rats.'[79]

Due to customs, norms and practices across various cultures, children who do not take part in armed conflict are usually spared from physical violence. There is evidence that in ancient India, customary practices existed that respected the principle that children should be shielded from war. Mahabharata states: '[y]ou should kill neither the aged nor the young nor yet the women'.[80] Islamic Jurists reached a

---

[78] Ibid., 98.   [79] Radio Mille Collines, Rwanda, 1994.
[80] Cited in Jenny Kuper, *International law Concerning Child Civilians in Armed Conflict* (Oxford: Clarendon Press, 1997), 75.

consensus that those 'who did not take part in fighting, such as women, children, monks ... were excluded from molestation'.[81] In the formation of Islamic Law it is documented that the Prophet Muhammad forbade killing or molesting women, infants and minors. In earlier times children were also excused from participating in Jihad. In West Africa, fighting was subject to a code of conduct and it was forbidden to kill women, children and old people. As Kuper suggests, the rules regulating the conduct of armed conflict in West Africa can be seen as 'nothing more than the expression of the same humanitarian principles which inspired the authors of the Geneva Conventions'.[82]

In modern history, the inadequacies of legislative measures, the lack of sincere commitment of parties caught up in conflicts, and a failure to form a strong and unified regulatory regime capable of dealing with children's rights in armed conflicts are some of the major difficulties in protecting children. Simply sparing children in the context of armed conflict clearly falls far short of providing for their wellbeing and development. During wars, children are in greater need of support and protection than in peacetime. Under IHL – a body of treaty law that regulates the conduct of hostilities[83] and the protection of victims during armed conflict[84] – specific measures can be taken to protect child civilians, and these are applicable to both international and non-international armed conflict. However, the deficiencies of international

---

[81] Ibid.   [82] Ibid.

[83] An armed hostility is broader than the customary definitions of armed conflicts and/or war. It includes any hostile act or attempted hostile act, if the severity rises to the level of an 'armed attack' or if it is intended to contribute to such acts. It is also relevant to note that the ICRC proposes the following definitions, which reflect strong prevailing legal opinion: '1. International armed conflicts exist whenever there is resort to armed force between two or more States. 2. Non-international armed conflicts are protracted armed confrontations occurring between governmental armed forces and the forces of one or more armed groups, or between such groups arising in the territory of a State (party to the Geneva Conventions). The armed confrontation must reach a minimum level of intensity and the parties involved in the conflict must show a minimum level of organisation.' ICRC Opinion Paper, 2008. Available at www.icrc.org/eng/assets/files/other/opinion-paper-armed-conflict.pdf.

[84] Françoise J. Hampson, 'Legal Protection Afforded to Children under International Humanitarian Law', Report for the Study on the Impact of Armed Conflict on Children, (May 1996). Available at www.essex.ac.uk/armedcon/story_id/000578.html.

law in this area are compounded by the problem that under the laws of war, the definition of a 'child' has yet to be clarified.[85]

The most significant IHL treaties are the Geneva Conventions drafted after World War II and the two Additional Protocols adopted in 1977. In the international context, prior to 1949 there was no specific mention of the vulnerability of children in conflict. The experiences of World War II demonstrated the inadequacies of existing laws to protect children in conflict zones. A major impediment with most of the Convention provisions was the lack of a legal definition before 1949 of children as persons under eighteen years of age. This was only accepted with the adoption of the UNCRC in 1989.

Child civilians

Since the 2003 invasion, various reports have noted that 39 per cent of those killed in Iraq by air raids were children. Forty-two per cent of fatalities caused by US, Iraqi and insurgent mortar shells were children. The statistics according to each belligerent nation are as follows. Iraq Body Count recorded that of the 45,779 violent deaths of civilians occurring between 2003 and 2011 for which it was able to obtain age-disaggregated data, 3,911 – 8.54 per cent – were children under the age of eighteen. Of the civilian victims killed by the coalition forces for whom age data was available, 1,201 – 29 per cent – were children.[86] Casualties from failed cluster sub-munitions rose between 1991 and 2007 from 5,500 to 80,000, 45.7 per cent between the age of fifteen and twenty-nine years of age, and 23.9 per cent were children under the age of fourteen. Both UNICEF and the United Nations Development Program (UNDP) believe these figures are underestimated.[87] There are also other sources of long-term and inter-generational harm to children caused by armed conflicts. For example, the destruction of military and industrial infrastructure in Iraq has released hazardous substances into the environment that cause deleterious health problems. News reports from Fallujah noted an unprecedented number of birth defects,

[85] See Chapter 1 of this book for the debates on the definition of who constitutes a child.
[86] Available at www.iraqbodycount.org/analysis/numbers/2011/.
[87] 'Iraqi Children: Deprived Rights, Stolen Future', Report published by the Center for Research on Globalisation (13 March 2013).

miscarriages and cancer in children. According to medical experts in Iraq, these have increased rapidly since 2005.

As noted earlier, while the majority of children affected by armed conflict are child civilians caught up in theatres of war, a disproportionate percentage of the international community's attention focuses on child soldiers. Even during the drafting of the UNCRC, stakeholders' considerations centred on the protection of child soldiers, most of whom are male. While the UNCRC Optional Protocols offer safeguards, legal theorists believe that the 'blinkered vision of the drafters of the Convention may have contributed to the weakening of standards in respect of child civilians'.[88]

Prior to the adoption of the UNCRC, IHL considered various legislative and innovative measures to protect child civilians. Children who do not take part in an international armed conflict are protected by the 1949 Geneva Convention IV – which exclusively provides protection for civilians during armed conflict – and the Additional Protocols I and II (API and APII). The Geneva Convention IV only provides limited protection for children. Still, it is applicable to all armed conflict because, not only are 194 states party to the 1949 Geneva Conventions, but these conventions are now largely considered to be customary international law. Articles 27 to 34 of the Geneva Convention IV and Article 75 of the API specify fundamental guarantees provided by the treaties, such as the right to life, and the proscription of coercion and torture. The API also provides rules for conducting hostilities, including a code requiring that civilians and combatants be distinguished, and prohibiting attacks against civilians (Article 48 and 51). Article 3 – common to the Geneva Conventions – and Article 4 and 13 of the APII further govern children's protection during regional and domestic armed conflicts. On the other hand, UNICEF and the ICRC have expanded the existing geographical concept of hospital zones to create a category of peace zones – or peace bridges – based upon the presence of children rather than on the demarcation of specific topographical boundaries. This strategy is intended to promote the idea of children as requiring protection by all parties regardless of existing safety and conflict zones; the adaptation of the concept of a safety zone to be applied not to a specific location

[88] Geraldine van Bueren, *The International Law on the Rights of the Child* (The Hague: Martinus Nijhoff Publishers, 1998), 341.

but to a specific group is an innovative way of applying international law[89] and is explored further in Chapter 9.

Recent international measures also include a combination of normative and innovative advocacy. The anti-landmine and cluster munitions and disability campaigns provide examples of this combined approach. As seen in Iraq, Sri Lanka, Cambodia and Burma, land mines and cluster munitions have had a huge impact on children, not only during, but also after armed conflict. Children are vulnerable to injury and death due to anti-personnel land mines. The International Campaign to Ban Landmines was involved in various innovative advocacy strategies at international, regional and national levels and succeeded in establishing a formal Mine Ban Treaty, the Convention on the Prohibition of the Use, Stockpiling, Production and Transfer of Anti-Personnel Mines and on their Destruction, which entered into force on 1 March 2009.[90] It specifies provisions for assistance in mine clearance, mine awareness and victim support.[91] The Anti-Personnel Mine Ban Convention (APMBC)[92] and the Convention on Cluster Munitions (CCM)[93] have also served as an important point of reference for subsequent negotiations on weapons.

Many children exposed to violence suffer physical deformities, diseases and trauma. They also experience serious post-traumatic stress: the everyday suffering of psychological disabilities, including

---

[89] Ibid.

[90] It was the result of the 'Ottawa Process', a freestanding process of treaty negotiation outside a United Nations-facilitated forum with the aim of outlawing anti-personnel mines. The process was launched in Ottawa by the Minister of Foreign Affairs of Canada in October 1996.

[91] International Bureau for Children's Rights, *Children and Armed Conflict*, (Montreal: Quebec, 2010).

[92] Anti-Personnel Landmines Convention. Available at www.unog.ch/80256E E600585943/%28httpPages%29/CA826818C8330D2BC1257180004B1B2E? OpenDocument. In particular, many of the provisions included in the Convention on Cluster Munitions, adopted in Dublin on 30 May 2008 and entered into force on 1 August 2010, are drawn from, or inspired by, those set out in the Anti-Personnel Mine Ban Convention.

[93] This Convention completely bans cluster munitions, their use, development, production, stockpiling and transfer; states must destroy their stockpiles within eight years; and clear remnants of cluster munitions within ten years of the treaty entering into force; the Convention also obliges states to provide comprehensive and age appropriate assistance to victims, including medical support, rehabilitation and psychological care, as well as providing for their social and economic inclusion. See Articles 1, 3(2), 4(1) and 5, Convention on Cluster Munitions.

memories of terror and behavioural problems. Article 2 of the UNCRC prohibits any discrimination on the ground of disability, and Article 23 recognises that children with mental and physical disabilities have a right to live with dignity and be involved in decisions relating to their care; it promotes self-reliance and children's active participation in the community. It further stipulates a child's right of access to comprehensive healthcare. The provisions set out in the UNCRC and complemented by the APMBC, the CCM, and the Convention on the Rights of Persons with Disabilities (CRPD) guarantees the rights of children, women and men whose lives irrevocably change through the use of weapons of modern warfare. The vast majority of states party to the CRPD are also signatories to the APMBC, including nineteen states that are responsible for significant numbers of land mine survivors.[94] Funding resources provided by the European Union (EU) allowed South Sudan, which is not yet a party to the CRPD, to include disability issues in its National Mine Action Strategy. The mine action funding leveraged the collection of disability data in various provinces of South Sudan that would be used in drafting its National Disability Strategy. The Ministry of Gender, Child and Social Welfare and the Ministry on Disability Issues are coordinating these efforts.

Children as combatants

The first international legal framework that introduced the question of child soldiers[95] was constituted by the loosely worded provisions of the API and APII.[96]

API, Article 77 stipulates:

2. The Parties to the conflict shall take all feasible measures in order that children who have not attained the age of fifteen years do not take a direct part in hostilities and, in particular, they shall refrain from recruiting them into their armed forces. In recruiting among those persons who have attained the age of fifteen years but who have not attained the age of eighteen years, the Parties to the conflict shall endeavour to give priority to those who are oldest.

[94] 'The Anti-Personnel Mine Ban Convention and The Convention on the Rights of Persons with Disabilities: A Common Agenda'. Available at http://reliefweb.int/report/world/anti-personnel-mine-ban-convention-and-convention-rights-persons-disabilities-common.

[95] For details on the child soldiers, see Chapter 5 in this book.

[96] Timothy Webster, 'Babes with Arms: International Law and Child Soldiers', *The George Washington International Law Review* 39(2) (2007), 227–54.

3. If, in exceptional cases, despite the provisions of paragraph 2, children who have not attained the age of fifteen years take a direct part in hostilities and fall into the power of an adverse Party, they shall continue to benefit from the special protection accorded by this Article, whether or not they are prisoners of war.

4. If arrested, detained or interned for reasons related to the armed conflict, children shall be held in quarters separate from the quarters of adults, except where families are accommodated as family units as provided in Article 75, paragraph 5.

5. The death penalty for an offence related to the armed conflict shall not be executed on persons who had not attained the age of eighteen years at the time the offence was committed.[97]

APII, Article 4(3) further stipulates:

Children shall be provided with the care and aid they require, and in particular:

(a) they shall receive an education, including religious and moral education, in keeping with the wishes of their parents, or in the absence of parents, of those responsible for their care;

(b) all appropriate steps shall be taken to facilitate the reunion of families temporarily separated;

(c) children who have not attained the age of fifteen years shall neither be recruited in the armed forces or groups nor allowed to take part in hostilities;

(d) the special protection provided by this Article to children who have not attained the age of fifteen years shall remain applicable to them if they take a direct part in hostilities despite the provisions of subparagraph (c) and are captured;

(e) measures shall be taken, if necessary, and whenever possible with the consent of their parents or persons who by law or custom are primarily responsible for their care, to remove children temporarily from the area in which hostilities are taking place to a safer area within the country and ensure that they are accompanied by persons responsible for their safety and well-being.[98]

---

[97] See www.icrc.org/ihl.nsf/WebART/470-750099?OpenDocument. Also note, Article 78 covers the evacuation of the children. Details available at www.icrc.org/ihl.nsf/WebART/470-750100?OpenDocument.

[98] Additional Protocol to the Geneva Conventions of 12 August 1949, relating to the Protection of Victims of Non-International Armed Conflicts (Protocol II), 8 June 1977. Available at www.icrc.org/ihl/WebART/470-750099.

While APII, Article 4(3) is more forceful than API, Article 77(2), the scope of the application of APII, Article 4(3) is much more restrictive. Together these provisions clearly indicate that children should not be recruited by warring factions: when detained they should be treated fairly and their protection must be ensured by all parties. Emphasis is on the duty to protect and assist children. It is also clear that the Geneva Conventions make distinctions between child civilians and child combatants. In non-international armed conflicts, ensuring this protection becomes particularly challenging. In addition to these provisions, as discussed below, the UNCRC and the ILO Convention No. 182 could also be applied to children's participation as combatants. However, in the context of international armed conflicts, children's protection when they are prisoners of war remains uncertain. Françoise Hampson argues that:

the silence of both provisions with regard to children between the ages of fifteen and eighteen years presumably means that they are to be treated in the same way as other fighters, unless they continue to benefit from the general protection afforded to children, being under eighteen years of age. Whilst Geneva Convention III on the treatment of Prisoners of War (PoW) contains a few references to women PoWs, no mention at all is made of child PoWs. This is not surprising when it is recalled that the issue of child soldiers was not addressed until the conclusion of the Protocols to the Geneva Conventions in 1977.[99]

Article 38 of the UNCRC deals specifically with armed conflict situations. It is significant because it brings together IHL and international human rights law. It states:

1. States Parties undertake to respect and to ensure respect for rules of international humanitarian law applicable to them in armed conflicts which are relevant to the child.
2. States Parties shall take all feasible measures to ensure that persons who have not attained the age of fifteen years do not take a direct part in hostilities.
3. States Parties shall refrain from recruiting any person who has not attained the age of fifteen years into their armed forces. In recruiting among those persons who have attained the age of fifteen years but who have not attained the age of eighteen years, States Parties shall endeavour to give priority to those who are oldest.

---

[99] Hampson, 'Legal Protection Afforded to Children under International Humanitarian Law', section 4.5.2.

4. In accordance with their obligations under international humanitarian law to protect the civilian population in armed conflicts, States Parties shall take all feasible measures to ensure protection and care of children who are affected by an armed conflict.

While it does confirm the prohibition of recruitment of children under the age of fifteen,[100] dissatisfaction with Article 38[101] was demonstrated in the Committee of the Rights of the Child second session in 1992 when a proposal was made for an Optional Protocol.[102] However, it was not until ten years after the UNCRC entered into force that UNGA adopted the Optional Protocol to the Convention on the Involvement of Children in Armed Conflict (OPAC), which entered into force on 12 February 2002.[103]

The OPAC raised the minimum age from fifteen years to eighteen years for both voluntary and compulsory recruitment and deployment. In the context of state objections, in particular from the United States, eighteen years has not universally been agreed as a minimum threshold; states are allowed to recruit under-eighteens provided that they volunteer to join the national army.[104] The OPAC consists of thirteen articles and includes provisions such as direct participation in hostilities (Article 1); military recruitment by the state (Articles 2 and 3) and by non-state armed forces (Article 4). Happold observes that the definition of armed forces does not appear to be limited to insurgent armed groups in conflict with the governments of states parties, but rather is wide enough to encompass armed groups allied with a state party's governments, but

---

[100] Convention on the Rights of the Child. Available at www.ohchr.org/Documents/ ProfessionalInterest/crc.pdf. Please note that Article 38(2) is not in line with the Article 3(1) principle of children's best interests.

[101] Concerns were raised that the UNCRC Article 38(2) refers to only 'all feasible measures' and the language was not strong enough to ensure that children would not be recruited. Debates before drafting considered that children's participation could be extracted in times of conflict. At the end, a compromise was reached that states should not recruit anyone under fifteen years of age into armed forces.

[102] Matthew Happold, *Child Soldiers in International Law* (Manchester: Manchester University Press, 2005), 74–80.

[103] Also, the Optional Protocol on the Sale of Children, Child Prostitution and Child Pornography (OPSC) was adopted in 2000 and entered into force on 18 January 2002. See http://childrenandarmedconflict.un.org/keydocuments/ english/UNCRCoptionalproto19.html.

[104] Chaditsa Poulatova, *Children and Armed Conflict* (Newcastle upon Tyne: Cambridge Scholars Publishing, 2013), 73.

which are not part of or under the control of its armed forces.[105] Article 4 is significant since it highlights the responsibilities of the armed groups that recruit child soldiers, in contrast with the UNCRC, which applies only to the state parties.[106]

In an alternative inventive measure, some of the impasses in the Optional Protocol Working Groups have been resolved in the context of the ILO Convention No. 182, which defines child soldiering as one of the worst forms of child labour. The ILO had further success in drafting regulations that deal with the minimum age of employment, working hours and conditions for children, and protection of children from dangerous work and hazardous substances. However, the United States – and a large number of other states that were not identified publicly – negotiated so that the ILO Convention No. 182 was restricted to covering compulsory and forced conscription and had no implications for other forms of military service.[107] Also, the ILO established conventions requiring member states to suppress or abolish child labour in both the state and the private sectors.[108] Happold also notes that, with the exception of the African Charter on the Rights and Welfare of the Child – which outlaws child soldiering and which is a regional rather than a global treaty – all the other conventions governing the recruitment of children use the 'lowest common denominator' provisions.[109]

'An era of application' and the UN resolutions

International human rights law governs the way states treat children, women and men – both citizens and non-citizens – who are in their jurisdiction. However, some human rights treaties can be suspended or restricted in national emergencies, as declared by the governing regimes in states parties. In reality, this possibility creates further vulnerability and allows political violence against the population. Most human rights treaties, including the UNCRC, do not allow the derogation of

---

[105] Matthew Happold, 'The Optional Protocol to the Convention on the Rights of the Child on the Involvement of Children in Armed Conflict', *Yearbook of International Humanitarian Law*, 3 (2000), 226–44, 239.
[106] Poulatova, *Children and Armed Conflict*, 76.
[107] Happold, *Child Soldiers in International Law*, 171–2.
[108] Achilihu, *Do African Children Have Rights?*, 21.
[109] Happold, *Child Soldiers in International Law*, 172.

rights, regardless of the situation of a state.[110] An important indication of rising international awareness of the pervasive nature of violence against children and the urgent need to address this is reflected in ongoing UN Security Council debates and a number of resolutions on children and armed conflict such as those listed in the Appendix.

Some international advocacy documents have significantly contributed to children's rights under IHL. For instance, the 1996 Machel Report enabled the possibility of incorporating children's concerns into the mainstream UN agenda, and highlighted a link between the proliferation of small arms and child soldiers.[111] Small arms proliferation increases the possibility of children's displacement and the rupture of traditional family life.[112] Small arms, such as handguns, light machine guns, revolvers and rifles increase the risk of children engaging in violence, as these are easily operable by a child. After conflict, small arms also become instruments of other forms of crime, and surplus weapons can contribute to a culture of violence that generates endless cycles of war.[113] The Machel Report used the UNCRC and the Optional Protocols to argue that children need to be protected during and after armed conflict.

The Office of the Special Representative has also been very active in conducting research, producing reports and initiating negotiations to halt the recruitment of child soldiers. For example, Olara Otunnu, the former UN Under-Secretary-General and the Special Representative for Children and Armed Conflict has stated: 'the Special Representative strongly believes that the international community must now redirect its energies from juridical tasks of developing standards to the political project of ensuring their application and respect on the ground. We must launch "an era of application" – the application of international and local norms for the protection of children in times of armed conflict.'[114] The agenda-setting work by the Special Representative

---

[110] International Bureau for Children's Rights, *Children and Armed Conflict*, 95.
[111] 'Children and Armed Conflict: Strategic Framework 2011–2013'. Available at https://childrenandarmedconflict.un.org/publications/StrategicFramework2011-2013.pdf.
[112] Rachel Stohl, 'Targeting Children: Small Arms and Children in Conflict', *The Brown Journal of World Affairs* 4(1) (2002), 281–92, 283.
[113] Ibid., 286.
[114] Olara Otunnu, 'Protection of Children Affected by Armed Conflict', Report of the Special Representative of the Secretary–General for Children and Armed Conflict, UNGA, Fifty-fifth session, agenda item 110 (3 October 2000), 3.

succeeded in the context of UN Security Council Resolutions 1261 (1999) and 1314 (2000), both of which recognise the consequences of conflict to children. Resolution 1314 advocates the demobilisation and reintegration of child solders, and the establishment of special child protection units.

Conclusion

Legal and normative frameworks provide the basis for protection of children during and after armed conflict. Specific frameworks such as the UNCRC constitute the primary mechanism for the protection of children, complemented by generally applicable international humanitarian and human rights instruments. This mechanism requires that children be provided with support and partnership from those protecting them. However, as discussed earlier in the chapter, anthropological and sociological scholarship on children in conflict zones provides the critical insight that children are capable of constructing and educating adults about their rights – an insight that is yet to be harnessed in constructing responsive, effective means of ensuring the rights of children in conflict.

The discourse of armed conflict and children's rights under international law mainly focuses on child soldiers. However, the principal victims of armed conflict are child civilians. At the international level, a combination of normative measures and innovative legal advocacy has increasingly become a strategic way of responding to the rights of the child. This combination of developing legal frameworks and a local regulatory mechanism has the benefit of ensuring that new norms are generally not breached. Significant energy has been directed towards drafting legislation and declarations that help to ensure children receive protection during international and domestic armed conflicts. Without restructuring of the monitoring, reporting and compliance regime for child protection it is impossible to ensure a sufficient level of protection for children.

While it is beyond the scope of this chapter to examine the monitoring and evaluation mechanisms of the UN, it is clear that without practical commitment from all parties involved in an armed conflict, the rights of the child cannot be guaranteed. Global inequality and the north–south divide means that significant challenges remain in including children in development policies and ensuring children's access to education, health and basic rights. Children's participation, access and agency in peace and development efforts are necessary to shape any comprehensive understanding of rights. While Chapter 7 looks at children and peace building the next chapter turns to the problem of child soldiers.

5 | Child soldiers: causes, solutions and cultures

KIM HUYNH

Introduction

We will fight until the last drop of blood![1]

This is what my father and uncle wrote on the wall of the family ancestral shrine, using blood that trickled from their freshly cut fingertips. Shortly afterwards, they left their village to become Viet Minh revolutionaries. At the age of twelve, my father was convinced that this was the best way for him to break free of poverty and attain an education. At the same time, he was eager to rescue his country from colonial oppression and was willing to sacrifice his life if need be.

This chapter examines some of the international, national, local and personal factors that motivate children to engage in war. Caretaker (or liberal humanitarian) and free-ranger (or critical childhood studies) perspectives are adopted to analyse the child soldier problem. From a caretaker position, no one is more vulnerable than a child and nothing is more senseless and destructive than war; therefore, the coalescence of the two in the form of a child soldier represents an injustice of the highest order. This perspective, which is prominent in international legal and advocacy circles, promotes a broad definition of child soldiers in terms of both age and activity and seeks to protect these victims of circumstance regardless of what they have done. When it comes to providing that protection, caretakers also take a global view in that 'everyone shares responsibility and a degree of blame'.[2] The free-ranger position, on the other hand, asserts that the caretaker understanding of the child soldier problem does not so much reflect the lawlessness and insecurities of the global south, but rather a deep-set anxiety and desire for control in the global north. While the differences between these two

---

[1] Kim Huynh, *Where the Sea Takes Us: A Vietnamese-Australian Story* (Sydney: Harper Perennial, 2008), 84.
[2] Machel, 'Impact of Armed Conflict on Children', UNICEF (1996).

camps are considerable, there is room for agreement in terms of how to address the child soldier problem. Specifically, indirect efforts that focus on socio-economic development, peace making and peace building can result in children and adults having less incentive to fight and can be more effective than direct efforts to save child soldiers which carry a high risk of cultural imperialism.

Being wary of cultural imperialism, however, does not necessitate cultural disengagement. On the contrary, the second part of the chapter proposes that cultural factors should be considered when assessing the causes of child soldiers and how best to address them, even and especially if the recognition of these factors refute the dominant image of children as vulnerable and of war as senseless and destructive. Such considerations should be made without rigid preconceptions of child soldier societies as irredeemably barbarous or, in contrast, heroic and spirited. One way to engage with child soldier cultures is by reading and listening to stories, including myths, folktales, biographies and propaganda. This chapter presents a case study of Vietnamese stories about child heroes and how they have animated generations of children to fight since the mythical time of Saint Giong – who grew from a toddler to a giant in order to drive away Chinese invaders – to the First Indochina War, when young Vietnamese, including my father, took up arms in the pursuit of national independence.

The problem of child soldiers: the caretaker position

> I know everything one can know about the wasting of youth, about the ways boys can be used. Of those boys with whom I walked, about half become soldiers eventually. And were they all willing? Only a few. They were twelve, thirteen years old, little more, when they were conscripted. We were all used.[3] (Valentino Achak Deng)

Child soldiers are commonly seen as an urgent and escalating problem in global affairs.[4] This is despite the fact that there are now, by best estimates, fewer child soldiers than there were in 1996 when Graça

---

[3] David Eggers, *What is the What: The Autobiography of Valentine Achak Deng* (a novel) (New York, NY: Penguin, 2007), 50.

[4] See, for instance, Donna Sharkey, 'Picture the Child Soldier', *Peace Review* 24 (2012), 263–4.

Machel released her ground-breaking report on the 'Impact of Armed Conflict on Children'.[5] At the turn of the century there were an estimated 300,000 child soldiers worldwide, a figure that has often been cited in NGO and scholarly work, in large part due to the absence of more reliable and up-to-date information.[6] There will always be a considerable margin for error in determining child soldier numbers due to the dangers of collecting data in conflict zones and the fact that recruiting forces are unlikely to be forthcoming with information. For this reason the peak NGO body in this field, Child Soldiers International, asserts that there are 'no exact figures' and that 'the numbers continually change'.[7] Nonetheless, taking into account the diminution of hostilities and demobilisation of child soldiers in Liberia, Sierra Leone and Angola, and the fact that there have not been substantial increases elsewhere, Gates has estimated that there were between 200,000 and 250,000 child soldiers around the world in 2010 and that this figure was unlikely to rise in the near future.[8]

How then are we to understand and assess the issue of child soldiers? What are the primary causes and what – if anything – should be done

[5] UNICEF, *Machel Study 10-Year Strategic Review* (2009).

[6] One of the earliest references to this estimate can be found in Rachel Brett, 'Child Soldiering: Questions and Challenges for Health Professionals', WHO Global Report on Violence, 1. Cited in Graça Machel, 'The Impact of Armed Conflict on Children: A Critical Review of Progress Made and Obstacles Encountered in Increasing Protection for War-Affected Children', presented at The International Conference on War-affected Children, Winnipeg, Canada (September 2000). Available at http://rsx23.justhost.com/~victimas/recursos_user/documentos/kb5736.pdf.

[7] Child Soldiers International, 'Who Are Child Soldiers?'. Available at www.child-soldiers.org/about_the_issues.php.

[8] Scott Gates and Simon Reich, 'Conclusion', in Scott Gates and Simon Reich (eds.), *Child Soldiers in the Age of Fractured States* (Pittsburgh, PA: University of Pittsburgh Press, 2010), 251. Poretti and Vautravers cite similar figures. Michele Poretti, 'Preventing Children from Joining Armed Groups', *Refugee Survey Quarterly* 27(4) (2009), 123; Alexandre J. Vautravers, 'Why Child Soldiers are Such a Complex Issue', *Refugee Survey Quarterly* 27(4) (2009), 96. Some of the changes in conflict that should be taken into account since those articles were published include the official cessation of hostilities in Sri Lanka, which has led to a reduction in child soldiers. There are reports, however, that children are increasingly being used in the Syrian civil war with a UN Panel estimating that by mid-2013 eighty-six child combatants had been killed, half of them in 2013. Nick Cumming-Bruce, 'U.N. Panel Reports Increasing Brutality by Both Sides in Syria', *The New York Times*, 4 June 2013. Available at www.nytimes.com/2013/06/05/world/middleeast/un-panel-reports-increasing-brutality-by-both-sides-in-syria.html?pagewanted=all&_r=0.

about the problem? It is useful to address these questions from caretaker – or liberal humanitarian – and free-ranger – or critical childhood studies – perspectives, noting that they represent ideal types on the edges of an ideological and epistemological spectrum. As outlined in Chapter 2, caretakers regard children as vulnerable, innocent, dependent and irrational. This position is prominent in UN bodies such as UNICEF, and NGOs such as Child Soldiers International and the Child Rights International Network (CRIN).[9] For them, children's involvement in conflict is fundamentally immoral and worthy of public outcry regardless of the numbers involved, the cultural context or individual choice. According to the child protection adviser for the ICRC, Kirstin Barstad, 'even so-called "voluntary" enlistment tends to be conditioned by factors beyond the child's control'.[10] A Save the Children field guide questions whether children can ever 'truly voluntarily' join armed groups given that the 'do not yet have the cognitive developmental skills to fully assess risks and choices' in a conflict-ridden milieu.[11] The UN High Commissioner for Human Rights urged all states and armed groups to stop recruiting children and to release those already in service: '[t]here can be no excuse for arming children to fight adult wars'.[12] The notion that children have no place in conflict is enshrined in the preamble to the UNCRC, which proclaims that children 'should grow up in a family environment, in an atmosphere of happiness, love and understanding' as ensured by adults.

Caretakers stress five points when it comes to defining and understanding the child soldier problem. For them, there is a crisis of child soldiers not only in moral terms but also because of persistent causal factors that mean the global situation has little chance of getting

---

[9] Kristen E. Cheney, '"Our Children Have Only Known War": Children's Experiences and the Uses of Childhood in Northern Uganda', *Children's Geographies* 3(1) (April 2005), 37.

[10] Barstad, 'Preventing the Recruitment of Child Soldiers: The IRCR Approach', 144.

[11] Save the Children, 'Child Soldiers: Care and Protection of Children in Emergencies: A field guide' (2001). Available at http://resourcecentre.savethe children.se/library/child-soldiers-care-protection-children-emergencies-field-guide.

[12] Cited in Yvonne Keairns, 'The Voices of Girl Child Soldiers: Summary', Quaker United Nations Office and Coalition to Stop the Use of Child Soldiers (2002). Available at www.quno.org/sites/default/files/resources/The%20voices%20of %20girl%20child%20soldiers_PHILIPPINES.pdf.

better and may well get worse. More specifically, there are socio-economic factors that have contributed to the proliferation of child soldiers since the end of the Cold War, and which could easily contribute to future increases notwithstanding the current downward trend. Underdevelopment is one of the most consistently cited causal factors, such that child soldiers are more likely to be found in societies where children are compelled by poverty to engage in gruelling and dangerous forms of labour.[13] In large part this explains why there are around 100,000 child soldiers in sub-Saharan Africa, where 48.5 per cent of the population subsists on US$ 1.24 per day or less and over 40 per cent of the population is below the age of fifteen.[14] In a telling survey of 300 demobilised child soldiers in the DRC, 61 per cent came from families with no income and more than half had at least six siblings.[15] Similarly, Podder's interviews with 101 Liberian ex-child soldiers found that only six had any form of employment before the war and eighty came from single income households with five to eight dependents.[16] And so, for caretakers whenever there is acute poverty and inequality, there is also the risk of children going to war in great numbers.

Secondly, caretakers point out that poverty and inequality interweave with other socio-economic factors, such as social exclusion, persecution, abuse and humiliation, to push children into joining militias and violent gangs.[17] Moreover, there are a range of concomitant pull factors that include the desire for social status, guns, consumer goods, friendship, surrogate families, partners, identity, revenge and the basic yearning for

---

[13] Scott Gates and Simon Reich, 'Introduction', in Scott Gates and Simon Reich (eds.), *Child Soldiers in the Age of Fractured States* (Pittsburgh, PA: University of Pittsburgh Press, 2010), 7; Jens Christopher Andvig and Scott Gates, 'Recruiting Children for Armed Conflict', in Scott Gates and Simon Reich (eds.), *Child Soldiers in the Age of Fractured States* (Pittsburgh, PA: University of Pittsburgh Press, 2010), 80.

[14] World Bank, 'Poverty'. Available at http://data.worldbank.org/topic/poverty; Vautravers, 'Why Child Soldiers are Such a Complex Issue', 103; Claude Rakisits, 'Child Soldiers in the East of the Democratic Republic of Congo', *Refugee Survey Quarterly* 27(4) (2009), 108.

[15] Cited in Brett and Specht, *Young Soldiers: Why They Choose to Fight*, 14.

[16] Krijn Peters, 'Group Cohesion and Coercive Recruitment: Young Combatants and the Revolutionary United Front of Sierra Leone', in Alpaslan Özerdem and Sukanya Podder (eds.), *Child Soldiers: From Recruitment to Reintegration* (Houndmills: Palgrave Macmillan, 2011), 56.

[17] Poretti, 'Preventing Children from Joining Armed Groups', 126.

power and protection from harm.[18] Thus, concerns that the global child soldier problem is at a crisis point are based on the unprecedented number of children who are likely to engage in armed conflict because they lack basic needs and opportunities in life.[19] However, while socio-economic factors are critical to understanding the child soldier problem, they are not the sole determinant. From a caretaker position, socio-economic factors can be viewed as the accumulation of ammunition that is set off by new wars.

Thirdly, therefore, caretakers stress that the rise of new wars makes the child soldier problem intractable and menacing. New wars are examined at length in Chapter 3 in the context of IR. They reflect a post-Cold War situation in which political and military violence has fragmented in terms of objectives, location, actors and strategies.[20] There is a high correlation between new wars and the use of child soldiers.[21] Of the thirty-one countries in which there were armed conflicts in 1998, child soldiers were used in twenty-seven. Children under the age of fifteen years were used in twenty-two of them.[22] This correlation has remained largely stable in the twenty-first century.[23] However, the number of state military forces enlisting child soldiers has dropped to ten, while the

---

[18] Ibid.

[19] Peter W. Singer, 'The Enablers of War: Causal Factors Behind the Child Soldier Phenomenon', in Scott Gates and Simon Reich (eds.), *Child Soldiers in the Age of Fractured States* (Pittsburgh, PA: University of Pittsburgh Press, 2010), 96.

[20] In this context, it is sufficient to point out that new wars can be distinguished from old wars in the following ways:

  1. In terms of timing and objective, they are commonly undeclared and driven by economic and identity-based objectives as much as political or ideological ones, and so, it is difficult to separate peace from conflict.
  2. In terms of location, they tend to be fought within states rather than among them.
  3. In terms of actors, they involve a wide array of groups beyond state-based armies including paramilitary forces, criminal syndicates, private military companies and foreign military contingents.
  4. In terms of strategies and tactics, there is a prevalence of insurgency activities (such as ambushes, assassinations, terrorism, kidnapping and blackmail) and counterinsurgency responses (such as resource depletion, torture, rendition and pacification). But in contrast to the anti-colonial conflicts of the twentieth century, new war combatants are often more concerned with terrorising and pillaging the populous than with winning hearts and minds.
  (Vautravers, 'Why Child Soldiers are Such a Complex Issue', 98.)

[21] UNICEF, *Machel Study 10-Year Strategic Review* (2009), 4.

[22] Vautravers, 'Why Child Soldiers are Such a Complex Issue', 96.   [23] Ibid.

number of non-state armed groups using child soldiers grew from twenty-three in 2002 to forty in 2006 and fifty-seven in 2007.[24]

Fourthly, the connection between new wars and child soldiers is attributable to the spread of small arms and light weapons, which include rifles, grenades, light machine guns, light mortars and land mines.[25] Small arms have proliferated since the end of the Cold War, undermining any prospect of a 'peace dividend' in the global south. Much of this is attributable to the greedy and unconscionable practices of rich countries. For instance, rather than destroying its surplus supplies, reunited Germany dumped them on the world market at US$ 60 for a machine gun and US$ 19 for a land mine.[26] Such actions resulted in a glut, so that at the turn of the century there were no less than 500 million small arms worldwide. These weapons were responsible for almost 90 per cent of wartime casualties in the decade after the end of the Cold War.[27]

As a strident opponent of the caretaker position, Rosen acknowledges the spread of small arms, but asserts there is 'virtually no hard evidence' that this has any connection with child soldiers.[28] Nonetheless, there is strong circumstantial evidence that small arms have enabled increased numbers of children to engage in direct combat. Specifically, there has been a steady shift from children acting in complementary roles – such as porters, messengers, scouts and cooks – to them becoming substitutes – indeed, sometimes favoured substitutes – for adult fighters.[29] Singer regards the proliferation of small arms as the 'key enabler' that has allowed the broadened pool of young recruits created by socio-economic factors to engage actively in war.[30] He cites technological advancements as having made portable weapons lighter, simpler, less expensive, more lethal and therefore conducive to use by children. Particularly popular is the Russian-designed Kalashnikov AK-47, which is regarded as 'the most used and available gun in the world'.[31] There were 6 million AK-47s in

---

[24] Ibid. Child Soldiers International, 'Louder than Words: An Agenda for Action to End State Use of Child Soldiers' (2012), 11. Available at www.child-soldiers.org/global_report_reader.php?id=562).
[25] Singer, 'The Enablers of War', 99.
[26] Cited in Singer, 'The Enablers of War', 101.   [27] Ibid., 100.
[28] Rosen, *Armies of the Young*, 14.
[29] Andvig and Gates, 'Recruiting Children for Armed Conflict', 79.
[30] Singer, 'The Enablers of War', 99.
[31] UNICEF, *Machel Study 10-Year Strategic Review* (2009), 9.

post-war Mozambique: one could be purchased for the price of a chicken in Uganda and Sudan, or twelve dollars in South Africa.[32] With only nine moving parts it requires thirty minutes of instruction to train a child to use it. The availability of small arms has not only militarised individual children, but also their societies, such that the Organization of African Unity's 2000 Bamako Declaration on Small Arms Proliferation states that they have entrenched a 'culture of violence' that replicates itself across generations.[33]

Finally, caretakers stress the imperviousness of new wars and particularly non-state actors to IHL in general and laws restricting the use of child soldiers in particular. They point out that in recent decades there have been extensive efforts to prohibit the use of child soldiers and to punish recruiters. There are five major legal documents and statements relating to children in combat zones (discussed in detail in Chapter 4), all of which have been widely supported by nation-states:

1. The 1997 Additional Protocols to the 1949 Geneva Convention IV, which apply IHL to civilian populations caught up in conflict.
2. The 2000 Optional Protocol to the UNCRC on the Involvement of Children in Armed Conflicts, Article 1 of which raises the minimum age for forced recruitment and direct participation in conflict from fifteen to eighteen years.
3. The 1998 Rome Statute of the International Criminal Court (ICC), which defines as a war crime enlisting children under the age of fifteen into 'national armed forces or using them to participate actively in hostilities'. Motions are afoot to raise this age limit to eighteen.
4. The ILO Convention No. 182 (1999) relates to the elimination of the worst forms of child labour and prohibits the recruitment, whether forced or voluntary, of children in armed conflict.
5. The 2007 Paris Commitments and Principles, which vow to protect children from unlawful recruitment or use by armed forces and groups and offer guidelines on the disarmament, demobilisation and reintegration of child soldiers.

Moreover, the use of child soldiers has been repeatedly condemned by the UN Security Council,[34] the UNGA, the UN Commission on Human

---

[32] Cited in Singer, 'The Enablers of War', 100–1, citing others on 101.
[33] Cited in Rosen, *Armies of the Young*, 14.
[34] UN Security Council Resolutions 1539 (2004) and 1612 (2005) call for the monitoring of children's rights and abuses against those rights in conflict zones.

Rights, the OSRSG-CaAC, UNICEF, the Organization for African Unity, the Economic Community of West African States, the Organization of American States, the Organization for Security and Cooperation in Europe, and the European Parliament, along with NGOs such as Child Soldiers International, the ICRC and Human Rights Watch.[35]

From a caretaker perspective, the problem is clearly not a result of under-regulation or insufficient effort on the part of the international humanitarian community, but rather noncompliance. The failed or failing states in which new wars are fought are largely immune to international law and are effectively no-go zones for liberal humanitarian forces. This is a consequence, caretakers argue, of the chaotic nature of new wars and the callousness of those who fight them.[36] The lethal mix of intense material need and encrusted ethnic hatred that fuels these conflicts results in a 'breakdown of the warrior's honor' and an eagerness to transgress the 'greatest taboo' of war; that is, allowing children to become involved.[37]

The problem of child soldiers: the free-ranger position

> You know, I come from a warrior's family; as far as I remember, my father has always been in the rebellion . . . I always wanted to be with my father, to listen to the stories, the plans; and then my brothers . . . When you are little, you want to do as if you were tall . . .[38] (Catherine, DRC)

According to free-rangers, childhood is a social construct that varies across time and place – as opposed to a fixed biological or psychological stage of development – and children are agents in their own right who have their own identity and values. Free-rangers are sceptical of caretakers who set out on missions to rescue children, considering them to be driven more by a desire to control and contain than to empower and emancipate. Free-rangers do not deny that there is a child soldier problem or that it has underlying socio-economic and

---

This is facilitated by the Security Council Working Group on Children and Armed Conflict.

[35] Singer, 'The Enablers of War', 95.

[36] Peter W. Singer, *Children at War* (Berkeley, CA: University of California Press, 2006), 4.

[37] Cited in Singer, 'The Enablers of War', 102–3.

[38] Brett and Specht, *Young Soldiers: Why They Choose to Fight*, 91.

military causes. However, they challenge the caretaker insistence that
children's participation in armed conflict is intrinsically wrong. More
precisely, they refute the claim that a child's engagement in conflict
constitutes the 'greatest taboo', conflicting with ethical norms that
have come into existence over the 'past four millennia of warfare'.[39]
They also contest pronouncements that child soldiers are products of
'failed adults' and 'failed communities' that have failed 'to learn the
humanity that they need to become successful neighbours and
parents'.[40]

For free-rangers, such blanket condemnations reveal a 'western
essentialist model of childhood' that condemns societies in which
child soldiers are regarded as necessary, if not normal, and in many
cases noble.[41] Rosen, for instance, asserts that during World War II,
Jewish child soldiers rightfully fought for their own lives and for the
survival of their people.[42] During the civil war in Sierra Leone,
moreover, it was entirely rational, says Rosen, for many children to
take up arms to overcome poverty. And, in joining the intifada,
Palestinian children expressed their desire for collective identity, pride
and vengeance. In such contexts, children's participation in war
represents an often regretful but nonetheless reasonable way for
children to grow up and make their mark on the world. Western
outrage over child soldiers, argue free-rangers, is deeply hypocritical
given that child soldiers commonly fought in the American Revolution,
the American Civil War and, to a lesser extent, during both World
Wars.[43] Drawing links back to Ancient Greece, Macmillan goes so
far as to speculate that 'children have been stock characters of
warfare since time immemorial'.[44] For Brocklehurst, the earliest
documented use of western children in active combat was in 1212
during the mythologised Children's Crusade to reclaim the Holy
Land.[45] Vautravers points out that children in modern Europe,

---

[39] Singer, *Children at War*, 4; Singer, 'The Enablers of War', 94.
[40] Maureen W. McClure and Gonzalo Retamal, 'Wise Investments in Future
Neighbours: Recruitment Deterrence, Human Agency, and Education', in
Scott Gates and Simon Reich (eds.), *Child Soldiers in the Age of Fractured States*
(Pittsburgh, PA: University of Pittsburgh Press, 2010), 223.
[41] Kristen E. Cheney, *Pillars of the Nation: Child Citizens and Ugandan National
Development* (Chicago, IL: University of Chicago Press, 2008), 209.
[42] See Rosen, *Armies of the Young*.   [43] Ibid., 8.
[44] Macmillan, 'The Child Soldier in North-South Relations', 36.
[45] Brocklehurst, *Who's Afraid of Children?*, 33–4.

especially impoverished or abandoned children, commonly joined field regiments and served on the frontline.[46] Van Emden records how English child soldiers were celebrated as 'brave young men' and how they were and continue to be honoured for their sacrifice as shown in gravestone inscriptions such as 'Oh So Young & Yet So Brave; Killed in Action 9th September 1916, aged 16.'[47] In an examination of fiction and film for alternatives to the child-as-victim model, Rosen and Rosen point to child characters, such as Gavroche in *Les Misérables* and Johnny Tremain, who are celebrated as courageous revolutionaries and fearless patriots.[48] They also laud the astuteness, sense of sacrifice and gladiatorial valour of Katniss Everdeen in *The Hunger Games* and have great respect for Harry Potter and his friends, who develop emotional fortitude, camaraderie and self-awareness through their confrontations with murderous evil. A similar assessment could be made of the crime-fighting Hit-Girl in *Kick-Ass* and the orphan Robin, who in the first Batman comics is taken under Bruce Wayne/ Batman's wing at the age of eight and trained to fight and kill.

According to free-rangers, caretakers overestimate both the manipulation of children in conflict and their own capacity to save and redeem child soldiers with nurturing and guidance. By constructing this victim–hero dichotomy they overlook children's capacity for agency, intrepidness, calculation and malice. On the basis of their studies of children in conflict zones, Boyden and de Berry argue that 'children and adolescents can be very active in defining their own allegiances during conflict, as well as their own strategies for coping and survival'.[49] There are, of course, situations in which child soldiers have been abducted, drugged, manipulated and abused. However, these instances attract a disproportionate amount of attention by caretakers, who are eager to declare a crisis or crime against humanity that demands humanitarian intervention. For free-rangers, the press-ganged, utterly indoctrinated and totally innocent child soldier is far closer to the exception than the norm.[50]

[46] Vautravers, 'Why Child Soldiers are Such a Complex Issue', 96.
[47] Richard van Emden, *Boy Soldiers of the Great War* (London: Headline Book Publishing, 2005), 53. Cited in Lee, 'Understanding and Addressing the Phenomenon of "Child Soldiers"', 3.
[48] Sarah Maya Rosen and David M. Rosen, 'Representing Child Soldiers in Fiction and Film', *Peace Review* 24 (2012), 305–12.
[49] Boyden and de Berry. 'Introduction', xv.
[50] Rosen, *Armies of the Young*, 16.

An ILO study of four central African countries supports their claim, finding that 'volunteers' accounted for two-thirds of child soldiers.[51] Brocklehurst adds that there is little evidence that children make ruthlessly effective soldiers because 'they don't ask questions'; in all likelihood, they do have questions and have opportunities to raise them. To suggest otherwise is not to empower children but to diminish them.[52] Hauge's interviews with one-time girl soldiers in Guatemala revealed that they joined after being informed and encouraged by family and friends who were already guerrillas.[53] The girls had also commonly experienced torture and massacres and were acutely aware of the prevalence of injustice in their communities and understandably wanted to do something about it. In short, they became armed rebels with a clear comprehension of the potential risks and rewards and commonly remained devoted to the cause well into adulthood. Peters points out that a considerable number of young abductees in the Revolutionary United Front (RUF) of Sierra Leone became true believers and loyal combatants as a consequence of ideological instruction, the affirmation of cultural identity and a realisation that armed conflict offered material and security benefits that could not be attained in their civilian lives.[54] Moreover, Podder's research suggests that during the Liberian civil wars (1989–1996 and 1999–2003) many children saw themselves and were seen by others as growing in maturity, resilience and prominence by participating in armed conflict.[55] In addition, recent interviews with child combatants from the Island of Mindanao in the Philippines found that they joined the military with the support of their families and communities along with a sense of duty to Allah.[56]

Thus, when it comes to what motivates child soldiers, free-rangers take note of the complex interaction between push and pull factors and

---

[51] Cited in Brett and Specht, *Young Soldiers: Why They Choose to Fight*, 3.
[52] Brocklehurst, *Who's Afraid of Children?*, 37.
[53] Wenche Hauge, 'Girl Soldiers in Guatemala', in Alpaslan Özerdem and Sukanya Podder (eds.), *Child Soldiers: From Recruitment to Reintegration* (Houndmills: Palgrave Macmillan, 2011), 97.
[54] Peters, 'Group Cohesion and Coercive Recruitment', 50–75.
[55] Cited in Peters, 'Group Cohesion and Coercive Recruitment', 57.
[56] Alpaslan Özerdem and Sukanya Podder, 'How Voluntary? The Role of Community in Youth Participation in Muslim Mindanao', in Alpaslan Özerdem and Sukanya Podder (eds.), *Child Soldiers: From Recruitment to Reintegration* (Houndmills: Palgrave Macmillan, 2011), 130.

the blurry distinction between voluntary and enforced recruitment.[57] Beyond trying to gain a more nuanced understanding of the nature and extent of the child soldier problem, free-rangers also seek to reconfigure and redirect the problem itself. Specifically, they argue that the problem reveals as much about anxieties in the global north as it does about the security of children in the global south. Macmillan makes a strident claim along these lines, asserting that a disproportionate amount of public and scholarly attention is directed towards the 300,000 or so child soldiers in the world vis-à-vis the billion poverty-stricken children living in both the global south and the global north.[58] Macmillan is sceptical of caretakers who assert that conflict robs children of their innocence and thereby undermines both the foundations and future prospects of a society. For her, liberal humanitarian efforts to protect foreign children from war are commonly aligned with conservative agendas to uphold family values on the home front. That is, caretakers either espouse or collude with those who bemoan the erosion of traditional western family values due to increased female participation in the workforce, higher divorce rates and gay marriage.[59] Therefore children – whether they are criminals, murderers, forced migrants, abuse survivors or soldiers – are a big issue because they putatively embody 'the last reliable source of love in postmodern societies'.[60] Along these lines it is also worth considering whether there is a link between the perceived need to do *something* about child soldiers in the global south and the perceived need to do *everything* for children in the global north that is encapsulated in the phenomena of helicopter parents and bubble-wrap kids.

In addition, this prevailing Anglo and Eurocentric anxiety is in all likelihood fed by demographic disparities and media hype about migration between the global south and the global north. Countries such as Italy, Germany, Spain and Greece are some of the fastest aging in the world, with average lifetime birth rates per woman at around 1.4, well below the replenishment rate of 2.1.[61] This would theoretically

---

[57] Brocklehurst, *Who's Afraid of Children?*, 35.
[58] Macmillan, 'The Child Soldier in North-South Relations', 47.   [59] Ibid.
[60] Ibid.
[61] Eurostat, 'Fertility Statistics'. Available at http://epp.eurostat.ec.europa.eu/ statistics_explained/index.php/Fertility_statistics; Lee Kuan Yew, 'Warning Bell for Developed Countries: Declining Birth Rates', *Forbes.com* 16 October 2012. Available at www.forbes.com/sites/currentevents/2012/10/16/warning-bell-for-developed-countries-declining-birth-rates/.

make the flow of young people from Africa and the Middle East to Europe a welcome necessity. However, the political reality is that an increasingly old Europe feels threatened and besieged by the youthful spiritedness and dynamism of countries to its east and south.[62] This anxiety is fed by fear-mongering about child soldiers who have already made their way to the global north as refugees. A stark example of such fear-mongering occurred in Australia in the lead up to the 2007 federal election when a nineteen-year-old Sudanese refugee was beaten to death in an outer Melbourne suburb by a man who shortly beforehand had been out on the street wielding a pole and pronouncing 'These blacks are turning the town into the Bronx. I am looking to take my town back. I'm going to kill the blacks.'[63] Much of the media commentary and government rhetoric that followed asserted that the problem was not racism, but rather the Sudanese, and child soldiers in particular who were imbued with violence. One journalist asserted that groups of young Sudanese were 'hunting in packs' and that because they had been 'brought up as warriors in their own country', it was a great 'culture shock' for them to 'suddenly have freedom'. Ultimately they were 'impossible to control'.[64]

For free-rangers, fears about the impossibility of controlling child soldiers over here nourish campaigns to contain or solve the child soldier problem over there. These campaigns are ineffective and harmful because they are infused with ethnocentrism and prosecuted with ill-directed evangelical zeal. The most prominent such instance is Invisible Children's *Kony2012* film, which fashioned the problem of child soldiers in Northern Uganda in a way that suited the global audience's craving for drama and a Hollywood happy ending. The film was wildly successful in its stated goal to 'make Kony famous', but did little to bring him to justice or empower child soldiers in the LRA. The fact that *Kony 2012* was accessed 100,000,000 times in less

---

[62] Klaus Eder, 'Europe's Borders: The Narrative Construction of the Boundaries of Europe', *European Journal of Social Theory* 9 (May 2006), 263.

[63] Norrie Ross, 'Two Jailed Over "Brutal and Unprovoked" Killing of Sudanese refugee Liep Gony in Noble Park', *heraldsun.com.au* 18 December 2009. Available at www.heraldsun.com.au/news/two-jailed-over-brutal-and-unpro voked-killing-of-sudanese-refugee-liep-gony-in-noble-park/story-e6frf7jo-1225811762854.

[64] Neil Mitchell, 'Above the Law in the Suburbs', *heraldsun.com.au* 4 October 2007. Available at www.heraldsun.com.au/news/above-the-law-in-the-suburbs/story-e6frfigo-1111114562102.

than a week reminds free-rangers of how it is easy to fetishise child soldiers and how dominant the caretaker ethos is in the popular consciousness.

An indirect approach to the problem of child soldiers

While there is a substantial gap between caretakers and free-rangers in terms of how they view the problem of child soldiers, there is considerable potential for bringing them together in terms of how to solve it. In particular, if both sides agree that there are fundamental socio-economic and military causes of the child soldier problem, then they can also agree on the socio-economic and military solutions. Focusing on socio-economic factors involves viewing the child soldier problem as a subset of the child labour problem. Thus, to the extent that it is conceivable that children rightfully work in certain contexts, it is also conceivable that they fight. Advocacy should thus be directed towards improving the conditions of that form of work or providing sustainable alternatives that would make such dangerous employment unattractive.

This indirect approach to addressing the child soldier problem represents a shift in degree and orientation rather than kind. For instance, UNICEF already stresses that conflict militates against countries achieving their MDGs.[65] An indirect approach recognises this nexus, but operates in the opposite direction, such that promoting the MDGs is an effective way to counter new wars that use child soldiers. As for the military triggers of the child soldier problem, Mack advocates ending wars in which there are high numbers of child soldiers rather than combating the use of child soldiers in war. Peace making and peace building have, he argues, done far more to reduce the number of children engaged in conflict than laws, resolutions and declarations.[66] Not focusing on the special needs of children can also be effective when it comes to demobilisation programmes. Shepler offers the example of demobilised 'child soldiers' in Sierra Leone, who felt aggrieved after being provided with counselling instead of a US$ 300 resettlement package provided to

---

[65] UNICEF, *Machel Study 10-Year Strategic Review* (2009), 26–9.
[66] Andrew Mack, 'Ending the Scourge of Child Soldiering: An Indirect Approach', in Scott Gates and Simon Reich (eds.), *Child Soldiers in the Age of Fractured States* (Pittsburgh, PA: University of Pittsburgh Press, 2010), 245.

demobilised adult soldiers.[67] None of this is to deny the deplorability of children being forced or manipulated to become soldiers or the need to prosecute recruiters. Nor is it to condemn all forms of international assistance on behalf of children.[68] Rather, it is to suggest that indirect solutions are generally better than direct ones when it comes to providing alternatives for both voluntary and forced child soldiers, along with the vast majority of child soldiers who are somewhere in between.

Caretakers are uncomfortable with indirect solutions because it means deprioritising their long-term solution of establishing a common ethic or universal norm which dictates that children have no place in conflict whatsoever.[69] However, caretakers themselves acknowledge that such measures have had a poor track record. By attributing this to the failed people and societies that they are trying to save rather than the inadequacies of their own approach, caretakers are prone to dogmatism and cultural imperialism. In response, caretakers assert that dogmatic and imperialist action is preferable to idleness in the face of manifest wrongs.

To this end, it is worth illustrating what an indirect approach to child soldiers would entail in a more concrete scenario. Poullard offers the example of child soldiers in the Mayi Mayi ethnic militia groups of the DRC.[70] From the outset he establishes a sense of caretaker urgency by equating child soldiers with 'press-ganged children' who may be 'abducted, killed, injured, mutilated or uprooted from their original community'.[71] His prescription is to 'restore the capacity of the state' so that it can ensure peace and security for children and allow them to be rehabilitated.[72] Poullard is sensitive to the tension between cultural absolutism and cultural relativism, acknowledging the complexity and

---

[67] Susan Shepler, Conflicted Childhoods: Fighting Over Child Soldiers in Sierra Leone, Thesis (Ph.D.), Department of Social and Cultural Studies in Education, University of California Berkeley (2005), 189. Cited in Lee, 'Understanding and Addressing the Phenomenon of "Child Soldiers"', 27.

[68] For example, the chapters on peace building and advocacy in this book outline the establishment by international forces of zones of peace for children in Nepal and Sri Lanka respectively. These were measured forms of intervention that provided emergency relief and protection to children during conflict.

[69] UNICEF, Machel Study 10-Year Strategic Review (2009), 1.

[70] Axel Poullard, 'Press-ganged Children', in 'Democratic Republic of Congo: Past, Present, Future?', Forced Migration Review 36 (November 2010), 24–5.

[71] Ibid., 24.   [72] Ibid.

multi-layered nature of the problem and advocating an approach that 'reconciles local needs and international imperatives'.[73] However, he understandably struggles with this tension, proclaiming that the problem is 'not as simple as demanding their exclusion from those conflicts' while at the same time asserting that the recruitment of child soldiers by Mayi Mayi is 'a practice that cannot be tolerated'.[74] Especially intolerable to Poullard is the fact that the use of child soldiers is deeply anchored in Mayi Mayi custom and tradition, whereby boys are often initiated from the age of sixteen to become men, husbands and warriors. Even more disturbing for him is the belief in magic that makes children not only eligible for war but highly desirable.

[Most] serious is the Mayi Mayi conviction that children have special protective powers. Mayi Mayi tradition dictates that they should be the first to be sent into battle to intimidate the enemy by crying and shouting, or by invoking their protective powers, which of course exposes them to grave danger.[75]

Poullard points out that attempts to address the child soldier problem in the DRC by denouncing and humiliating those who engage in such socio-cultural practices have been largely ineffective. Concomitantly, external forces promoting international standards have had limited success in rehabilitating children so that they can return to 'normal living'. One of the possible reasons for this is that initiation, magic and child warriors are part of what Mayi Mayi regard as normal living. While war and child warriors are undesirable and often lead to tragic outcomes, neither is necessarily aberrant or indicative of a community's failure. In recognition of this, an indirect approach involves shifting efforts away from eradicating these established beliefs and practices and focusing on other causal factors that Poullard himself suggests go to the root of the problem – poverty and chronic insecurity; the assumption being that a rise in development and security levels would render the cultural connection between children and war harmless. These indirect efforts to improve socio-economic and security conditions may well incorporate their own tensions, but the risk of cultural imperialism is smaller than the risk involved in denouncing and trying to redefine what it means to be normal for the Mayi Mayi. Taking an indirect approach to child soldier problems does

[73] Ibid.   [74] Ibid., 25.   [75] Ibid.

not necessitate approving all of the established beliefs and practices that place children on the battlefront. It merely requires realisation that effectively changing traditions necessitates deep engagement with them, and will most likely be achieved by the direct efforts of cultural insiders, or in the long-term via the soft power influence of outsiders.

Child soldier cultures

> War was our culture. We used to have breakfast, lunch and dinner with war.[76] (Mozambican child soldier)

This section argues that while cultural imperialism is to be eschewed, cultural engagement can provide a more fulsome understanding of what causes the problem of child soldiers – beyond socio-economic and military factors. Indeed, such engagement should also be a prerequisite for anyone considering intervention and peace building on their behalf. Much of the scholarship on child soldiers tends to avoid or discount culture. Gates and Reich assert that searching for cultural explanations as to why children fight in wars can lead to unpalatable conclusions such as 'Those people do not value their children as we do' or 'It's an African thing.'[77] There is no thread, they argue, 'that links the use of child soldiers to particular national cultures or set of historical experiences' nor – with the possible exception of Liberia – any evidence of child soldiers being consistently deployed in a country across different conflicts.[78] In this sense, Gates and Reich assume that cultures are static and rooted in the past. Chapter 4 of this volume on 'The rights of the child' points out that culture does not only encompass heritage and traditions, but also reflects contemporary power flows and hopes for the future. Understanding culture as dynamic allows us to recognise that it can contribute to the use of child soldiers in one or some conflicts in a particular society without it being a persistent or inescapable influence over time. Moreover, as discussed above, culture is only one of several causes of child soldier problems; so its impact may well be consistent without child soldiers being consistently used.

---

[76] Victor Igreja, 'Cultural Disruption and the Care of Infants in Post-War Mozambique', in Jo Boyden and Joanna de Berry (eds.), *Children and Youth on the Front Line: Ethnography, Armed Conflict and Displacement* (New York, NY: Berghahn Books, 2004), 26.
[77] Gates and Reich, 'Introduction', 9.   [78] Ibid.

Caretakers tend to view cultural practices that condone or encourage violence as antithetical to their universal ethic and logic. For Poretti, societies that 'legitimize violence as a way to resolve conflicts send a symbolic message to children'.[79] This message, he argues, is generally false in the sense that it involves the selective manipulation of history by political authorities along with indoctrination and propaganda. From this perspective, child soldier cultures are also malevolent in that they divert children from peace-loving norms towards hatred and the dehumanisation of others. Caretakers would therefore argue that Mayi Mayi beliefs that put children on the front line and stories that valorise child warriors are vestiges of a barbarous past that need to be discarded. This aligns with a biomedical framework for addressing child soldiers that presumes that they are victims of trauma, manipulation and abuse who have to be isolated from their surroundings if they are to have any chance of being nurtured back to good health.[80]

Some critics of caretaker and biomedical perspectives stress that children often make rational choices to engage in conflict. For instance, Peters and Richards conclude from their interviews with child soldiers in Sierra Leone that they are 'rational human actors' with a 'surprisingly mature understanding of their predicament'.[81] Sometimes organisation theory is incorporated into such analysis to show how flows of material and human resources regulate decisions by children, their families and communities to mobilise for war.[82] This perspective highlights the volition of child soldiers but, like caretakers, removes them from their social and historical contexts so that they fit within a rational actor model.

In contrast, free-rangers argue that to gain a nuanced and grounded picture of why and how children fight wars, culture must be taken into account. Free-rangers question whether child soldiers and the cultures that animate them are a problem that can or even should be fixed. Instead, they argue for the need to engage with these cultures for two

---

[79] Poretti, 'Preventing Children from Joining Armed Groups', 134.
[80] Boyden and de Berry, 'Introduction', xv.
[81] Cited in Rosen, *Armies of the Young*, 17.
[82] See, for instance, Scott Gates, 'Why Do Children Fight? Motivations and the Mode of Recruitment', in Alpaslan Özerdem and Sukanya Podder, *Child Soldiers: From Recruitment to Reintegration* (Houndmills: Palgrave Macmillan, 2011), 29–49; Jeremy M. Weinstein, 'Resources and the Information Problem in Rebel Recruitment', *Journal of Conflict Resolution* 49(4) (2005), 598–624.

major reasons. First, we cannot understand the impact of conflict on children without examining how 'culture, social power and identity' shape their experiences of suffering, triumph, healing and recovery.[83] Secondly, we cannot grasp the full impact of children on conflict and peace without taking into account cultural factors that propel them to 'the forefront of value formation and attitudinal change' as opposed to many adults who are more likely to cling to idealised notions of the past.[84] In sum, cultural engagement is a prerequisite for us to help child soldiers and for us to realise how they might help us. The next section twists the focus and format of the chapter in order to demonstrate how stories can serve as an avenue for engaging Vietnamese child soldiers, one of whom was my father.

Vietnam's child soldiers: fathers, giants and emperors

KIM: Tell me about when you went to the Viet Minh school.

DAD: I learnt about communism.

KIM: What exactly did you learn?

DAD: You know, capitalism is bad. Marx is good. Lenin is great. Ho Chi Minh is the best. That sort of thing.

KIM: Can you give me a few more details?

DAD: No, not really. It was almost fifty years ago you know. I can't remember everything.

KIM: Well, what did you do there? Did you study communism all day?

DAD: No. There were maths and history classes. Sometimes we sang songs and danced. At other times we split up into small groups and did military training. We made punji sticks.

KIM: What's a punji stick?

DAD: It's a sharpened piece of bamboo that you put in the ground to kill French soldiers.[85]

I was stunned when my father revealed to me in the most nonchalant manner how he filled his days as a young Viet Minh revolutionary. My discomfort grew when soon afterwards he recalled how he used to soak the punji sticks in buffalo dung and urine so as to ensure that his victims' wounds would become infected. As a twelve-year-old, my

---

[83] Boyden and de Berry, 'Introduction', xv.   [84] Ibid., xvii.
[85] Huynh, *Where the Sea Takes Us*, 71.

father relished the prospect of French white devils falling into his trap and writhing in pain. At the same time he calculated that it was best to maim rather than kill them as, in addition to disabling one colonial soldier, two others would be forced to carry him from the battlefield. In this section I attempt to address my anxiety over my father's experiences as a child soldier by exploring the events, figures, forces, strategic contexts and stories that influenced his and many other Vietnamese children's decisions to fight in the First and Second Indochina Wars, and which still shape Vietnamese children's identities today. I aim to show that Vietnam's child soldier culture is not necessarily alien or backward, but rather very much worth studying and engaging with.

As a child my father was never far from war. His first memory is of fleeing his village and being displaced for almost a year. During this time his family was continually dogged by bombs and bullets, and his oldest brother died of malnourishment and disease. So the question is not so much how my father became involved with war – he had no choice – but rather why he decided, against his mother's best wishes, to become a trainee guerrilla fighter. At a personal level he was eager to follow in the footsteps of his remaining older brother and an uncle, both of whom had become convinced that only Ho Chi Minh could save the nation from French colonialism. Moreover, they helped him realise that by joining the Viet Minh and defeating the French, they could avenge his oldest brother's death and establish an era of peace and prosperity. This would allow him to go to school and escape the poverty and backwardness that he had begun to associate with village life. My father's personal motivations to fight thus dovetailed with his larger vision for a modern Vietnam. From a young age he was drawn to the city lights and dearly wanted to be independent while also supporting his family and developing the nation.

To his and my great fortune, the First Indochina War ended in 1954 before my father saw combat. During the punctuated peace that followed, he channelled his energies towards work and study. He moved to Saigon to complete a diploma in electrical design, secured a job with the electricity authority and met my mother. These opportunities aided not only in his demobilisation and demilitarisation, but also in his de-radicalisation. As a consequence, over a period of years and without coercion or will, my father shifted from the extreme left of the ideological spectrum to the mild right. The conclusiveness of this shift was evident in 1979 when his dedication to individual liberty, free markets and, above all, his young family, motivated us to leave our homeland. That is, as they say, another story. The point of this one is to suggest that cultural forces were tied up with the personal decisions and socio-economic factors that contributed to my father becoming a child soldier. Moreover, vestiges of these cultural beliefs and practices can be found in my father's, the Socialist Republic of Vietnam's, and in all likelihood my own identity today. Of course, determining and recording cultural influence is not a matter of clear-cut account keeping. For Antonio Gramsci, culture leaves in us 'an infinity of traces without an inventory'.[86] This does not so much make cultural inquiry impossible, but rather all the more invigorating and rewarding.

One way of engaging with my father's child soldier culture is via stories of young warriors that he and many other Vietnamese have known and cherished. Galway adopts a broadly similar approach in considering the extent to which, and the means by which, representations of boy soldiers as both victims and heroes in World War I children's literature made many young people eager to 'take part in the action'.[87] Understanding Vietnamese child soldier stories, however, requires some comprehension of the part that stories play in Vietnamese history and culture. There are five points that must be noted in this regard.

Firstly, stories mean a great deal to the Vietnamese. The renowned scholar Alexander Woodside famously asserted that 'Vietnam is and always has been one of the most intensely literary civilisations on the face of the planet'.[88] Most Vietnamese can recount with enthusiasm and authority a great many folktales and legends and can recite a wide range of songs, poems and proverbs. For centuries the fact that their libraries were preserved in their hearts and souls was wilfully ignored by colonisers to the detriment of all concerned. The related second

---

[86] Antonio Gramsci (edited by Quentin Hoare and Geoffrey Nowell Smith), *Prison Note: Selections* (London: International Publishers Company, 1971), 324.

[87] Elizabeth A. Galway, 'Competing Representations of Boy Soldiers in WWI Children's Literature', *Peace Review* 24 (2012), 298–304; see also Kimberley Reynolds, 'Words about War for Boys: Representations of Soldiers and Conflict in Writing for Children before World War I', *Children's Literature Association Quarterly* 34(2) (2009), 255–71.

[88] Alexander B. Woodside, *Community and Revolution in Modern Vietnam* (Boston, MA: Houghton Mifflin Company, 1976), ix.

point is that traditionally, popular Vietnamese culture has been preserved and transmitted orally; that is, until European missionaries fashioned a Latinised alphabet in the 1600s and the Viet Minh instituted mass literacy programmes in the mid-1900s. As a consequence – and this is the third point – popular Vietnamese stories are shaped in a collective and protean manner. So while there are recurring themes, characters and messages, stories are commonly modified according to person and place with relatively little concern for any western-oriented commitment to authenticity and originality. Similarly and fourthly, in the Vietnamese mind-set there is no clear border between factual history and fictional legends, myths and folktales. For instance, the historical fact that eighteen generations of Hùng kings established the nation between 2879 BC and 258 BC sits comfortably beside the belief that the first Hùng king was the eldest son of Lac Long Quan, the Dragon Lord, and Au Co, the mountain fairy. Moreover, the last Hùng king, An Duong Vuong, held the Chinese at bay with a crossbow made from a magical turtle claw. The final point to make about Vietnamese stories – and Vietnam's identity more generally – is that many of them are at once derived from China as the country's cultural progenitor while also being defined against it as its most enduring threat and enemy.

With this in mind, we can now turn to an articulation of these five points in the story of Saint Giong.[89]

In the reign of the sixth Hùng king, a boy was born to a middle-aged woman who grew eggplants. The woman did not have a husband, but one day when she was out in the fields she stepped in a giant footprint and after that her stomach began to grow. Nine months later she gave birth to a baby boy whom she named 'Giong'. Giong was not like other babies. He did not cry, laugh, gurgle, say 'Mama' or make the slightest sound. Nor did he wriggle, roll, sit up or crawl, choosing instead to lie perfectly still. None of this mattered to his mother, who was grateful for the gift of a child and loved him all the same.

At the time that Giong was born, the royal court was frantic because gangs from the Shang Dynasty to the north were crossing the border, massacring

---

[89] This story is derived from a number of sources. First, the story as it has been told to me and my father. Secondly, an interactive app that I purchased for my son and my nephew. Thirdly, Thich Nhat Hanh, 'The Magical Warrior', in Thich Nhat Hanh, *The Dragon Prince: Stories and Legends from Vietnam* (Berkeley, CA: Paralax Press, 2007), 115–22.

Vietnamese, pillaging their belongings and razing their crops. Concerned that the Shang were preparing for a full-scale invasion, the king called together his advisers. They informed him that while the Vietnamese army was fierce, it was no match for the Shang forces, which were far larger in number and had a vast supply of weapons. The desperate king prayed and made offerings to the Dragon Lord for guidance. When the Dragon Lord came down from the heavens he informed the King that the Shang were still occupied in battle on other frontiers and that they would not launch a full invasion for another three years.

'Use this time to prepare for war', commanded the Dragon Lord. 'Everyone must commit themselves to the safety and wellbeing of the kingdom. The farmers must give up their crops. The tailors must give up their cloth. The carpenters must give up their timber. You must also train an elite squad of warriors who will confront the Shang head on.'

'Thank you Dragon Lord', said the king. 'But, with respect, even with all our efforts we would not be able to turn back the invaders. For every one of us there are ten of them. When we fire a single arrow at them they respond with a quiver full.'

'Do not underestimate my powers or the power of the Vietnamese people,' replied the Dragon Lord. 'As you sight the Shang soldiers on the border, you must seek a general to lead your warriors into battle. Now listen carefully. It is important that you do not ignore the person who stands up in this dark and dangerous time. It does not matter whether he is rich or poor, tall or small, old or young. You must put your faith in him and do exactly as he says.'

Three years later, just as the Dragon Lord predicted, the Shang began their invasion. Vietnam's elite warriors were deployed to repel them at the border. At the same time, envoys were sent out across the kingdom to look for a hero to save them.

When the three-year-old Giong heard a passing envoy's call he suddenly stood bolt upright and sung out with a voice like a temple bell. At first the envoy could not believe his eyes. But the toddler commanded him with booming authority.

'Behold, I am Giong! Send word to the king that you have found his general. Tell him to collect all of the iron in the land and gather the very best blacksmiths. They must forge for me a suit of armour that is ten metres tall along with an iron horse and staff of like proportions. Hurry! There is no time to waste.'

The messenger scurried back to the king, convinced that he had witnessed a miracle. When he arrived at the capital he was afraid that the king would not believe him. But the king remembered the Dragon Lord's pronouncement and set about fulfilling Giong's demands.

In the meanwhile, Giong called for food. His mother was astonished to see that in his first sitting, Giong ate enough rice to fill 100 men. Still he called for more. Supplies were brought in from nearby villages as word spread that there was a young boy who would save the kingdom from the advancing Chinese. The amazing thing was that Giong grew with each serve of rice until he stood ten metres tall. At that point he let out a mighty burp that turned back the waves in the Eastern Ocean: Bbbbuuuurrrrpp!!! Then he put down the fence palings that he was using as chop sticks and the wooden bath tub that had served as his bowl and bounded off to the capital.

Giong's freshly cast armour, horse and staff were waiting for him. After paying his respects to the king, he mounted the iron horse. Suddenly, it came to life, kicking up great clumps of dirt. As the horse snorted and snarled, flames shot out of its enormous nostrils. Giong grabbed his staff and made his way to the border where the Shang Chinese and Vietnamese soldiers were engaged in battle. The giant Giong and his iron stallion leapt right into the midst of the enemy hordes. Again and again and again, he swung his staff, cutting through Shang soldiers as a sickle cuts through straw. Waves of Chinese troops arrived to replace those who had fallen and every weapon in the Middle Kingdom was directed at the mighty Giong. But they did not even dent his armour.

The giant battered, cut and killed so many of the invaders that his staff eventually broke into pieces when it struck one of the especially thick-headed Chinese. But this did not stop Giong. He rode into the forest, where he tore out of the ground the thickest and tallest pieces of bamboo, which he wielded to finish the job. As the remaining Chinese fled north, Vietnamese forces cheered and sung tributes to the boy hero. Knowing that his people were safe and his glory assured, Giong and his horse flew up to the top of Soc Son Mountain and then ascended to the heavens.

Not long afterwards a temple was built in Giong's village of Phu Dong in honour of the eggplant farmer's son who saved the kingdom. The king pronounced Giong the patron saint of harvests and national peace. To this day, a festival is held for Saint Giong during the fourth month of the lunar year, at which time people can see the gigantic hoof-marks left behind from his fearsome stallion and the yellow bamboo which was scorched by the flames from its nostrils.

This story shares an underlying message with the award-winning children's book, *The Very Hungry Caterpillar*, by Eric Carle. Both the caterpillar and Saint Giong demonstrate to children how important it is for them to eat so that they can grow and develop. However, whereas the caterpillar eats ferociously so that it can become a beautiful butterfly, the very hungry Giong consumes bathtubs of rice so that he might defend his people against injustice and foreign occupation. Moreover, Giong informs young and old Vietnamese alike that passivism and inertia are not options when war is at hand: that they must be enlivened when duty calls. The child-turned-general also reinforces a powerful Davidic motif in Vietnamese culture, whereby the small and unassuming can overcome the large and menacing.

In more recent Vietnamese history there have been noble and famous children who, like Giong, have stood at the very centre of the nation's struggles. For instance, in 1777 at the age of fifteen, Prince Nguyen Anh was forced into hiding after a peasant uprising killed his family. He found refuge with French missionaries and colonists who helped Nguyen Anh to modernise his armed forces and reconquer Vietnam in its entirety by 1802. Subsequently, Nguyen Anh anointed himself Emperor Gia Long, establishing the Nguyen Dynasty, which lasted thirteen generations until the end of World War II. Known for his Confucian orthodoxy and for paving the way for French colonialism, Gia Long is condemned by the contemporary Vietnamese regime.

The eighth Nguyen emperor of Vietnam, Ham Nghi, also engaged in conflict as a child, but is seen in a far more favourable light by the Socialist Republic of Vietnam. Having a mother who was a commoner and being only thirteen years old, Ham Nghi was not an obvious choice for emperor. Nonetheless, he was installed on the throne in 1884 by French colonial forces who believed that he would be easy to control. Ham Nghi did not possess the good graces and classical education of his siblings, but quickly became known for his sharp mind and sense of principle. After one year as emperor he was captured by two regents, Nguyen Van Tuong and Ton That Thuyet, during an uprising against foreign occupation. Thereafter he joined the rebels and became the figurehead of the patriotic 'Can Vuong' ('Restore the King') movement, which launched attacks on the French and their Vietnamese collaborators from mountain bases on the Laos border. Lacking in coherence and resources, the Can Vuong movement proved little match for the newly installed Emperor Dong Khanh. Thus in 1888 Ham Nghi was captured and exiled to Algeria. He died in 1943 having never returned to his homeland.

Vietnam's child soldiers: total war, new heroes and martyrs

When the Viet Minh came to my father's village to proselytise their cause and recruit soldiers, they presented themselves as the modern manifestation of past heroes who had fought for Vietnamese independence. Conscious, however, that past uprisings like the Can Vuong movement had been soundly defeated, the president of the Democratic Republic of Vietnam (DRV) Ho Chi Minh knew that appeals to the past would not be enough. They also needed to maximize the DRV's human and material resources and draw from the strategic successes of their comrades abroad. Ancient and classical Vietnamese patriots were thus harnessed in the pursuit of a Maoist-style total war and carefully adapted to suit the Viet Minh's Marxist–Leninist ideology. This interchange of culture, strategy and ideology created a milieu that encouraged ordinary children such as my father to take up arms.

During the second half of the First Indochina War (1946–1954), the DRV's leadership orchestrated a strategic shift from a low-intensity insurgency to a general counter-offensive in accordance with Mao's model of revolutionary warfare. It was time, judged the General Secretary of the Vietnamese Communist Party, Truong Chinh, for total war. Goscha points out that this was 'one of the most socially totalizing wars' in modern history.[90] On 4 November 1949 the DRV created the People's Army of Viet Nam (PAVN) by enacting compulsory military service for all men aged between eighteen and forty-five. In preparation for engaging in set-piece battles, the DRV also implemented a logistics system to transport food supplies, ammunition, weapons and medicine. The hundreds of thousands of Vietnamese porters pushing bicycles that had been modified to carry loads of up to 200 kilograms would prove crucial in the final victory over the French at Dien Bien Phu in 1954. By that time the PAVN had mobilised 1.7 million people, around one-fifth of the Central and Northern Vietnamese population that made up the DRV.[91] Truong Chinh's command at the outset of the transition to total war had been all but successfully implemented: 'We must mobilize all of our military, political, economic, administrative, and cultural forces.'[92]

The success of the general counter-offensive turned not only on increasing the numbers of people engaged in the resistance, but also on the quantity and quality of each individual's contribution. For

---

[90] Christopher Goscha, 'A "Total War" of Decolonization? Social Mobilization and State-Building in Community Vietnam (1949–1954)', *War & Society* 31(2) (August 2012), 136.
[91] Ibid., 157.   [92] Ibid., 140.

Truong Chinh a 'total people's resistance' required that 'those who have riches must contribute money, those who have manpower must contribute their strength, those with talents must donate them'.[93] However, it was not sufficient for people merely to offer surplus goods or even their skills; for the resistance to be successful they had to be willing to sacrifice their lives. This was especially true for the peasants who constituted the vast majority of the population and who often had few resources to contribute to the war effort. The upshot was that in the early 1950s the distinction between citizens and combatants in the DRV was effectively abolished. Indeed, according to Goscha, this is precisely what constitutes total war.[94] And so, the compelling message that filtered down to my father at secret night-time rallies through animated talks, songs and plays was that if the Vietnamese were going to honour their heroic past, fight present injustice and construct a glorious future, then 'every citizen must be a soldier'.[95]

This conflation is critical with respect to DRV children who in this most 'socially totalizing war' were considered citizen-soldiers capable of making great sacrifices and deserving of honour and praise.[96] The children of the DRV were, in a sense, like the bicycles that were acquisitioned and modified to carry heavy loads during wartime. Once peace and independence were in place, they could go back to their routine function having hopefully been hardened rather than damaged by the extra strain that had been placed upon them. In my father's case, he recounts joining the Viet Minh as both an initiation into adulthood and also the ideologies of Marx, Lenin and Ho Chi Minh. This logic and process worked in reverse, such that Vietnamese who fought alongside the French were diminished and infantilised. This is evident in a popular memoir with a strong socialist realist bent by Pham Thang.[97] In

---

[93] Ibid., 143.   [94] Ibid., 157.   [95] Huynh, *Where the Sea Takes Us*, 80.

[96] Goscha, 'A "Total War" of Decolonization?', 157.

[97] Pham Thang, *Doi Tinh Bao Thieu Nien (The Youth Intelligence Squad)*, 2nd edn (Hanoi: So Van Hoa, 1972). Apparently, seven editions and 100,300 copies of this story have been sold, with each edition being modified to suit the socialist realist 'art as life' conditions of the time. So, for instance, the post-1975 edition was revised to suit both a southern audience and the need to ideologically 'Northernise' the south. Nguyet Ha, '"Doi vien tinh bao Bat Sat": Huyen thoai giua doi thuong' (The Bat Sat Intelligence Squad: Common life legends)', *cand. com.vn* 2 April 2013. Available at http://vnca.cand.com.vn/vi-vn/truyenthong/2013/3/57912.cand. Phung Quan's *Tuoi Tho Duoi Doi (A Fierce Childhood*

The Youth Intelligence Squad, Pham Thang recounts the 1946–1948 adventures of a squad of twelve to fifteen-year-old boys who, because they are small and appear unassuming, are tasked with scouting out paths for Viet Minh guerrillas to make incursions upon occupied Hanoi. The pledge that they sing with great gusto goes as follows:

> The members of the squad here pledge,
> To overcome every hardship in fulfilment of our duties.
> Better to die than surrender to the enemy
> If caught, no matter how terrible the torture, we'll never fess up.[98]

One member of the squad is captured by a French-aligned Vietnamese 'puppet', who is described as having acquired the face of a German fascist. More importantly, the adult soldier is referred to as 'thang nguy'. 'Nguy' denotes someone who is false and unpatriotic – a title assigned to my family after the fall of Saigon. 'Thang' is the slightly pejorative and mocking personal pronoun reserved for boys. By this account, armed conflict created a context in which children on the side of revolutionary justice could grow up, while men on the side of the comprador capitalists devolved into mere boys.

Thus while DRV military conscription focused on adult men, boys and girls were also actively encouraged to join the armed forces. In fact, they had their own fighting units, such as the Youth Guerrillas (*Du kich Thieu Nhi*) and Ho Chi Minh's Child Pioneers (*Doi Thieu nien Tien phong Ho Chi Minh*). Most notably, the Youth Shock Brigades (*Thanh Nien Xung Phong*) were established in 1950 with the revolutionary mission 'to produce, to fight and to educate [politically]'.[99] Celebrated for their volunteerism, becoming a brigade member meant devoting one's 'body and soul' to the

---

(NXB Văn Học, 2011) is perhaps the most well-known child soldier memoir. It tells the story of thirty-one thirteen- and fourteen-year-old boys who were messengers in the war against France. The lead character's name is 'Mừng' which means 'Happy'. Phung Quan was also a child soldier during the resistance, but was officially banned from publishing for almost thirty years due to his involvement with an independent literary movement. As a result, *A Fierce Childhood* was not published until 1988. It was awarded the National Prize for Literature in 2007.

[98] Pham Thang, *Doi Tinh Bao Thieu Nien*, 15.

[99] François Guillemot, 'Death and Suffering at First Hand: Youth Shock Brigades During the Vietnam War (1950–1975)', *Journal of Vietnamese Studies* 4(3) (1 October 2009), 19.

DRV.[100] They had always to be ready to launch an attack and willing – as the Youth Shock Brigades' oath stated – to 'sacrifice oneself unconditionally for the fatherland'.[101] The Youth Shock Brigades was active throughout the second half of the First Indochina War and into the Second Indochina War, attracting a total membership of between 220,000 and 350,000 that was evenly male and female.[102] Most were fifteen to twenty years old, but there are stories of children as young as twelve lying about their age in order to enlist. Brigade members served various roles, including as porters, messengers and intelligence gatherers, but were also actively engaged in combat; around 8,000 children were involved in the battle at Dien Bien Phu. The popular expression at that time was that the Youth Shock Brigades 'went in first' – to open the road to battle – and 'returned last' – after transporting the wounded and burying the dead.[103] Monuments have been erected for Youth Shock Brigades heroes who died in battle. But beyond the mythology there are also accounts of how child soldiers were often ill-prepared, annihilated in battle, ravaged by living in the jungle, and how those who survived suffered persistent trauma and found it difficult to reintegrate into society.[104] In this regard, they were arguably no different to adults.

The representation of child soldiers in the DRV during the Indochina Wars highlights the complex interaction between the agency of child soldiers, the influence of culture and the power of political indoctrination. As noted above, it should not be assumed that the Vietnamese populace as a whole was amenable or pliant to the DRV leadership's push for total war, even if many were sympathetic to the justice of the cause or the promise of material reward and national progress. In the early 1950s, peasants understandably 'did not want to take part in this increasingly deadly conflagration putting them at the mercy of some of the most lethal industrial weapons of the twentieth century'.[105] The DRV leadership sought to overcome the population's preoccupation with self-preservation, or what they regarded as a 'sluggish attitude' (*ue aoi*), using mass mobilisation techniques adopted from Moscow and Beijing. These techniques included land reform, ideological rectification classes, cults of personality rituals, emulations of

---

[100] Ibid., 18.   [101] Ibid., 24.   [102] Ibid., 24.   [103] Ibid., 19.
[104] Ibid., 18.   [105] Cited in Goscha, 'A "Total War" of Decolonization?', 146.

past campaigns, and the veneration of new heroes.[106] Child soldiers and martyrs were especially important to the patriotic emulation campaigns and propagation of new heroes which were designed to promote revolutionary warfare, nation building and social reform.

After withstanding a French onslaught during the initial years of the First Indochina War, the DRV communist leadership grew concerned about the prospect of the colonists establishing a competing nation-state under the leadership of the thirteenth Nguyen Emperor, Bao Dai. The 'Patriotic Emulation Campaigns' were aimed at addressing this threat and involved sending cadres out into the countryside to build support for the DRV. According to Ho Chi Minh, the goal of patriotic emulation was 'to fight famine and poverty, to fight ignorance, and to fight the foreign invaders'.[107] The emulation campaigns sought to seduce the populace rather than compel and conscript them. Cadres worked alongside and co-opted existing mass organisations of farmers, women and youth, welding their revolutionary cause to social objectives, such as the eradication of illiteracy and increasing the production of food and supplies.[108] Medals, certificates and meagre prizes were given to high-achieving individuals and villages. Often the cadres appealed to regional and village patriots and martyrs as being worthy of emulation. They knew that Vietnamese have a long history of venerating martyrs going back to the Trung sisters, who in 43 AD are thought to have drowned themselves in the Red River rather than submit to Chinese rule.[109] In my father's village, for instance, the cadres referred to the example of Mr Ich Duong, who was captured by the French but refused to submit to them even as his head was placed upon the block. 'The People of Vietnam are like grass,' Mr Ich Duong defiantly yelled, 'if you pluck one blade a thousand more will sprout!'[110]

Initially, the emulation campaigns were not successful because although many people revered saints, princes and esteemed gentlemen such as Mr Ich Duong, the thought of emulating them was daunting. The exemplars of old were seen by common Vietnamese to 'inhabit the realm between myth and reality', a situation that made it harder to

[106] Ibid., 146.
[107] Benoît de Tréglodé (trans. Claire Duiker), *Heroes and Revolution in Vietnam* (Singapore: NUS Press, 2012), 39.
[108] Goscha, 'A "Total War" of Decolonization?', 147.   [109] Ibid., 13, 24–5.
[110] Huynh, *Where the Sea Takes Us*, 76.

mimic their qualities and actions in everyday life.[111] One villager at the time said that, 'We men of the people, we often dream of becoming heroes but we are simple people ... It's just too hard.'[112] The campaigns were thus remodelled from a strictly vertical orientation to a more horizontal one via the construction and promotion of new heroes. These heroes were 'new' in at least three senses. First, new heroes were ordinary 'peasants, soldiers, workers, women and youth who had distinguished themselves in their selflessness, productivity, bravery, and devotion to the party and the nation'.[113] The DRV leadership thus retained the Confucian tradition of using heroic stories to guide and educate the people, but greatly expanded the pool of characters so as to facilitate mass mobilisation.[114] Secondly, there were also new means by which stories about the heroes were constructed and promulgated. Specifically, while often based on real people, the character and lives of new heroes were highly curated according to the ideological dictates of the DRV and their concerted propaganda techniques.[115] Thirdly, many new heroes were ordinary child soldiers who, by dedicating their lives to the nation, inspired both children and adults alike. The lives and sacrifices of some of the most noteworthy child soldiers who were active at around my father's time and who, as mythologised new heroes, are very much alive in Vietnam today are summarised below.[116]

Ly Tu Trong (1914–1931)

Coming from a revolutionary background, Ly Tu Trong was terrorised by the French from birth and had to flee to Thailand when he was small. Upon moving to China he became one of seven youth who were cultivated by Ho Chi Minh from 1925–1927. At the age of fifteen, he returned to Vietnam to mobilise other young people in and around Saigon. He was captured after killing a French secret agent. During his incarceration, Ly Tu Trong was tortured and also seduced with promises of trips to France, money, power and women – none of which dented his

---

[111] Ibid., 96.   [112] Ibid., 49.
[113] Goscha, 'A "Total War" of Decolonization?', 149.
[114] Cited in Goscha, 'A "Total War" of Decolonization?', 149. de Tréglodé, *Heroes and Revolution in Vietnam*, 39.
[115] Goscha, 'A "Total War" of Decolonization?', 149.
[116] The following stories can be readily found in children's books and on the internet.

resolve. During his court case, his attorney claimed that he should be treated leniently because he was too young to know what he was doing. In response, Ly Tu Trong is thought to have proclaimed, 'Truly, I may not have come of age, but I am old enough to know that there is only one true path to adulthood, and that is the revolutionary one!' He was executed the next day as he sung 'The Internationale'.

Kim Dong (1929–1943)

Kim Dong was of the Nùng ethnic minority and came from Cao Bang Province in northeast Vietnam. His family were poor peasants and his father and older brother died when he was young. Kim Dong joined the Viet Minh when he was twelve, and was stationed at the famous hideout near Pac Bo village in Cao Bang Province where Ho Chi Minh had returned and was hiding after thirty years of exile. One day, while delivering a message, Kim Dong observed French troops closing down on one of Ho Chi Minh's hideouts. He lured them away with a gunshot and was killed on the bank of a picturesque stream that Ho Chi Minh named after Vladimir Lenin.

Vo Thi Sau (1933–1952)

Born in the southern province of Ba Rịa, Vo Thi Sau is remembered for being full of song and cheer, adept at sewing and embroidery, having a passion for flowers, and for unwavering revolutionary determination. At the age of twelve she followed her brother and joined the Viet Minh insurgency. Two years later she tossed a grenade at a unit of French soldiers, killing one of them and injuring at least twenty others. A year later, during another assassination mission, she was captured and was transferred to various jails, the final one being the infamous Con Dao island prison. Even then, she was known by other inmates for her high spirits. When Vo Thi Sau was finally led to the guillotine, the executioner demanded that she kneel. To this she responded, 'I only know how to stand, I do not know how to kneel.' The French shot her instead.

Le Van Tam (-)

Le Van Tam made a living by selling peanuts in the street. One day his devotion to his people drove him to charge into a colonial fuel depot where he set himself alight. Just as horrifying was a revelation by esteemed Hanoi National University History Professor, Phan Huy Le, that the Le Van Tam story had been fabricated by another scholar, Tran Huy Lieu, when he was Ho Chi Minh's Minister for Propaganda and Information. The revelation did not spark a great debate or widespread outrage in Vietnam. In part, this was because both scholars upheld a distinction between the rightful duty of historians to truth and the rightful duty of leaders to propagandise. They agreed that during wartime in particular, the latter duty takes precedence.

According to de Tréglodé, martyrs offer the Vietnamese state 'a finished picture of the revolutionary ideal' that can never be tarnished.[117] Stories of child martyrs are especially effective because they encase in cultural amber a sense of national innocence and pride that is threatened by foreign aggression and protected by the sacrifices – violent if need be – of youth. In the popular Vietnamese mind-set it remains undesirable and unfortunate that children have to engage in conflict. However, this situation is born of desperate and intolerable circumstances for which foreign enemies, as opposed to patriotic comrades, must be condemned. Indeed, the domestic population, their culture and their child soldiers deserve praise and admiration for combating these enemies. It should be no surprise then that today there are parks, schools and theatres named after Le Van Tam, and the story of his fiery courage can be found in English language primers – much to the fright of western tutors. Students go on excursions to the grave of Vo Thi Sau, where they lay flowers, and a play was recently produced that tells of her glorious life and death. The area where Kim Dong was killed is now a heritage zone, and a major children's literature publishing house is named in his honour. In one region, poor students who have overcome the odds to succeed in high school are awarded the Ly Tu Trong medal. At the same time, the Vietnamese regime professes to be, 'committed to protecting children's rights and interests and facilitating children's exercise of those rights' particularly through education and socio-economic development.[118] Indeed, the Socialist Republic of Vietnam was one of the first countries to sign

---

[117] de Tréglodé, *Heroes and Revolution in Vietnam*, 111
[118] Child Rights International Network, 'VIETNAM: Children's Rights References in the Universal Periodic Review', (8 May 2009). Available at www.crin.org/resources/infoDetail.asp?ID=21681.

the UNCRC and the second to ratify it on 28 February 1990.[119] More importantly, it has made significant efforts to reduce abusive forms of child labour and there are no reports of children serving in the Vietnamese armed forces. This is worth noting not to highlight a heinous contradiction, but rather to illustrate the workable coexistence between a child soldier culture and a commitment to children's rights.

Conclusion

This chapter has examined what causes children to engage in armed conflict. It argues that there is little evidence to show that the problem of child soldiers is growing, but that the socio-economic factors of underdevelopment and marginalisation, along with the unruly nature of postmodern warfare, make it a persistent problem that has the potential to foster widespread insecurity. This chapter also makes a case for considering cultural factors when it comes to comprehending and addressing the problem of child soldiers. For instance, reading stories about child soldiers in Vietnam provides a means of engaging with the broader culture, of considering how that culture shapes conflict, and of understanding why my father went to war. To say that 'culture counts' when it comes to comprehending why children become involved in global conflict is not to make a slam-dunk case. Rather, it is like throwing up a three-pointer and watching the arc of the ball as it makes its way towards the hoop. The result is less emphatic, but more rewarding. Deeper cultural engagement militates against wayward and colonial interventions and opens up pathways for more measured and effective criticism. For example, reading and listening to stories about Vietnamese child heroes and martyrs highlights how precious independence is to the Vietnamese and the extent that they have gone to over the millennia to protect it. Delving into the Le Van Tam scandal may also offer a means for Vietnamese and non-Vietnamese alike to criticise the political manipulation of both child soldier stories and the general population in contemporary Vietnam.

[119] 'United Nations Treaty Collection', *treaties.un.org*, 28 June 2013. Available at http://treaties.un.org/Pages/ViewDetails.aspx?mtdsg_no=IV-11&chapter=4&lang=en.

This general framework for cultural engagement can be applied to other militarised and conflict-ridden societies. Horrific schoolyard shootings in the United States are often followed by worldwide condemnation of American gun culture and its impact on children. Such critics should be open-minded to the possibility that there are elements of gun culture that are embedded in American society and which are worthy of respect and preservation. For instance, the gun is arguably an important symbol of American individualism and serves as the ultimate protection against a society and a state that should never be fully trusted. These values are exemplified in the folk hero Davy Crockett, who from the age of eight supposedly expressed a desire go hunting with a rifle. This does not mean that there is no room to criticise the corporate and political power that promotes guns and violence for narrow material interests in the United States. Rather, deep cultural engagement adds force, sophistication and legitimacy to such criticisms. As has been demonstrated in this chapter, a light-handed approach to cultural intervention can coincide with deeper cultural engagement and is also valuable because it fosters a fuller understanding of oneself.

6 | Child forced migrants: bio-politics, autonomy and ambivalence

KIM HUYNH

Introduction

Children are on the move, covering great distances and facing daunting obstacles, increasingly without adults by their side. Fleeing conflict-ravaged and destitute regions of Latin America, children risk drowning, dehydration and imprisonment en route to the United States. From Africa and the Middle East, they are crossing the Mediterranean and hiding inside or under trucks and even on planes in the hope that Europe will fulfil promises of fraternity and civilisation that stretch back to the colonial age. In recent years, Afghan, Iranian, Iraqi and Sri Lankan children have risked their lives on overcrowded boats to reach far-flung destinations such as Australia and Canada. These movements are propelled by a mix of global, local and personal forces and raise fundamental questions of liberty and justice.

This chapter examines children's political exclusion and agency in the contemporary Age of Forced Migration.[1] The first section outlines the

---

[1] A number of alternative terms can be adopted to describe people who have been displaced by persecution and conflict. 'Humanitarian migrant' evokes an image of a person who has a claim to protection and assistance based on humane grounds. It was rejected because it does not sit well with the critical examination of humanitarianism that is to come. McNevin defines 'irregular migrants' as 'people whose movements are increasingly cast as illegitimate and/or unwanted (even though their labour may service the demands of the global economy) and whose plight is indicative of new global hierarchies of mobility'. While useful, this definition places too much emphasis on economic migration for the purposes of this chapter. To this end, 'forced migrant' has been adopted with the caveat that 'forced' does not deny the existence of agency or subjective decision-making on the migrant's part. The International Association for the Study of Forced Migration (IASFM) defines 'forced migration' as, 'a general term that refers to the movements of refugees and internally displaced people (those displaced by conflicts) as well as people displaced by natural or environmental disasters, chemical or nuclear disasters, famine, or development projects'. For an outline of forced migrant categories see: Forced Migration Online, 'What is Forced Migration?'. Available at www.forcedmigration. org/about/whatisfm/what-is-forced-migration; Anne McNevin, 'Ambivalence and

159

global dynamics of forced migration and develops explanations from Agamben and Fassin as to why liberal democracies are fearful of and fearsome towards unauthorised arrivals, especially children. However, the profound objectification and mistreatment of forced migrants does not mean that they are totally superfluous to contemporary politics in the sense that they have no place in or impact upon it. Rather, they are highly politicised as warnings to people both outside and within borders of what happens to those who do not belong. Moreover, drawing from the work of Anne McNevin, it is argued that forced migrants, both adults and children, retain and fashion a degree of political autonomy even in contexts where their power is tightly constricted and the outcomes of their actions are ambiguous. The second section focuses on the demographics of child forced migration and sets out the push, enabling and pulling factors that have contributed to their prominence. The third and fourth sections apply the insights from the first two sections to an Australian context in which the bio-political contest over the suffering and resistance of irregular migrant children reflects a much larger struggle over what it means to be a liberal democracy in the twenty-first century.

The Age of Forced Migration

Immediately after the Cold War, Mikhail Gorbachev envisioned a new world order in which, more and more, cooperation replaced force, globalisation yielded unprecedented growth, and human rights took precedence over state sovereignty.[2] In such a world fewer people would be compelled by conflict, persecution and hardship to flee from their homes. At the same time, the crumbling of ideologically constructed barriers would make it easier for asylum seekers to cross borders and find refuge. However, Gorbachev was no idealist, acknowledging in his 1991 Nobel Prize acceptance speech that '[t]he melting ice of the Cold War reveals old conflicts and claims, and entirely new problems accumulate rapidly'.[3] Forced migration was one such problem which,

Citizenship: Theorising the Political Claims of Irregular Migrants', *Millennium – Journal of International Studies* 41(2) (January 2013), 183.
[2] Mikhail Gorbachev, 'Nobel Speech', Nobelprize.org, 5 June 1991. Available at www.nobelprize.org/nobel_prizes/peace/laureates/1990/gorbachev-lecture.html.
[3] Ibid.

while not entirely new, grew rapidly in terms of both numbers and political significance.

The late 1980s and 1990s saw a profound increase in forced migration. According to the Office of the UNHCR, the global number of refugees grew from 11.9 million in 1985 to 14.7 million in 1989, and in 1992 reached a high of 17.8 million.[4] This figure fell to around 10 million after the post-Cold War conflicts in the former Yugoslavia and Afghanistan drew to a close; however, since then there has been an increase in instances of internal displacement and statelessness, largely due to high rates of intra-state conflict, state failure and environmental emergencies.[5] Forced migration in general is thus at a historic high with 35.8 million people being of concern to the UNHCR at the conclusion of 2012, the second highest number on record.[6]

The problem of irregular migration has also intensified, in that increasing numbers of people have absolutely no place to go. In the philosopher Hannah Arendt's terms, they have lost the 'right to have rights' or 'right to belong', upon which she insisted all others are predicated.[7] There are Rohingyas in Burma, Thailand and Bangladesh, Afghans in Pakistan and Iran, and South Sudanese and Somalis in Northern Kenya who have been displaced and alienated for generations. Many of the camps in which they hoped to reside temporarily have become permanent fixtures and yet remain highly insecure. Recent estimates put the number of refugees in protracted situations at 6.4 million across twenty-five countries overwhelmingly

---

[4] UNHCR Statistical Online Population Database. Available at www.unhcr.org/statistics/populationdatabase, data extracted: 22 August 2011.

[5] According to data collected by the UNHCR the number of stateless people rose from 559,107 in 2000 to 6,578,826 in 2009, falling back to 3,484,139 in 2010. However, the UNHCR stresses that the problem is difficult to quantify and estimates that statelessness may be as high as 12 million people. According to the Internal Displacement Monitoring Centre the number of IDPs rose from 16.5 million in 1989 to an estimated 27.5 million in 2010. This has meant that the population of concern to the UNHCR has increased from 23 million at the end of 1993 to 33.9 million at the end of 2011. UNHCR Statistical Online Population Database. Available at www.unhcr.org/statistics/populationdatabase: data extracted: 22 August 2011; Internal Displacement Monitoring Centre, 'Global IDP estimates'. Available at www.internal-displacement.org/publications/2013/global-overview-2012-people-internally-displaced-by-conflict-and-violence.

[6] UNHCR, 'Global Trends 2012', 5.

[7] Hannah Arendt, *The Origins of Totalitarianism*, 3rd edn (London: Allen & Unwin, 1967), 295.

located in the global south.[8] In light of the minuscule odds of formal resettlement, millions of migrants have found unauthorised ways to enter the global north. Those who succeed more often than not exist in the shadows with little prospect of becoming regularised. When captured by the authorities, they can be summarily deported or detained with little regard for due process and human rights.

The popular impression that arises from such statistics in rich industrialised countries is that they are being inundated by the developing world's flotsam and jetsam. However, the vast majority of refugees, 83 per cent, remain in their regions of origin.[9] Moreover, most of these people have no expectation of crossing continents, but instead want to return to secure homes. The UNHCR estimates that of the 42.5 million displaced people in the world, around 800,000 are in need of immediate resettlement, with the best and most durable solution for the rest being repatriation or reintegration into host communities.[10] Considering that the United States alone took in over half a million Vietnamese as part of the Orderly Departure Program after the Vietnam War, accommodating 800,000 people is by no means beyond the capabilities or interests of the world's wealthiest countries. However, instead of directly confronting this difficult but surmountable challenge, popular rhetoric in the global north constructs an existential threat posed by 42.5 million migrants who are either poised on the doorstep or already barging in. Within this fearful context, the EU, North America and Australia, amongst others, have constructed a new 'Wall around the West' and react with brutal calculating force against those who try to scale it.[11] The problem, again to paraphrase Arendt, is not one of space, but of political organisation.

Giorgio Agamben is among the most prominent thinkers who have sought to explain and critique the forms of political organisation that

---

[8] UNHCR, 'Global Trends 2012', 12. The UNHCR defines a protracted refugee situation as 'one in which 25,000 or more refugees of the same nationality have been in exile for five years or longer in any given asylum country'.

[9] Moreover, the fact is that rich nations play a critical role in shaping and exacerbating the problem of forced migration.

[10] UNHCR, 'Global Trends 2012', 19.

[11] Judith Kumin, 'Orderly Departure from Vietnam: Cold War Anomaly or Humanitarian Innovation?', *Refugee Survey Quarterly* 27(1) (1 January 2008), 104.

exclude forced migrants.[12] Agamben shares Arendt's premonition of refugees as the 'symptomatic group in contemporary politics'.[13] However, while she was preoccupied with the events of the twentieth century and the deportation and rejection of Jews in particular, Agamben contends that Arendt's dark vision only fully manifested itself on a global scale after the Cold War. Introducing his argument in straightforward terms, the east/west divide that demarcated political belonging during the later twentieth century has been replaced with a human/nonhuman divide. From the more optimistic Mikhail Gorbachev, or from democratic peace theory perspectives, this opens up the prospect of global unity, given that all of us belong to the club of humanity. Agamben, however, is deeply pessimistic about the prospects of encroaching humanitarianism. Despite all the chatter about the responsibility of liberal democracies to protect the rights and advance the liberties of others, he highlights the failure of Anglo–European countries to move beyond a form of identity politics that centres upon drawing distinctions between friends and enemies. This instinctive practice stretches back to the beginnings of human society when, by necessity, strangers were conceived of as enemies seeking to raid or kill the tribe.[14] Friend–enemy politics was most infamously promoted by Nazi philosopher and jurist Carl Schmitt. For Agamben, humanitarian virtues do not mark the transcendence of such distinctions and suspicions, but rather their exemplification; that is, the supposedly expansive human fraternity that is embodied in liberal democracies is predicated upon the conjuring-up of nonhuman enemies – those whose humanity can be lawfully disregarded and politically demonised – especially in the form of forced migrants.[15]

Forced migrants are thus critical to contemporary politics because their uncertain, solitary and wretched condition is the mirror in which liberal democratic states and citizens puff up and preen their sense of security, solidarity and civility. What makes this Age of Forced Migration particularly bleak is that there is no refuge for the enemies

[12] Giorgio Agamben, (trans. Daniel Heller-Roazen), *Homo Sacer: Sovereign Power and Bare Life* (Stanford, CA: Stanford University Press, 1998).

[13] Giorgio Agamben, (trans. Michael Rocke), 'We Refugees', *Symposium* 49(2) (1995), 114–19.

[14] Carl Schmitt, *The Concept of the Political* (Chicago, IL: University of Chicago Press, 1996); Jared Diamond, *The World Until Yesterday: What Can We Learn from Traditional Societies?* (New York, NY: Viking, 2012), 134, 210.

[15] Agamben, 'We Refugees', 114.

of twenty-first century liberal democratic states. Whereas being exiled
from a tribe, city-state or empire left open the possibility of finding
another place to belong, this prospect is closed off to those who have
been judged nonhuman. In effect, the exceptional condition that
Arendt ascribed to the Jews during World War II of being 'totally
superfluous', 'undeportable' and yet 'symptomatic to politics' is
becoming the norm for those trapped between borders and on the
margins of liberal democracies. For this reason, Agamben propounds
that modern politics is not inspired by Athens, but rather by Auschwitz;
and moreover that because of the infectious nature of this politics there
is no escape for any of us from the camp.[16]

Didier Fassin provides concrete and detailed accounts of some of
Agamben's sweeping claims via his examination of the bio-politics of
forced migration in France. In recent years the meaning of political
asylum, Fassin argues, has been radically warped.[17] The crumbling of
east/west divisions has meant that the refugee is no longer accepted and
held up as the heroic exile, prisoner of conscience or ideological trophy.
Instead, asylum is determined according to strict bio-political
determinations. It follows that the legitimacy of an asylum claim does
not turn on the existence of political persecution as determined by
interviews and testimony, but rather manifest evidence of the
'suffering body'.[18] The upshot for asylum seekers in states such as
France is that they must display marks of profound physical or
psychological abuse. In their bid for legal status such figures are,
Fassin argues, only recognised through their pathology.[19] Liisa
Malkki observes a similar reduction of social parameters to biological
ones in refugee camps where the distribution of humanitarian relief and
refuge is dependent upon the capacity of people to display scars.[20]
Importantly, migrants' bodies are not assessed to determine whether
they fulfil the membership requirements of citizenship, protection or

---

[16] Giorgio Agamben (trans. Kevin Attell), *State of Exception* (Chicago, IL:
University of Chicago Press, 2005).
[17] Didier Fassin and Estelle d'Halluin, 'Critical Evidence: The Politics of Trauma in
French Asylum Policies', *ETHOS* 35(3) (2007), 309.
[18] Didier Fassin, 'The Biologics of Otherness: Undocumented Foreigners and
Racial Discrimination in French Public Debate', *Anthropology Today* 17(1)
(2001), 3.
[19] Ibid., 4.
[20] Liisa H. Malkki, 'Speechless Emissaries: Refugees, Humanitarianism and
Dehistoricization', *Cultural Anthropology* 11(3) (1996), 383.

humanity. This would require acknowledging the voice and will of the stranger and conflicts with the primary purpose of asylum screening in the twenty-first century, which is to amplify the power and humanity of the host. The necessary evidence for a successful claim reflects the host's determination to protect only those whose physical and psychological depletion is so severe as to demonstrate the very absence of will that is required to be human and a citizen. The effect is to protect or 'let live' only those who are not human.

While attentive to how human rights and humanitarianism have created new categories of outsiders, McNevin's conception of the ways in which forced migrants' claims are deeply ambiguous offers a nuanced perspective of identity politics in the contemporary age.[21] She argues that Agamben's notion of power is reductive in that it overstates the potency and coherence of border security measures in liberal democracies as exercised by a multitude of actors: border police, officials, concerned citizens among others. At the same time, Agamben understates the potential of forced migrants to influence prevailing notions and expressions of liberty, obligation and citizenship.[22] Nor does McNevin fully embrace the opposing 'Autonomy of Migration' perspective which lauds migrants' persistent agency and subjective decision-making in all contexts.[23] Instead, the legal and political claims of forced migrants should be understood in terms of an 'ambivalence' that, while often severely constrained by sovereign power, has the potential to generate new forms of political belonging both within and across borders.[24] The next section explains how children became prominent in the Age of Forced Migration, and is followed by the final section, which explores the bio-politics and ambivalence of child forced migrants in Australia.

Children and the Age of Forced Migration

Children play a central role in the Age of Forced Migration both in terms of sheer numbers and political significance. In her pivotal 1996 Report on the 'Impact of Armed Conflict on Children', Graça Machel

---

[21] McNevin, 'Ambivalence and Citizenship', 182–200.   [22] Ibid., 188.
[23] Ibid., 184.
[24] For a similar argument see Giorgia Doná and Angela Veale, 'Divergent Discourses, Children and Forced Migration', *Journal of Ethnic and Migration Studies* 37(8) (2011), 1273–89.

estimated that around half of the people displaced by war were under the age of eighteen.[25] While there is significant regional variation, this accords with more recent UNHCR statistics, which estimate that children make up 44 per cent of refugees, 48 per cent of internally displaced persons (IDPs), and 55 per cent of stateless people.[26] Moreover, three years after the outbreak of hostilities in Syria, the UNHCR estimates that slightly over 50 per cent of people of concern to the Refugee Agency are children.[27]

There is also growing awareness of unaccompanied and separated children who are travelling to industrialised countries via irregular channels.[28] According to Bhabha, in 2004 around 8.8 per cent of the asylum claims in the United Kingdom were made by separated children.[29] The figure was similar and rising in the United States even while overall asylum claims were in decline.[30] In 2011, 17,700 asylum applications – up from 15,600 in 2010 – mostly from Afghans and Somalis were lodged by unaccompanied or separated children across sixty-nine countries.[31] This figure increased to 21,300 in 2012 and then 25,300 in 2013.[32] The profound marginalisation of such minors, who have limited support from adults and no place to call their own, has prompted Bhabha to refer to them as 'Arendt's children'.[33]

Not only are children being displaced on a massive scale, they are also confronting debilitating conditions. After being uprooted from

---

[25] Machel, 'Impact of Armed Conflict on Children', UNICEF (1996), 17.
[26] UNHCR, 'Global Trends 2012', 3.
[27] UNHCR, 'Syria Regional Refugee Response', Inter-Agency Information Sharing Portal. Available at http://data.unhcr.org/syrianrefugees/regional.php.
[28] 'Unaccompanied children' have separated from their parents or primary caregivers and are totally alone. 'Separated children' includes 'unaccompanied children' but also may be accompanied by extended relatives, friends or acquaintances.
[29] Jacqueline Bhabha and Nadine Finch, 'Seeking Asylum Alone: Unaccompanied and Separated Children and Refugee Protection in the U.K.', (November 2006), 22. Available at www.childmigration.net/files/SAA_UK.pdf.
[30] Jacqueline Bhabha and Susan Schmidt, 'Seeking Asylum Alone: Unaccompanied and Separated Children and Refugee Protection in the U.S.' *Journal of the History of Childhood and Youth* 1(1) (Winter 2008), 128.
[31] UNCHR, 'Global Trends 2012', 3.
[32] UNCHR, 'Global Trends 2013: War's Human Cost', 3. Available at http://unhcr.org/trends2013/.
[33] Jacqueline Bhabha, 'Arendt's Children: Do Today's Migrant Children Have a Right to Have Rights?' *Human Rights Quarterly* 31(2) (2009), 410–51.

their homes, children are more likely to face poor education prospects and future unemployment, alcoholism and domestic violence, all of which entrench hopelessness and anomie. As Cheney observed in Uganda, '[t]he children don't know their villages, they think that life is living in a camp'.[34] The potential for this sense of disenfranchisement to cross continents is evident in Somali refugee children who, because they came to the United Kingdom by way of East African camps, are referred to by other refugees as 'sijui', Swahili for 'I don't know' because this was how they replied when asked where they came from.[35]

The widespread and worsening condition of child forced migration stands at odds with the popularity of the UNCRC. The UNCRC was unanimously approved by the UNGA in 1989 without even requiring a vote and, with 194 states parties, is more widely adopted than any other treaty. On the face of it, this would suggest that child forced migrants are comprehensively protected by international law. However, as Boyden points out, 'far from being a positive step, early ratification has in many cases signified a public relations exercise – the countries that ratified quickly were often those with the least intention of implementing in full'.[36] The point being that states have adopted the UNCRC with alacrity in order to promote themselves to other states and their own citizens as being on the right side of the post-Cold War human/nonhuman divide. Ratification demonstrated reverence for the welfare of all children, which was 'an international gauge of a state's modernity and progress'.[37] Lee argues that during the 1990s the child and children's rights served as an 'integrative symbol' and unifying moral and political force for the international humanitarian community, citing Machel's declaration that children 'present us with a uniquely compelling motivation for mobilisation'.[38]

Referring to the same compelling motivation but from a more critical perspective, Fassin argues that humanitarian sentiments – especially around children – elicit a 'fantasy of a global moral community' that

---

[34] Cheney, 'Our Children Have Only Known War', 32.
[35] Deborah Sporton, Gill Valentine and Katrine Bang Nielsen, 'Post Conflict Identities: Affiliations and Practices of Somali Asylum Seeker Children', *Children's Geographies* 4(2) (2006), 212.
[36] Jo Boyden, *Families: Celebration and Hope in a World of Change* (Sydney: Doubleday, 1993), 3.
[37] Macmillan, 'The Child Soldier in North-South Relations', 39.
[38] Lee, 'Understanding and Addressing the Phenomenon of "Child Soldiers"', 7; Machel, 'Impact of Armed Conflict on Children', UNICEF (1996), 89.

enshrines rather than combats global inequality.[39] This is because children themselves, particularly those who are moving between borders, have proven to be superfluous. This is evident with respect to prevailing approaches to asylum claims – especially but not exclusively claims from children – which are not regarded as evoking basic human rights and duties, but rather, pleas from vulnerable victims for 'charity and generosity'.[40] The shift in perceiving refuge as a gift bestowed by benevolent states, rather than a duty – albeit with an element of self-interest in play – is reflected in a recent trend by which Organization for Economic Cooperation and Development countries are diverting funds away from foreign aid to pay for the accommodation and processing of asylum seekers within their territory or region.[41]

The politicisation of childhood in global affairs is not new. Wells asserts that since the nineteenth century, notions of childhood and the nation-state have been intricately connected.[42] She points out that modern governments are distinguished by their attempt to take greater control of the health and welfare of their populations. In so doing they have turned their attention to children, 'their conception, their gestation, their birth, their infancy, the contours of their normal and abnormal development'.[43] It follows that a nation-state that cannot protect its children loses legitimacy amongst other nation-states and within the humanitarian community. What distinguishes the politicisation of children in the twenty-first century is that this need to protect children who belong to the nation-state is mirrored by the need to harm those who do not.

Thus, in liberal democracies around the world, child forced migrants have been harmed and harnessed to create a political and moral division between the human 'us' and nonhuman 'them'. Children are by no

---

[39] Didier Fassin, *Humanitarian Reason: A Moral History of the Present* (Berkeley, CA: University of California Press, 2011), xii.

[40] Marita Eastmond and Henry Ascher, 'In the Best Interest of the Child? The Politics of Vulnerability and Negotiations for Asylum in Sweden', *Journal of Ethnic and Migration Studies* 37(8) (2011), 1196.

[41] Sabra Lane, 'Foreign Spending Boosted and Aid Money Capped for Onshore Asylum Costs', *AM*, ABC Radio National, 13 May 2013. Available at www.abc.net.au/news/2013–05–13/foreign-spending-boosted-and-aid-money-capped-for/4685104?section=business.

[42] Karen Wells, 'The Politics of Life: Governing Childhood', *Global Studies of Childhood* 1(1) (2011), 15–25.

[43] Ibid.,18.

means exempt from this division. Indeed the humanitarian devotion professed towards children by liberal democracies can quickly transform into fear and hate.[44] In Ireland for instance, the hysteria around a small number of babies of African descent led to a national referendum that overturned longstanding birth-right citizenship laws.[45] Shandy refers to the alarm surrounding these infants as depicting a 'particular sort of potent agency', evidence that the new-borns in question could 'impact the surrounding world'.[46] However, the impact upon these children is not self-generated, but rather insidiously imposed. The image and 'pre-verbal cries' of these 'babes in arms' are manipulated to be at best ignored and more often detested. In this way, child forced migrants become a 'malignancy to the body politic' from which citizens must be protected and against which they can unite.[47] Governments that promote their border security credentials and commitment to cultural stability can thereafter reap the political dividends.

The numerical prominence of children in the Age of Forced Migration can be attributed to push and pull factors. Poverty is one of the most discernible factors that push children to migrate. Children are highly prevalent among poor and marginalised populations, so much so that Castells argues that there has been a 'dramatic reversal of social conquests and children's rights'.[48] Specifically, there is an abundant supply of children from developing countries created by high birth rates, family breakdown and material destitution, which results in large numbers of children running away from their homes or being sold and trafficked.[49] Children are also pushed to migrate because of encroaching conflict and violence. Other chapters in this book deal with the development of 'new wars', which are fought through non-traditional means by non-traditional actors and for non-traditional ends. These wars often involve criminal syndicates and

---

[44] Klaus Neumann, 'The Politics of Compassion', *Inside Story*, 1 March 2012. Available at http://inside.org.au/the-politics-of-compassion/ (accessed 17 June 2014).

[45] Dianna J. Shandy, 'Irish Babies, African Mothers: Rites of Passage and Rights in Citizenship in Post-Millennial Ireland', *Anthropological Quarterly* 81(4) (October 2008), 803–31.

[46] Shandy, 'Irish Babies, African Mothers', 806.   [47] Ibid.

[48] Manuel Castells, *The Information Age: Economy, Society, and Culture, Volume III: End of Millennium* (New York, NY: Wiley, 1998), 162.

[49] Ibid., 163.

engulf civilian populations, including and especially children. Universal notions of childhood and rights have little currency in contexts that one author has described as 'roving orphanages of blood and flame'.[50] Importantly, as new wars have borne down on children, increasing numbers of children have sought a means of escape. For instance, the high number of Afghan minors claiming asylum in Europe during the early twenty-first century can be attributed to the Taliban's practice of abducting boys to serve in the army. The continuation of these asylum claims after the Taliban was removed from power reflects the threat of retribution should boy soldiers return home.[51]

The destination of child forced migrants is influenced by powerful pull factors. Castells asserts that a voracious demand is generated in many countries by the pervasive sexualisation of children and facilitated by globalised criminal networks that profit from their trade and exploitation.[52] This is underpinned by a market logic according to which children are a cheap and expendable resource and the regulation or obstruction of their movement is counter-productive to growth. Children are also drawn to rich industrialised countries because they have access to television, the internet and communications technology. Young people are increasingly aware of how others live, which impacts upon their perceptions of how they themselves should be living. North African children cite television and stories from those who made it across the Mediterranean as contributing to their vision of a European El Dorado that promises riches, education and freedom from traditional cultural constraints.[53] Similarly, Uehling illustrates how young migrants from Central America see Wal-Mart as an icon of the American dream.[54]

---

[50] Daniel Bergner, *In the Land of Magic Soldiers: A Story of Black and White in West Africa* (New York, NY: Farrar, Strauss and Giroux, 2003), 43.

[51] Bhabha and Finch, 'Seeking Asylum Alone: Unaccompanied and Separated Children and Refugee Protection in the U.K.', 24.

[52] For a discussion of child sexualisation see Emma Rush and Andrea La Nauze, 'Corporate Paedophilia Sexualisation of Children in Australia', *The Australia Institute*, Discussion Paper 90 (October 2006).

[53] Najat M'Jid, 'The Situation of Unaccompanied Minors in Morocco', 10. Paper presented at the 'Migration of Unaccompanied Minors: Acting in the Best Interests of the Child' Conference, 27–28 October 2005. Available at www.coe.int/t/dg3/migration/archives/Source/MalagaRegConf/MG-RCONF_2005_3_Report_Morocco_en.pdf. Cited in Watters, *Refugee Children*, 43.

[54] Greta Lynn Uehling, 'The International Smuggling of Children: Coyotes, Snakeheads, and the Politics of Compassion', *Anthropological Quarterly* 81(4) (October 2008), 849.

The aspirations of many Chinese have become so transnational that children who are reluctant to go abroad are chastised as having 'no great future'.[55] In these and many other cases the driving message is that although the journey may hold great dangers and difficulties, it is worth the risk.

Of course adults and children have always moved in search of security. However, these push and pull factors have coalesced in the Age of Forced Migration to create a context in which destitute and vulnerable individuals can repeatedly cross borders and even continents if they are desperate enough. Nazario provides a stark example of this precarious hyper-mobility in her account of unaccompanied children from Latin America trying to reunite with their mothers working in the United States by riding on the roof tops of freight trains.[56] In so doing they confront gang and state violence and endure acute hunger and thirst. Often the children are caught, imprisoned or deported, only to attempt the perilous journey again and again. In 2014, an estimated 60,000 unaccompanied children will flee their violent and poverty-stricken societies in Latin America, making their way to the United States.[57] In 2015, this figure is estimated to grow to over 100,000.[58] Koser's work is also important in this regard because it illustrates how families and entire villages of displaced Afghans living in exile in Pakistan can decide that the best hope for their collective future is to pool their resources and invest in a selected person or people – often young men – to travel across the world in search of asylum.[59] Commonly their journeys stretch over months or even years and are made up of both authorised – visa-sanctioned – and unauthorised – smuggler-assisted – components. Asylum seekers thereby become part of a mixed-migration flow in which they are not easily distinguished from other forced or economic migrants. This makes it even more difficult for governments and the UNHCR to discharge their protection responsibilities, and easier for

---

[55] Uehling, 'The International Smuggling of Children', 858.
[56] Sonia Nazario, *Enrique's Journey* (Melbourne: Scribe, 2006).
[57] Tom Ashbrook, 'U.S. Borders Swamped by Child Migrants', *Onpoint*, 9 June 2014. Available at http://onpoint.wbur.org/2014/06/09/child-migrants-border-patrol-mexico (accessed 19 June 2014).
[58] Ibid.
[59] Khalid Koser, 'Why Take the Risk? Explaining Migrant Smuggling', in Tariq Modood and John Salt (eds.), *Global Migration, Ethnicity and Britishness* (Basingstoke, Hampshire (UK): Palgrave Macmillan, 2011), 65–83.

forced migrants to be portrayed as greedy illegals who do not know their place.

To outline the global push, pull and enabling factors that influence child forced migrants is not to deny their autonomy of movement or to suggest that they have been swept up by a whirlwind of globalisation. Indeed, for Fass 'the loosening of youth from their moorings in the past is part and parcel of what globalization is all about'.[60] She stresses that, notwithstanding the perilous existence of child forced migrants, it is both inaccurate and disempowering to construe them as inert components in international mechanisms of change.[61] The often well-meaning western assumption that 'the normal state of a child's life is stability' denies children's dynamic agency.[62] Fass argues that child forced migrants should be lauded as rebels and entrepreneurs. Unlike their sedentary parents who 'cling to their homes and possessions', children on the move 'cling to hope of the future'.[63] The following case study highlights the hope embodied in child forced migrants against the backdrop of the severe violence committed against them by modern liberal democracies such as Australia.

The view from down under: nonhuman children

No problem has been more fiercely contested in twenty-first century Australian politics than the arrival of asylum seekers by boat. This is in part due to spikes in what the Immigration Department refers to as Illegal Maritime Arrivals (IMAs).[64] However, even when IMAs were at their highest, the pressure posed by asylum seekers upon the Australian government and community has been small compared to other industrialised countries such as Italy, Germany and Greece, let alone developing countries, for example, Pakistan and Kenya.[65] This has led some scholars to attribute the widespread fervour over boatpeople to a deep anxiety about whether Australia truly belongs in the region. This anxiety grows out of the country's failure to come to grips with the

---

[60] Paula S. Fass, 'Children in Global Migrations', *Journal of Social History* 38(4) (July 2005), 949.
[61] Ibid.   [62] Ibid., 937.   [63] Ibid.
[64] They were previously referred to as Suspect Unlawful Non-Citizens (SUNCs) who arrived on board Suspect Illegal Entry Vessels (SIEVs). The acronym that was used during the Rudd and Gillard Labour governments was IMA.
[65] UNHCR, 'Global Trends 2012', 15.

traumatic dispossession of its indigenous population and an uncertain standing as a white western outpost in Asia.[66] A more recent explanation relates to identity politics in post-Cold War Australia. McNevin points out the 'liberal paradox' at the core of not only contemporary Australian politics but also many other liberal democratic administrations, whereby an openness to the free movement of money coincides with a violent aversion to the free movement of people.[67] In explaining Australia's liberal paradox, successive administrations have offset the public insecurity caused by the denationalisation of the economy by promoting exclusionary forms of national identity. This push to renationalise the country has been evident on sporting fields, in class rooms and during commemorative occasions, but is most pronounced with respect to asylum seekers. The following examples illustrate how child forced migrants in particular have – in ways that echo the foreboding of Hannah Arendt – become both symptomatic figures in modern Australia and also totally superfluous.

The insecurity cast upon migrants to bolster a sense of security among Australians is most evident in efforts to deter asylum seekers from making their way to Australia by boat. It is important to recognise that until 2005 no formal distinction was made in Australia between minors and adults, despite Australia signing the 1951 UN Refugee Convention and the UNCRC. This distinguished it from other countries that instituted legal measures to identify child forced migrants and services in order to cater for their distinct needs. In making their way to Australian territory, however, adults and children alike have been turned back or transferred to isolated locations where legal protections, welfare provisions and public scrutiny are highly restricted. The deterrence logic and identity politics that underpin these measures and the objectification of child forced migrants are examined below.

As a matter of policy and with the general support of the populous, the conservative governments of John Howard (1996–2007) and Tony Abbott (2013-) have interdicted boats of asylum seekers at sea and

---

[66] Anthony Burke, *Fear of Security: Australia's invasion anxiety* (Port Melbourne: Cambridge University Press, 2008); Don McMaster, 'Asylum-seekers and the Insecurity of a Nation', *Australian Journal of International Affairs* 56(2) (July 2002), 279–90.

[67] Anne McNevin, 'The Liberal Paradox and the Politics of Asylum in Australia', *Australian Journal of Political Science* 42(4) (December 2007), 611–30.

turned them away regardless of whether children are aboard. According to their deterrence logic and strategy, such measures are necessary to protect citizens from migrants who have not undergone health and security checks, and are particularly critical in the aftermath of terrorist attacks. Acting as a Good Samaritan towards irregular arrivals is irrational and dangerous because of the 'upstream' consequences. Specifically, Australian compassion will be regarded as weakness by forced migrants and thereby attract more needy and persecuted people, many of whom pay smugglers to help them achieve their migration goals. It follows that everyone on IMAs – from the frail and elderly to helpless infants – is perceived as threatening to the security of Australians and their standard of living.

Politicians have also argued that deterrence is ultimately beneficial for the security of genuine forced migrants, particularly children. Days before announcing a policy by which all IMAs who were found to be refugees would be resettled by the Australian government in Papua New Guinea, the Labour Immigration Minister, Tony Burke, proclaimed that, '[t]he consequences for children are horrific and too often end in tragedy. There is no stronger argument for combating people smuggling with a serious regional approach than the impact on children.'[68] His logic was that if Australia is seen by forced migrants to be soft when it comes to protecting its borders or provides special treatment for child forced migrants, then this will encourage more parents to put their children's lives in peril via dangerous sea voyages. Of course, this assumes that forced migrants have safe and viable options other than coming to Australia. The logic of deterrence relies upon the objectification of forced migrants as mere means towards the state's ends. The politically malevolent end that underpins this logic, as conceived by Carl Schmidt, is that the creation of external enemies is the surest way to solidify the certainties of friendship within.

Klaus Neumann argues that even seemingly compassionate pleas for child forced migrants can have the effect of advancing an identity politics agenda that aggrandises the all-powerful 'Us' as asylum givers over the hapless 'them' as asylum seekers.[69] Specifically, the progressive case that is commonly made in favour of showing benevolence towards child

---

[68] Cited in Gemma Jones, 'Save Boat Babies', *The Herald Sun*, 9 June 2013, 4.
[69] Neumann, 'The Politics of Compassion'.

asylum seekers is based on the view that they, as vulnerable and dependent beings, had no choice in making the journey.[70] This may well understate the agency of children on the move. Just as critical is the corollary that adult asylum seekers, unlike children, have a distinct choice and therefore do not deserve compassion. Indeed, the logic that often follows is that adult asylum seekers in exercising that choice are taking advantage of humanitarian law and Australia's good will. The effect is to cast kind-hearted Australians as having the option of assisting children, but in the process detracting attention away from the asylum seekers' legitimate claims and Australia's obligations. In this vein, Neumann cites Didier Fassin's argument that humanitarian reason operates to govern and preserve precarious lives; that is, by militating against the questioning of inequality and exposing its root causes, the politics of compassion tends to enshrine or even exacerbate power disparities between those who belong and those who do not.[71]

Australia's deterrence of forced migrants does not only involve driving them away from its borders but also inflicting physical and psychological harm upon those whose claims are being assessed onshore. Mandatory detention has been a central pillar of Australian asylum policy since it was introduced in 1992 and requires that all asylum seekers who arrive without a visa be incarcerated throughout the application process. Consequently, children have been detained for years in isolated locations and under what Australia's human rights watchdog describes as 'cruel, inhumane and degrading' conditions that are 'fundamentally inconsistent' with the UNCRC.[72] In 2003, children in Australian Immigration Detention Centres (IDCs) had been detained on average. 619 days, with the longest period being almost five and a half years.[73] Moreover, a series of landmark cases passed down by the

---

[70] See, for instance, a comment from former Labour government minister Craig Emerson. Craig Emerson, 'Refugee Politics with Kim Huynh' *Emmo Forum*, Episode 14, 19 January 2014. Available at http://craigemersoneconomics.com/blog/2014/1/19/emmo-forum-ep-14-refugee-politics-w-kim-huynh.

[71] Neumann, 'The Politics of Compassion'.

[72] The Australian Human Rights and Equal Opportunity Commission, 'A Last Resort? National Inquiry into Children in Immigration Detention', (2004), 5–6. Available at www.humanrights.gov.au/publications/last-resort-national-inquiry-children-immigration-detention.

[73] Sev Ozdowski, 'An Absence of Human Rights: Children in Detention', Human Rights Law and Policy Conference, Melbourne, 17 June 2008. Available at www.uws.edu.au/equity_diversity/equity_and_diversity/tools_

High Court of Australia in 2004 affirmed that, in the absence of a bill of rights, asylum seekers could be lawfully detained indefinitely in harsh and inhumane conditions.[74] This is a stark example of the profound disempowerment of those who are bereft of what Arendt regarded as 'the right to have rights'. And it illustrates how the refugee condition is far more perilous and removed from human society than that of the criminal who is still afforded his or her humanity in the form of legal protections against indefinite detention. For Giorgio Agamben, the absolute power of the modern state is intrinsically linked to the absolute disempowerment of the forced migrant, a disparity that occurs not in spite of liberal democratic principles of countries like Australia, but rather because of them.

Recounting Shayan Badraie's ordeal serves to personalise the objectification of child forced migrants in Australia.[75] Five-year-old Shayan arrived with his family in 2000 from Iran to seek asylum. After being sent to Woomera IDC in outback South Australia, he witnessed riots and acts of self-harm that left him deeply disturbed. As a consequence, Shayan spent three months in hospital receiving treatment for post-traumatic stress disorder before being returned to a Sydney detention centre. He was later released into foster care without his family, who remained in detention. When questioned about the boy's plight, Immigration Minister Philip Ruddock intimated that his condition was due to the fact that he was being raised by his stepmother, not his biological mother.[76] In the media frenzy that followed, there were unfounded reports that Shayan's stepmother had stolen him and that he was being coached to refrain from eating and to draw disconcerting pictures so that his family could be allowed into the community. In another interview, Minister

and_resources/speeches_-and-_articles_by_dr_sev_ozdowski/
an_absence_of_human_rights_children_in_detention.

[74] In the *Al-Kateb* and *Al Khafaji* cases the High Court ruled that the government could use the 'aliens' power under s. 51 (xix) of the Australian Constitution to detain asylum seekers for as long as it deemed necessary. In the *Behrooz* case the Court declared that harsh and inhumane conditions was no defense to a charge of escaping from immigration detention.

[75] This story is recounted in Jacquie Everitt, *The Bitter Shore: An Iranian Family's Escape to Australia and the Hell They Found at the Border of Paradise* (Sydney: Macmillan, 2008). See also Debbie Whitmont, 'The Inside Story', *4Corners*, 13 August 2001. Available at www.abc.net.au/4corners/stories/2011/08/08/32885 32.htm.

[76] Margot O'Neill, *Blind Conscience* (Sydney: UNSW Press, 2009), 76.

Ruddock referred to Shayan as 'it': 'I understand it receives food and it receives liquids.'[77] This, he much later reflected, was the only action that he regretted during his time as Immigration Minister.[78] Yet he always maintained the logical necessity of his government's actions with respect to child asylum seekers: allowing them out of detention would mean separating them from their loved ones or releasing entire families into the community, which could undermine the deterrence value of mandatory detention. Neither option was acceptable.

Shayan's case illustrates the lengths that a liberal democratic state will go to in order to deter and exclude forced migrants. Furthermore, 'it' points to some of the discursive strategies that not only justify these measures, but dehumanise forced migrants for political gain. To this end, it is worth examining the politicisation of child forced migrants in the lead up to the 2001 national election. In October 2001, days after the election campaign was formally announced, an overcrowded fishing boat carrying 223 asylum seekers including fifty-six children, was intercepted by an Australian Navy vessel.[79] Machine guns were used to try to force the SIEV 4 (Suspect Illegal Entry Vessel) back to Indonesia. When the engine failed – most likely due to tampering by asylum seekers – the boat was boarded and towed around the Indian Ocean as Navy personnel awaited orders. The terrified asylum seekers held up their children to show that there were minors on board. When the stricken boat started to sink, children and adults alike were forced to

---

[77] Ibid.

[78] After having their initial application rejected the Badraies were granted protection visas. Shayan became the 'first child in Australia to be formally recognised as having his rights breached' under the UNCRC. Ibid., 78.
    The key provisions in the UNCRC are as follows:

- the best interests of the child shall be a primary consideration (Article 3(1));
- detention must be as a measure of last resort and for the shortest appropriate period of time (Article 37(b));
- children in detention have right to be treated with humanity and respect (Article 37(a), (c));
- children have the right to enjoy, to the maximum extent possible, development and recovery from past trauma (Articles 6(2) and 39);
- asylum-seeking and refugee children are entitled to appropriate protection and assistance (Article 22(1)).

[79] David Marr, 'Truth Overboard – the Story that Won't Go Away', *The Sydney Morning Herald* (28 February 2006). Available at www.smh.com.au/news/nati onal/truth-overboard–the-story-that-wont-go-away/2006/02/27/11410200236 54.html.

enter the water. While there remains some doubt over what the government knew and when, its most senior members were clearly eager to portray the asylum seekers as manipulative and threatening.[80] The migrants were, by extension, un-Australian in the sense that their values were utterly alien and contemptible, especially with regard to how they treated their own children. Immigration Minister Ruddock was the first to claim that, 'disturbingly, a number of children have been thrown overboard'.[81] The Foreign Minister added, '[t]hey're not types of people we want integrated in our community, people who throw children overboard. It's simply just appalled people in this country'.[82] Along similar lines, Prime Minister Howard expressed his anger and incomprehension at 'how genuine refugees would throw their children overboard'.[83] The asylum seekers were all rescued and transferred to Papua New Guinea to be processed as part of the 'Pacific Solution'. Eventually, the vast majority were found to be refugees and, having served their political purpose, quietly resettled in Australia.

The view from down under: re-humanising children

While there is strong evidence of the acute dehumanisation of child forced migrants in Australia, this process has not been as totalising as Agamben suggests. Nor has liberal democracy been harnessed at all times and in every way to erode the autonomy of outsiders. On the contrary, there have been significant instances of liberal politicians, advocates, and forced migrants themselves appealing to notions of human rights and the universal child in order to rescue forced migrants from the fringes.

One of the most influential individuals in the struggle for child forced migrants in Australia is a former federal parliamentarian, Petro Georgiou. Along with a small group of fellow Liberal Party backbenchers – the

---

[80] Andrew Herd, 'Amplifying Outrage over Children Overboard', *Social Alternatives* 25(2) (2006) 59–63. Available at www.uow.edu.au/arts/sts/bmartin/pubs/bf/06saHerd.html. Two parliamentary committee inquiries have been held into this incident. The 2002 'Select Committee for an inquiry into a certain maritime incident' and the 2004 'Senate Select Committee on the Scrafton Evidence'.

[81] Tracey Bowden, 'Navy Chief Enters Asylum Seekers Debate', *ABC 7:30 Report*, 8 November 2001. Available at www.abc.net.au/7.30/content/2001/s412083.htm.

[82] Ibid.   [83] Ibid.

Liberal Party constituting the main conservative party in Australia – Georgiou lobbied tirelessly to free child asylum seekers from detention. He appealed to progressive small-'l' liberal principles emphasising the sovereign person rather than the big 'L' variety, privileging the party and the state. This drew fierce criticism, especially from his own side of politics. One parliamentarian accused Georgiou of being a 'political terrorist' who wanted to undermine his own government. In what was their greatest achievement, Georgiou and his fellow dissenters pressured the government to release child asylum seekers and their families into the community in 2005. This involved bringing the Australian Migration Act more into line with the UNCRC so that children should only be detained 'as a measure of last resort'. For Georgiou, children's rights are self-evident and should speak for themselves. As he retired from a lifetime in politics, Georgiou reflected upon how getting children out from behind razor wire 'was not a huge step for humanity, but it was a step forward'.[84]

In the Australian community there has also been a groundswell of support for asylum seekers, reflected in the formation of a handful of voluntary organisations that focus exclusively on promoting the welfare of child forced migrants. Most prominently, ChilOut was formed in August 2001 by parents and citizens who had seen Shayan Badraie's breakdown on television. ChilOut seeks to increase public awareness of what is happening to children in detention with a view to improving their conditions and securing their release. It lobbies for changes to policy and law so that 'Australia treats every child seeking asylum with dignity and in line with our international obligations'.[85] O'Neill chronicles the astonishing dedication of refugee advocates in a wide range of Australian organisations, including those colloquially – and somewhat mockingly – referred to as 'doctors' wives'.[86] These middle-class, middle-aged women who often lean towards the ideological right and have never been politically active, are some of the most fervent champions of child asylum seekers in Australia.[87] O'Neill records the combined humanitarian and patriotic sentiments of the advocates at witnessing 'deliberate cruelty towards powerless people': '[i]t leaves

[84] Petro Georgiou, 'Petro Georgiou: It's War Without Blood', speech to Cranala in Melbourne, 14 April 2010. Available at www.culturaldiversity.net.au/index.php?option=com_content&view=article&id=551:petro-georgiou-its-war-without-blood&catid=14:human-rights-articles&Itemid=24.
[85] ChilOut, 'Our Goals'. Available at www.chilout.org/our-goals.
[86] O'Neill, *Blind Conscience*.   [87] Ibid., 2.

you feeling angry and ashamed. Because it was state-sponsored, it also leaves you feeling a little scared. Not here. Not in "fair go" Australia.'[88] Such women visit and succour youth in detention centres, smuggle in phone cards and food, raise funds for legal appeals and petition their members of parliament. Their dedication, at times bordering on obsession, has strained their relationships with family and friends. In many cases they have become convinced that the child forced migrants are no different from their own. They represent a valuable and powerful manifestation of the politics of compassion.

The notion of the child as the ward of humanity has been heavily promoted by asylum seeker advocates. Indeed, child forced migrants have become the key battleground on which the rights of other forced migrants might be secured. It follows that if the battle for children cannot be won, there is little hope for adults. In a 2011 effort to deter asylum seekers, the Australian government devised a 'swap scheme' in which 800 boatpeople who reached Australian territory would be transferred to Malaysia for processing. Even if found to be refugees, none of these 800 people would be resettled in Australia. In return, Australia would accept 4,000 refugees from Malaysia. Criticising this new deterrence measure, a Greens senator claimed that the 'big question' for Australians is, 'What happens to children at the centre of all of this? Why are we using children as pawns in this awful human chess game?'[89] The 'Malaysia Solution' was challenged and a landmark ruling in the High Court found that sending asylum seekers to countries where they would not be properly processed and protected contravened Australian and international law.[90] Importantly, because one of the plaintiffs was a sixteen-year-old unaccompanied minor, the Court stipulated that he/she was under the guardianship of the Immigration Minister, who was required to act in the child's best interest. While this requirement was later circumvented through legislative amendment, the campaign against the Malaysia Solution nonetheless illustrates that concerted appeals to liberal humanitarian

[88] Ibid., 1–2.

[89] Barrie Cassidy, 'Greens to Pursue Manus Island Inquiry', *Insiders*, Australian Broadcasting Corporation, 21 August 2011. Available at www.abc.net.au/insiders/content/2011/s3298357.htm.

[90] This leaves Australian law in the position where an asylum seeker can be theoretically detained indefinitely under inhumane conditions in Australia, but cannot be deported to another country where their protection is under question.

principles have had a substantial impact on politics and law in Australia, and that children have been critical to this process. Indeed, this more positive politicisation of children on the grounds of compassion reflects a variation of Fassin's observations about contemporary asylum claims, whereby childhood is likened to the 'suffering body' as a testimony that cannot be dismissed.[91] The fact that these children are protected and allowed to 'let live' – using Agamben's term – because they are incomplete and diminished humans reveals how advocates can push liberal democratic states to live up to their own principles.

A similar assessment can be made of child forced migrants who have promoted their own rights and those of other forced migrants by appealing to humanitarian concepts and ideals. An instructive example from the Australian political context involves the *Jaya Lestari 5*, a boat carrying 255 Tamil asylum seekers that was intercepted by the Indonesian Navy in October 2009 en route to Australia. The boat was forced to dock at the Javanese port of Merak as a result of a direct request from the Australian Prime Minister, Kevin Rudd. Rudd had been warned of the boat's movements and was concerned about the coverage it would generate if it reached Australia. However, when the *Jaya Lestari 5* docked at Merak, the boatpeople refused to disembark and the adults subsequently went on a hunger strike. One of the key figures in the crisis that ensued was nine-year-old Brindah. In an impassioned plea for assistance that was broadcast through the international media she evoked the image of the universal child in need: 'We are Sri Lankan

---

[91] Fassin, 'The Biologics of Otherness: Undocumented Foreigners and Racial Discrimination in French Public Debate', 3. Of course the veracity of an asylum seeker's claim to being a child can be doubted, sometimes with great bio-political force. In 2011 the popular newspaper, *The Herald Sun*, ran a front page article with secret pictures that it had obtained of asylum seekers who claimed to be children but showed, 'obvious signs of ageing, including crow's-feet, wrinkles around their eyes and receding hairlines'. A forensic anatomist was enlisted to assert that the asylum seekers were not juveniles. Refugee lawyer David Manne raised concerns about the improper processing of the asylum seekers and the hysteria around them, referring to 'deeply institutionalised suspicion, bordering on paranoia'. Anne Wright, 'Asylum Seekers Pretending To Be Teenagers for Faster Processing', *The Herald Sun*, 16 May 2011. Available at www.heraldsun. com.au/news/asylum-seekers-pretending-to-be-teenagers-for-faster-processing/ story-e6frf7jo-1226056354628; Andrew Tillett, 'Asylum Seekers "Lie About Age"', *The West Australian*, 7 January 2011. Available at http://au.news.yahoo. com/thewest/a/-/breaking/8607237/asylum-seekers-lie-about-age/.

refugees, please take us to your country, we can't live in Sri Lanka. Please help us and save our lives. We are your children, please think of us, please, please.'[92]

While Brindah exercised a great deal more power than Shayan Badraie, the mixture of will and compulsion along with the ultimate efficacy of her and other child forced migrant pleas are difficult to assess for at least three reasons. Firstly, it is unclear to what extent these children assert their own considered claims and the extent to which their voices are mediated through their families and communities. Brindah was probably coached to some extent by her parents into making her eloquent statements, which for some people in the popular media made them and her less legitimate. Secondly, the capacity of child forced migrants to express their helplessness and beg for mercy is arguably antithetical to political agency. However, if they are playing up to humanitarian preconceptions of constituents in receiving countries and trying to evoke sympathy, this might equate to a form of 'victimcy' or everyday resistance as outlined in Chapter 2. Thirdly, agency itself can be detrimental in the sense that child forced migrants who demonstrate an ability to shape their own destiny along with others risk losing the sympathy and care commonly associated with being 'children' and 'forced'. This is especially apparent when children engage in hunger strikes, lip-sewing or protest activities that can alienate them from the people they are appealing to.

The vexed nature of child forced migrants' agency is illustrated in the *Jaya Lestari 5* crisis. Despite Brindah's global exposure, the stand-off between the boatpeople and the governments of Indonesia and Australia lasted for six months, during which time one of the boatpeople died. In April 2010, the protesters were forcibly moved to an Australian-funded detention centre in Indonesia from where they were eventually transferred to a range of resettlement countries. The very fact that the crisis was prolonged demonstrates the potential power of child forced migrants' appeals to human rights, but also their ultimate limitations. This case thus illustrates McNevin's point about the problem with fixating on either the preponderance of bio-political power or the inalienability of migrants' autonomy in

---

[92] Geoff Thompson, 'Asylum Seekers Issue Personal Plea to PM', *AM*, ABC Radio National, 15 October 2009. Available at www.abc.net.au/am/content/2009/s2 714594.htm.

circumstances that are deeply ambivalent because they incorporate such desperation, compulsion, will and despair.[93]

Ambivalent conclusions

This chapter has illustrated how forced migrants have become symptomatic figures in contemporary politics and how children are symptomatic forced migrants. The struggle to define, secure and liberate such children aligns with fundamental questions of 'Who belongs?' in liberal democracies. To argue, however, that children have been at the centre of this political struggle is not to say that they have been active and free agents. Indeed, the twenty-first century has seen the profound objectification and displacement of child forced migrants as threats, victims, aliens and pathologies. At the same time their exclusion is not so complete as to make politics, defined as a contest of empowered agents, impossible. An examination of contemporary Australian politics highlights the extreme material, legal and rhetorical lengths that a liberal democracy will go to in order to – as Giorgio Agamben puts it – *ban* child forced migrants and thereby bolster its corporate identity. Yet politicians, Australian civil society – both individuals and organisations – and child forced migrants themselves have rallied and, to paraphrase Petro Georgiou, made small steps forward for humanity.

The bill that Georgiou initiated stipulating that children should only be detained as a matter of last resort was followed in 2008, after a change of government, by 'Key Immigration Detention Values'. According to these values children and where possible their families would not be detained in detention centres, and indefinite or otherwise arbitrary detention was unacceptable.[94] Since then, a rise in IMAs has meant that these values have been pushed aside by the logic of deterrence. As a consequence, child forced migrants have again been transferred to inhospitable camps in Nauru and Papua New Guinea where they will stay for potentially indefinite periods of time so as to

---

[93] McNevin, 'Ambivalence and Citizenship', 184.
[94] Department of Immigration and Citizenship, 'Key Immigration Detention Values'. Available at www.immi.gov.au/managing-australias-borders/detention/about/key-values.htm. It is worth noting that the first 'value' is, 'Mandatory detention is an essential component of strong border control.'

prove to others – both outside and inside Australia – that IMAs receive 'no advantage' and that the Australian government will 'Stop the Boats' at all costs.[95] According to government statistics, as of February 2013 there were 1,062 children in IDCs and makeshift detention centres known as Alternative Places of Detention (APODs).[96] The fact that every step forward for humanity carries with it the potential for going backwards, and vice versa, affirms the ambivalent situations in which forced migrants act in the post-Cold War world. The challenge for them, and for advocates and scholars, is not only to recognise and navigate through this ambivalence, but also to harness it 'as a political resource, rather than a strategic handicap'.[97]

[95] Debbie Whitmont and Janine Cohen, 'No Advantage', *4Corners*, 29 April 2013. Available at www.abc.net.au/4corners/stories/2013/04/29/3745276.htm.
[96] Department of Immigration and Citizenship, 'Immigration Detention Statistics', Available at www.jrs.org.au/files/documents/test/Resources/fact_sheets__ immigration_detention_values.pdf.
[97] McNevin, 'Ambivalence and Citizenship',185.

7 | Children and peace building: propagating peace

KATRINA LEE-KOO

Children and young people must play a key role in [the peace] process – not only because peace and security are basic ingredients for the full realization of children's rights, but because children are such a large proportion of the world's people.[1]

Introduction

In October 2012, a Taliban assassin boarded a girls' school bus in Pakistan's Swat Valley. The gunman asked: 'Which one of you is Malala?' When the fifteen-year-old Malala Yousafzai was identified, she was shot in the face. This child had been targeted for assassination; she was a threat to the Taliban because she deigned to believe that her homeland might be better than it is, and because her activism had the power to influence others. Prior to the attack, Malala had been a long-time activist for girls' rights to education in Pakistan. When the Taliban issued an edict banning girls from school in her region, she and many of her classmates continued to attend. She had expressed her views as a blogger for BBC Urdu and became the subject of a *New York Times* documentary about her life in the Swat Valley.

Though a child, Malala understood conflict. She wrote on her blog in January 2009:

I had a terrible dream yesterday with military helicopters and the Taleban. I have had such dreams since the launch of the military operation in Swat. My mother made me breakfast and I went off to school. I was afraid going to school because the Taleban had issued an edict banning all girls from attending school.[2]

---

[1] UNICEF, *Machel Study 10-Year Strategic Review* (2009), 172.
[2] Malala Yousafzai, '"Saturday 03 January: I Am Afraid" – Diary of a Pakistani Girl', *BBC News*, 19 January 2009. Available at http://news.bbc.co.uk/2/hi/south_asia/7834402.stm.

185

As she wrote her blog, the Pakistani Army and the Taliban battled for control of her homeland and the Taliban in particular targeted civilian women and girls for gender-based violence. During the conflict, Malala had witnessed the public shooting of celebrated Pakistani female dancer Shabana,[3] and Malala herself was the victim of several threats of violence. This reinforced her already well-established and vocal commitment to defy the conflict that engulfed her community and seek a better future for herself and her schoolmates. She was later quoted as saying: 'They cannot stop me . . . I will get my education' and 'I would like to be a politician. Our country is full of crisis . . . I would like to . . . serve the nation.'[4]

Since her recovery from major surgery following her attack, Malala, still fifteen years old, has begun to fulfil that promise. With the support of others she established the Malala Fund, which provides financial support to the families of Pakistani girls who wish to attend school. With the attention of the global media, she has also become an icon for girls' rights, universal education, peace and the power of individual activism. She has received the Nobel Peace Prize, Pakistan's first National Youth Peace Prize, and has been named one of *Time* magazine's 2013 one hundred most influential people.

There is no doubt that Malala's story is extraordinary. It is not the commonplace experience of children living amidst conflict. Unlike most children living in conflict zones, Malala is given unique access to the global stage and support from the international community to advance her agenda. Yet, while her experience may be uncommon in this regard, the theme of her story is not, and it demonstrates a familiar and clear point: children do imagine peace. Moreover, they strive for it. They may not have the opportunities, support, or even the intelligence and determination of Malala, but they have demonstrated the capacity to be peace builders and to contribute to cultures of peace within their societies. These children may not be nominated for peace

---

[3] Dean Nelson and Emal Khan, 'Taliban Underlines Its Growing Power with Killing of "Dancing Girl" in Pakistan', *The Telegraph*, 11 January 2009. Available at www.telegraph.co.uk/news/worldnews/asia/pakistan/4217690/Taliban-underlines-its-growing-power-with-killing-of-dancing-girl-in-Pakistan.html.

[4] Quoted in Marie Brenner, 'The Target', *Vanity Fair*, April 2013. Available at www.vanityfair.com/politics/2013/04/malala-yousafzai-pakistan-profile.

prizes, but they exercise the agency they possess – often supported by others – to contribute to everyday peace. The other girls on Malala's school bus that October afternoon, and the millions of children around the world who form children's clubs and youth forums, who challenge the entrenched and violent views of older generations, or who simply seek to survive and protect others amidst conflict are examples of the positive and enduring role that some children can play in building peace.

Yet while this is true, it is important not to universalise Malala's story. It would be incorrect to present children as innately peaceful; such claims only reinforce unhelpful and untenable stereotypes of children's real-life experiences in conflict zones. It is similarly important not to romanticise children's agency with regards to their peace building capacities. As this book has argued, children have agency. However, as in wartime, children's agency during times of conflict transformation is contingent upon the action of adults, the behaviour of their peers, the extent and nature of the violence around them, their own personal circumstances and experiences, and their evolving capacities. Thus their agency as peace builders exists in a dynamic and often simultaneous relationship with their other experiences in conflict – as victims and witnesses of war and, possibly, as perpetrators of violence.

Consequently, there is just as much capacity for children – and young people – to use that activism not to build peace, but instead to support the re-ignition of conflict.[5] For example, in the aftermath of Timor Leste's 2002 independence, a major threat to the peace was the proliferation of male-dominated youth gangs. High unemployment and poverty, political disenfranchisement, limited educational opportunities and social manipulation of gendered identities led one analyst to suggest that '[i]t's hardly surprising that seven out of ten young men find their way to the various clubs and gangs'.[6] This culminated in crisis in 2006 when widespread street violence broke out across Timor Leste between so-called eastern and western gangs, causing the destruction of 6,000 homes in gang-related violence.

---

[5] Lyndsay McLean Hilker and Erika Fraser, 'Youth, Exclusion, Violence, Conflict and Fragile States', Report Prepared for DFID's Equity and Rights Team, 30 April 2009, 4. Available at www.gsdrc.org/docs/open/CON66.pdf.

[6] Ausaid, 'East Timor Youth Status', *Focus*, June–September 2008. Available at www.ausaid.gov.au/publications/focus/june08/focus_June08_03.pdf.

Timor Leste-based social worker Justin Kaliszewski was quoted as saying: 'many young people are resorting to violence because they don't know any other way of achieving political change'.[7] Such comments speak of exclusion and missed opportunities to engage children and young people in political change in positive and peaceful ways.

Whether as contributors or spoilers, this chapter argues first that children are central to the success of sustainable peace. If the values of peace in a post-conflict society are to endure beyond the present adult population, it will require today's children to transmit it to tomorrow's generations. To phrase this in terms of a generational, fecund conceit, children are the flowers of fruiting trees; they already possess the individual capacity which, when nurtured, will become the fruit that sustains and propagates a balanced and peaceful society into the future.

Secondly, this chapter argues that children are capable peace builders. As will be demonstrated, children can and do contribute to the everyday practices of peace which, in turn, provide the foundation for a strong and organic culture of peace. The UNGA declared the first decade of the twenty-first century to be the 'International Decade for a Culture of Peace and Non-Violence for the Children of the World'. In so doing the UN described a culture of peace as the 'values, attitudes, modes of behaviours and ways of life that reject violence and prevent conflicts by tackling their root causes to solve problems through dialogue and negotiation among individuals, groups and nations'.[8] In this sense, building a culture of peace can be performed through simple and informal everyday acts such as going to school, talking to others, impromptu play, or dreaming of the future. It is also performed through formal and adult-facilitated activities such as joining youth groups or clubs, participating in peace forums, or petitioning leaders for change. These activities can play an important role in both negative and positive peace. They can contribute to breaking cycles of violence in post-conflict zones by discouraging children from reigniting conflict and instead encouraging children to invest in their community and its

---

[7] Anne Barker, 'Drugs fuelling East Timor Gangs, Youth Workers Say', *ABC, The World Today*, 30 October 2006. Available at www.abc.net.au/worldtoday/content/2006/s1776961.htm.

[8] UN, 'Building a Culture of Peace for the Children of the World', (2001). Available at www.un.org/events/UNART/panel_culture_of_peace04.pdf.

future. Furthermore, it creates the circumstances which enable human security and personal safety, justice and reconciliation.[9]

Finally, this chapter argues that both local and international adult communities need to support and facilitate children's roles as peace builders. This requires not just advocacy on behalf of children, but action to empower children to become responsible custodians of peace.[10] The relationship between children and peace therefore operates in both directions: peace shapes the opportunities that children have to live healthy, happy and safe lives where their rights are protected, while children shape the possibility that peace will exist and persist beyond current adult generations. In short, this chapter argues that far from the high-stakes end of internationally sponsored formal peace negotiations, peace is found equally in the everyday – the primary location of children – where a commitment to supporting children as peace builders is akin to propagating peace.

This chapter begins by identifying the gaps in the literature with regards to children and peace building. It considers the current state of significant literature on peace building, which dedicates little theorising to the role of children, while the literature on children and conflict dedicates little space to the question of children's role in peace building. It further notes that the dominance of the liberal peace project, outlined in Chapter 3, stifles curiosity about the specifics of local and everyday peace building, instead preferring to focus upon the global and universal values of liberal peace. Where children are considered in either of these literatures it is in two guises: firstly, in the liberal humanitarian view developed in Chapter 3, as victims of conflict whose protection can be facilitated by peace or, secondly, in a realist view, as spoilers of peace – unrehabilitated youth who have the capacity to destroy hard-won peace. After challenging this literature, this chapter then moves on to theorise the everyday role that children can and do play in peace building. It highlights the emerging research that evidences children's positive role in peace building activities, and examines recent international efforts to facilitate children's participation. In doing so it considers the

---

[9] Johan Galtung, *Peace by Peaceful Means: Peace and Conflict, Development and Civilisation* (London: Sage, 1996), 31–3.

[10] Stephanie Schwartz, *Youth in Post-Conflict Reconstruction: Agents of Change* (Washington, DC: United States Institute of Peace Press, 2010), 23.

question of what participation might mean for children and the societies in which they live, and how it can best be achieved.

Searching for children in international peace building

Building a sustainable peace – one that endures beyond the present generation – is a major challenge for the international community. In 2009, the World Bank claimed that 40 per cent of all conflicts reignite within the first decade of peace.[11] This highlights the need for concerted international effort focused not just on ending conflict, but upon post-conflict peace building. Since the 1992 publication of former UN Secretary-General Boutros Boutros-Ghali's *An Agenda for Peace*, this has been an agenda increasingly – though not always consistently – spearheaded by the UN. Most recently, the December 2005 establishment of the UN Peace Building Commission (UNPBC) has taken on the role of coordinating global peace building efforts. The Commission's mandated peace building responsibilities are defined as coordinating and advising on integrated strategies for post-conflict peace building and recovery; focusing on reconstruction, institution-building, and the foundation for sustainable development; and developing international best practices for international involvement in post-conflict societies.[12] This suggests a serious attempt to institutionalise international peace building activities at the global level. The question for this chapter is how well children, and children's rights, have been mainstreamed into this agenda.

It is important to keep in mind that peace building is a process which is distinct from other UN activities such as peace making, peace keeping, or peace enforcing.[13] In May 2007 the UN Secretary-General's Policy Committee described peace building as involving:

a range of measures targeted to reduce the risk of lapsing or relapsing into conflict by strengthening national capacities at all levels for conflict

---

[11] The World Bank, 'Crisis Impact: Fragile and Conflict-affected Countries Face Greater Risks', (2 October 2009). Available at http://web.worldbank.org/ WBSITE/EXTERNAL/NEWS/0,,contentMDK:22337380~pagePK:64257043~ piPK:437376~theSitePK:4607,00.html.

[12] See UN Peace Building Commission, 'Mandate of the Peacebuilding Commission'. Available at www.un.org/en/peacebuilding/mandate.shtml.

[13] See Alex J. Bellamy and Paul D. Williams, *Understanding Peacekeeping*, 2nd edn (Cambridge: Polity, 2010), 14.

management, and to lay the foundations for sustainable peace and development. Peacebuilding strategies must be coherent and tailored to the specific needs of the country concerned, based on national ownership, and should comprise a carefully prioritized, sequenced, and therefore relatively narrow set of activities aimed at achieving the above objectives.[14]

Peace building, in its idealised type, is therefore dedicated to addressing the social, political and economic triggers that enable conflict in any conflict-prone setting. Moreover, it is a process that is designed to be specific to the context of a local conflict, has substantial input and ownership by the local populations, and pursues a focused and achievable agenda. Yet, as the field has developed – both in theory and in practice – the art of peace building has become contested. Particularly in the post-9/11 world, struggles between key stakeholders for the vision, the control, and the implementation of the peace building agenda have led to re-questioning of how to achieve sustainable peace.[15] These struggles suggest contestation at the ontological heart of peace building between global and local agendas, liberal and non-liberal visions, and top-down and bottom-up approaches.

Critical scholars argue that contemporary UN and international peace building practices have tipped the balance in favour of the ambitions and visions of the global north. They argue that there has been a co-option of the peace building agenda by the liberal peace project. This project has distorted the international peace building priorities and goals towards global, top-down, institutional and bureaucratic programming for peace building. While the rhetoric of local ownership, sustainability and context specificity remains present in the discourse, the practice, critical scholars argue, has become much more technocratic in its approach.[16] In this sense, local specificity is allowed so long as it does not disrupt the primary liberal vision of a post-conflict society whose practices are democratic, whose values are liberal, and whose economy can be eventually integrated into the global marketplace. Consequently, 'what is being constructed [as peace building] is ... a liberal peace led by hegemonic powers, who may be concerned more to stabilize a world

---

[14] UN Peacebuilding Support Office, 'UN Peacebuilding: An Orientation', (September 2010), 49. Available at www.un.org/en/peacebuilding/pbso/pdf/peacebuilding_orientation.pdf.
[15] Oliver Ramsbotham, Tom Woodhouse and Hugh Miall, *Contemporary Conflict Resolution*, 3rd edn (London: Polity, 2011), 230.
[16] Newman, '"Liberal" Peacebuilding Debates', 42.

order dominated by the rich and powerful than to enable a liberating transformation out of violence'.[17] Newman, Paris and Richmond describe this as a problem-solving and policy-oriented approach to peace building that seeks merely to redirect the path of ongoing problems within an existing global system; its emphasis is on improving the coordination and efficiency of actors and approaches[18] rather than reconceptualising the nature of peace itself. While these activities are labelled 'peace building', Richmond argues that they should more accurately be referred to as 'state-building'.[19] In this sense, the UN's bureaucratic and institutionalised approach to peace building provides little opportunity to stray from the global liberal peace project. This has the potential to decouple peace building from a local emancipatory ethic.[20] In practice, this threatens the capacity for peace building efforts to have local ownership and therefore to persist beyond any international presence that drives the agenda – a point most recently demonstrated in Iraq and Afghanistan.[21]

Building upon this critique, critical scholars argue that 'peacebuilding should reflect and be a product of a negotiated discursive practice and not the outcome of a technically defined and externally imposed blueprint'.[22] Critical scholars therefore advocate a return to Johan Galtung's early definition of peace building as a process that involves identifying the root causes of conflict and supporting the capacities of local actors to build enduring cultures and structures of peace.[23] A bottom-up approach to international peace building is therefore driven by an ethic of facilitating agency within conflict-affected communities. Through co-operation and assistance it seeks to build agency within local communities to design and implement a context-specific and inclusive peace. Similarly, it is an approach that

---

[17] Ramsbotham, Woodhouse and Miall, *Contemporary Conflict Resolution*, 232.
[18] Edward Newman, Roland Paris and Oliver P. Richmond, 'Introduction', in Edward Newman, Roland Paris and Oliver P. Richmond (eds.), *New Perspectives on Liberal Peacebuilding* (Tokyo: United Nations University Press, 2009), 3–25, 23.
[19] Oliver P. Richmond, 'Becoming Liberal, Unbecoming Liberalism: Liberal-Local Hybridity via the Everyday as a Response to the Paradoxes of Liberal Peace building', *Journal of Intervention and Statebuilding* 3(3) (2009), 330.
[20] Newman, '"Liberal" Peacebuilding Debates', 38.
[21] Ramsbotham, Woodhouse and Miall, *Contemporary Conflict Resolution*, 230.
[22] Ibid., 231.
[23] Johan Galtung, *Peace by Peaceful Means, Peace and Conflict, Development and Civilization*, 271.

considers local cultural values and sensitivities as crucial factors in designing a legitimate peace. This does not make the international community irrelevant, but it does suggest a fundamental shift in its peace building role from architect to partner. It implies 'a grassroots, bottom-up activity involving engaging with societies, cultures and identities'.[24] Thus for critical scholars, peace building is a necessarily emancipatory practice.[25] It is driven by immanent critique – 'a critique of an existing order from within, rather than relying on an ahistorical point of reference'.[26] This approach encourages a deliberative and inclusive process that includes multiple visions of peace and a range of invested stakeholders.

In practice, international peace building is therefore about striking a balance. This balance is between the norms and goals of the international community and the needs and values of the local community. Undeniably, this balance is not easy to strike: this is particularly the case when the two are in contradiction. On the one hand, an internationally designed peace building programme that claims to be universal and is externally imposed may be critiqued as 'formulaic, top-down and ethnocentric'.[27] On the other hand, it is important not to romanticise the local; as with all politics, local cultures can be 'sites of power asymmetry, patriarchy and privilege'[28] that may readily marginalise disempowered groups such as children. Like the concept of childhood discussed in Chapter 1, there is a clear tension between universalised conceptualisations of peace and peace building claimed by a liberal agenda, and competing ones based on local values, histories and experiences. Yet, also like childhood, it is important to recognise that peace is a socially constructed concept, one that is capable of both imbibing and resisting international and local pressures. For MacGinty the key to understanding these tensions is the concept that he refers to as 'hybrid peace', a 'composite of exogenous and indigenous forces'.[29] MacGinty argues that the practice of peace building cannot

---

[24] Richmond, 'Becoming Liberal, Unbecoming Liberalism', 330.
[25] Oliver P. Richmond, 'A Post-Liberal Peace: Eirenism and the Everyday', *Review of International Studies* 35(3) (2009), 557.
[26] K. M. Fierke, *Critical Approaches to International Security* (Cambridge: Polity Press, 2007), 167.
[27] Newman, '"Liberal" Peacebuilding Debates', 42.
[28] Ramsbotham, Woodhouse and Miall, *Contemporary Conflict Resolution*, 236.
[29] Roger MacGinty, 'Hybrid Peace: The Interactions between Top-Down and Bottom-Up Peace', *Security Dialogue* 41(4) (2010), 392.

be truly dominated by the international community, but rather is constantly shaped and adapted by local actors, and vice versa. He argues that local and international actors are 'rarely able to act autonomously' and are instead 'compelled to operate in an environment shaped in some way by others'.[30] As these sites of contestation between the local and the global, and the universal and the specific, play out in scholarly debate and in practice, the question for this chapter concerns the type of impact it has upon the possibilities for children to be visible, and to participate in local peace building activities.

As with the disciplinary study of IR discussed in Chapter 3, children are virtually absent from scholarly debate within the peace building literature. While there is a growing literature on the role of gender, culture, religion and language in peace building,[31] the issue of children as a significant and unique identity group remains largely unexplored.[32] As Watson argues:

> most approaches to building peace marginalise issues surrounding children: they are little discussed in peacebuilding policies, seldom asked to participate in peacebuilding projects and peacebuilding strategies are rarely informed by knowledge regarding either their wartime experiences or their post-conflict needs.[33]

Yet the debates raised above have a clear impact upon children. Attending the liberal peace project is a caretaker approach to children's rights. As outlined in Chapter 2, this can manifest in a number of ways. First, it conceptualises children as apolitical beings and passive victims of a conflict that has been brought to bear upon their lives. This prioritises a protection agenda for children in peacetime, one that focuses upon protecting children from the post-conflict processes, whether it is ongoing sporadic violence, violence from peace keepers, or ensuring access to food, shelter, family and healthcare.[34] This is evident in UN Security Council resolutions

---

[30] Ibid.
[31] See, for example, Ramsbotham, Woodhouse and Miall, *Contemporary Conflict Resolution*, which provides chapter-length analysis on gender, culture and religion, and linguistics, but only briefly mentions children.
[32] See Watson, 'Can There Be a "Kindered" Peace?', 35–42 and Schwartz, *Youth in Post-Conflict Reconstruction*, 17.
[33] Watson, 'Can There Be a "Kindered" Peace?', 36.
[34] Schwartz, *Youth in Post-Conflict Reconstruction*, 8; see, for instance, ICRC, *Children in War* (Geneva: ICRC, November 2009), 6.

which, among other practices, prioritise a role for Child Protection Advisers to fulfil this primary function. While these are necessary occupations for the global community in post-conflict zones, they nonetheless focus upon children's passivity and vulnerability in the face of conflict transformation. Protection is promoted as the singular agenda for the international community's engagement with children, excluding any sense that children have a role to play as participants in peace building activities.

This protection focus is perhaps most evident in the work of the OSRSG-CaAC. As noted in Chapter 1, the OSRSG-CaAC is mandated primarily with the protection of children in situations of armed conflict. This is reinforced by its focus upon the six grave violations against children in armed conflict, which were outlined in Chapter 1. In fact, its work in its nine key areas – advocacy, mainstreaming children's rights across the UN system, monitoring and reporting, naming and shaming, establishing action plans, release and reintegration, dealing with persistent violators, working to end impunity for those who commit crimes against children, and sanctions – focuses on the protection obligations made by the Security Council in its resolutions. However, the Office engages in little sustained research or advocacy on the issue of children as actors or agents of peace. The peace building agenda with regards to children is focused almost entirely on managing the impact that conflict has had upon children's lives, rather than considering the impact that children can have upon the transition to peace. While this is not true of all areas of the UN – as will be discussed later in the chapter – the OSRSG-CaAC has certainly demonstrated an exclusive focus upon child protection.

The failure to advocate for children's participation in peace building processes is a significant oversight of the top-down and institutionally focused liberal approach. This is particularly the case in light of the demographics of contemporary post-conflict zones. Children and young people in certain post-conflict zones have outnumbered adults.[35] According to the World Bank's statistics for 2008–2012, Afghanistan, Angola, the Central African Republic, the DRC, Côte d'Ivoire, Eritrea, Ethiopia, Iraq, Liberia, Mali, Mozambique, Rwanda, Sierra Leone, Solomon Islands, Somalia, Timor Leste, Uganda and the West Bank and Gaza are just some of the post-conflict

[35] See UNICEF, *Machel Study 10-Year Strategic Review* (2009), 172.

and fragile countries where children under the age of fourteen represent at least 40 per cent of the entire population.[36] Where statistics include all children under the age of eighteen or all young people, the numbers further increase. For example, at the end of the Kosovo conflict, half of the population was under the age of twenty.[37] These statistics immediately suggest that children, by virtue of their sheer numbers, will impact the day-to-day success of peace building. The failure of the liberal peace project to acknowledge openly and engage with this issue is therefore a significant oversight.

The youth bulge thesis

While the liberal peace project may largely overlook the political agency of children, other orthodox approaches to IR do not. Some realist scholars have recognised that children and young people constitute a sizable proportion of post-conflict populations and therefore constitute a demographic excess that has led realist scholars to develop the so-called 'youth bulge thesis'. Invoked in the pejorative sense, this thesis acknowledges young people's agency, but not as positive and active participants in peace building. Rather, they are identified as potential spoilers of peace. This alarmist literature presents the youth bulge as comprising under-educated, unemployed, conflict-affected and disempowered young people, primarily male, who become a threat to the peace. This thesis has been provocatively spread by Samuel Huntington and Robert Kaplan. Huntington argues that societies become war prone when the number of young people aged between fifteen and twenty-four reaches a critical level of 20 per cent of the entire population of a country.[38] Similarly, in Kaplan's influential 1994 article 'The Coming Anarchy', the proliferation of young men in West Africa is presented as the dry kindling that needs only the slightest provocation to explode: '[i]n cities in six West African countries' Kaplan writes, 'I saw . . . young men everywhere – hordes of

---

[36] World Bank, 'Data: Population Ages 0–14 (% of total)'. Available at http://data. worldbank.org/indicator/SP.POP.0014.TO.ZS.

[37] Siobhan McEvoy-Levy, 'Youth as Social and Political Agents: Issues in Post-Settlement Peace Building', *Kroc Institute Occasional Paper* 21(2) (December 2001), 7.

[38] Samuel P. Huntington, *The Clash of Civilisations and the Remaking of World Order* (New York, NY: Simon & Schuster, 1996), 261.

them. They were like loose molecules in a very unstable social fluid, a fluid that was clearly on the verge of igniting.'[39] For some, the rise of violent youth gang problems in post-conflict societies such as Timor Leste – or in the ongoing conflict in Columbia – provides fuel to the 'moral panic propagated by youth bulge theorists'.[40]

This image of the youth bulge has the effect of separating children from youth as one of two distinct identity groups. As noted in Chapter 1, the analytical distinction is often usefully employed to acknowledge the more developed capacities of the latter, who, depending upon the definition used, may age between twelve and thirty-five.[41] Older children and younger adults do have different experiences, needs and abilities. Furthermore, they will pose challenges to a post-conflict society that are significantly different from those posed by younger children.[42] McEvoy-Levy argues that a focus upon youth is therefore important because, as a group, they embody the key post-conflict challenge: they are 'at once potential threats to peace and significant peace building resources'.[43] Indeed, as children become older the balance between the protection and participation agendas in peace building should shift towards participation.

While the separation of children and youth may enable some analytical clarity, it has also been attended by a negative and cautionary public discourse regarding young people, particularly young men, and their role in post-conflict societies. The youth bulge thesis is evidence of this. It creates a dichotomy between children and youth whereby children remain the passive and apolitical recipients of protection, while youth become a mistrusted and unpredictable force that needs to be contained. McEvoy-Levy notes that the term 'youth' is pejoratively deployed in familiar references to 'youth gangs', 'youth violence' and 'youth

---

[39] Kaplan, 'The Coming Anarchy'.

[40] Jo Boyden, 'Children, War and World Disorder in the 21st century: A Review of the Theories and the Literature on Children's Contribution to Armed Violence', Working Paper No. 138, (November 2006), 1. Available at www3.qeh.ox.ac.uk/pdf/qehwp/qehwps138.pdf.

[41] See Siobhan McEvoy-Levy, 'Introduction: Youth and the Post-Accord Environment', in Siobhan McEvoy-Levy (ed.), *Trouble Makers or Peace Makers? Youth and Post-Accord Peacebuilding* (Notre Dame, IN: University of Notre Dame Press, 2006), 3–5.

[42] Schwartz, *Youth in Post-Conflict Reconstruction*, 4 and McEvoy-Levy, 'Youth as Social and Political Agents'.

[43] McEvoy-Levy, 'Introduction: Youth and the Post-Accord Environment', 2.

delinquency', while 'child' highlights the victimisation children suffer as 'child soldiers' and in 'child poverty' and 'child labour'.[44] For instance, throughout the riots involving young people in Timor Leste in the years after independence, headline news reports read: 'Rival Youth Gangs Clash in East Timor',[45] 'Timorese Pray for Peace as Youth Gangs Rampage',[46] and Reuters' coverage included: '[w]ith names like "Cold Blooded Killers", "Provoke me and I'll smash you", and "Beaten Black and Blue"; such titles insist that East Timor's youth gangs promise mayhem on streets which not so long ago offered hope.'[47] Moreover, it is important to note that this is a highly gendered discourse that focuses upon the belligerency of young men, but which excludes any role for young women. Consequently, the primary discourse posits youth as threats to society and spoilers of peace rather than as forces that can be harnessed for peace building.

However, efforts to test the youth bulge thesis, particularly as outlined by Huntington, have failed to prove the validity of claims linking the number of youth with the failure of peace programmes or the propensity towards violent conflict. Urdal has argued that there is no evidence to support Huntington's claim that there is a critical level of 20 per cent of youth, at which point peace is threatened, and similarly finds that there is no supporting evidence for Kaplan's and others' more evocative discourse of desperate youth.[48] Schwartz's analysis also finds 'that a high proportion of youth in the population does not automatically presage instability'.[49] In agreement, Boyden argues that a 'large number of young people with guns undoubtedly do have the power to challenge adult authority and adult society, but in many cases

[44] Ibid., 4.

[45] 'Rival Youth Gangs Clash in East Timor', ABC Radio Australia, 16 November 2006. Available at www.radioaustralia.net.au/international/2006–11–16/rival-youth-gangs-clash-in-east-timor/730128.

[46] Reuters, 'Timorese Pray for Peace as Youth Gangs Rampage', *The Epoch Times*, 28 May 2006. Available at www.theepochtimes.com/news/6–5–28/42043.html.

[47] Rob Taylor, 'Timor Gangs Promise Mayhem on East Timor's Streets', *Reuters*, 6 March 2007. Available at www.reuters.com/article/2007/03/06/us-timor-australia-gangs-idUSSYD9080920070306.

[48] Henrik Urdal, 'The Devil in the Demographics: The Effect of Youth Bulges on Domestic Armed Conflict, 1950–2000', Social Development Papers: Conflict Prevention and Reconstruction, The World Bank, Paper No. 14, (July 2004), 16. Available at www-wds.worldbank.org/servlet/WDSContentServer/WDSP/IB/2004/07/28/000012009_20040728162225/Rendered/PDF/29740.pdf.

[49] Schwartz, *Youth in Post-Conflict Reconstruction*, 22.

the moral panic incited by young people is wholly disproportionate to the threat they pose'.[50] Thus there is no evidence – credible or otherwise – to suggest that there is a predetermined causal link between the large number of young men in a post-conflict society and the likelihood that peace will break down.

While the youth bulge thesis encodes an unproven determinism in the behaviour of youth, the underlying premise within the thesis is worthy of further consideration, namely: some youth do continue cycles of violence in peacetime. Schwartz's research suggests that youth gangs in South Africa have had a significant destabilising impact in the post-apartheid era, young militancy continues to plague the Niger Delta, and 'children and youth represent a central contributing factor in the ongoing instability' in the DRC.[51] 'Youth rebellion' against 'elder power' has also been described as a central problem in a number of African conflicts[52] and, as demonstrated above, in Timor Leste after its 2002 independence.

There may be a number of reasons why young people return to violence. Firstly, some young people have only known war. For instance, a child or young adult born and raised in Afghanistan in the past two decades has lived through Taliban rule and the post-2001 international intervention. Moreover, the child's parents have most likely lived through the 1979 Soviet invasion and subsequent civil conflict. A lifetime of conflict and militarised violence may also be the primary frame of reference for children living in Burma, Colombia, Darfur, Iraq, North-West Pakistan, Palestine, Somalia and Southern Thailand, among other states that have endured protracted wartime violence. If conflict constitutes children's primary framework for social structure, they may reasonably be at risk of continuing cycles of violence.[53]

Secondly, as outlined in Chapter 5, some young people may have made political investments in conflict as active combatants or otherwise. McEvoy-Levy's research demonstrates that in cases of protracted conflict, children and young people can imbibe the political prejudices and conflict cultures of older generations. She

---

[50] Boyden, 'Children, War and World Disorder in the 21st Century', 22.
[51] Schwartz, *Youth in Post-Conflict Reconstruction*, 2–3, 113.
[52] Wagnsson, Hellman and Holmberg, 'The Centrality of Non-traditional Groups for Security in the Globalized Era', 10.
[53] Wessells, 'Children, Armed Conflict, and Peace', 643.

notes that in Northern Ireland, 'by the age of three children ... are able to identify and attribute positive and negative characteristics to a Catholic or Protestant person'.[54] When left unchallenged by an emerging culture of peace, conflict ideologies can resurface. Thirdly, throughout conflict young people may have exercised reasonable power and autonomy, as heads of households, leaders within armed groups, or as economically independent individuals. Schwartz argues that 'in peacetime youth are likely to lose much of the power they once held, face inadequate economic opportunity, and lack access to a political forum to make their voices heard'.[55] The risk here is that a proportion of young people will become increasingly disempowered and disenfranchised from society in ways that encourage them to struggle against an emerging culture of peace.

Finally, opportunities may not exist for young people to be positively invested in their societies. Schwartz argues that a lack of employment opportunities, insufficient or unequal access to education, poor governance, gender inequalities, and legacies of past violence provide the structural conditions that increase the likelihood of young people's engagement with renewed violence.[56] Yet, to again highlight the critiques of the youth bulge thesis, this is a possibility, not an inevitability. The key to avoiding re-ignition of violence by children and youth is to facilitate their investment in the emerging peace and to imbue them with a responsibility to build a culture of peace, a point that is developed further below.

However, the two literatures reviewed here – the liberal humanitarian approach and the realist youth bulge thesis – present children's relationship to peace building in binary ways. In the case of the former, children are protected from the violence and tumult associated with the transition to peace. Their relationship to any element of the peace building agenda is mediated for them by the international/adult community. Alternatively, the youth bulge thesis presents young people as a super-empowered and malevolent force capable of directly disrupting the peace. The focus of these two literatures fails to acknowledge a middle ground. In this sense, both literatures have a case to make, but the extremities of their case demonstrate two

---

[54] McEvoy-Levy, 'Youth as Social and Political Agents', 20.
[55] Schwartz, *Youth in Post-Conflict Reconstruction*, 14.
[56] Hilker and Fraser, 'Youth, Exclusion, Violence, Conflict and Fragile States', 4.

fundamental flaws. First, they both offer a simplistic and determinist account of children's agency. In reality, children are neither wholly vulnerable nor super-empowered when it comes to their experiences in post-conflict zones. As will be demonstrated below, their agency can certainly be circumscribed by their age and situation, but it is nonetheless dynamic. Simultaneously – or at various stages of their lives – they can be victims of violence and agents of peace; this agency is neither predetermined nor universal. Secondly, such claims fail to consider the 'everydayness' of the lives of children who negotiate their way through social, political, economic and cultural life during peace. Children are presented as apart from their societies rather than as engaged members of it. In this sense, both literatures fail to demonstrate curiosity regarding how society shapes the political values of children and how children in return might then engage with and challenge those social values.

Children and everyday peace

The chapter now turns to a critical account of children's role as peace builders. While this book advocates a role for children's voices at all levels of the peace building process, this chapter focuses specially upon the role of children as everyday peace builders. The idea of the 'everyday' in politics is particularly useful in theorising the unavoidable political role that children play. As outlined in Chapter 2, it is in the practices of the everyday that de Certeau argues people are able to shape, reorganise or resist prevailing and dominant structures and forms of power.[57] When applied to peace building, the everyday becomes a site in which locals in post-conflict zones can use their proximity and the power derived by their local knowledge and relationships to shape the culture of peace. Moreover, this may or may not support cultures of peace being imposed from outside. Richmond describes this everyday peace building as:

a space in which local individuals and communities live and develop political strategies in their local environment, towards the state and towards international models of order. It is not civil society, often a Western-induced artifice, but it is representative of the deeper local-local. It is often

---

[57] de Certeau, *The Practice of Everyday Life*, 14.

transversal and transnational, engaging with needs, rights, custom, individual, community, agency and mobilisation in political terms.[58]

Read within this context, children's everyday acts become sites of political participation: attending school, caring for their family, or even playing provide an opportunity for them to contribute to a culture of peace and provide the groundwork for a post-conflict social order. Read in this way, children's everyday lives at home, in school and in their communities 'then becomes a site of politics and represents a move from subjects to active citizens, from de-politicisation to self-government and self-determination'.[59] As much as adults, children engage in everyday activities that materially influence the likelihood of ongoing peace.

Consideration of the role of the everyday in producing sustainable peace reflects the bottom-up and emancipatory approach to peace building discussed earlier. This project not only sees a role for locally inspired peace projects, but also an inclusive role for all members of society. In Richmond's words, it 'would more likely be participatory, empathetic, locally owned, and self-sustaining, socially, politically, economically speaking'.[60] In terms of promoting participation, critical scholars can point to the often neglected elements of the UNCRC that support children's rights to participation in decisions affecting their lives. These are clearly outlined in Articles 12 to 17 of the UNCRC, which address the role of children as social actors. Article 12 states that parties to the UNCRC 'shall assure to the child who is capable of forming his or her own views the right to express those views freely in all matters affecting the child, the views of the child being given due weight in accordance with the age and maturity of the child'. Following from this, Article 13 enshrines children's right to freedom of expression, Article 14 addresses children's right to freedom of thought, conscience and religion, and finally, Article 15 'recognises the rights of the child to freedom of association and to freedom of peaceful assembly'. In this sense, the UNCRC provides the foundation for children's rights to participate in peace building processes, although they are not universally applied. What is further needed, therefore, is a framework for how this participation might more broadly be achieved.

[58] Oliver P. Richmond, 'Resistance and the Post-Liberal Peace', *Millennium: Journal of International Studies* 38(3) (2010), 670.
[59] Richmond, 'A Post-Liberal Peace', 571.   [60] Ibid., 572.

Participation is central to establishing the possibilities for children's investment in peace. While the logistics of facilitating the participation of children in peace building activities differ from those of adults, the meaning of participation remains the same. Participation as a concept begins with notions of presence, inclusion and involvement, but in order for it to be meaningful it needs to be much more than this. Once again, the question of agency is central. In order for participation to be meaningful, children must have the capacity to be politically transformative. They must not only be heard, but also listened to, and their contributions to peace must be understood and respected. They must see their ideas take shape and have the capacity to influence their communities. Participation is therefore primarily about giving children a role to play in decisions affecting their own lives and their own living conditions. In order for this to be the case, the idea of children's participation needs to overcome both practical and socio-cultural barriers. As discussed in further depth below, overcoming the first of these barriers requires creating spaces and opportunities for children to participate in their communities. Overcoming the second requires a conceptual shift in the ideas that adults – including those in the international community – have about children. The concept of children as peace builders needs to be taken seriously by adults. This requires overcoming stereotypes of children as victims of war, as apolitical beings and as irrational creatures unable to conceptualise the future.

In practice, children's participation can take both informal and formal forms. Informally, children's everyday actions can contribute to a culture of peace. According to Save the Children (Norway), children describe peace as 'life and survival. It is to live in our houses . . . It is reflected in how we treat each other and how we work and live. It is to respect each other's silence and listen to each other's song; to respect and realise that every single human being has got a worth.'[61] While it may not necessarily be conscious, children's everyday actions can be seen as a site of political resistance to the conflict that has gone before and as a commitment to a culture of

---

[61] Quoted in Save the Children, 'Adult's War and Young Generation's Peace: Children's Participation in Armed Conflict, Post Conflict and Peacebuilding' (2008), 89. Available at http://resourcecentre.savethechildren.se/library/global-report-adults-war-and-young-generations-peace-childrens-participation-armed-conflict.

peace. This is also true of children who make active choices to defy cultures of violence. The busload of Pakistani girls in Swat Valley who attended school despite the Taliban's prohibition is an example of children's informal resistance to violence. In rebuilding social relationships and social structures, children's 'contributions play a role in reconciliation, in the search for truth and justice, and in rebuilding education, the economy and livelihood'.[62]

Formal participation by children in peace building requires adults in both the local and the international community to facilitate, not dominate, children's peace building activities. This facilitation can come in the form of supporting children to create groups or communities where they can meet together and talk about their experiences and the issues that affect them. This might involve organising children's activities or clubs where children can talk about conflict transformation, their hopes for the future, and practice and develop skills of respect, independence, dialogue and conciliation. Children's clubs have been active in a number of post-conflict zones including Nepal, Northern Uganda, Bosnia-Herzegovina, Guatemala and Mindanao (Southern Philippines).[63] Such forums are opportunities for children to learn about their rights, and to identify and discuss issues such as discrimination, violence – including domestic violence – and corruption within their local communities. For younger children it may be a safe place to play and to express themselves through games, singing, dancing and acting.[64] Save the Children argues that facilitating meaningful social participation for children 'can give children strength and increase their life skills and self-confidence – especially in situations

---

[62] Claire O'Kane, Clare Feinstein and Annette Giertsen, 'Children and Young People in Post-Conflict Peacebuilding', in David Nosworthy (ed.), *Seen, But Not Heard: Placing Children and Youth on the Security Governance Agenda* (New Brunswick: Transaction Publishers, 2009), 274.

[63] See Clare Feinstein, Annette Giertsen and Claire O'Kane, 'Children's Participation in Armed Conflict and Post-Conflict Peacebuilding', in Barry Percy-Smith and Nigel Thomas (eds.), *A Handbook of Children and Young People's Participation: Perspectives from Theory and Practice* (Abingdon: Routledge, 2010), 56–7 and Aimyleen Velicaria and Maria Cecil Laguardia, 'Building Bridges of Peace for Mindanao: A Role for Children', in World Vision, *Children and Peacebuilding: Experiences and Perspectives, September 2012* (London: World Vision, 2012), 20.

[64] Feinstein, Giertsen and O'Kane, 'Children's Participation in Armed Conflict and Post-Conflict Peacebuilding', 55.

characterised by conflict or insecurity'.[65] Moreover, supporting children's participation within their own and broader communities provides them with 'the political space to take a progressive role in their own societies'.[66] With regard to the youth assemblies sponsored by World Vision in Mindanao, the NGO reports that 'the impact of events such as ethnically mixed children's and youth assemblies should never be underestimated, as the young have proven to be enthusiastic peacebuilders capable of influencing others positively'.[67]

Increasingly, the international NGO sector and sections of the UN have demonstrated a commitment to facilitating children's role in peace building.[68] Hilker and Fraser argue that this has led to the development of a 'youth lens' in programming around children in post-conflict zones.[69] While this is an important step forward in ensuring a more consistent approach to children's participation in peace building, it requires a number of necessary preconditions. First, it must avoid securitising children: focus must be on the productive role children play in peace building, not their potential to continue cycles of violence. What this means in practice is that programming around children as peace builders should not focus solely on those that are seen to be a threat. This requires that opportunities for participation be provided both to girls and boys, combatants and non-combatants, children from all sides of a conflict, and all children regardless of age. Secondly, while a youth or child-focused approach recognises the similarities of children's experiences, it should also be prepared to adapt to children's differences. In this sense, former child combatants may require different forms of engagement than refugee children, children with disabilities or child heads of households. This requires complex engagement with the multiple skill sets, experiences, ages and needs of children in post-conflict zones, which will shape their capacity and possibly their willingness to be peace builders.

UNICEF notes, for instance, that integrating former combatants into a culture of peace requires specific programming. It must acknowledge the roles that children have played in war. This requires developing an

---

[65] Ibid.
[66] World Vision, *Children and Peacebuilding: Experiences and Perspectives, September 2012* (London: World Vision, 2012), 57.
[67] Velicaria and Laguardia, 'Building Bridges of Peace for Mindanao', 20.
[68] See Hilker and Fraser, 'Youth, Exclusion, Violence, Conflict and Fragile States', 5.
[69] Ibid., 5–6.

understanding of what motivated children to participate in violence in the first instance. For example, UNICEF's research demonstrates that children in South Africa during the apartheid era and Palestinian children in the Occupied Palestinian Territories have joined struggles fully understanding the pursuit for political freedom.[70] This political consciousness, outlined in depth in Chapter 5, must be taken seriously in moves towards peace. As UNICEF reports, 'addressing the experiences, frustration, needs and aspirations that move children to participate in violence is vital in transitioning away from conflict'.[71] Secondly, child advocates need to acknowledge the skills, the knowledge, and the abilities that child combatants develop through participation in conflict, and find avenues for them to be deployed towards peace. For instance, after Timor Leste's gang violence in 2006, actor Jackie Chan toured the region, engaging thousands of young men and women in martial arts training. In doing so, Chan imparted a philosophy of peace around the use of martial arts techniques: '[t]raining for martial arts helps you to strengthen your eyes, your mind and your body' he told Timor Leste's youth. 'When you have a good body and mind, let's help people. Don't harm them.'[72] This visit complemented extended efforts by local and global civil society to the engage young people who had been involved in the violence in peace building initiatives ranging from sporting activities to human rights education. Finally, as discussed in the next chapter, former child combatants must also have access to 'inclusive and appropriate processes of transitional justice'.[73] In this sense, while a child-focused approach to peace building shares some common values, the programming by which children are supported to become peace builders may differ according to their experiences.

The concept of 'children as zones of peace' (CZOP) demonstrates the opportunities provided by a child-focused and child-driven approach to peace building. While this practice has been evident around the world, as discussed in Chapter 9, it has seen recent successes in the post-conflict peace building processes in Nepal. The Nepalese civil conflict between the government and Maoist rebels lasted from 1996

---

[70] UNICEF, *Machel Study 10-Year Strategic Review* (2009), 37.   [71] Ibid., 38.
[72] Quoted in Sheila Oviedo, 'Jackie Chan Takes on Timor's Karate Kids', *Asia Times*, 18 September 2008. Available at www.atimes.com/atimes/Southeast_Asia/JI18Ae01.html.
[73] UNICEF, *Machel Study 10-Year Strategic Review* (2009), 38.

to 2006 and has had a significantly negative impact upon children. The Watchlist on Children and Armed Conflict reported that children were subject to killing and maiming, forced recruitment, abduction, detention, and torture.[74] Throughout the conflict children, with adult partners, implemented the programme of CZOP. This movement promotes the idea that adults and their institutions should respect and protect children's rights during armed conflict in a bipartisan manner. It 'envisions a Nepali society where children are respected as zones of peace and all actors take maximum possible steps to protect children's rights even in conflict situations'.[75] In practice, this has led to widespread advocacy by children, local adults, and international organisations, including UNICEF. They have petitioned all parties to the conflict to ensure that children are not recruited or in any way involved in conflict, and that they retain uninterrupted access to education, health care services, water and sanitation. While the idea did not receive universal support, in May 2011 the Nepalese Ministry of Education declared all schools and school buses to be zones of peace. This campaign has sought to protect schools from outside attack and ensure they are not used for political purposes. Moreover, children have been active participants in promoting and monitoring the zones of peace by documenting their school attendance and experiences in diaries, and covering over political slogans that appear on school grounds with child-friendly paintings. Furthermore, children's clubs in Nepal have promoted an understanding among children of the concept of CZOP and helped them to advocate for it more broadly. Children have organised peace campaigns, rallies, workshops and public events to speak about how violations of children's rights affect their lives.[76] Children and their representatives have also been vocal in

---

[74] Partnerships for Protecting Children in Armed Conflict, The Monitoring and Reporting Mechanism on Grave Violations against Children in Armed Conflict in Nepal, 2005–2012: A Civil Society Perspective, September 2012, 5. Available at http://watchlist.org/wordpress/wp-content/uploads/PPCC-Nepal-MRM-Study-FINAL-16p.pdf.

[75] National Coalition for Children as Zones of Peace and Child Protection, 'Coalition's Visions', 2012. Available at http://resourcecentre.savethechildren.se/library/national-coalition-children-zones-peace-national-campaign-protect-children-armed-conflict.

[76] Feinstein, Giertsen and O'Kane, 'Children's Participation in Armed Conflict and Post-Conflict Peacebuilding', 56.

negotiations of Nepal's new constitution and its truth and reconciliation commission.

Another child-driven peace initiative – referred to as the 'High School Refusenik' movement – began in Israel in October 2004. During its initial protest more than 300 Israeli high school students signed a letter denouncing Israel's occupation of the Palestinian territories and refusing to accept military service. In March 2005 they petitioned the Prime Minister, the Minister of Defence, the Minister of Education and the Military Chief of Staff to say, '[w]e are here to [put an] end to the occupation and bring freedom, security and peace to all Israelis and Palestinians. We refuse to take part in the occupation, which is against our basic values … We believe there is another way.'[77] This is one of a number of movements which includes Israeli and Palestinian children and young people who work individually and collaboratively to end the Israeli occupation in Palestine, to discourage young people from investing in the culture of violence, and to bring about peace.[78]

The conflict in the former Yugoslavia also sparked initiatives to build communities where children and young people could share a 'safe space'. Gillard's analysis of the Mladi Most youth brigade – which operated in Mostar in the Croatian-controlled part of Bosnia and Herzegovina from September 1994 to 1995 – is one such example. While its premises were eventually closed due to harassment and police raids, it had served as an open house where young people could meet 'free of the nationalistic pressure and antagonisms of the city outside, and could interact with one another in a "normal" way, irrespective of nationality'.[79] Gillard argues that while we must be wary of exaggerating the overall influence of such examples, they nonetheless provided sites for 'damage limitations' among ongoing social tensions.[80] Similarly, Pruitt's analysis of the role that music plays in building youth communities demonstrates that such youth-focused initiatives provide an important foundation for young people's

---

[77] Quoted in Celina Del Felice and Andria Wisler, 'The Unexplored Power and Potential of Youth as Peace-builders', *Journal of Peace, Conflict and Development*, 11(November 2007), 15.

[78] See, for example, the OneVoice movement in Israel and Palestine.

[79] Steve Gillard, 'Winning the Peace: Youth, Identity and Peacebuilding in Bosnia and Herzegovina', *International Peacekeeping* 8(1) 2001, 79.

[80] Ibid., 79.

participation in peace building.[81] Pruitt examines youth groups in Australia and Northern Ireland that use musical participation – music-making and dancing – as the primary method of bringing together young people from ethnically and religiously diverse backgrounds. She finds that rather than perpetuating the prejudices and violence of older generations, young people themselves reported that music and dance had been a useful tool with which to bring them together and build the foundations of peace. Coupled with peace building workshops and education, Pruitt found that the use of music and dance by these groups facilitated young people's active participation.[82]

More broadly, local and international NGOs report positively upon their facilitation of children's peace building activities worldwide. Save the Children, World Vision, and UNICEF are only a few of the organisations that have adopted child-focused peace building initiatives. These have taken the form of creating opportunities for children to speak to political leaders, staging dramatic performances, promoting children's rights through education and training to children and adults, and building ethnically mixed children's communities. According to analysis conducted by NGOs, these programmes have increased children's self-confidence, education and investment in society. This has in turn contributed to cultures of peace. These findings have been supported by the research conducted by international organisations including UNICEF, UNHCR, the ILO and the World Bank, which argues that it is essential for 'an organisation to recognise the importance of youth as both partners in and beneficiaries of development and conflict prevention'.[83]

Conclusion

Facilitating or simply allowing children's involvement in peace building activities is part of a much broader momentum towards inter-connected post-conflict peace building. As custodians of the future, as significant proportions of the current population, and as individuals capable of exerting political agency, children are central

---

[81] Pruitt, *Youth Peacebuilding.*   [82] Ibid., 69.
[83] Hilker and Fraser, 'Youth, Exclusion, Violence, Conflict and Fragile States', 5.

to sustainable peace. As they grow, they will determine whether a society transitions permanently into peace or relapses into armed conflict. McEvoy-Levy observes that 'the youth of a peace process receive their political education even as they create their political futures, and so live and create one of the many paradoxes of peace building'.[84] Not only, therefore, should post-conflict societies seek to engage positively with children's peace building capacities, but children should also take their increasing social responsibilities seriously.

As demonstrated in this chapter, it is only recently, and only in certain NGO and academic quarters, that this cyclical relationship between children's agency and peace is being realised. Within the mainstream approaches and analyses of peace building, children remain marginalised or are considered in only an ad hoc manner. The liberal humanitarian approach continues to regard children as apolitical victims of war who should be protected from the tumult associated with transitions to peace. The realist approach similarly accepts this view of children, but creates a separate category for youth, who it perceives as a bulging and unruly force in post-conflict societies, ready to re-ignite their worlds into conflict. While the capacity for young people to engage in violence – and indeed to ignite it – cannot be denied, this chapter has demonstrated that it is not predetermined. Instead, engaging children and young people as peace builders and providing them with opportunities to express themselves offers the most promising way forward.

Consequently, this chapter has argued that not only can children be everyday peace builders, they already are. The informal activities of – often – younger children – such as going to school, asking questions, or playing with others – are simple acts that create the groundwork for peace. Socially, they build the cultures of cooperation, interaction, respect and dialogue that are necessary cornerstones of peace. Individually, they help children to develop self-confidence, negotiation, participation and social investment that are the necessary skills for peace builders. The formal and co-ordinated activities of – often – older children, such as peace forums, engaging with political leaders, and attending peace workshops, help to build young people's commitment to peace and their society. In this sense,

---

[84] Siobhan McEvoy-Levy, 'Youth, Violence and Conflict Transformation', *Peace Review: A Journal of Social Justice* 13(1) (2001), 95.

they prepare them to become the custodians of a positive peace that sustains society into the future. Crucial to the international community is the need to adapt to the constantly shifting balance between its obligations to protect children from further harm, and to prepare children for their future roles.

8 | Children and justice: past crimes, healing and the future

BINA D'COSTA

Introduction

Narrated by Death, who is haunted by humans, Marcus Zusak's *The Book Thief* is a powerful story about Liesel Meminger, a nine-year-old German girl. Liesel is given up by her mother to live with Hans and Rosa Hubermann shortly before World War II. Hans then agrees to hide twenty-four-year-old Max Vandenburg, who befriends Liesel. After Max is taken to a concentration camp, Liesel falls into despair and starts to disdain the written word, seeing Hitler's words as the source of her suffering:

The words. Why did they have to exist? Without them, there wouldn't be any of this. Without words, the Führer was nothing. There would be no limping prisoners, no need for consolation or wordly tricks to make us feel better. What good were the words? She said it audibly now, to the orange-lit room. 'What good are the words?'[1]

Zusak represents children as having a remarkably creative ability to analyse a world that is at times too brutal even for adults to comprehend. Liesel realises that *Mein Kampf* and Hitler's propaganda are fuelling the war around her, and therefore constitute the ultimate cause of her grief. Liesel's struggles and the unbearable choices that the war forces upon her and her family echo questions about the justice and injustice of war.

Moving away from fiction, the real-life tale of thirteen-year-old Jewish girl Anne Frank has become an iconic account of the Holocaust, especially of children bearing witness to violence. The Frank family went into hiding in July 1942 in the top two floors and attic that formed part of their Amsterdam family business. Assisted by Dutch friends they managed to remain undetected until August 1944,

---

[1] Marcus Zusak, *The Book Thief* (New York, NY: Alfred A. Knopf Books, 2006), 521.

when they were betrayed and sent to the concentration camps. The father, Otto, survived the ordeal and after his return was given Anne's diary, kept safe by their friends. Anne died in Bergen-Belsen in 1945, just six months before the end of the war.[2] In 1947, the first version of the diary, edited by Otto, was published as *The Annex: Diary Notes from 14 June 1942 – 1 August 1944*. The English translation became available in 1952. Her diary demonstrates the extraordinary capability of children to exert their agency when all choices are forcibly taken from them:

Although I'm only fourteen, I know quite well what I want, I know who is right and who is wrong. I have my opinions, my own ideas and principles, and although it may sound pretty mad from an adolescent, I feel more of a person than a child, I feel quite independent of anyone.[3]

Holocaust researchers have estimated that 1.1 million Jewish children in Europe did not survive World War II.[4] A German girl and a Jewish girl, placed on opposite sides of a war, in both their imagined and real lives, epitomise a world in which compassion and humanity become the central themes in children's understanding of justice and injustice. Evident as these themes are in discourse concerning racism in Nazi Europe and the extermination of the Jews, there are also subtle situations in which it becomes clear, through the examination and comparison of everyday lives, how children live and interact during the height of hostilities, terror and suspicion. While the Holocaust was the climatic episode of a long history of persecution against the Jews[5] and was the first mass-scale genocide to be addressed before an international military tribunal, children received limited attention as

---

[2] The Dutch state considered the situation of hidden Jewish children and family unification after the war. The state's insensitivity was demonstrated by a new law regarding parental guardianship that had also been proposed by members of the Resistance and put into effect soon after the war. It notes that if parents did not return to claim their children following a brief absence, they would lose the right of guardianship over their children. For details, see Diana L. Wolf, *Beyond Anne Frank: Hidden Children and Postwar Families in Holland* (Berkeley, CA: University of California Press, 2007), 8.

[3] *Anne Frank: The Diary of a Young Girl* (first published 1 January 1947; Ealing: Bantam 1993), 191.

[4] Nicholas Stargardt, *Witnesses of War: Children's Lives under the Nazis* (New York, NY: Alfred A. Knopf, 2006), 9.

[5] See, for example, the Introduction in Rebecca Joyce Frey, *Genocide and International Justice* (New York, NY: Infobase Publishing, 2009).

victims and witnesses in the trials that took place in Nuremberg. On the other hand, childhood witnessing, as exemplified by Anne, her sister Margot and as expressed through the character of Liesel, could be understood by their readers as advocating for political action in the struggles against injustices faced by children and adults alike.

Unlike the post-World War II context, in contemporary conflict situations children's roles and responsibilities in transitional justice processes are finally being viewed as crucial for sustainable peace and justice. However, this realisation is fairly recent and remains underdeveloped. Practices of including children in transitional justice mechanisms across various regions of the world remain culturally specific, with children continuing to feature at the bottom of the social hierarchy. This chapter is based on the premise that children's expressions, recollections and inclusion are crucial in developing justice measures and processes in any society, particularly in societies influenced by and constructed through violence.

A report by the UN Secretary-General on the rule of law and transitional justice published in 2004 defines transitional justice as:

The full range of processes and mechanisms associated with a society's attempts to come to terms with a legacy of large-scale past abuses, in order to ensure accountability, serve justice and achieve reconciliation. These may include both judicial and non-judicial mechanisms, with differing levels of international involvement (or none at all) and individual prosecutions, reparations, truth-seeking, institutional reform, vetting and dismissals, or a combination thereof.[6]

Drawing from this definition, this chapter argues that meaningful transitional justice must be conceptualised in order to 'ensure accountability, serve justice and achieve reconciliation'. Furthermore, justice for children must include protection measures and mechanisms for children who are accused of crimes. In order to illustrate these points, the first part of this chapter discusses child welfare and law reform in the context of juvenile justice systems and how these systems have evolved to inform an international juvenile justice standard. The role of international criminal law in framing children's responsibility in international crimes is then considered, and relevant cases are examined. Finally, the chapter

---

[6] UN Security Council, 'The Rule of Law and Transitional Justice in Conflict and Post-Conflict Societies', Report of the Secretary-General, UN Doc S/2004/616, 23 August, 2004, 4, para. 8.

reviews children's participation in societies' restorative justice systems, including truth-seeking and healing processes.

The evolution of juvenile justice systems

Worldwide, minors under the age of five have one of the highest conflict-related mortality rates of any age group. The impact of war on children extends much further than those killed as a direct result of violence. Children caught up in armed conflict are much more likely to be malnourished. In contrast, youth – defined by the UN as those aged between fifteen and twenty-four years of age – are affected by armed conflict in a variety of different ways. While they can be 'formidable assets in innovation and creativity, able to promote equality and justice in society',[7] they can also be perpetrators of violent crimes. Studies demonstrate that children who witness violent crimes are most at risk of engaging in delinquent and violent behaviour in the future.

For example, the 1994 genocide in Rwanda claimed more than 800,000 lives. Children who survived the brutal violence retained physical and emotional scars. The tragedy orphaned an estimated 95,000 children. The fact that the genocide involved children both as victims and offenders posed a serious challenge in Rwanda's efforts to punish the perpetrators of the genocide and to reform its juvenile justice system. The dilemma of dealing with children accused of genocide illustrates the complexity of balancing culpability, a community's sense of justice, and the best interests of the child. A UNICEF document published in 2000 estimated that in Rwanda there were 300,000 children living in child-headed households; 120,000 children in foster families; and up to 3,000 in correctional centres and orphanages. An estimated 4,500 children and young adults between the age of fourteen and eighteen were imprisoned, most of whom were formally charged for their alleged involvement in the genocide.[8] These children were held for years in overcrowded prisons and communal detention centres in dreadful conditions while they awaited court hearings. The UNICEF report further noted that in 1999:

---

[7] UN, Fact Sheet on Youth and Juvenile Justice. Available at www.un.org/esa/ socdev/unyin/documents/wyr11/FactSheetonYouthandJuvenileJustice.pdf.
[8] Peter van Krieken, 'Rwanda: Children in Conflict with the Law', Report published by UNICEF Rwanda (2000) 7, 10.

- eighty minors, who had been provided with legal assistance during their trials, received sentences ranging from one to ten years of imprisonment;
- 196 minors who were under fourteen at the time of the alleged crime were released in 1999 and reunited with their families;
- 1,097 minors lived in *les cachots* – dungeons and cells – together with adults;
- 3,357 minors remained in prisons, mainly in wings separate from adults;
- 125 infants lived with their mothers in sixteen different prisons.[9]

These figures exemplify an alarming situation in post-conflict juvenile justice that is not unique to Rwanda. The severity of the charges facing children in Rwanda did not justify reducing the fundamental human rights and legal safeguards accorded to children under the UNCRC. Maintaining these rights and safeguards was all the more important under circumstances such as those that prevailed in Rwanda, in which the society was trying to re-establish the rule of law and a sense of normalcy.[10] Smith argues that the *gacaca* courts[11] in Rwanda failed to comply with the international juvenile justice standards and thereby failed to achieve the objectives of ending impunity and promoting a culture of reconciliation in Rwanda.[12] Smith notes that these courts had no authority to deal with war crimes and deliberately overlooked the crimes committed by the Rwandan Patriotic Front (RPF).[13]

---

[9] Ibid., 10, 12.

[10] Author's interviews with the Witness and Victim Support Section (WVSS) staff at the ICTR in Arusha, Tanzania, March 2010.

[11] The *gacaca* court is a form of community justice mechanism for conflict resolution that was developed based on the informal traditional justice system to resolve disputes over land rights, marital issues, theft and property damage. After the genocide it was adopted as Rwanda's transitional justice mechanism to prosecute genocide suspects: approximately 120,000 suspects were detained in jails around the country. For details, see Phil Clark, *The Gacaca Courts, Post-Genocide Justice and Reconciliation in Rwanda* (Cambridge: Cambridge University Press, 2010).

[12] Alison Smith, 'Basic Assumptions of Transitional Justice and Children', in Sharanjeet Parmar et al. (eds.), *Children and Transitional Justice: Truth-Telling, Accountability and Reconciliation* (Cambridge, MA: Harvard University Press, 2010), 60.

[13] The genocide trials have not addressed the war crimes committed by the (then rebel) Rwandan Patriotic Army (RPA), the armed wing of the RPF, which is now in power.

Moreover, she argues that some of the operational weaknesses of the courts, particularly those related to corruption and incompetence, contributed to the courts' inability to deal with juvenile crimes.[14]

On the other hand, what Smith means when she refers to international juvenile justice standards and, in particular, how these apply to states in transition, has not been clarified. The three significant international instruments relating to juvenile justice are the UN Standard Minimum Rules for the Administration of Juvenile Justice 1985 (Beijing Rules), the UN Rules for the Protection of Juveniles Deprived of their Liberty 1990 (JDL), and the UNCRC. The key protections afforded by the international juvenile justice standards include: due process and the right to a fair trial; privacy; the right to a hearing in an appropriate setting; the right to participate; the best interests of the child; prevention of deprivation of liberty; prohibition of corporal punishment; and suitable detention conditions, such as separation from adults.

Rwanda and other states in transition have experienced significant obstacles to revitalising national juvenile justice programmes, despite the pressing need to respond to children's and young adults' justice concerns. As discussed in Chapter 5 the context of financial difficulties, social and political exclusion, the availability of firearms, and fragile political environments – especially those where children's rights are violated and their lives put at risk – their resentment and dissatisfaction may influence their decisions to participate in and perpetrate violence. Adding to these challenges is the fact that research on best practices in relation to juvenile justice systems in post-conflict states is limited. Bearing this in mind, it is important to shift our gaze to national child welfare policies and law reforms that either inform or are informed by international juvenile justice standards, making reference to two examples: the first is the regime of child welfare policies in Germany; and the second is a US Supreme Court case *Roper* v. *Simmons*.[15]

The first example illustrates that rehabilitation programmes – which are grounded in a long history of national and regional practices – are a more effective means with which to deter juvenile crime in post-conflict

---

[14] Smith, 'Basic Assumptions of Transitional Justice and Children', 60–2.
[15] In the Supreme Court of the United States, *Donal Roper* (Petitioner) v. *Christopher Simmons*, Brief for the American Psychological Association as *Amici Curiae* Supporting Respondent, 19 July 2004. Available at www.apa.org/about/offices/ogc/amicus/roper.pdf.

states than incarceration. Throughout the post-World War II years until the early 1980s, juveniles in Europe were incarcerated in religious institutions and reformatories. There were more than 3,000 such prison-like institutions in West Germany, which assumed guardianship of children from poor families, single mothers and mothers from underprivileged backgrounds. These institutions employed various forms of punishment to discipline children, such as incarceration, caning, flogging, humiliation, forced labour and depriving children of food. Scholars contend that rigid social controls have caused a continuous upward trend in the number of juvenile offenders during the post-war period.[16]

The introduction of more innovative, less retributive ways of dealing with crimes committed by children was influenced by a shift from child saving to public accountability practices. In a fascinating analysis of Germany's child welfare policies, Edward Dickinson argues that following the war, social dislocation and hardship created a sense of moral collapse for many Germans.[17] The fathers of approximately 16 per cent of German children were either dead or in captivity and, by 1952, about 94,000 illegitimate children were fathered by occupation troops.[18] In addition, one-third of households were headed by single women, a situation which Dickinson observes created moral panic across the political spectrum, including conservatives, Catholic and Protestant groups, and secular progressives. The concern that the wellbeing and the psychological and moral development of millions of children were threatened increased in response to a sharp rise in juvenile delinquency. The Christian lobby believed that children who grew up without fathers would not develop an understanding of God's authority, or of that of teachers, magistrates and the law. The perception that post-war youth suffered from 'an alarming infantalism', that 'they shunned responsibility, and that they were interested only in gaining the most narrow professional training',[19]

[16] Felipe Estrada, 'Juvenile Crime Trends in Post-War Europe', *European Journal on Criminal Policy and Research* 7(1) (1999), 23–42, 23.

[17] Edward R. Dickinson, *The Politics of German Child Welfare from the Empire to the Federal Republic* (Cambridge, MA: Harvard University Press, 1996), 250.

[18] Ibid. Policymakers were also worried about the rising illegitimacy rates, 7.1 per cent in 1941 and 10.6 per cent in 1948.

[19] Dickinson, *The Politics of German Child Welfare from the Empire to the Federal Republic*, 253–4.

strongly influenced interventionist juvenile justice programmes in which churches and charities played a central role.

In contrast, child welfare advocates, especially those on the left, argued that public programmes needed not only to sustain familial socialisation, but also to complement it. There was a perception that although modern families were shaped by economic and legal realities that have largely transformed traditional and patriarchal family structures, out-dated hierarchical and authoritarian family values remained in Germany. Among those who rebuilt post-war German sociology, Gerhard Wurzbacher went as far as to state that patriarchal families were 'almost oppressive'.[20] It was also believed that children raised in such family environments were neither groomed for life in a democracy, nor prepared for civic participation, responsibility and initiatives that are crucial to the survival of a democratic state. Germany's strategy in the early 1960s, therefore, was to cease the operations of the Youth Bureau as a special police agency for problem groups of children. Instead, the agency was remade as a social and pedagogical institution offering services deemed appropriate for the political socialisation of children. These debates and changes influenced the operations of church institutions, charities and reformatories, and a gradual shift occurred that placed more emphasis on children's education and psycho-social support in responding to juvenile delinquency.

Through such changes the regulators and reformers in Europe constructed the governance of juvenile offenders to differentiate between older children and those who were under the age of fourteen. Juvenile justice procedures took a dual approach: corporal punishment was combined with distinctive psycho-social support and education programmes for minors who needed care and protection.[21] Some new approaches demonstrated the transformation of punishment – such as that carried out in church institutions and reformatories – into welfare discipline with the aim of exerting appropriate influence on minors. One of these was to make the juvenile justice system more effective through diversionary programmes that served as an alternative to incarceration. These programmes were 'an attempt to divert, or channel out, youthful

---

[20] Translation cited in Dickinson, *The Politics of German Child Welfare from the Empire to the Federal Republic*, 263.
[21] It should be noted that the national approaches to the age of criminal responsibility vary widely.

offenders from the juvenile justice system'.[22] The concept of diversion is based on the theory that processing certain youth through the juvenile justice system may do more harm than good.[23] Diversion programmes were developed in the late nineteenth century as a response to concerns that prisons were inappropriate and counter-productive environments for youth offenders. Similarly, the UNCRC advocates diversion programmes, which prevent young people from being convicted for petty offences and encourage effective education and communication. The Convention insists that institutionalisation should be the last resort. Criminology and restorative justice experts such as John Braithwaite have considered South Africa as an example of how to transform restorative justice principles into a functioning child justice system by placing diversion at the centre of the regime.[24]

Another example – which illustrates the major advances in juvenile justice and customary international law – is reflected in a crucial judicial decision by one of the world's most influential national constitutional courts.[25] In March 2005, the US Supreme Court in *Roper* v. *Simmons* ruled that the death penalty is a disproportionate punishment for offenders under the age of eighteen. By a five–four majority this decision overruled the Court's prior ruling upholding such sentences for offenders above or at the age of sixteen.[26]

In his analysis on customary international law and children's rights, William Schabas observes that *Roper* v. *Simmons* was a defining moment 'not only in the history of the United States but also in the development of customary international law concerning the rights of children'.[27] The original court judgment was delivered on 13 October 2004. The appeal challenged the constitutionality of capital

---

[22] J. E. Bynum, and W. E Thompson, *Juvenile Delinquency: A Sociological Approach*, 3rd edn (Needham Heights, MA: Allyn and Bacon, 1996), 430.

[23] R. J. Lundman, *Prevention and Control of Delinquency*, 2nd edn (New York, NY: Oxford University Press 1993).

[24] John Braithwaite, 'Principles of Restorative Justice', in A. Von Hirsch et al. (eds.), *Restorative Justice and Criminal Justice* (Portland: Hart Publishing, 2003).

[25] It should be noted that the first juvenile court in the world was established in Cook County, Chicago in 1899. By 1920, the United States had 300 full-time juvenile courts.

[26] *Stanford* v. *Kentucky*, 492 U.S. 361 (1989), overturned statutes in twenty-five states that had the penalty set lower.

[27] William A. Schabas, 'The Rights of the Child, Law of Armed Conflict and Customary International Law: A Tale of Two Cases', in Karin Arts and

punishment for persons who were juveniles when their crimes were committed, citing the Eighth Amendment protection against cruel and unusual punishments including torture. In maintaining the 'national consensus' position, the court noted the decreasing frequency with which states were applying capital punishment to juvenile offenders. The court also examined practices in other countries to support its arguments. Amnesty International reported that between 1979 and 1998, there were only eight juveniles under the age of eighteen who were executed around the world, three of those eight were executed in America.[28] The other five adolescents were executed in Bangladesh, Barbados, Pakistan and Rwanda.[29] Schabas argued that the Supreme Court's reliance on the Eighth Amendment to the Constitution meant that the *Roper* v. *Simmons* judgment was also relevant to the application of the spectrum of national and international human rights instruments[30] that prohibit torture or cruel, inhuman and degrading treatment or punishment. The judgment makes reference to international condemnations of juvenile executions[31] and the virtual universal abolition of the practice.[32]

Legal theorists in general agree that the development of an effective juvenile justice system is integral to law reform in post-conflict environments.[33] The UN has provided various kinds of policy advice and technical assistance to juvenile justice systems in Afghanistan,

Vesselin Popovski (eds.), *International Criminal Accountability and the Rights of Children* (The Hague: Hague Academic Press 2006), 19–35, 21.

[28] Since 1642, at least 366 juvenile offenders were executed, an average of almost exactly one per year and twenty-two of these were carried out between 1973 and 2005, until the crucial Supreme Court decision. For details see, Victor I. Streib, 'The Juvenile Death Penalty Today: Death Sentences and Executions for Juvenile Crimes, January 1, 1973–February 28, 2005', Periodic Report on Death Penalty Information 2005. Available at www.deathpenaltyinfo.org/juveniles-and-death-penalty.

[29] John Watkins, *The Juvenile Justice Century: A Sociological Commentary on American Juvenile Courts* (Durham, NC: Carolina Academic, 1998), 221.

[30] Article 5, UDHR; Article 7, ICCPR; CAT, annex.

[31] These condemnations could be traced back to the Fourth Geneva Convention, adopted on 12 August 1949, Article 77(5) of the Additional Protocol 1, Article 6(5) ICCPR and Article 37(a) UNCRC. In recent years, the prohibition of executions for crimes committed under the age of eighteen is a norm of customary international law.

[32] Schabas, 'The Rights of the Child, Law of Armed Conflict and Customary International Law', 19–35, 29.

[33] Claire Morris, 'Developing a Juvenile Justice System in Bosnia and Herzegovina: Rights, Diversion and Alternatives', *Youth Justice* 8(3) (2008) 197–213.

Cambodia, Ecuador, Haiti, Jordan, Lebanon, Libya and South Sudan. The objectives of these assistance programmes include: youth crime prevention; diversion of children away from the juvenile justice system; ensuring that children's rights are protected throughout the criminal justice process; ensuring that deprivation of liberty is a measure of last resort and for the shortest period of time; improving conditions of detention; and improving the social reintegration of children in conflict with the law.

Based on these objectives, the benefits of one of the practices of the juvenile justice system is evident in UN-administered Kosovo. The state has emphasised rehabilitation rather than punishment to deal with juvenile crimes. Based on good practices in the EU member states, the European Agency for Reconstruction (EAR) has collaborated with UNICEF to support the reforming of Kosovo's juvenile justice system. Pivotal to rule of law reforms in Kosovo, the Juvenile Justice Code (JJC), adopted in 2004, is expected to bring better standards for implementation by the courts, prosecution and the probation system. There is a notable congruence between the principles and provisions laid down in the JJC, the UNCRC, and international juvenile justice standards such as those stipulated in the Beijing Rules.

Despite massive international assistance, the juvenile justice system in Afghanistan remains in a dire condition. The age of criminal responsibility in Afghanistan is thirteen.[34] Based on government data, in March 2012 a total of 891 juveniles – 818 boys and seventy-three girls – were in Juvenile Rehabilitation Centres (JRCs) in Afghanistan. Of these children, only 119 had been sentenced. Another 152 were suspected and 620 accused of crimes.[35] Most of the children were arrested for 'moral' or 'ethical' crimes,[36] crimes against national

---

[34] Juvenile Code, Article 5.1. Only 10 per cent of children in Afghanistan are registered during birth and many lack the necessary ID cards to prove their age. Also, methods to establish age by the criminal justice agencies are not always accurate.

[35] The Ministry of Justice, Afghanistan, International Juvenile Justice Observatory, 'Afghanistan: Child Justice Brief', (June, 2012). Available at www.ipjj.org/fileadmin/data/documents/reports_monitoring_evaluation/JusticeStudio_AfghanistanChildJusticeBrief_2012_EN.pdf.

[36] These include running away, adultery or *zina* (sex outside marriage), pederasty (sex between an adult male and a child), kidnapping, accompaniment or prostitution. K. M. Motley, 'An Assessment of Juvenile Justice in Afghanistan',

security, and theft.[37] In addition to Afghanistan's obligations under the UNCRC, which it signed in 1994, recent national laws such as the Juvenile Code (2005) and the Law on Juvenile Rehabilitation and Correction Centres (2009) include provisions ensuring children's protection. Human rights groups have expressed concern that widespread physical and verbal abuse of children occurs at the time of arrest by the Afghan National Police.[38] Also, although Article 22 of the Afghan Juvenile Code and Article 5 of the Interim Criminal Procedure Code (ICPC) provide children with the right to be represented and advised by a lawyer, in reality only a small minority of children are afforded one when appearing in court. It has been reported that the juvenile correction centres frequently fall below internationally accepted standards. Overcrowding and lack of sanitation, the poor condition of cells, and the incarceration of children with adults are in breach of the UNCRC, which obliges a state to treat the child with humanity and to respect their dignity.[39] International observers have warned that competing concepts of justice in Afghanistan, such as those underlying the formal justice system and those embedded in the informal justice system and cultural and religious traditions enable the country to maintain a 'presumption of guilt throughout the criminal justice system and a different understanding about the function of detention and procedural protections'.[40] The experience of Afghanistan shows that in the absence of major shifts in cultural and traditional approaches

---

Report published by Terre des homes, 2010. Available at www.crin.org/docs/Tdh_Juvenile_justice_web.pdf. Most of these cases are perpetrated by adults on children and in reality are cases of sexual abuse.

[37] The Ministry of Justice, Afghanistan, 'Afghanistan: Child Justice Brief' (June, 2012).

[38] See, for example, the Afghanistan Independent Human Rights Commission (AIHRC) 2008 report. 'AIHRC and UNICEF, Justice for Children: The Situation of Children in Conflict with the Law' (Kabul: AIHRC, 2008).

[39] Nisrine Abiad and Farkhanda Zia Mansoor, 'Criminal Law and Rights of the Child in Afghanistan', in Nisrine Abiad and Farkhanda Zia Mansoor (eds.), *Criminal Law and the Rights of the Child in Muslim States: A Comparative and Analytical Perspective* (London: British Institute of International and Comparative Law, 2010), 85–100, 94–5.

[40] UNAMA, 'Understanding and Combating Arbitrary Detention Practices in Afghanistan: A Call for Action, Vol. II., Human Rights, Kabul' (2009). Available at www.unama.unmissions.org/Default.aspx?ctl=Details&tabid=12254&mid=15756&ItemID=31488.

towards dealing with juvenile justice, introducing international standards and regulations in national settings would not be effective.[41]

A comparison of juvenile justice systems in different countries draws attention to the gap between the discourse of juvenile justice standards and national and traditional systems. The international criminal justice processes documented in the next section demonstrate that the international community is taking important steps to redress this gap while advancing the rights of the children.

The child in international criminal justice

> We must not close our eyes to the fact that child soldiers are both victims and perpetrators. They sometimes carry out the most barbaric acts of violence. But no matter what the child is guilty of, the main responsibility lies with us, the adults. There is simply no excuse, no acceptable argument for arming children.[42]

The Cape Town Principles and Best Practices (1997) provide a broad definition of child soldiers as:

> any person under eighteen years of age who is part of any kind of regular or irregular armed group in any capacity, including but not limited to cooks, porters, messengers, and those accompanying such groups, other than purely as family members. It includes girls recruited for sexual purposes and forced marriage. It does not, therefore, only refer to a child who is carrying or has carried arms.[43]

---

[41] While this is beyond the scope of this chapter it should also be noted that child detainees held by the National Directorate of Security (NDS) Department 90/ 124 in the name of national security, use a variety of techniques amounting to torture. Following personal interviews with six children, UNAMA concluded that five of them were tortured during interrogation for purposes of obtaining confessions. One child reported that the interrogators squeezed his testicles, while another child reported threats of sexual assault. All of them claimed that they signed false confessions under duress. UNAMA, 'Treatment of Conflict-Related Detainees in Afghan Custody' (Kabul: UN OHCHR, October 2011), 21.

[42] Archbishop Desmond Tutu cited in Christina Clark, 'Juvenile Justice and Child Soldiering: Trends, Challenges, Dilemmas', in Charles W. Greenbaum, Philip Veerman and Naomi Bacon-Shnoor (eds.), *Protection of Children During Armed Political Conflict: A Multidisciplinary Perspective* (Oxford: Hart Publishing, 2006), 311–28, cited in 311.

[43] UNICEF, 'Cape Town Principles and Best Practices (April 1997)', adopted at the Symposium of Recruitment of Children into the Armed Forces and on

This definition is consistent with Article 1 of the Optional Protocol to the UNCRC.

In 2007 UNICEF initiated a review of the Cape Town Principles and subsequently published the Paris Principles. It states:

Children who are accused of crimes under international law allegedly committed while they were associated with armed forces or armed groups should be considered primarily as victims of offences against international law; not only as perpetrators. They must be treated in accordance with international law in a framework of restorative justice and social rehabilitation, consistent with international law which offers children special protection through numerous agreements and principles.[44]

It further states: '[w]herever possible, alternatives to judicial proceedings must be sought, in line with the Convention on the Rights of the Child and other international standards for juvenile justice'.[45]

Drawing from the 1996 Machel Report, the Cape Town Principles and the Paris Principles, this chapter provides an overview of three practices in international criminal law relating to children bearing arms, children as witnesses, and girls as survivors of sexual and gender-based violence. It must be noted that these may often be overlapping categories and that the distinctions between these classifications are not decisive.

The armed child

The civil war in Sierra Leone that began in 1991 between the government and the rebel RUF formally ended in 1999 with the signing of the Lomé Peace Accords. The UN and the Sierra Leone government established the Special Court for Sierra Leone (SCSL) in 2000. Estimates of the number of child soldiers that were involved at any one time in the civil war range between 5,000 and 10,000, some of whom were as young as eight years old. Responding to widespread concerns, customary international law prohibits the recruitment of children by armed forces, especially those who are under the age of

Demobilisation and Social Reintegration of Child Soldiers in Africa. Available at www.unicef.org/emergencies/files/Cape_Town_Principles(1).pdf.

[44] UNICEF, 'The Paris Principles: Principles and Guidelines on Children Associated with Armed Forces or Armed Groups' (February 2007), para. 3.6. Available at www.unicef.org/emergencies/files/ParisPrinciples310107English.pdf.

[45] Ibid., para. 3.7.

fifteen. The prosecution of former child soldiers under national legislation must follow international standards of juvenile justice. However, as discussed earlier in this chapter, these standards are not always applied in practice. Military law, special legislation, captured or demobilised child soldiers, and post-conflict environments affect the process and effectiveness of juvenile justice systems. Adding to these challenges is conflicting opinion regarding accountability for the crimes committed by children.

Legal scholars argue that states are required to establish a minimum age of criminal responsibility, and that children being held accountable for their actions must be treated differently from adults.[46] The trial, conviction and sentencing of four child soldiers by the Court of Military Order in the DRC attracted global attention and the intervention of international human rights organisations. Human Rights Watch urged the government of the DRC to withdraw the sentence of capital punishment given to four child soldiers aged between fourteen and sixteen years old at the time of their arrest.[47] While in this instance the government changed its decision, in 2000 it executed a fourteen-year-old child soldier.[48]

A persistent challenge exists in dealing with the criminal responsibility of children for international crimes. The case of Dominic Ongwen, the commander of the Sinia Brigade of the LRA, Uganda, is perhaps the most challenging of all because he could be considered equally a victim and a perpetrator. The ICC issued an arrest warrant for him in October 2005 for war crimes and crimes against humanity, including enslavement of children.[49] Ongwen was abducted when he was ten years old for the purposes of child soldiering, and then rose in the ranks of the LRA, becoming

---

[46] Matthew Happold, 'The Age of Criminal Responsibility for International Crimes under International Law', in Karin Arts, and Vesselin Popovski, (eds.), *International Criminal Accountability and the Rights of Children* (The Hague: Hague Academic Press, 2006), 69–84.

[47] Human Rights Watch, Letter to Foreign Minister of Democratic Republic of Congo, (2 May, 2001), cited in Happold, 'The Age of Criminal Responsibility for International Crimes under International Law', 69. Also see, www.hrw.org/news/2001/05/02/congo-dont-execute-child-soldiers.

[48] See www.hrw.org/news/2001/05/02/congo-dont-execute-child-soldiers.

[49] Jurisdiction by the court does not extend to crimes committed by people under eighteen, and before 2002 when the Rome Statute entered into force. The crimes cited are for when Ongwen was an adult. For details see, www.irinnews.org/Report/93900/Analysis-Should-child-soldiers-be-prosecuted-for-their-crimes.

'responsible for devising and implementing LRA strategy, including standing orders to attack and brutalise civilian populations'.[50] Baines examines this case and ICC strategies in detail and argues that '[c]learly Ongwen is a perpetrator and by virtue of his rank and position in the LRA high command bears great responsibility. He made certain choices to commit crimes against humanity – choices others did not make (by escaping, by refusal to kill, by melting into the background, by choosing death).'[51] Baines categorises Ongwen as a 'complex political perpetrator', meaning those youth who 'occupy extremely marginal spaces in settings of chronic crisis, and who use violence as an expression of political agency'.[52] Grover disagrees with this assessment, commenting that determining Ongwen's conduct in committing atrocities as his choice when he was under threat since early childhood is as problematic as categorising a victim as a 'complex political perpetrator'.[53] Grover argues that attributing choice to those who are forcibly recruited poses a serious challenge to the precepts of IHL, while the victim-perpetrator category simply sidesteps the issue of accountability.

Whereas it is still unclear where the line should be drawn in international law with respect to the minimum age threshold for child victim-perpetrators and criminal responsibility, the jurisprudence developed by the SCSL and the ICC has made significant contributions to the criminalisation of recruiting children. The SCSL is the first of the international hybrid tribunals to have focused on crimes committed against children.[54] The ICC has indicted twelve senior commanders including: Thomas Lubanga Dyilo, who led the Union of Congolese Patriots in the DRC; Joseph Kony; Vincent Otti and Okot Odhiambo of the LRA, Uganda; and Bosco Ntaganda of the

---

[50] Warrant of Arrest for Dominic Ongwen (2005), ICC-02/04-01/05-57, para. 9.
[51] Erin K. Baines, 'Complex Political Perpetrators: Reflections on Dominic Ongwen', *The Journal of Modern African Studies* 47(2) (2009), 163–91, 182.
[52] Ibid., 163.
[53] Sonja C. Grover, *Child Soldier Victims of Genocidal Forcible Transfer: Exonerating Child Soldiers Charged with Grave Conflict-related International Crimes* (Springer: Heidelberg, 2012), 252–4.
[54] Cécile Aptel, 'International Criminal Justice and Child Protection', in Sharanjeet Parmar et al. (eds.), *Children and Transitional Justice: Truth-Telling, Accountability and Reconciliation* (Cambridge, MA: Harvard University Press, 2010), 67–111, 70.

Congolese armed group National Congress for the Defence of the People, on charges related to the enlistment or use of child soldiers.

The decision of the Appeals Chamber of the SCSL in *Prosecutor* v. *Samuel Hinga Norman* in May 2004 is significant in establishing the relevance of national and international norms in prohibiting the practice of child recruitment. In this case the defendant was national coordinator of the Civil Defence Forces, a pro-government paramilitary group. He was charged with war crimes and crimes against humanity, including the recruitment of child soldiers. Recruitment of children under the age of fifteen is expressly referred to as a crime against humanity in the Rome Statute of the ICC, 1998. The Special Court Prosecutor's jurisdiction began in 1996: thus Norman argued that he could not be tried for recruiting child soldiers because it was not a crime under international law during the years that the Prosecutor cited. An Amicus Curiae[55] brief prepared by UNICEF and submitted to the SCSL Appeals Chamber established that customary international law recognised this as a crime well before it was set out in the Rome Statute.[56] Citing the UNCRC and the African Charter on the Rights and Welfare of the Child, the Appeals Chamber subsequently found that 'a norm need not be expressly stated in an international convention for it to crystallize as a crime under customary

---

[55] 'Friends of the court' who could be invited to provide expert briefs on various judicial matters, such as the concerns of the international community.

[56] UNICEF's Amicus Brief provides some examples of national legislation criminalising child recruitment prior to 1996. For example:

'1. Ireland's Geneva Convention Act provides that any "minor breach" of the Geneva conventions [...], as well as any "contravention" of Additional Protocol II, are punishable offences. Ireland, Geneva Conventions Act as amended (1962), Section 4(1) and (4).

2. The operative Code of Military justice of Argentina states that breaches of treaty provisions providing for special protection of children are war crimes. Argentina, Draft Code of Military Justice (1998), Article 292, introducing a new article 876(4) in the Code of Military Justice, as amended (1951).

3. Norway's Military Penal Code states that [...] anyone who contravenes or is accessory to the contravention of provisions relating to the protection of persons or property laid down in [...] the Geneva Conventions [...] [and in] the two additional protocols to these Conventions [...] is liable to imprisonment'. Norway, Military Penal code as amended (1902), para. 108.'
UNICEF, 'The Prosecutor against Sam Hinga Norman, Amicus Curiae of the United Nations Children's Fund (UNICEF)', 21 January 2004. Available at www.refworld.org/docid/49aba9462.html.

international law'.[57] The Chamber noted that the protection of children is one of the fundamental guarantees articulated in the Second Additional Protocol of the Geneva Conventions and reflected in the Special Court Statute, and therefore violating that guarantee by recruiting child soldiers resulted in individual criminal responsibility.[58]

Based on this decision, the first convictions for recruiting and using children as soldiers took place in 2007, when the tribunal found three senior commanders of the Armed Forces Revolutionary Council guilty of enlisting children under the age of fifteen.[59] Subsequently, after a five-year trial, former Liberian President Charles Taylor was convicted on 26 April 2012. Judges at the SCSL found Taylor guilty of eleven counts of war crimes and crimes against humanity, and he was sentenced to fifty years in prison. His crimes included murder, rape, slavery and the use of child soldiers, which Taylor was found to have enabled by trafficking weapons to rebels in exchange for blood diamonds.

The first case appearing before the ICC also involved the unlawful recruitment of children. The charge against Congolese warlord Thomas Lubanga Dyilo of conscripting and using child soldiers in 2002 and 2003 was criticised as too narrow since he committed numerous other international crimes including killings and sexual crimes.[60] Lubanga's trial nonetheless allowed the ICC to develop nascent international norms prohibiting the recruitment of child soldiers. This example is also examined below with a view to arguing that the international courts need to pay special attention to the protection of children who appear as witnesses in such trials.

---

[57] *Prosecutor v. Sam Hinga Norman*, SCSL-2004–14-Ar72(E), para. 38.

[58] The SCSL ruling, however, is not without shortcomings. There were disagreements about child recruitment in customary international law. In his Dissenting Opinion, Justice Robertson was 'in no doubt that the crime of non-forcible enlistment did not enter international criminal law until the Rome Treaty'. Judge Robertson: *Prosecutor v. Norman*, Case No. SCSL-2004–14-Ar72(E), Dissenting Opinion of Justice Robertson, 31 May 2004, para. 32. Schabas also suggests that 'there cannot be much doubt that the drafters of the Rome Statute believed that by adding child recruitment to the list of war crimes in Article 8, they were making new law and not codifying existing law'. Schabas, 'The Rights of the Child, Law of Armed Conflict and Customary International Law', 34.

[59] Judgment, SCSL-04–14-T, 2 August, 2007; Judgment, SCSL-04–16-T, 20 June, 2007.

[60] *Prosecutor v. Thomas Lubanga Dyilo*, ICC-01/04-01/06. For a more developed critique, see Aptel, 'International Criminal Justice and Child Protection', 75–83.

The child as witness

On the first day of the Lubanga trial the principal child soldier witness collapsed with fear after facing his former commander and recanted his testimony. After reassurance by the court authorities that he would no longer be subjected to Lubanga's direct gaze, the witness was able to recount his experience, but only after a two-week sojourn. Lubanga was reputed to have enlisted about 3,000 child soldiers under the age of fifteen in his militia.[61] During the Lubanga trial the prosecution requested image and voice distortion and pseudonyms to protect child witness identities.[62]

That children require special protection as witnesses has been accepted by the international criminal justice institutions. Child soldiers who have testified at the ICC as witnesses in criminal proceedings have benefited from safety protection and healthcare. Despite the provision of such benefits, the absence of wide-ranging measures with respect to child witness protection and victim support programmes – in the SCSL and ICC in particular – underlines how little had been done until very recently. In addition, very little systematic analytical work exists regarding children as witnesses in international criminal justice.

The distress of a child giving evidence in a criminal trial and the value of protecting child witnesses was first recorded in a Middlesex Court in 1919. The accused father was convicted of assaulting, ill-treating and neglecting his eleven-year-old daughter.[63] When the girl was called to provide evidence, her father was asked by the court to move out of sight of the witness while she spoke. The presiding judge believed that the presence of the father would intimidate the witness and impede the judicial process. Another landmark case before the US Supreme Court in 1990 ruled that one-way closed-circuit television could be used to present the testimony of an alleged child sex-abuse victim. The Court ruled that the Sixth Amendment's Confrontational Clause, which provided defendants with a right to confront witnesses against them, did not bar the use of transmitted testimony.[64]

[61] *Prosecutor* v. *Thomas Lubanga Dyilo*, ICC-01/04-01/06.
[62] See www.lubangatrial.org/2009/06/26/witness-protection-successes-and-challenges-in-the-lubanga-trial/.
[63] *R* v. *George Smellie*, 1919, 14 Cr App R 128. Cited in Allan Levy 'Children in Court', in Julie Fionda (ed.), *The Legal Concept of Childhood* (Oxford: Hart Publishing, 2001), 99–110, cited 99–100.
[64] *Maryland* v. *Craig*, 497 U.S. 836 (1990).

The first international tribunals in Nuremberg and Tokyo paid almost no attention to crimes committed against children. However, in learning from recent conflicts, the international community now widely accepts that children – and more specifically former child soldiers – are very important witnesses. Children often possess the best and sometimes only evidence of a crime.[65] However, they are also vulnerable witnesses who need special protection. Ann Michels, the former Head of the Psychosocial Support Team of the Witnesses and Victims Unit of the SCSL (2003–2005) states that from a psychological point of view, 'every witness who might face risk of being retraumatised by the judicial process, because of his or her history and/or mental state, can be considered a vulnerable witness'.[66] Evidentiary and procedural innovations have been crucial in making certain that children's voices are included in legal proceedings. Rule 96 of the ICTY Rules of Procedure and Evidence specifically provides that no corroboration is required for victims of sexual assault. The SCSL developed comprehensive support for vulnerable witnesses, including children. Similarly, the ICC (Rome Statute, Articles 36, 42, 43 and 68) requires courts to take appropriate measures in protecting child witnesses, particularly victims of sexual violence.

As indicated earlier, the literature on child witnesses in international criminal courts is relatively thin. During the Lubanga trial, Chief Prosecutor of the ICC, Luis Moreno-Ocampo, argued that Lubanga 'stole the childhood of the victims by forcing them to kill and rape'.[67] Michael Wessells, however, observes that depicting child soldiers only as 'emotionally crippled and damaged for life'[68] emphasises deficits and ignores the resilience of children. IR scholars have observed that

---

[65] Stuart Beresford, 'Child Witnesses and the International Criminal Justice System: Does the International Criminal Court Protect the Most Vulnerable?', *The Journal of International Criminal Justice* 3 (2005), 721–48.

[66] Ann Michels, '"As If It Was Happening Again": Supporting Especially Vulnerable Witnesses, in Particular Women and Children, at the Special Court for Sierra Leone', in Karin Arts and Vesselin Popovski (eds.), *International Criminal Accountability and the Rights of Children* (The Hague: Hague Academic Press. 2006) 133–45, 134.

[67] Luis Moreno-Ocampo, Opening Statement, *The Case of the Prosecutor v. Lubanga*, ICC-01/04-01/06 (The Hague, 26 January 2009), 29.

[68] Michael Wessells, *Child Soldiers: From Violence to Protection* (Cambridge, MA: Harvard University, 2006), x, 4.

child soldiers have become media shorthand for all that is irrational and brutal in warfare raging in the global south.[69] Such views propose that the perception of children only as victims of savage warfare in Africa need to be contested, as they undermine children's agency in the process of justice. The child victim as witness should be provided with the opportunity to take part in international judicial processes. Nevertheless, a balance must be found between child participation and child protection.

Girls in conflict zones

Feminist scholars working on child protection and international law have examined the inadequacies of many traditional academic disciplines in overlooking the issues informing this topic of research. These issues include gender, identity politics, race, religion, caste and class. Feminist analyses have contributed to our understanding of sexual violence in armed conflict, women's roles in peace building, masculinities and violence, gender and national identity politics, and testimonies and memory.[70] Elsewhere, the authors of this volume have articulated women's everyday resistance[71] and what a feminist emancipatory future[72] might look like. However, it is worth noting that not enough attention has been given to girls' special protection rights in conflict zones, either in feminist IR or in international law. It is arguable not only that girls encounter armed conflict in different ways than boys, but also that their experiences of marginalisation and vulnerability are distinct from those experienced by women and boys.

An assessment of jurisdiction, law and evidence validate that a challenge remains in prosecuting sexual and gender-based violence as

---

[69] For details, see Lee-Koo, 'Horror and hope', 725–42.

[70] Kelly Askin, *War Crimes Against Women: Prosecution in International War Crimes Tribunals* (Hague: Kluwer Law International, 1997); Christine Chinkin and Hilary Charlesworth, 'Building Women into Peace: The International Legal Framework', *Third World Quarterly* 27(5) (2006), 937–57.

[71] Kim Huynh, 'One Woman's Everyday Resistance: An Empowering Yet Cautionary Tale from Vietnam', in Bina D'Costa and Katrina Lee-Koo (eds.), *Gender and Global Politics in the Asia-Pacific* (New York, NY: Palgrave, 2009), 129–42.

[72] Katrina Lee Koo, 'Security as Enslavement, Security as Emancipation: Gendered Legacies and Feminist Futures in the Asia-Pacific', in Anthony Burke and Matt McDonald (eds.), *Critical Security in the Asia-Pacific* (Manchester: Manchester University Press, 2007), 246.

an international crime. In a conference marking the tenth anniversary of the ICTR judgment in the *Akayesu* case, the UN High Commissioner for Human Rights, Navenethem Pillay – who also served as a member of the Trial Chamber – explained:

> rape and sexual violence are sustained by the patterns of gender inequality which cut across geo-political, economical and social boundaries. Justice is needed on the individual and national level to redress rape and other expressions of sex inequality that women experience as a part of their everyday lives, as well as on the international level for sexual violence and other crimes perpetrated in times of conflict and war that are not effectively addressed at the national level.[73]

This case significantly expanded the international community's ability to prosecute gender-based war crimes; the jurisprudence it has provided has formed the starting point for review of rape laws elsewhere.[74] A collection of essays deriving from the conference provides critical appraisal of recent developments in rape laws across a range of diverse jurisdictions. Jurisprudential analysis in this collection reveals that wide-ranging efforts have been carried out that allow for a diversity of approaches and traditions.[75] The contributing authors explain national and international rape law developments and concerns. A particular insight offered by a number of the authors and relevant to our discussion is that constant pressure from feminists has led to rape law reforms. For example, in post-conflict Croatia, voices of feminism and women's activism have been crucial in placing concerns of sexual violence on the political agenda;[76] while in both Australia and the United States sustained feminist activism has achieved changes in formal laws and policies on rape.[77] However, it has also been noted that England and Wales have one of the lowest rape conviction rates in

---

[73] Navanethem Pillay, 'Foreword', in Clare McGlynn and Vanessa E. Munro (eds.), *Rethinking Rape Law: International and Comparative Perspectives* (New York, NY: Routledge, 2010), xiv.

[74] Ibid., xv.

[75] See generally Clare McGlynn and Vanessa E. Munro (eds.), *Rethinking Rape Law: International and Comparative Perspectives* (New York, NY: Routledge, 2010), 137–251.

[76] Ivana Radaèiæ and Ksenija Turković, 'Rethinking Croatian Rape Laws: Force, Consent and the Contribution of the Victim', in Clare McGlynn and Vanessa E. Munro (eds.), *Rethinking Rape Law: International and Comparative Perspectives* (New York, NY: Routledge, 2010), 168–82.

[77] McGlynn and Munro, *Rethinking Rape Law*, 10–11.

Europe, and that despite feminist pressure, reforms, and convictions, the sentencing of individuals has been inadequate. Moreover, the occurrence of derogatory comments about child victims made by judges illustrates that the enactment of progressive legislation can often be undermined by existing attitudes and assumptions.[78]

Some of the prejudices inherent in national laws, such as the divide between the private and public spheres – which usually denies protection against domestic abuse by national law – are also present in foundational international law, which considers the treatment of citizens as a private matter for each state.[79] As both a woman and a child, the two main international legal frameworks applicable to girls are the Convention on the Elimination of All Forms of Discrimination against Women (CEDAW) and the UNCRC. Although both guarantee limited protection, the conventions do not inclusively overlap and girls 'risk falling between the cracks of the age-neutral' provisions of CEDAW and the gender-neutral provisions of the UNCRC.[80] In the CEDAW, the term 'girls' is used only once in the entire Convention (Article 10).[81] Although Cohen considers the UNCRC a feminist landmark, as the Convention treats boys and girls equally, for Nura Taefi, the gender-neutral language of the UNCRC limits the articulation of their specific experiences.[82] However, Walsh fittingly observes that the failure to recognise and address girls' interests in

---

[78] See, Clare McGlynn's analysis on child rape cases in England and Wales, in ibid., 144–6; Clare McGlynn, 'Feminist Activism and Rape Law Reform in England and Wales: A Sisyphean Struggle?', in Clare McGlynn and Vanessa E. Munro (eds.), *Rethinking Rape Law: International and Comparative Perspectives* (New York, NY: Routledge, 2010), 139–53.

[79] Alison Cole, 'International Criminal Law and Sexual Violence: An Overview', in Clare McGlynn and Vanessa E. Munro (eds.), *Rethinking Rape Law: International and Comparative Perspectives* (New York, NY: Routledge, 2010), 46–50.

[80] Annelotte Walsh, 'International Criminal Justice and the Girl Child', in Lisa Yarwood (ed.), *Women and Transitional Justice: The Experience of Women as Participants* (London: Routledge, 2013), 54–74, 56.

[81] Walsh also reflects on Nura Taefi's argument that the Convention's reference to parent-child relations (Articles 5, 9 and 16) may contribute to a deepening division between girls and adult-women and a misperception that girls are equal rights holders. Nura Taefi, 'The Synthesis of Age and Gender: Intersectionality, International Human Rights Law and the Marginalisation of the Girl-Child', *The International Journal of Children's Rights* 17(3) (2009), 356.

[82] Cynthia Price Cohen, 'The United Nations Convention of the Rights of the Child: A Feminist Landmark', *William and Mary Journal of Women and the Law* 3(1) (1997), 45; Taefi, 'The Synthesis of Age and Gender', 357.

practice does not mean that the legal framework of the UNCRC is inadequate, but it does indicate a failure to enforce the framework effectively.[83]

International norms and regulations explicitly prohibit rape and sexual abuse in situations of armed conflict. Article 77 of The First Additional Protocol to Geneva Conventions specifies that '[c]hildren shall be the object of special respect and shall be protected against any form of indecent assault. The Parties to the conflict shall provide them with the care and aid they require, whether because of their age or for any other reason.'

The UNGA adopted the Declaration on the Protection of Women and Children in Emergency and Armed Conflict in 1974. Although not legally binding on the parties to a specific armed conflict, it illustrated the vulnerability of children in conflicts, especially in internal conflicts. However, the wars in Rwanda, the Balkan region, Sierra Leone, Sri Lanka and Burma show that various parties have violated this Declaration repeatedly.[84] It took decades for the international community to consider and investigate sexual crimes seriously. Four international criminal justice institutions, namely the ICTR, the ICTY, the SCSL and the ICC played a key role in acknowledging that rape, forced marriage, sexual slavery and forced prostitution are war crimes, crimes against humanity, and in some instances acts of genocide.[85] The ground-breaking *Akayesu* case heard before the ICTR was the first time that an international court recognised that rape constituted an act of genocide. The text of the *Akayesu* judgment made a discursive shift

---

[83] Walsh, 'International Criminal Justice and the Girl Child', 57. For example, in the Afghan customary justice system, in cases of serious crimes such as murder, the *jirga* (tribal jury system) could recommend either revenge or the marriage of a girl from the family of the murdered person to a relative of the victim. This customary practice is known as *bad* and the settlement is done in the name of punishing the whole family and community of the offender's family and community. *Badal* is also another form of dispute resolution where parties could settle by agreeing to give a girl in marriage as part of the settlement. Despite Afghanistan being a party to the UNCRC and both customs contravening the Afghan national laws these are still practised widely.

[84] For details, see Chapter 1 and Chapter 3 in this book.

[85] See for details Annelotte Walsh, 'International Criminal Justice and the Girl Child', 62–5. For an overview of the jurisprudence addressing sexual violence in international courts and hybrid tribunals, see Bina D'Costa and Sara Hossain, 'Redress for Sexual Violence Before the International Crimes Tribunal in Bangladesh: Lessons from History and Hopes for the Future', *Criminal Law Forum* 21(2) (2010), 331–59.

by naming both women and girls as victims of violence. The *Tadić* case heard before the ICTY was the first case in which a defendant was specifically charged with rape and sexual violence as crimes against humanity and war crimes.[86] Also, the *Kunarac (Foča)* case in the ICTY resulted in the first international conviction for rape, torture and enslavement of women and girls as crimes against humanity.[87]

All of the current trials before the ICC include charges of sexual crimes, and so far twelve individuals have been charged with gender-related crimes.[88] The SCSL was the first international court to recognise forced marriage as a crime against humanity in the *RUF* case. An estimated 60 per cent of girls involved in the armed conflict in Sierra Leone were 'bush wives'.[89] While the term denotes 'forced marriage', scholars and human rights organisations note that more accurately the term refers to sexual and domestic slavery.[90] Such girls' experiences in the fighting forces were different from boys who were recruited. Scholars have observed that invariably the wives in the war in Sierra Leone were not women but girls.[91] Augustine Park reflects that the indictment of 'forced marriage' by the SCSL is significant as it condemns the bush-wife phenomenon – which is also carried out in many other countries – as a crime against humanity. It focuses on gender-specific crimes against humanity perpetrated within an armed group; because forced marriage is overwhelmingly perpetrated against girls, it addresses the age-specific experience of

[86] *Prosecutor* v. *Tadić*, ICTY, Case No. IT-94-1-A (15 July, 1999).
[87] Dragoljub Kunarac is one of the eight individuals named in the first indictment, issued in June 1996, dealing with sexual offences. This significant indictment covers the brutal regime of gang-rape, torture and enslavement which Muslim women and girls of *Foča* and elsewhere were subjected to between April 1992 and February 1993 by Bosnian Serb soldiers, policemen and members of paramilitary groups, including some coming from Serbia and Montenegro. *Prosecutor* v. *Kunarac* (Trial Judgment), ICTY, Case No. IT-96-23-T and Case No. IT-96-23/1-T (22 February, 2001).
[88] Walsh, 'International Criminal Justice and the Girl Child', 64.
[89] Susan McKay and Dyan Mazurana, *Where Are the Girls? Girls in Fighting Forces in Northern Uganda, Sierra Leone and Mozambique: Their Lives During and After War* (Montreal: International Center for Human Rights and Democratic Development, 2004), 92.
[90] Augustine S. J. Park, '"Other Inhumane Acts": Forced Marriage, Girl Soldiers and the Special Court for Sierra Leone', *Social and Legal Studies* 15(3) (2006), 315–37.
[91] See McKay and Mazurana, *Where Are the Girls?*, 93, and Park, '"Other Inhumane Acts"', 316.

girls in war zones.[92] However, legal precedents are not enough to oppose the marginalisation and vulnerabilities of girls. The capacity of girls to be involved in designing their own empowering activities is crucial in any effective justice approach.

The final section discusses children's role in restorative justice and provides a brief overview of child-sensitive and child-responsive restorative justice measures.

Truth and healing through restorative justice

The young are not afraid of telling the truth.[93]

In September 2005, the Dutch railway system formally apologised for its role in transporting over 100,000 Jews – about 75 per cent of its Jewish population – to transit camps, from which they were moved to concentration camps.[94] A great proportion of these victims were children, a minute percentage of whom survived as witnesses forced to live with their horrific experiences of the Holocaust. As discussed at the beginning of this chapter, children use words, but also play, art and other creative endeavours to cope with their trauma. While the role of children in healing processes and restorative justice mechanisms is crucial, children's healing through transitional justice measures must be grounded in local contexts. In this sense, it is necessary to acknowledge that their role must also be informed by cross-cultural knowledge. The international community generally agrees that in societies recovering from their traumatic past, acknowledging the crimes children had to bear not only promotes their best interests but may also help in preventing recurring cycles of violence.[95] However, there are limitations in current restorative justice processes. Firstly, it is necessary to observe that children's inclusion in justice measures primarily focuses on speech acts and how children can perform these efficiently without being retraumatised by restorative justice mechanisms. Secondly, based on the premise that vocalising trauma is healing for children, the

[92] Park, '"Other Inhumane Acts"', 328.
[93] Frances Goodrich, *Anne Frank: The Diary of Anne Frank* (Boston, MA: Houghton Mifflin, 1989), 189.
[94] Wolf, *Beyond Anne Frank*, 10.
[95] See generally, The UNICEF Innocenti Research Centre, Children and Truth Commissions, (2010). Available at www.unicef-irc.org/publications/pdf/truth_commissions_eng.pdf.

centrality of verbal recollection[96] may be counter-productive if it is not implemented in tangible ways to ensure child-centred justice.

Following the wave of violence at the end of the twentieth century, recent literature into the history of genocide[97] has contributed to the area of restorative justice. Likewise, active involvement in human rights movements and mobilisation around human rights issues has intensified, focusing on struggles of people generating demands for truth and justice, and the acknowledgement of war crimes.[98] The realisation that only a limited number of perpetrators could be held accountable by judicial bodies such as war crimes tribunals led to serious consideration of other complementary processes. Galtung argues that social reconstruction, rehabilitation and reconciliation are necessary for sustainable peace.[99] Similarly, a growing body of international literature examines various aspects of the need to come to terms with the past in order to create a peaceful political and social future.[100] Scholars and practitioners generally accept that it is necessary to examine, acknowledge and account for violence that occurred in the past in order to ensure national reconciliation and rebuilding. Again, significant disagreement exists regarding how to deal with the past, exactly what kind of healing is necessary for a nation, and whether or not these approaches ensure justice and sustainable peace for post-conflict states. Truth commissions, reparations, apology and amnesty are some of the most common forms of reconciliation.[101]

---

[96] For details on this line of argument see, Rosalind Shaw, 'Rethinking Truth and Reconciliation Commissions: Lessons from Sierra Leone', Special Report, 130 (Washington, DC: United States Institute of Peace (USIP), 2005). Also, Rosalind Shaw, 'Memory Frictions: Localizing the Truth and Reconciliation Commission in Sierra Leone', *The International Journal of Transitional Justice* 1(2) (2007), 183–207.

[97] Robert Gellately and Ben Kiernan (eds.), *The Specter of Genocide: Mass Murder in Historical Perspective* (Cambridge: Cambridge University Press, 2003); Askin, *War Crimes Against Women*.

[98] Robert I. Rotberg and Dennis Thompson (eds.), *Truth v. Justice: The Morality of Truth Commissions* (Princeton, NJ: Princeton University Press, 2000).

[99] Johan Galtung, *After Violence: 3R, Reconstruction, Reconciliation, Resolution; Coping with Visible and Invisible Effects of War and Violence* (New York, NY: Transcend, 1998).

[100] Elazar Barkan, *The Guilt of Nations: Restitution and Negotiating Historical Injustices* (Baltimore, MD: Johns Hopkins University Press, 2000) and Rotberg and Thompson, *Truth v. Justice*.

[101] For details see D'Costa, *Nationbuilding, Gender and War Crimes in South Asia*.

The prevailing form of reconciliation is the truth commission. Priscilla Hayner highlights some of the dominant purposes of a truth commission: to investigate past human rights violations of a country; to punish perpetrators; establish truth; prevent further abuses; promote national reconciliation; reduce conflict over the past; and highlight a new government's concern for human rights.[102] The highly publicised South African Truth and Reconciliation Commission stressed that reconciliation and social healing were imperative to repair societal relationships and to address fundamental causes of repression and human rights abuses. Chile, Argentina and Guatemala have organised truth commissions despite government indifference or hostility. Most of the literature on reconciliation processes and justice has focused on the more publicised case studies in Africa and Latin America; truth and reconciliation commissions in South Africa, Sierra Leone, Argentina, Chile, El Salvador and Guatemala have been examined extensively.[103] In Africa and in Latin America, processes of restorative justice have developed innovative ways of including children in restorative justice mechanisms.

Practitioners often cite Sierra Leone as a good example of a child-friendly truth commission. International jurisprudence was extremely influential in shaping the Sierra Leone Commission, which was established as a condition of the Lomé Peace Accord in 1999 and was the first truth and reconciliation commission to mention children explicitly in its mandate. Child rights organisations were systematically consulted to assist in shaping the scope, processes and outcomes of the programmes.[104] During a multi-phase process in 2002–2003, the Truth and Reconciliation Commission collected over 9,000 statements and conducted reconciliation activities. From testimonies concerning the war in 2002 and 2003, the Commission submitted its 1,500 page document and 3,500 page annex in October 2004. The Commission concluded that Sierra Leonean children were

---

[102] Priscilla Hayner, *Unspeakable Truths: Confronting State Terror and Atrocity* (New York, NY: Routledge, 2001) 11.

[103] Ibid.

[104] Dyan Mazurana and Khristopher Carlson, 'Reparations as a Means for Recognising and Addressing Crimes and Grave Rights Violations against Girls and Boys during Situations of Armed Conflict and Under Authoritarian and Dictatorial Regimes', in Ruth Rubio-Marín (ed.),*The Gender Reparations: Unsettling Sexual Hierarchies While Redressing Human Rights Violations* (New York, NY: Cambridge University Press, 2009) 162–214, 176.

drugged, especially by Foday Sankoh's RUF, compelled to become perpetrators of crimes ranging from amputating limbs – a favourite of the Armed Forces Revolutionary Council – to forced cannibalism – a ritual imposed by the Kamajor militias. Girls were raped, forced into sexual slavery, and endured torture including bodily mutilation and a range of other cruel and debasing acts. Child victims were forced to become perpetrators and rejected by their communities after the war. The victims turned perpetrators lost childhood opportunities for education, and many were rejected by their families because of their violent past. In determining reparations, the seven-member Truth and Reconciliation Commission recommended meeting victims' needs in health, housing, pensions, education, skills training and micro-credit, community reparations and symbolic reparations.

The Sierra Leone Truth and Reconciliation Commission adopted a conscious approach to assist children to come to terms with their past. Children contributed throughout the process, helping to give shape to a report that would bring about positive action, for and by children. Children's participation in the drafting process came from three children's networks: the CFN, the Voice of Children Radio and the Children's National Assembly. Over one hundred children were involved in the drafting, of whom fifteen worked closely with the Commission. Discussions of the child-friendly report, led by children, were also aired on the Voice of Children Radio. During the first-ever Children's National Assembly, held in Freetown in December 2003, meetings were convened to discuss the child-friendly report, which brought children together from districts across the country. Excerpts from the discussions on the child-friendly report that took place at the Children's National Assembly were broadcast on national television and radio.[105]

While the Truth and Reconciliation Commission process made serious attempts to be inclusive, its impact on the larger society is yet to be seen. It is widely reported that the Truth and Reconciliation Commission lacked adequate funding and suffered from serious mismanagement and staff hiring difficulties. Participation of children in the Truth and Reconciliation Commission was provided with a great

---

[105] See the methodology section, TRC Report, children's version, produced by the UNICEF. Available at www.unicef.org/infobycountry/sierraleone_23937.html.

deal of attention, but only up to the period leading to the operation of the Commission. Children's testimonies were taken in closed hearing sessions to avoid retraumatisation and stigmatisation by their family and community. Disappointingly, the public hearing on children only attracted a very small attendance in Freetown.[106]

Similar to the South African Truth and Reconciliation Commission, the Sierra Leone process also valorised a particular kind of memory practice – truth-telling. The Truth and Reconciliation Commission Act 2000 noted that truth was the primary means by which the TRC pursued five goals of its mandate, 'to create an impartial historical record of violations and abuses . . . to address impunity, to respond to the needs of the victims, to promote healing and reconciliation and to prevent a repetition of the violations and abuses suffered'.[107] It is worth noting that the SCSL states that the 'major role for children in proceedings will be to testify to the atrocities they witnessed and experienced both as victims and perpetrators'.[108] Both the restorative justice and the criminal justice processes in Sierra Leone focused on speech acts, testimonies and memories; this focus typifies reconciliation programmes for children, which have largely categorised children as victims and witnesses. While the Truth and Reconciliation Commission specified that its role was to prevent future violations and to promote social healing, the implications of 'truth' in the Commission's title remained unclear. Children's inclusion in the Truth and Reconciliation Commission primarily focused on speech acts and children's performance that avoided retraumatising them. Healing often takes a long and difficult path, and typically does not occur as the result of a limited number of speaking, remembering and counselling sessions. It has been reported that children were pressured to testify voluntarily before the Truth and Reconciliation Commission and were told that their testimony would bring peace to Sierra Leone.[109] Truth-telling was suggested as the only way to heal the traumas of the society's recent past. The Truth and Reconciliation

[106] Beth K. Dougherty, 'Searching for Answers: Sierra Leone's Truth and Reconciliation Commission', *African Studies Quarterly* 8(1) (2004), 40–56, 47.

[107] Cited in Shaw, 'Rethinking Truth and Reconciliation Commissions'.

[108] Witness to Truth: Report of the Sierra Leone Truth and Reconciliation Commission, Vol 3B, 2004, Sierra Leone: Truth and Reconciliation Commission. Available at www.sierraleonetrc.org/.

[109] Philip Cook and Cheryl Heykoop, 'Child Participation in the Sierra Leonean Truth and Reconciliation Commission', in Sharanjeet Parmar et el. (eds.),

Commission Report and the related strategies suggest that children's healing was one of the goals of the truth-telling process in Sierra Leone; nonetheless, the process can also be seen as an opportunity to bring together the dual intentions of restoring peace – a socio-political concern – and the psycho-social concern of countering individual suffering. Having said this, it is reasonable to concede that it is too early to evaluate whether the outcome of the Truth and Reconciliation Commission's strategies of combining reconciliation – in the interests of the state – with truth-telling and healing – as the best interests of the child – has reflected positively in shaping the future of Sierra Leone.

Experiences of the commissions in Africa and Latin America have contributed well-informed procedures to the construction of recent justice mechanisms. For instance, although not all countries in the Asia-Pacific have formed their own restorative justice bodies and commissions, various measures have been adopted that combine retributive and restorative justice approaches. The scholarship on Asian justice processes largely focuses on judicial mechanisms,[110] traditional approaches of justice,[111] comparative reconciliation processes of countries,[112] and regional identities and peace.[113] While the functions of these justice processes in the Asia-Pacific differ, the underlying objective of speech acts such as truth-telling and testimony comprise a central theme. This suggests that while commissions are important mechanisms with which to consider peace in post-conflict societies, it is tangible outcomes that are required to ensure child-centred justice and children's reconciliation.

The UN Transitional Authority in East Timor (UNTAET) issued regulation 2001/10 to establish the Commission for Reception, Truth and Reconciliation (CAVR) to deal with crimes committed between

---

Children and Transitional Justice: Truth-Telling, Accountability and Reconciliation (Cambridge, MA: Harvard University Press, 2010), 159–91.

[110] Suzannah Linton, 'Cambodia, East Timor and Sierra Leone: Experiments in International Justice', *Criminal Law Forum* 12(2) (2001), 185–246.

[111] Dionisio Babo-Soares, 'NaheBiti: The Philosophy and Process of Grassroots Reconciliation (and Justice) in East Timor', *The Asia-Pacific Journal of Anthropology* 5(1) (2004), 15–33.

[112] Wendy Lambourne, 'Justice and Reconciliation: Postconflict Peacebuilding in Cambodia and Rwanda', in Mohammed Abu-Nimer (ed.), *Reconciliation, Justice and Coexistence: Theory and Practice* (Lanham, MD: Lexington Books, 2001), 311–37.

[113] Ranabir Samaddar and Helmut Reifeld (eds.), *Peace as Process: Reconciliation and Conflict Resolution in South Asia* (New Delhi: Manohar, 2001).

1974 and 1999 in East Timor. In addition to this, despite the UN Commission of Enquiry's suggestion for a tribunal, the UNTAET established instead the Serious Crimes Unit pursuant to the UN Security Council Resolution 1272, to investigate and prosecute war crimes, crimes against humanity and individual offences of rape, torture and killing committed in East Timor between 1 January and 25 October 1999. The mandate of the Serious Crimes Unit ended in May 2005.[114]

The CAVR process, which covered crimes committed between 1974 and 1999, collected 7,669 statements, conducted more than 1,000 interviews, and conducted public hearings. The CAVR's Report, *Chega!*, became public in October 2005 and includes testimony from seven national public hearings. Over 2,500 pages, *Chega!* makes 205 recommendations based on its findings in relation to justice, reconciliation, human rights, and the relationship between Timor Leste and other countries, including Indonesia. However, then President, Xanana Gusmao, and Foreign Minister, José Ramos-Horta, rejected this and warned that any attempt to prosecute every crime committed between 1975 and 1999 would bring political anarchy and social chaos.[115] On 14 December 2004, Indonesia and East Timor concluded a bilateral agreement on the establishment of a Commission of Truth and Friendship to 'seek truth and promote friendship'.[116]

The CAVR investigated crimes committed against children and interviewed many Timorese children who were forcibly recruited into the TBO (*Tenaga Bantuan Operasi*), a civilian group formed by Indonesia to support its forces in Timor Leste.[117] In addition to being forcibly recruited by the Indonesian security forces, children were tortured, sexually abused, detained, forcibly displaced and killed.

---

[114] In accordance with paragraph 4(i) of Security Council Resolution 1704 (2006) to assist the Office of the Prosecutor-General of Timor Leste, the UN Integrated Mission in Timor Leste created the Serious Crimes Investigation Team (SCIT). The investigations in the thirteen districts of Timor Leste were resumed after 12 February 2008. As of December 2012, the SCIT completed 311 investigations.

[115] Jeffrey Kingston, 'Balancing Justice and Reconciliation in East Timor', *Critical Asian Studies* 38(3) (2006), 271–302.

[116] Report to the Secretary-General of the Commission of Experts to Review the Prosecution of Serious Violations of Human Rights in Timor Leste (the then East Timor) in 1999, 26 May 2005.

[117] See Ch. 7 and Ch. 8 in '*Chega!* Report of the Commission of Reception, Truth and Reconciliation in East Timor' (2005). Available at www.cavr-timorleste. org/en/chegaReport.htm.

Similar to Latin American military juntas, especially those in Argentina and El Salvador, the Indonesians forcibly transferred many Timorese children to Indonesia. While it is not clear if this was a formalised policy, the CAVR report stated that these children's whereabouts were not known.

The interviews conducted by the Commission confirm that in situations of massive and systematic violence, children suffer from acts of aggression perpetrated by those directly targeting them, and indirectly by those targeting their family, caregivers and communities. Physical, sexual, gendered and community rights violations were found to have profoundly affected children's lives. The recommendation section of the report includes all the appropriate schemes such as ensuring a better future for children, identifying and promoting positive role models for children, allocating sporting infrastructure, and developing reproductive health education programmes.[118] However, the report does not clarify the extent to which these interactions with the Commission helped children to come to terms with their past. It recounts the testimony of child survivors and victims, noting that, 'the truth contained in this Report comes largely from the words of those who directly experienced the years of conflict'.[119] Supported by the UNTAET, in June 2000, representatives of Timorese civil society, the Catholic Church and community leaders came together to consider transitional justice mechanisms. As *Chega!* states, the group agreed that reconciliation is central to moving forward and to initiate the healing process for Timorese society:

> Reconciliation is a process, which acknowledges past mistakes including regret and forgiveness as a product of a path inherent in the process of achieving justice; it is also a process which must involve the People of Timor-Leste so that the cycle of accusation, denial and counter-accusation can be broken. This process must not be seen only as a conflict resolution or mere political tool which aims at pacification and reintegration of individuals or groups in the context of their acceptance of independence and sovereignty of Timor-Leste but, above all, must be seen as a process where truth must be the outcome.[120]

A close reading of the Commission report, especially Chapter 7.8, reveals that the CAVR truth-telling initiative was intended to determine and document abuses against children. However, the

[118] Ibid., Part 11: 13–14 and 34–5.   [119] Ibid., 9   [120] Ibid., para. 38, 10.

Commission's apparent methodology of assessing and identifying strategies that could be developed into future child-friendly procedures protecting the rights of children is not obvious from the report or the follow-up measures. It is also not clear what motivated children to come forward to share their stories in the hearings. How truth-telling and healing would ensure children's justice was not described anywhere in the lengthy report. In the aftermath of the 2006 stand-off between the military and the rebel forces, about 130 children were charged, constituting approximately 10 per cent of all criminal cases. This period highlighted the gaps in Timor Leste's juvenile justice system[121] and the child protection rhetoric set out in its truth commission report.

The report states that many East Timorese children were separated from their families during the Indonesian occupation of Timor-Leste, including some 4,500 in 1999. Many in the pre-1999 category are now adults and include some who are looking for their families but may not know where they come from. Most of those who became separated from their families during the violence of 1999 have either been reunited with their families or have continued to stay with caretakers.[122] To date there has been no systematic collection of records concerning the missing children.[123] Some have estimated that possibly as many as 4,000 Timorese children were taken to Indonesia.[124] The ICRC maintains a register of 400 cases of children who disappeared, many of which qualify as enforced disappearances.[125] The mandate of the Commission of Truth and Friendship, the first of its kind to be established between two states, was to uncover the truth regarding the events of 1999, to heal wounds

---

[121] The minimum age of criminal responsibility is only sixteen years. In 2009, Timor Leste established its National Commission of Child Rights designed to be guided by children and young people. A Youth Parliament was also organised that provided policy recommendations on education, health, employment and recreation.

[122] *Chega!*, Chapter 11, 14.

[123] For details on children's transfer in Indonesia, see Helene van Klinken, *Making them Indonesians: Child Transfers Out of East Timor* (Clayton: Monash University Publishing, 2012).

[124] Authors' interviews with CAVR officials carried out in Canberra, Australia, 2006. While not confirmed, the Christian lobby in Timor Leste also note that more than 1,000 children were forcibly converted to Islam.

[125] Press briefing of the UN Working Group on Enforced or Involuntary Disappearances visit to Timor Leste. Available at www.ohchr.org/en/News Events/Pages/DisplayNews.aspx?NewsID=10729&LangID=E.

and promote friendship. Based on the Commission of Truth and Friendship recommendation to establish a disappearance commission in 2011, a memorandum of understanding was signed between the Indonesian National Human Rights Commission and the Provedor's Office in Timor Leste. The memorandum of understanding intended that the Commission would focus on the children who disappeared and possibly now reside in Indonesia. To date, no progress has been made to establish the Commission, to gather forensic evidence or to find those children who disappeared. This illustrates that while a child-friendly truth and reconciliation commission may be skilled in recommending measures to redress past injustice, in reality the implementation of children's justice is immensely challenging. Similar to the Sierra Leone Truth and Reconciliation Commission, the centrality of truth-telling is evident in the CAVR process. The notion that speaking the truth heals the nation and allows it to develop in spite of the trauma of the past, comes into direct conflict with the task of addressing the grey zones of victims' justice, which is very much typified by the unresolved disappearances of children in Timor Leste.

Conclusion

Returning to Zusak's novel *The Book Thief*, the author describes how Ilsa Hermann, the wife of the village Mayor, gave Liesel a blank book and encouraged her to write. At a fevered pace Liesel recounts tragedy and beauty in the story of her life; she finally realises that words can cause both violence and comfort. Liesel struggles to portray the truth she has witnessed, thereby combating the publicly accepted lacunae of wartime propaganda.

Before World War II commenced, the Frank sisters, Anne and Margot, had begun correspondence with two sisters in a small Iowa town. Although Anne did not mention anything about the political situation in Europe, in her letter to Betty Ann Wagner, Margot wrote of the Netherlands, stating that, 'we often listen to the radio as times are very exciting, having a frontier with Germany and being a small country we never feel safe'.[126] She further remarked in reference to

---

[126] Cited in Shelby Myers-Verhage, 'Postmarked from Amsterdam – Anne Frank and Her Iowa Pen Pal', in Harold Bloom (ed.), *The Diary of Anne Frank* (New York, NY: Infobase Publishing, 2010) 37–44, 39.

visiting her cousins in Switzerland, '[w]e have to travel through Germany which we cannot do or through Belgium and France and in that we cannot do either. It is war and no visas are given.'[127]

For Liesel, Margot and Anne, communicating to their readers – both imagined and real – became the most symbolic means of making sense of their trauma, forced displacement and dislocation. Their understanding of the world in conflict is not only age-specific but it is also shaped by their gender identity. It is a short step from understanding the brutal world of Anne and Margot Frank to realising that girls' age and gender-specific experiences are not always visible in the justice measures and the mechanisms implemented by the international community and its signatory states. Adrienne Kertzer observes that readers and writers of children's literature concerning the Holocaust rarely ask about the meanings and significance of the words.[128] However, reading such literature and being exposed to children's expressions and experiences of trauma, loss and helplessness can hopefully compel us to reconsider children's ability to comprehend and cope with narratives of injustice. The Holocaust has been a critical event in shaping international justice processes. Nonetheless, it took decades for the international community seriously to recognise that children need special attention and protection in local and international justice processes.

This chapter has argued that while children are disproportionately affected by violence, the focus on the rights of children in transitional justice remains narrowly defined. In international and national judicial processes there exists limited understanding that children bearing arms are victims of conflict and not those who bear the greatest responsibility. Conversely, it is also suggested that international processes are not designed to prosecute children who have allegedly committed crimes under international law. This chapter stresses that not only appropriate regulations, but also child-sensitive and child-responsive mechanisms, are necessary to promote and protect the rights of children in transitional and post-conflict settings.

---

[127] Ibid.
[128] Adrienne Kertzer, 'What Good are the Words?: Child Memoirs and Holocaust Fiction', in Daniel Thomas Cook and John Wall (eds.), *Children and Armed Conflict: Cross Disciplinary Investigations* (Basingstoke: Palgrave Macmillan, 2001), 22–38.

In closing this chapter, it is worth emphasising that the international community has a special responsibility in pursuing justice for children. It is critical to ensure that children are able to rely on systems of justice in order to preserve and develop their capacity as national and global citizens. Children are often at the heart of the struggles and oppressions of armed conflict. As participants, witnesses, victims and perpetrators, their role in healing and coming to terms with the past is critical. While it is early in regards to the development of truth and enquiry commissions, for the foreseeable future these might constitute the most effective means of approaching the guilt experienced by child perpetrators.

9 | Who speaks for children? Advocacy, activism and resistance

BINA D'COSTA

I do not intend to return children to murderers because it would not be fair. They do not have the right to have them. So, I will `rule not to return any children to you. It does not make sense to disturb those children that are in the hands of decent families that will be able to educate them right, not like you educated your children. Only over my dead body will you obtain custody of them.[1]

Introduction

The Argentine Grandmothers with Disappeared Grandchildren was formed in 1977 by grandmothers who organised themselves to locate children taken during Argentina's Dirty War. The children were systematically abducted for adoption by military families and the allies of the regime as part of a plan to control the subversiveness of future generations.[2] The search for the missing children in Argentina, El Salvador, Chile and Guatemala developed one of the most symbolic and effective transnational human rights networks in contemporary history. Keck and Sikkink emphasise that networks are characterised by the prominence of principled ideas and the central role of NGOs.[3] They articulate how grandmothers travelled to Europe, the United States and Canada to denounce human rights violations and to seek international solidarity.[4] The solidarity framework is one of the most important pillars of advocacy and

---

[1] Dr Delia Pons, a judge from the juvenile court in Buenos Aires in her comments to the Grandmothers of the Plaza de Mayo in Rita Arditti, *Searching for Life: The Grandmothers of the Plaza de Mayo and the Disappeared Children of Argentina* (Berkeley, CA: University of California Press, 1999), 57.
[2] Arditti, *Searching for Life*.
[3] Margaret E. Keck and Kathryn Sikkink, *Activists Beyond Borders: Advocacy Networks in International Politics* (New York, NY: Cornell University Press, 1998).
[4] Ibid., 92–5.

activism among NGOs and other human rights actors, involving 'relationships between oppressed peoples and those in a position to support them'.[5]

Drawing from Keck and Sikkink's ground-breaking study of advocacy and activism, this chapter explores the norm-setting and framing agenda for children's rights and protection in conflict zones. This chapter seeks to identify some of the factors mobilising global and local movements in responding to children's concerns in conflict zones. It considers the initiatives used to protect children from abuse and exploitation in various regions, and the tensions that exist within advocacy and activism for children, especially with regard to the political processes and shifting dynamics of conflict zones. The first part of the chapter provides a brief overview of civil society and advocacy.

This chapter also reflects on the paradox of the term 'post-conflict'; Junne and Verkoren observe that post-conflict is shorthand for conflict situations in which open warfare has concluded.[6] Commonly, discussion of the relations between state and society in terms of 'post-conflict' is problematic, as it does not take into consideration the complex identity politics and power struggles that are produced and reproduced in specific social contexts once conflict formally ends. Actors often move from one sector to another: a retired military general or a senior bureaucrat might start an NGO committed to child protection, or accept a position in an educational institution, importing their own ideas, connections, and biases to that institution. This illustrates the impossibility of establishing a clear-cut distinction between state and society: they overlap with one another. Some of the examples in this chapter underline the need for special programmes for children to be anchored in broader plans to support entire communities without singling out those children who have perpetrated violent crimes. The following sections of this chapter explores children's representation in global advocacy, their role as activists and as political subjects.

---

[5] Ibid., 95.
[6] Gerd Junne and Willemijn Verkoren, 'The Challenges of Postconflict Development', in Gerd Junne and Willemijn Verkoren(eds.), *Postconflict Development: Meeting New Challenges* (Boulder, CO: Lynne Rienner Publishers, 2005), 1–18.

Civil society

The role of civil society in fostering child-responsive and child-sensitive mechanisms is widely recognised. While a number of experts have provided extensive analysis on the idea of civil society,[7] for the purposes of this chapter it is useful to turn to Mary Kaldor's categorisation of the concept. Historically, the concept was described 'as a rule of law and a political community, a peaceful order based on implicit or explicit consent of individuals',[8] and also as a zone of civility that is understood not only in terms of good behaviour and politeness of a society, but also as a state of affairs that reduces violence as an approach for organising social relations. Kaldor proposes that there are five different views of civil society in general usage. She argues that the first historical version – *societas civilas* – could not be separated from the state classically defined as having a public monopoly of violence, but rather could be differentiated from non-civil societies – 'the state of nature or absolutist empires – and from war'.[9] In its second version, bourgeois society, civil society was a historical phenomenon associated with capitalism. For Hegel and Marx civil society in this sense was a ground of ethical life existing between the state and the family and distinct from the state. The other three types occur in contemporary usage, which Kaldor classifies as activist, neoliberal, and postmodern versions of civil society. The activist perspective denotes active citizenship and the development of alignments beyond formal political circles; through political pressure it insists not only on containing state power, but also on its redistribution. Activists are more concerned with public affairs and public debates, and emphasise shared cosmopolitanism and political emancipation. For activists, whether or not groups advocating violence can be included in civil society is open to discussion. The *laissez-faire* politics embedded in the neoliberal version of civil society refers to a nonprofit, voluntary third sector that in addition to restraining state power also performs

---

[7] For a variety of philosophical traditions and practical contexts in how the notion of civil society is invoked, see, Simone Chambers and Will Kymlicka, (eds.), *Alternative Conceptions of Civil Society* (Princeton, NJ: Princeton University Press, 2002); Sudipta Kaviraj and Sunil Khilnani, (eds.), *Civil Society: History and Possibilities* (Cambridge: Cambridge University Press, 2001).

[8] Mary Kaldor, *Global Civil Society: An Answer to War* (Cambridge: Polity, 2003), 7.

[9] Ibid., 7

certain welfare and security functions traditionally understood as the state's responsibility. The NGOs involved in the development, human rights and humanitarian sectors offer these additional functions. Departing from both activist and neoliberal views of universalism, Kaldor's final version of civil society – postmodern civil society – subscribes to one particular universal principle: tolerance. Postmodernists call attention to identity politics and multiple layers of interests based on national, religious and other forms of allegiance. As such, this form of civil society incorporates and emphasises pluralism and networks – including religious and diaspora-based networks, and rights-based linkages.[10]

In Kaldor's theorisation of global civil society, groups, networks and movements, both formal and informal, comprise mechanisms in which individuals negotiate social contracts or political bargains at a global level. These processes occur through interactions with the institutions of global governance. Kaldor defines such interactions as global politics; that is, the domestication of the international beyond the realm of diplomacy, high-level meetings and military strategies to a realm of dialogue and public pressure.[11] Moving on from theoretical conceptualisation to the practical challenges, the diverse cultural and intellectual settings of civil society – and its transformation through protracted and uneven processes of diffusion – have been raised in particular in development discourse. As the contributions from Keck, Sikkink and Kaldor suggest, civil society encompasses a wide variety of actors, ranging across local and international, independent and quasi-governmental players, networks, movements, groups and individuals. But it is not only cultural and intellectual formations that structure civil society: conflict constitutes a significant means by which civil society's actions and identity develop.

It is now widely accepted that a number of international advocacy reports and conventions have significantly contributed to the advancement of children's rights in conflict zones. The 1996 Machel Report opened up the possibility of incorporating children's concerns in the UN agenda. The report used the UNCRC and the Optional Protocols to argue that children need to be protected during and after armed conflicts. The OSRSG-CaAC, as discussed in

---

[10] Ibid., 7–12.   [11] Ibid., 78–82.

Chapter 1, has also been active in conducting research, producing reports and initiating negotiations to halt the recruitment of child soldiers. This agenda-setting work resulted in the UN Security Council Resolutions 1261 and 1314, both of which recognise the consequences of conflict on children. Resolution 1314 also advocates the demobilisation and reintegration of child solders, meeting special needs of former child soldiers, and the necessity of establishing special child protection units. NGO activism in transnational networks and global campaigns has also successfully raised the profile of children's rights.

Over the past two decades the rising importance of NGOs has attracted considerable attention. Yet scholarly opinion remains deeply divided over the extent to which they are able to act as a progressive force for political and social change. In the absence of greater efforts to conduct empirical research, especially in the developing world, these perspectives are likely to remain polarised. Although much work has been done on the ways in which NGOs interact with the state and multilateral organisations to bring about reform, current understanding of the diverse influences of NGO actors and their behaviour in practice remains limited. The comparative advantage of NGOs lies in their capacity to function effectively at the local level, and often at the margins of the state in social spaces that are not clearly defined. In so doing, they are critical to the implementation of global justice norms relating to human rights, gender equity and sustainable livelihoods. However, the strategies that are employed by local activists and, indeed, their interpretation of what global justice means in practice differ widely according to the local culture and political and socio-economic context.

Scholars have also argued that in the context of a higher degree of politicisation and a less-structured institutional setting, conflict societies could generate a more intense mobilisation of NGOs and other actors of civil society. In conflict the role of civil societies could be recognisably different from society during peacetime. Marchetti and Tocci suggest that instead of calling these conflict actors 'civil society', it is useful to use the term 'conflict society'.[12]

---

[12] Raffaele Marchetti and Nathalie Tocci, 'Conflict Society: Understanding the Role of Civil Society in Conflict', *Global Change, Peace and Security*, 21(2) (2009), 201–17.

For them, conflict society comprises all local civic organisations within conflict contexts as well as those third countries, international, transnational and civic organisations involved in particular conflicts.[13] Using this definition, they emphasise that in conflict contexts, particularly in structural conflicts, both civil and non-civil groups are involved in the formation of civil society; this is useful in our analysis of children's involvement in advocacy movements and activist groups. Similar to state and non-state armed groups, civil society has the potential to use children to advance its goals regardless of whether it is beneficial or detrimental to children's empowerment. Movements use children to advance their political goals. It has been argued that the images of children in extreme poverty used by international organisations, such as World Vision, Save the Children and UNICEF, to attract contributions from people living in the global north generate a politics of pity rather than establishing a productive understanding of children in conflict and beneficial relationships between those willing to help and those children requiring it.

NGOs and pro-child rights networks working in protracted conflicts, and actors involved in children's issues almost without exception advocate for peace as a necessary precondition for children's rights and protection. Marchetti and Tocci do not make it clear whether in the instance of a state transitioning from conflict to peace it would be reasonable to expect it to revert to a framework of civil – rather than conflict – society. This chapter does not consider business persons, professional associations, and organised crime networks since these actors primarily and visibly operate in the market sector. However, trade unions include child labour rights advocacy strategies, and therefore are considered. Marchetti and Tocci's typology of key actors in conflict situations is provided in Table 9.1.[14]

The next section provides accounts of global advocacy for children's rights and protection. For the most part, these advocacy strategies do not include children's direct participation. However, as will be discussed, contemporary advocacy efforts have opened up a space for children's voices to be directly represented in issues that primarily concern their safety, rights and wellbeing.

[13] Ibid., 206.   [14] Ibid..

Table 9.1 *Key Civil Society Actors in Conflict Situations*

Types of activities	Actors
Professional	Technical experts consultants
Business	Trade unions
Private citizens	Individual citizens
	Diaspora groups
	Families and clans
Research, training and education	Special interest research centres
	Think tanks
	Universities
Activism	NGOs
	Lobby groups
	Grass-roots social movements
	Local communities
	Combatant groups
Religion	Spiritual communities
	Charities
	Religious movements
Funding	Foundations
	Individual philanthropists
Communication	Journalists
	Media operators

The transformative politics of advocacy: naming and shaming

UN agencies and various other international humanitarian actors have made it abundantly clear that contemporary identity-based domestic armed conflicts abuse and consciously target children, leaving them physically scarred and psychologically traumatised. UNICEF, ICRC, Save the Children and Plan International have referred to the lack of accountability of those wielding military, economic and political power as the root cause of violence against children.[15] International advocacy

[15] See, for example, reports and press releases by agencies on child protection, such as UNICEF 'Conflict Creating Unprecedented Threats to Children's Lives' (12 June 2011). Available at www.unicef.org/media/media_69614.html; ICRC, workshop report, 'Children Affected by Armed Conflict and other Situations of Violence', (March 2011). Available at www.icrc.org/eng/resources/documents/publication/p4082.htm; Save the Children, 'Childhood Under Fire: The Impact

to resolve children's vulnerability in conflicts has adopted four specific approaches: publicly naming those who target children; establishing children's peace zones; lobbying for a more rigorous normative framework; and establishing international alerts to ensure that states and non-state actors comply with existing humanitarian and human rights norms. The law and justice chapters in this book discuss in detail the normative frameworks and international laws with which various agencies are involved. Below, this chapter considers the strategies of naming and shaming and CZOP. It is important to note that the strategy of naming and shaming through monitoring processes does not involve the direct participation of children. Although NGOs were first resented and viewed with suspicion by governments, an ad hoc working group on the UNCRC gradually emerged as a positive source representing NGOs at the UN level. At the international level, NGOs have become significant actors and norm-shapers. The experience of NGOs – especially child rights organisations at local levels – became crucial to ensuring the compliance of state and non-state actors during times of conflict. The mainstreaming of children's concerns through the UN protection agenda for children affected by armed conflict has focused on four specific elements defining the specificities and the scope of application of its campaign.[16] These are:

systematic monitoring and reporting of grave violations against children as a basis for action to end the impunity of those committing abuses; mainstreaming of CAAC [children affected by armed conflict] concerns into the policies, priorities, and programs of the entities and institutional processes of the UN and beyond; strategic advocacy, awareness raising, and dissemination of CAAC norms and standards; recognition, support, and enhancement of local civil society actors, organisations, and networks who represent the front line protection and rehabilitation of CAAC.[17]

This programme emphasises that a significant limitation in ensuring accountability and countering impunity is the silence and invisibility of children in international global advocacy discourse. The UN

---

of Two Years Conflict in Syria', (2013). Available at www.savethechildren.org. uk/resources/online-library/childhood-under-fire.

[16] See Chapter 4 in this book.

[17] Tonderai W. Chikuhwa, 'The Evolution of the United Nations' Protection Agenda for Children', in Scott Gates and Simon Reich (eds.), *Child Soldiers in the Age of Fractured States* (Pittsburgh, PA: University of Pittsburgh Press, 2010), 37–55, 39.

Security Council therefore determined to list publicly the identity of perpetrators, their location and area of activity.[18] This is covered by Resolution 1261 (2001), and is applicable to those who continue to recruit and use children as child soldiers. The perpetrators were to be included in an annex of named parties in the Secretary-General's Annual Report on Children and Armed Conflict. This practice has continued since 2002, and has brought some success in terms of compliance. The most recent annual report of the Secretary-General consists of fifty-seven parties in fifteen countries, including seven government forces; seventeen perpetrators have been on the list for at least five years and count among the most persistent violators.[19]

Human rights organisations such as Amnesty International have frequently named actors responsible for violating international norms. One of the most visible means of naming and shaming has been through NGO evaluations of states parties to the Committee on the Rights of the Child for the Convention (the Committee) – see Table 9.2. The CRIN data on NGO Alternative Reports suggest that a total of 446 NGO reports were submitted to the Committee up until 2010.

Table 9.2 *The Principal International NGOs Submitting Reports on the UNCRC*

Number of Reports	International NGO
28	Child Helpline International
28	Coalition to Stop the Use of Child Soldiers
27	Human Rights Watch
17	Global Initiative to End All Corporal Punishment of Children
17	Defence for Children International
12	Save the Children
9	Organisation Mondiale Centre la Torture
8	NGO Group for the UNCRC
6	Children's Rights Alliance

Source: Poulatova, *Children and Armed Conflict*, 196.

[18] OSRSG-CaAC, 'Naming and Shaming'. Available at http://childrenandarmed conflict.un.org/our-work/naming-and-shaming/.
[19] Ibid.

These reports submitted by the major international NGOs reflect that in their advocacy strategies at the global level, NGOs either evaluate the states parties' performance with regard to the UNCRC or adopt an issue-specific approach. In relation to Article 38, which bans the recruitment of children under the age of fifteen in war and armed conflicts, for example, Poulatova classifies NGO reporting on children's concerns into three groups.[20] Referring to these classifications, the following discussion provides concrete examples of how children are represented and their everyday lives documented in global lobbying. The first category comprises NGOs that emphasise specific issues of the UNCRC instead of directly evaluating states parties' performance with regard to Article 38. The NGOs in this category generate pressure by reproducing case material on children's vulnerabilities. For example, the Global Initiatives to End All Corporal Punishment for Children refers in its reports to evidence of the prevalence of corporal punishment in private and public spaces, such as the home, alternative care and penal systems cases. Its main aim is to ban all forms of corporal punishment and provide support for public education programmes. Its Afghanistan report in 2011 noted, 'we hope the Committee will urge the government of Afghanistan to enact legislation to prohibit corporal punishment of children in all settings, including in the family and in the penal system under Islamic law, and to support law reform with relevant public awareness raising and education'.[21]

The NGOs in Poulatova's second category are concerned with children's protection in armed conflicts. A transnational alliance of NGOs, the Coalition to Stop the Use of Child Soldiers, is an archetypical example in this category. This coalition is committed exclusively to ending the recruitment and use of child soldiers, whereas other NGOs that look at child soldiering conduct their advocacy on other aspects of child rights violations as well. In its 2011 submission, the coalition brought attention to Southern Thailand and informal armed groups. It stated that unlike the armed opposition groups, which actively seek out and indoctrinate children in order to secure their participation in acts of armed violence, the

---

[20] Ibid., 197–202.
[21] Child Rights International Network, 'Briefing from Global Initiative to End All Corporal Punishment of Children –Afghanistan'. Available at www.crin.org/resources/infoDetail.asp?ID=23838&flag=legal.

recruitment of boys to the *Chor Ror Bor* (Village Defence Volunteers) is not formal policy. Instead it arises primarily from a lack of vigilance on the part of the Thai authorities and a lack of awareness at the village level of relevant government regulations and directives, or alternative, more appropriate options for young people.[22]

In the third category are those NGOs that advocate for enforcement of all the UNCRC provisions. Poulatova observes that a majority of these NGOs refer to Article 22 on refugee children, and Article 39 on rehabilitative care, recovery and social integration of children, while a third of the NGOs in this category explicitly report on Article 38. However, NGOs are increasingly drawing attention to a broader range of UNCRC rights violations and using interviews with images of children to represent those violations. For example, in its submission to the 62nd–63rd session of the Committee, the Palestinian Centre for Human Rights included in its report images of children who have survived horrific injuries. The report offers supplementary information on Israel's second periodic UNCRC report, addressing the following issues with regard to children in the Gaza Strip:

- illegal attacks by the Israeli army on the Gaza Strip resulting in the deaths and injury of children, violating Article 6 (survival and development) of the UNCRC;
- the country's failure to provide a safe and clean environment, negatively impacting on health, in violation of Article 24 (on health and health services) of the UNCRC;
- Israeli attacks against school buildings, denying children's rights to education and negatively affecting the mental health of school children, violating Articles 24 and 27 (adequate standard of living) of the UNCRC;
- Israel's unlawful arrest and subsequent detention of children, in violation of Article 37 (on detention and punishment) of the UNCRC.[23]

---

[22] Child Soldiers International, 'Report Priority to Protect Preventing Children's Association with Village Defence Militias in Southern Thailand', March 2011. Available at www.refworld.org/docid/4d79f35b2.html.
[23] Palestinian Centre for Human Rights, Submission to the 62–63rd Session of the Committee on the Rights of the Child: Report of Israel under the Convention on the Rights of the Child, (15 July, 2012). Available at www.bettercare network.org/resources/infodetail.asp?id=29707.

The report includes testimonies of victims and their families. Children and young people's statements are taken in the presence of supportive family members rather than in isolation. This indicates that some NGOs also pay attention to ethical methodology in their research:

My name is Mohammed Salman Mubarak al-Sweirki. I am 17 years old. I live in Juhr al-Dik area. I started to collect iron and aluminum three days ago. This activity is the only living resource for me and for my family. I make around 60 NIS daily. At around 06:00 am on Monday, 03 October 2011, I went with two of my friends Saed Ali al-Sawarkah (17) and Ahmed Fawzi al-Sawarkah (15) to the dump site in the east of Juhr al-Dik around 400 meters from the border. I started to collect iron and aluminum ... We were nearly 500 meters from the border. At approximately 09:00 am on the same day, we were surprised by a single bullet fired by one of the Israeli soldiers who were positioned at the border. We ran away but another bullet was fired and wounded me in my left foot.[24]

The Arakan Project in its alternative report on Burma's country report raised Article 2 (non-discrimination), Article 7 (registration, name, nationality, care), Article 24 (health and health services), and Article 28 (right to education). Similar to the Palestinian organisation's report, it uses children's images and interviews to focus on country violations of the UNCRC. In Part II of this report – titled 'Rohingya Children in Their Own Words' – the NGO also includes interviews of five children, aged between nine and twelve. With regard to the interviews it is explained:

The Arakan Project met them while they were on a short visit to Bangladesh. All these children are currently living and growing up in Northern Rakhine State, Myanmar. They were afraid that they or their family would face problems back home because they talked to us. For this reason, we have omitted their real names as well as the name of their village and we have not included their photographs.[25]

The five respondents were asked various questions about documentation of citizenship, restriction on movement, rights to basic needs, arrest and detention, forced labour, and about their future. The official report of the state had made no reference to the

---

[24] Ibid., 13.
[25] Arakan Project, 'Submission to the Committee on the Rights of the Child: For the Examination of the Combined 3rd and 4th Periodic State Party Reports' (January 2012), 13. Available at www.crin.org/docs/Myanmar_AP_CRC%20 Report%20UPDATED.pdf.

Muslim population of the Northern Rakhine state and ignored specific recommendations that were made by the Committee adopted on 30 June 2004 relating to the concerns faced by the Muslim population:

Do you understand the word 'stateless'? What does it mean to you?
    Anwar (9 yrs)
    Stateless, what is this? You say people who have no country are stateless. I have a country. My country is Burma.[26]
    Abdullah (11 yrs)
    I don't know the word stateless. You say that someone who has no country is stateless. Burma is my country. I am not stateless. I live in a country called Burma. If someone is born and brought up in a country then he belongs to that country. All people are born in some country and that is their country. Why should one be stateless?[27]
    Enayet (11 yrs)
    ... You say that stateless people are people without a country. What do stateless people look like? When I think about it, Magh[28] boys can travel without any travel document and they can go wherever they want to go but I can't do that. Maybe this is because the country belongs to them and does not belong to me. Is that why we face so many problems to visit people in a different village? Or maybe it is because Burma is only for Buddhists, not for Muslims. Does this mean that I am stateless? I don't understand this.[29]

The report also provides insights on children's experiences in forced labour.

Rafique (12 yrs)
    I must work to support my family. I first worked for a farmer and then I started working for myself as a fisherman in a shrimp farm and catching fish in the river. Sometimes I also collect firewood. I earn between 1,000 and 1,200 Kyat a day, sometimes more. I spent all that I earned for my brothers and sisters. For the farmer I used to work 12 to 14 hours a day. Now I work on average 8 to 10 hours a day fishing or collecting firewood ... I also have to work at least once a week in the NaSaKa camp ... sometimes twice a week. This NaSaKa camp is about 1.5 miles from my house.[30]

Karim Ali (11 yrs) knew it would be tough but he took forced labour duties to help his family just before he turned ten years of age.

[26] Ibid., 15.   [27] Ibid., 19.
[28] Pejorative term used to identify Rakhine Buddhists. Muslims on the other hand are often called *kala* – meaning dark-skinned people.
[29] Arakan Project, 24.   [30] Ibid., 33.

Once I had to carry sand, bricks and gravel downhill and then again uphill, because the Army was building a house on top of that hill. Many people had to work for many months for this new building on the hill. The hill was very high and climbing it carrying a load was too difficult for me. I will never forget this all my life. I could hardly carry 5 bricks at a time to the top of that hill. I fell sick and got fever because this work was too hard and my whole body was painful.[31]

These examples illustrate that NGOs are not only being creative in their advocacy strategies by representing children's direct voices in high-level documentation, but also giving careful consideration to questions of ethics in their fieldwork methodology.

The transformative politics of advocacy: CZOP

In the second approach, children's visibility is raised in both global and local advocacy by drawing attention to their vulnerabilities and marginalisation. However, this approach also includes initiatives to integrate children's voices into advocacy programmes, and from early 2000 in encouraging children's peace movements.

In the early 1980s, Nils Thedin, then a delegate of Sweden to the Executive Board of UNICEF, lobbied for children's organisations to stress 'children as a conflict-free zone in human relations'.[32] In Lebanon, many children from different communities and factions – Druze, Shiite, Christian, Palestinian and others – attend summer camps for a period for several years as part of a peace education campaign. As the idea of promoting CZOP developed through these initiatives in different parts of the world, prominent individuals supported negotiation processes in a number of conflict societies. For example, in the early 1980s, James P. Grant, then Executive Director of UNICEF, joined forces with Archbishop Arturo Rivero Damas of El Salvador to broker 'days of tranquillity' between the government and the rebel forces, which allowed health workers to carry out vaccination programmes throughout the country.[33]

The protection of children from harm is enshrined in the last paragraph of the Machel Report, which urges the need to claim

---

[31] Ibid., 37.
[32] Varindra Tarzie Vittachi, *Between the Guns – Children as a Zone of Peace* (London: Hodder and Stoughton, 1993).
[33] Nigel Fisher, 'Leadership and Impunity: The Politics Behind the Traumatization of Children During Armed Conflicts', *Traumatology* 8(3) (2002), 146–59, 151.

CZOP.[34] This was embraced enthusiastically by the UNICEF office in Colombo in early 2000. A study conducted by the Reflecting on the Peace Practice Project in 2001 recorded that people felt that children's voices could influence the dominant attitudes regarding the conflict in Sri Lanka.[35] In the first phase, UNICEF Colombo initiated a series of consultations with a wide range of stakeholders from, for example, the Ministry of Defence, the Liberation Tigers of Tamil Eelam (LTTE), religious organisations, local and international NGOs, schools, and communities directly affected by the conflict. The agreement stipulated that CZOP would provide a positive advocacy function and bring attention to the effects of conflict on children. A loose coalition of interested agencies and individuals was formed as a result of this consultation process, with over 250 participants from civil society. The result was a booklet titled: 'The Children as Zones of Peace: A Call for Action, Promoting and Protecting the Rights of Children Affected by Armed Conflict in Sri Lanka', which was closely based on the Machel Report and published in English, Sinhala and Tamil. The booklet recorded that by 1998 an estimated 380,000 children were displaced – many of them repeatedly – and up to 250,000 remain displaced. Land mines and unexploded weapons created several civilian victims every month, the majority being children. Approximately 900,000 children living in the war zones experience a variety of problems, from reduced medical care to displacement, rape and recruitment as soldiers.[36]

Sixteen agencies working in Sri Lanka endorsed the CZOP initiative. However, the different mandates across the agencies constrained the extent to which CZOP could succeed. There were disagreements about CZOP's public stand as a group against the recruitment of child soldiers. These concerns also affected how Sri Lankans perceived the CZOP, and ultimately the initiative was not very effective: 'CZOP is not controversial enough; the concept is too obvious (we can all agree that children are important) and therefore easy to dismiss or ignore'.[37]

Practitioners have taken the phrase apart, pointing to the political and cultural inappropriateness of each of the words. For example, in the interviews given to the Reflecting on the Peace Practice Project, some

---

[34] See Chapter 1 of this book.
[35] Luc Zandvliet and Orion Kriegman, 'Reflecting on Peace Practice Project', Report published by Life and Peace Institute, Uppsala, 2001, 5.
[36] Ibid., 5–7.   [37] Ibid., 14.

observers noted that even though children made choices to join military forces at times of conflict, they could not easily be separated from the family sphere. Adults continued to form a part of their world and to offer safety. Death of a parent, a family member or a teacher affected a child's peace. Also, the term 'zone' was politically loaded. Earlier, UNESCO declared Jaffna as a 'zone of peace' that the LTTE dismissed since there was an implication that Jaffna could not be attacked. Some worried that 'zone of peace' could mean an anti-Tamil Eelam position. Others questioned whether children could constitute zones of peace; whether zones were geographical locations; and even whether adults should tell children they were zones of peace, particularly when they experienced violence on a daily basis. The implicit message for children in this naming process could be that adults were out of touch with children's everyday realities. In addition, NGOs pointed out that it is not only armed conflicts that affect children's security. Challenging issues of class, caste and minority identities must be included in the broader definition of peace. The term as a whole did not make much sense to Sinhala, whereas the Tamil translation was closer to the spirit of the phrase – 'children are sacred places' in seeking to establish an umbrella of protection.[38]

In Sri Lanka, the concept was understood as one that was owned by UNICEF, which limited local legitimacy. CZOP in Sri Lanka did not emerge following a needs assessment of the country, but rather was an outcome of a report commissioned by the UNGA. This example of an advocacy effort initiated by international organisations in a local context raises questions regarding the extent to which a concept with universal implication and applicability needs to be tailored to suit specific political and cultural settings, or even whether it is practically possible to do so. UNICEF's approach in Sri Lanka was careful not to offend the warring factions, including the government. While the strategy was to transform the attitude towards children, the top-heavy operational design of the CZOP as led by UNICEF was criticised as not being forceful enough. For example, in May 1998, the Special Representative of the Secretary-General of the UN for Children and Armed Conflict, Olara Otunnu, visited Sri Lanka. Prior to his visit, UNICEF ran a print media campaign that included narratives of four children affected by violence in conflicts in Sri Lanka. The campaigns were run via television and radio channels

---

[38] Ibid., 14–16.

with the understanding that they should be informative but non-confrontational.

As such, children were present at the first stage of the CZOP in Sri Lanka only as subjects of international advocacy efforts. Children's vulnerabilities in conflict situations in Sri Lanka were highlighted by representing them primarily as victims in need of protection, but they were given no say in designing the protection mechanisms. The politics of the armed conflict in Sri Lanka influenced the success of the CZOP programme and constrained children's ownership and participation at a minimal level. The staff at the UNICEF Colombo office believed that the ongoing conflict seriously undermined the traditional importance given to education, as schools were used for recruitment centres for both the LTTE and the paramilitary forces of the government. One of its initiatives was to sponsor theatre groups that allowed children to express themselves and motivated parents to send them to school. However, some parents were not satisfied with UNICEF's approach of encouraging children to take initiative and support each other to go to school, believing that financial support for children was more important.[39] At this time, although children participated in theatre groups, it was adults – their families, the local and international NGOs and other stakeholders – who were the primary beneficiaries of these programmes.

By 2005, a transformation was visible in the CZOP approach as children's voices began to be directly included as a result of increasing awareness of effective ways of including children. The CZOP initiative considered that the global and local norms and perspectives of integrating children's voices in the design was a more effective way of carrying out its agenda. As a result, whereas in 1998 the images of children were used to raise awareness of their vulnerabilities, by 2005 there was a conscious shift to include children's thoughts in the promotion of peace. The CZOP initiative carried out a nationwide survey of 1,500 children between the ages of nine and sixteen, from different religions, ethnic groups and socio-economic classes. A poll released in May of that year revealed that if they were president, only 3 per cent of Sri Lankan children would be in favour of fighting a war.[40]

---

[39] Ibid., 6.
[40] CZOP Media Release, 'Sri Lankan Children Overwhelmingly Support Peace, Finds New Poll'. Available at www.unicef.org/srilanka/activities_1677.htm.

Most children would instead prefer to promote peace and bridge political and ethnic differences. Children responding to the survey felt that if the armed conflict was resolved, the money otherwise spent on the war could be used to develop schools; help children from different ethnic groups coexist; allow children in the north and east to return to school; and rebuild schools destroyed by war. In addition to measuring children's attitudes towards war and peace in Sri Lanka, the poll aimed to take a vital first step in ensuring children a voice in the peace building process. The UNICEF Representative in Sri Lanka was quoted by the press: '[a]lthough child rights are now on the peace process agenda, children are not given the opportunity to effectively participate in the peace process, this poll should act as a starting point to enable greater representation of children in peace building'.[41]

Sri Lanka's twenty-six years of protracted conflict ended after extremely violent battles in 2009. The UN estimates that 40,000 civilians died in the five months before the war formally ended in May 2009, when the LTTE surrendered. Other estimates suggest that a minimum of 70,000 died in these five months, while the government of Sri Lanka claimed that the number was 10,000.[42] The government declared a No Fire Zone (NFZ) on 20 January 2009 on a thin strip of land estimated to be 35 square km in Mullaithivu, on Sri Lanka's northeast coast.[43] During these five months the government violated international norms and systematically subjected these areas to aerial and artillery bombardment. On the other hand, the LTTE also committed war crimes by not allowing civilians to move out of the NFZ. Its fighters prevented civilians from leaving LTTE territory, and in the final weeks shot those trying to flee to safety. It forcibly recruited children as young as fourteen and used forced labour to build its

---

[41] Ibid.
[42] See the report by the Expert Panel on Sri Lanka, April 25, 2011. Available at www.un.org/News/dh/infocus/Sri_Lanka/The_Internal_Review_Panel_report_on_Sri_Lanka.pdf.
[43] Following heavy shelling, the international organisations left the no-fly-zone (NFZ) along with the Red Cross on 25 January. On 12 February, another NFZ was declared covering a 12 km coastal strip that was packed with 300,000 children, women and men. On 27 April, the government declared the third NFZ, where an estimated 100,000 people were crammed together. The government claimed that there were 10,000 civilians and the military deliberately restricted emergency supplies to the area. For details see the report by the Expert Panel on Sri Lanka, April 25, 2011, 8–14. Available at www.un.org/News/dh/infocus/Sri_Lanka/The_Internal_Review_Panel_report_on_Sri_Lanka.pdf.

defences.[44] While no age-disaggregated data exist for the last stage of the battle, all reports confirm that many children perished in 2009 despite remaining in the NFZ. In 2012, Channel 4, UK showed footage of twelve-year-old Balachandran Prabhakaran, the son of the LTTE leader, Velupillai Prabhakaran. He was executed while in military custody along with five men, believed to be his bodyguards.[45] The documentary showed how Balachandran was given a small final meal and then shot dead at a close range.

While CZOP is valuable for negotiation and even humanitarian intervention, the Sri Lankan example illustrates that international advocacy of CZOP has certain limitations. Lack of political will, violation of international and local norms, and labelling children as enemies and hostages could break down the gentle image of CZOP, which appears to be successful only at times when warring factions are willing to compromise. Educational programmes, however, are one of CZOP's more successful advocacy strategies. According to UNESCO, there are currently 67 million children not receiving schooling throughout the world, and over 40 per cent of them are in conflict-affected countries.[46] Representatives of Côte d'Ivoire, India, Liberia, Nepal and South Sudan met in Nepal in May 2012 to work on the Schools as Zones of Peace programme. The strategies that the forty participants discussed included: community ownership; the use of art-based therapy in conflict-affected areas of Chhattisgarh, India; child-friendly teachers in Liberia; and involving students in building drinking water taps in South Sudan.[47] Stressing that education is crucial to peace, this five-country initiative focused on the transition to peace by linking schools to the family and the community. The programme

[44] Ibid.
[45] Channel 4 film, *No Fire Zone: The Killing Fields of Sri Lanka*. Also see, film-maker Callum Macrae's comments, available at www.independent.co.uk/ voices/comment/no-fire-zone-the-truth-is-out-about-sri-lanka-despite-official-efforts-to-stop-it-8931603.html.
[46] Megh Raj Ale and Rupa Joshi, Media Release, 'As strikes grip Nepal, children demonstrate against efforts to close schools' (Kathmandu: UN Children's Fund) 25 May, 2012. See www.unicef.org/infobycountry/nepal_62457.html? p=printme.
[47] Rupa Joshi, Media Release, 'Countries learn from Nepal's 'Schools as Zones of Peace' programme', (Kathmandu: UN Children's Fund) May 16, 2012. See www.protectingeducation.org/news/countries-learn-nepals-schools-zones-peace-programme.

was also implemented in Nepal through collaboration between the government and local and global civil society actors. UNICEF in Nepal asserts that the Schools as Zones of Peace initiative succeeded in ensuring that more than 1 million Nepali children in more than 4,000 schools directly benefited from schools being kept open at times of political unrest.[48]

A very important outcome of CZOP has been the promotion of the role of children in peace movements. While CZOP has targeted education and health programmes, the constant reference to children's role in peace building has also allowed the programme to move beyond strategic interventions. However, as discussed below, it is not only CZOP that succeeded in effecting this change: a range of local and global advocacy strategies have promoted children's roles and responsibilities as peace activists.

Children as activists

> We can't change the whole world alone, but if I can teach people that if you put your hand in mine and little by little we join more hands, maybe we can construct a new world.[49]

When her friend Jorge died, Farlis Calle was traumatised and deeply shaken by the civil war in Colombia. In April 1996, the UN sent Graça Machel to investigate the impact of the conflict on Colombian children. Machel's call to children asking them to express in their own words how they felt about the war sparked a spirit of activism in Farlis. With research undertaken by her school student council, a children's movement was formed that worked within the national constitution to contest local elections and form a local government of children in her town municipality of Apartadó. Farlis and other young activists demonstrated unwavering courage in calling for a national ceasefire. Amidst death threats, Farlis averred 'You can't kill the hopes of kids!'[50] On 25 October 1996, 2.7 million children voted for peace. The Colombian Children's Movement for Peace succeeded in establishing peace zones in schools and parks.

---

[48] Ibid.
[49] Farlis Calle, aged 15, Colombian, in Janet Wilson, *One Peace: True Stories of Young Activists* (Victoria: Orca Book Publishers, 2008), 11.
[50] Ibid.

Almost no peace activism existed in Colombia until the early to mid-1990s.[51] Although various political regimes initiated peace talks with guerrilla groups, organised citizens' networks were rarely invited to be part of these negotiations. Citizen's groups organised the first peace week in September 1987, which involved a variety of educational and social awareness events. After the collapse of peace talks between the government and the *Fuerzas Armadas Revolucionarias de Colombia* (FARC) and *Ejército de Liberación Nacional* (ELN) in 1992, peace activists organised themselves throughout the country and formed the National Network of Initiatives for Peace and against War (REDEPAZ) in 1993. Supported by REDEPAZ and UNICEF, children, including Farlis Calle and the Apartadó students, symbolically voted for peace. A year later, on 26 October 1997, in a non-binding ballot measure during municipal elections, 10 million adults also voted for peace, pledging their support for the Children's Mandate for Peace. Peace groups, church leaders and other members of civil society joined hands to organise a 'Citizen Mandate for Peace'. The Colombian Children's Movement for Peace was nominated three times for the Nobel Peace Prize.[52] The organisation has grown to more than 100,000 members from 400 different youth organisations throughout the country. These events demonstrate that politicised environments can compel children to take action. Children have the power to mobilise and lead their communities towards positive change.[53] The issue of children in peace building is dealt with in greater detail in Chapter 7 in this book.

Children's activism also involves their voluntary participation in resistance movements and protests, some of which are violent in nature. Critics have claimed that media and education are responsible for motivating children to participate in demonstrations and resistance movements. Voluntary participation of children in protests receives impetus from a number of causal factors, among them children's perception of danger; their daily witnessing of the impunity enjoyed

[51] Adam Isacson and Jorge Rojas Rodríguez, 'Origins, Evolution, Lessons of the Colombian Peace Movement', in Virginia M. Bouvier (ed.), *Colombia: Building Peace in a Time of War* (Washington, DC: United States Institute of Peace, 2009), 9–38, 20.

[52] Ibid., 21–22.

[53] Sara Cameron, 'Children as Leaders: Lessons from Colombia's Children's Movement for Peace', *Peace News*, 2444 (2001), Available at http://peacenews.info/node/3928/children-leaders-lessons-colombias-childrens-movement-peace.

by government forces and rebel groups; and in-group loyalties. In both the Israel-Palestine and the Kashmir conflicts children have been involved in civil disobedience movements that at times have involved violent protests. The stone-pelting practices of protest movements for many children and youth have been voluntary, while in the case of Kashmir, the Indian government has maintained that foreign states were responsible for instigating youth violence.

Prior to President Barack Obama's visit to Israel on 20 March 2013, twenty-seven young Palestinian boys between seven and fifteen years were arrested in the West Bank city of Hebron for wearing Obama masks in public. The Israeli human rights group *B'Tselem*[54] sought legal advice, and the Israeli Defence Force (IDF) released an official statement, claiming that '[d]ue to recent stone-throwing incidents toward the security forces and citizens in the city, the IDF arrested Palestinian youth who pelted stones. Seven have been taken for a police interrogation.'[55] Precedents of stone pelting in civil disobedience have long been visible in Palestinian movements, beginning with the resistance campaigns against the British between 1936 and 1939. Nevertheless, organised stone pelting by children and young adults took a new direction during the first intifada, from December 1987 until the signing of the Oslo Accords in 1993. At this time, youth – many of whom joined the resistance movement voluntarily – were also involved in a range of community activities. As a result of the Israeli siege, assaults and restrictions on the Palestinian press, many of them resorted to writing graffiti on walls as a means of political resistance. In the Palestinian uprising against the Israeli occupation of Palestinian territories, the youth in Gaza, the West Bank and East Jerusalem initiated a programme of civil disobedience, pelting stones, rocks, bricks and petrol bombs. Cheap and accessible slingshots were effective in attracting international attention, as they emphasised the radically uneven level of resources available to the combatant parties, and the IDF's use of excessive force to curb public violence. In the absence of anti-riot troops, the IDF and the Border Police were provided with protective helmets, plastic and rubber ammunition,

---

[54] See www.btselem.org/press_releases/20130320_minors_detained_in_hebron.
[55] Ynet news, 'IDF arrest 7 children for throwing stones in Hebron', 20 March 2013. See www.ynetnews.com/articles/0,7340,L-4359014,00.html.

batons and gas canisters. The Israeli government also invented a gravel-throwing vehicle with which to disperse rock-throwing mobs.[56]

The Indian state has been equally hard on stone-pelting youth in the State of Jammu and Kashmir (J&K). In June 2010, the Indian army killed three Kashmiris on a 'fake encounter' mission, later claiming that they were Pakistani infiltrators. The anti-India protest movements began when the opposition demanded the demilitarisation of Kashmir. In March 2011, the State government admitted that over 5,228 young protesters were arrested in 2010 in Kashmir, of which 4,900 were later released. In a press release in May the Jammu and Kashmir State government revealed that over 1,811 youth – against whom 230 cases were registered for 'involvement' in stone pelting during the 2010 and 2011 unrest in Kashmir – had been granted amnesty under a scheme announced by the Chief Minister Omar Abdullah.[57] The Chief Minister made it clear that the amnesty would not extend to those who were involved in arson and damage to public and private property.

We have decided to give the youths a second chance. Cases against all the youths arrested on charges of stone-pelting, but not involved in arson, registered during last year's disturbance will be withdrawn ... Their involvement in these [stone pelting] cases may not affect adversely in the verification of these youths for obtaining passport [sic],[58] service verification and for obtaining loans for education/jobs.[59]

A child's or a young adult's social, cultural and political identity is shaped by the world she or he is exposed to. In her ground-breaking work on children and the politics of culture, Sharon Stephens wrote:

the notion of children's culture is also important within less universalizing approaches to the study of young people as social actors in their own right, engaged in making sense of and recreating the social worlds they inherit.

---

[56] Hemda Ben-Yehuda and Shmuel Sandler, *The Arab-Israeli Conflict Transformed* (New York, NY: State University of New York, 2002), 146.

[57] Muddasir Ali, '1800 "stone pelting" youth granted amnesty: Govt, Greater Kashmir' (12 March, 2013). See www.greaterkashmir.com/news/2013/Mar/12/1800-stone-pelting-youth-granted-amnesty-govt-84.asp.

[58] It is incredibly difficult for Kashmiri political and human rights activists to get a passport. Many of the activists have not been allowed to leave India for years.

[59] Muddasir Ali, '1800 "stone pelting" youth granted amnesty'.

Children creatively live from inside complex mixtures of languages and social domains that are external structures for many adults.[60]

Stephens suggests that through their experiences children know many things that adults are unaware of or unable to comprehend. For Palestinian and Kashmiri children, stone pelting and writing graffiti are rituals of resistance through which they make choices in their everyday lives and take back a modicum of control from the authorities. In both cases childhood is militarised, and the political framing of movements make children's role politicised as well. As these examples illustrate, the issue of children's activism in protest movements is complex and often impelled by how they perceive their state's actions. The Israel-Palestine and Kashmir conflicts demonstrate that political movements have the potential to harden children's social and cultural identities, politicising their actions and encouraging children to participate willingly in violent protest movements.

Stephens states:

The crucial task for researchers now ... is to develop more powerful understandings of the role of the child in the structures of modernity, the historical processes by which these once localized Western constructions have been exported around the world and the global, political, economic, and cultural transformations that are currently rendering children so dangerous, contested, and pivotal in the formation of new sorts of social persons, groups, and institutions.[61]

As the final section in this chapter will reveal, Stephen's words are relevant more than a decade later in this discussion of childhood; particular kinds of childhood are perceived as dangerous and contested, and hence undesirable.

Children as political subjects – babies as political objects[62]

As discussed at the beginning of this chapter, disappeared children in Latin America were very much perceived as embodying great political

---

[60] 'Introduction' in Sharon Stephens, *Children and the Politics of Culture* (Princeton, NJ: Princeton University Press, 1995), 24.

[61] Ibid., 13–14.

[62] This section primarily draws from D'Costa, *Nationbuilding, Gender and War Crimes in South Asia*. For details of these case studies see Chapters 2 and 4 of this book.

potential. They were abducted for adoption by rich and powerful families, ostensibly to curb and discourage resistance by future generations. This section discusses a similar example in which undesirable babies were removed from their parents for racist, genocidal motives; that is, to preserve the purity of the state and the sanctity of the family. In this way, the babies are politically objectified to curb or even eradicate their potential to become political subjects as children and adults.

Sexual violence perpetrated during conflict as a reproductive crime has received significant attention following the Balkan wars. Conceived in conflicts around the globe, children referred to as 'war babies' face stigma, discrimination and often infanticide.[63] Humanitarian NGOs have shown interest in integrating the children born of sexual violence during conflict into their communities in any post-conflict humanitarian efforts, migration policies or refugee settlement programmes. However, the role of states has been analysed in depth without much attention being given to its relationship with the family. Feminists have discussed the family's role in gender oppression, inequality and the prevalence of domestic violence. Concomitantly, socialists have highlighted how family has been used as an instrument 'in conjunction with the institution of private property, for the reproduction of structured socio-economic inequality'.[64] In normal circumstances there is a deep unwillingness by the state to exercise its authority in how a family should function. The family is a valuable social institution and in most societies there exists an implicit assumption that it is appropriate for parents and adult family members to exercise their rights in family life. The presence of a child often provides the family with legitimacy to function as part of society as a family unit. However, when the child's legitimacy is in question, especially in a conflict targeting the community, the inviolable, private structure of the family also breaks down. As the example from South Asia below demonstrates, notions of honour and purity are crucial in constituting families and the nation through the control of the identity of children. Specifically, children born of fathers of the opposing culture and religious faith – Muslim or Hindu – in the aftermath of

[63] Charli Carpenter, 'Women, Children and Other Vulnerable Groups', 295.
[64] David William Archard, *Children, Family and the State* (Hampshire: Ashgate, 2003), 67.

India's Partition in 1947, and after the independence war of Bangladesh in 1971, were rejected because they were perceived as politicised objects. Civil society actors have assisted state schemes of social engineering through their active involvement in framing a particular kind of political identity, such as refugees, who are frequently regarded as undesirable and a threat to a nation's integrity and identity.

After Partition, children in India and Pakistan were destined to belong with their fathers, whereas in post-conflict Bangladesh abortion and international adoption sealed their futures. Carpenter points out that feminist scholars often place exclusive importance on the violation of maternal rights in understanding the politics of children conceived in war, and argues that such complexities must instead be explained in terms of children's human rights discourse.[65] This is an important ideological shift that responds to the repeated aspiration of states to re-formulate children's identities and citizenship claims in terms of political subjectivity. Civil society actors, such as social workers, volunteers and, in Bangladesh's case, international agencies, have all been involved in state-sponsored nation building projects. Through active support from civil society, the state has often controlled the legitimate space of upbringing for children regarded as 'illegitimate'. Separated from their mothers, their narratives have been ignored or erased.

The 1947 partition of India sparked widespread riots, during which brutal mass killings occurred, and thousands of women and girls on both sides of the newly formed borders were subjected to rape, abduction and forced marriage.[66] Children born of sexual violence during this period constituted a novel political problem for the two nations. Indian and Pakistani authorities used the term 'recovery operation' to describe the forced retrieval and return of abducted women and girls to their own communities, which in turn required determination of their children's legal status. The Indian and Pakistani governments entered into an Inter-Dominion Agreement in November

---

[65] R. Charli Carpenter, 'Surfacing Children: Limitations of Genocidal Rape Discourse', *Human Rights Quarterly* 22(2) (2000) 428–77 and R. Charli Carpenter, *Forgetting Children Born of War: Setting the Human Rights Agenda in Bosnia and Beyond* (New York, NY: Columbia University Press, 2010).

[66] The official estimate of the number of abducted women was placed at 50,000 Muslim women in India and 33,000 Hindu and Sikh women in Pakistan.

1947 to recover abducted persons. Between December 1947 and December 1949, Rameshwari Nehru's Women's Section in India's Ministry of Relief and Rehabilitation recovered 6,000 women and girls from Pakistan and returned 12,000 from India. Most recoveries were made from East and West Punjab, followed by Jammu, Kashmir and Patiala. Approximately 30,000 Muslim and non-Muslim women and girls were recovered by both countries over an eight-year period. The total number of Muslim women recovered was significantly higher – 20,728 as against 9,032 non-Muslims. While most recoveries occurred between 1947 and 1952, women were being returned as late as 1956. In order to expedite the process, instead of relying on the military the governments involved prominent women as social workers and a small number of agencies: civil society actors in India and Pakistan, such as female volunteers, social workers and welfare associations, were given a primary role.

Some of the close associates of Mahatma Gandhi, such as Mridula Sarabhai (Chief All India Organiser), Rameshwari Nehru (Honorary Adviser), Anis Kidwai and Sushila Nayar also worked for the recovery operation of the Indian government. While the Women's Section maintained overall responsibility for the operation, volunteers from the National Council of Women, the International Red Cross and the Friends Service Unit were also involved. Urvashi Butalia, Ritu Menon and Kamla Bhasin conducted ground-breaking historical research in this field, recording the Constituency Assembly Debates in which members of the Indian Parliament argued over the fate of the children. Their research highlights how the policymakers used religious identity as the primary criterion by which to determine where the children would belong. In an effort to restore moral order, the narratives of sexual violence prevalent during the Partition riots had to be reversed. This was achieved through redefinition of children's identity by implicitly acknowledging that the child belonged with the father, Hindu or Muslim, and should be left behind when women were being recovered from the enemy community.

However, as far as the recovery operation was concerned, removing women without their children proved to be a difficult task. While leaders were actively delineating boundaries and dividing communities and territories, social workers faced the appalling problem of separating women and children like 'oranges and grapes'.[67] Communities regarded children born of rape as the visible instantiation of the impurity of their mothers, and as such saw these children as posing a serious threat to national identity. The Indian and Pakistani governments had agreed that neither forced conversions nor forced marriages would be recognised by either country. It followed that children born of such unions would be illegitimate and in legislation were defined as 'abducted persons' if they were born within the time-frame specified in the Act. There was a firm belief that the children should remain with their natural fathers.[68] The policymakers and the practitioners in India concluded that Hindu fathers should be allowed their right of guardianship, but that children born of Muslim fathers could not be accommodated in majority Hindu India.[69] The children, who were the living proof of rape, could neither be socially acknowledged nor legally sanctioned.[70] The extent of each state's anxiety regarding the recovery of women and concomitant renunciation of their children was limited to concern over the legitimacy of citizenship of a child born of violence, and the intrinsic link of the identity of those children to the nation's notions of purity and honour.

Two decades after Partition, another brutal war resulted in East Pakistan seceding as the newly formed state of Bangladesh. In addition to mass killings, a large number of Bangladeshi women were subjected to sexual violence; the official figure is some 200,000. Official documents suggest that there were at least 25,000 cases of forced pregnancy in the aftermath of the war. Bangladeshi leaders entrusted social workers and medical practitioners with the primary responsibility of dealing with the raped women; as a result, International Planned Parenthood, the Red Cross and the Catholic Church became involved in rehabilitation programmes. These

[67] Ritu Menon and Kamla Bhasin, *Borders and Boundaries: Women in India's Partition* (New Delhi: Kali for Women, 1998), 118.

[68] Urvashi Butalia, *The Other Side of Silence: Voices from the Partition of India* (New Delhi: Penguin Books India, 1998), 215–17.

[69] As a result, not only women's sexuality but also their right to parenthood was violated by the state. Men, many of whom had actually committed the violence, were given the sole right to raise the children in Indian society, as fathers and legitimate guardians of the children. Menon and Bhasin, *Borders and Boundaries*.

[70] Veena Das, *Critical Events: An Anthropological Perspective on Contemporary India* (Oxford: Oxford University Press, 1995).

organisations also became responsible for carrying out the task of dealing with pregnancies. Two programmes thus began to occur simultaneously: that which allowed pregnant women to have abortions, and the programme for the adoption of war babies. From interviews with prominent social workers and medical practitioners directly involved with war babies, it is clear that while many of these social workers were genuinely committed to supporting the victims, there were occasions when decisions to terminate a pregnancy or relinquish the baby for adoption were contrary to the women's own choices. In addition, there were instances in which the resolute preferences of young pregnant girls were ignored, with girls being considered too young to make mature decisions. Confusion over how to deal with war babies appears to have reached high levels of government. Then Prime Minister of Bangladesh, Sheikh Mujibur Rahman, repeatedly referred to these *birangona* (valiant) women as his 'daughters', and asked the nation to welcome them back into their communities and families.[71] However, he also declared that 'none of the babies who carry the blood of the Pakistanis will be allowed to remain in Bangladesh'.[72] Nilima Ibrahim, a prominent social worker and feminist author, recalls meeting with Sheikh Mujibur in her book, *Ami Birangona Bolchi*.[73] When questioned about the status of war babies, the Prime Minister responded: 'Please send away the children who do not have their father's identity. They should be raised as human beings with honour. Besides, I do not want to keep those [*sic*] polluted blood in this country.' Perhaps such statements aided the push for adoption.[74]

In her research into the aftermath of the Balkan wars, Charli Carpenter investigates why most of the key organisations central to advocacy around children and armed conflict ignored children of rape between 1991 and 2007.[75] Carpenter identified that transnational gatekeepers – the organisations primarily associated with children's

[71] D'Costa, *Nationbuilding, Gender and War Crimes in South Asia*, 133.
[72] Ibid.
[73] Nilima Ibrahim, *Ami Birangona Bolchi* (Dhaka: Jagriti Prokashoni, 1998).
[74] In addition, through state-sponsored programmes, International Planned Parenthood and the International Abortion Research and Training Centre, local clinics helped women to carry out abortions. Clinics were set up with the support of the Bangladesh Central Organisation for Women's Rehabilitation in Dhaka and seventeen outlying areas, to cope with unwanted pregnancies.
[75] Charli Carpenter, *Forgetting Children Born of War*, 164.

issues – perceived the issue of children born of war to be too sensitive and complicated for direct advocacy. It is interesting to observe that while advocacy in other matters has advanced considerably, contemporary discourse on children born of war has made little progress since the conflicts of late 1940s, or even since the 1970s. Carpenter argues that championing the human rights of children in some cases has also generated anxiety about the extent to which it might detract attention from advocacy regarding sexual violence.[76] Similarly, in the South Asian context described above, the organisational, practical and tactical constraints of civil society groups, combined with the state's ideals of sovereignty and political belonging, play a critical role in recasting the role of babies as political objects and children as political subjects.

Conclusion

In Sierra Leone's post-war child rights programmes, UNICEF has sought to ensure that children can participate and raise their concerns. While UNICEF has been dedicated to this process, children have nonetheless been overwhelmed as they have been taught to regard it as culturally inappropriate to speak in front of adults.[77] Familial and social structure in different cultural contexts affects children's participation in social awareness campaigns; this chapter has demonstrated that cultural, political and social contexts matter in children's participation in advocacy.

This chapter documents children's struggles, activism and advocacy and their relation to civil society actors. While this is not a comprehensive global review of relevant examples, the cases chosen illustrate important insights about children's struggles that are often linked with a variety of advocacy strategies and social and political movements. It is sufficient that the chapter has considered children's rights in the context of interventions and policymaking in relation to a host of post-Cold War 'new wars' – mainly intra-state civil conflicts with regional dynamics. The general consensus – itself building on the legacy of the multilateral post-1945 conflict management experience – would appear to be that the likelihood, duration, severity and recurrence of violent conflict can be decreased by the

[76] Ibid., 173.   [77] Susan Shepler, 'The Rites of the Child', 197–211.

careful intervention of civil society. The second point is the correlation increasingly discerned between development and security discourse in protecting children and securing their rights in, for instance, education and health programmes.

While images of children have historically been used to frame advocacy measures, children's direct participation until comparatively recently has been almost non-existent in advocacy and activism. The rationale was that while it was critical to advocate for children's agency and empowerment, ultimately it was adults who framed policies. Such an advocacy approach was universal in global governance, including in transnational movements, anti-trafficking networks, and in state governance mechanisms. The brief overview provided here has outlined the status of children as participants in political movements – both peace and protest movements. Finally, this chapter has discussed how social workers, NGOs and advocacy networks have dealt with the sensitive issue of children born of conflict. State's rights to construct legitimate citizens have been supported by civil society's approach of preserving culturally appropriate measures, and engaging families and local communities. Children's representations in global and local advocacy strategies – their participation and the political framing of their identities – illustrates that the multifaceted and sometimes paradoxical engagement of civil society in child protection and child rights discourse is an ongoing and significant factor that must be recognised in order to understand and properly accede to the rights of children in post-conflict society.

On a final note, while we are completing the manuscript for this book, images of children affected by conflicts in Gaza, Syria, Iraq, Afghanistan and elsewhere continue to fill our television screens; indiscriminate attacks on civilian areas or attacks directly targeting civilians have taken a terrible toll on children. They were killed by explosive weapons, air strikes or the use of terror tactics in places where intensifying hostilities included widespread grave violations against children. However, we must question the selective moral outrage of the international community and the focus of various advocacy efforts to respond to crimes committed against children.

On the night of 14–16 April 2014, Boko Haram, an extremist group abducted 276 female students from the Government Secondary School in Chibok, Borno province of Nigeria. Though violence has occurred in Nigeria for years, the massive abduction shocked the international community into assisting the search for the missing girls. The reporting in various international media thoroughly captured the public opinion in the United States. It deployed eighty troops in Chad to assist in the search for the schoolgirls. Marking one hundred days since the incident, Gordon Brown, the UN Special Envoy on Global Education and the former Prime Minister of the United Kingdom writes: '[f]or an adolescent with plans, dreams and ambitions, 100 days must seem an eternity. But they are not alone. The world has not forgotten these girls. Not in 100 days, not for one day.'[78] Organised by the Global March against Child Labour, on 23 July 2014 demonstrations were held in Africa, Asia and Latin America. For example, led by *Idara-e-Taleem-o-Aagahi* (ITA), schoolgirls in Pakistan campaigned for girls' right to education. Similar campaigns were organised by the *Bachpan Bachao Andolan* group, which rescues children from bonded labour in India, and Walk Free, the anti-slavery organisation in different parts of the globe.

Conversations and debates surrounding the kidnap of the Nigerian girls range from the resurgence of al Qaeda to the persecution of minority Christians to the deprivation of education opportunities for women. The International community also took note of the social media #BringBackOurGirls campaign which effectively began to raise awareness of the crisis. On the other hand, the civil war in Syria claimed 11,420 of its children by December 2013. Further, an estimated 130 children were kidnapped by the Islamic State of Iraq and Syria (ISIS) in Manbij, a Syrian town, in early 2014. In May 2014, according to the Human Rights Watch another 153 children were abducted by ISIS from the mostly anti-Kurdish town of Ain-al-Arab. Some critics observe that the horrific experiences of children in Syria and Iraq do not make the lead news anymore and could not shock the international community into action.

The international community has often supported education and health projects in conflict zones and in countries in transition to rebuild societies. Similarly, in recent conflicts extremist groups tended to have targeted educational and health facilities such as schools, hospitals and health clinics. Schools and hospitals have also been

---

[78] Gordon Brown, 'Kidnapped Nigerian Girls Not Forgotten', (CNN news, 23 July 2014). Available at http://edition.cnn.com/2014/07/23/opinion/brown-nigeria-boko-haram-girls/.

bombed during the most recent offensive of Israel against Hamas in Gaza in July 2014. Human rights organisations in Gaza such as Al Mezan Centre for Human Rights and the Palestinian Centre for Human Rights continued to update the number of Palestinian death that included 249 children by the third week of the offensive. The Israeli government and Palestinian NGO disagreement over the numbers or the questions of who is child, or how should one distinguish between child/minor civilians and child/minor combatants; mixed reaction of the international community; and sharp criticisms from the UN Secretary-General, Ban Ki Moon, directed towards Israel after an airstrike that targeted the UN school in Gaza indicate that there are also tensions in the international advocacy efforts about how best to respond to children's experiences in conflict zones. Images of children are also used as a propaganda tool by different warring factions. The face of an injured or a dead child invokes more emotions then the image of an adult. While the role of civil society, including children's groups, has important potential it cannot compensate for the failures of international, regional and national policy efforts to end conflicts and achieve peace. One important lesson from these examples and insights is that civil society efforts to curb violence against children and to involve children in peace initiatives are also embedded in the national and global political history of various conflicts and their multiple representations.

Conclusion

KIM HUYNH

William Ross Wallace's (1819–1881) poem, 'The Hand that Rocks the Cradle is the Hand that Rules the World' glorifies motherhood as a divine mission of 'strength and grace'. The infant in Wallace's poem is almost entirely invisible and inert. It is mentioned only once when likened to a 'tender fountain'. This concluding poem asks us to consider how children rock the cradle in their own right and how they might rule the world in their own way.

The cradle it rocks

Against
My best wishes,
Our best efforts,
its best interests.

The cradle it rocks.
From inside,
it stirs.

Breaching the crib to
Slap my cheek,
Blubber my lips,
Chatter my teeth.

its shrewd little hands,
Like butterfly wings,
Stroking my hair,
Molesting my lids.

The cradle it rocks.
Outside,
The world stirs.

Oblivious *it* is
To conflict and slurs.

To small arms new wars
And gasses uprising.

Soon *it* will emerge
With virtue admiring,
With justice by sceptre
By sword and by shield.

The cradle it rocks.
We cannot
But yield.

Appendix

I. UN human rights instruments

a. Treaties and protocols

- Convention on the Rights of the Child, 1989.
- Optional Protocol I to the Convention on the Rights of the Child on the Sale of Children, Child Prostitution and Child Pornography, 2002.
- Optional Protocol II to the Convention on the Rights of the Child on the involvement of children in armed conflict, 2002.
- ILO Convention No. 182 concerning the Prohibition and Immediate Action for the Elimination of the Worst Forms of Child Labour, 1999.

b. Security Council resolutions

- Security Council Resolution 1261 (August 1999, Children and armed conflict)
- Security Council Resolution 1314 (August 2000, Children and armed conflict)
- Security Council Resolution 1325 (October 2000, Women, Peace and Security)
- Security Council Resolution 1379 (November 2001, Children and armed conflict)
- Security Council Resolution 1460 (January 2003, Children and armed conflict)
- Security Council Resolution 1539 (April 2004, Children and armed conflict)
- Security Council Resolution 1612 (July 2005, Children and armed conflict)
- Security Council Resolution 1820 (June 2008, Women, Peace and Security)
- Security Council Resolution 1882 (August 2009, Children and armed conflict)

- Security Council Resolution 1888 (September 2009, Women, Peace and Security)
- Security Council Resolution 1889 (October 2009, Women, Peace and Security)
- Security Council Resolution 1960 (December 2010, Women, Peace and Security)
- Security Council Resolution 1998 (July 2011, Children and armed conflict)
- Security Council Resolution 2068 (Sep 2012, Children and armed conflict)
- Security Council Resolution 2106 (June 2013, Women, Peace and Security)
- Security Council Resolution 2143 (March 2014, Children and armed conflict)

c. Resolutions by the General Assembly related to children and armed conflict

- Resolutions on the rights of the child introduced by the EU, jointly with Group of Latin America and Caribbean Countries (GRULAC), in the Human Rights Council and Third Committee of the UN General Assembly on a yearly basis. These resolutions contain paragraphs on children and armed conflict.

II. IHL, refugees and IDPs

- Geneva Convention relative to the Treatment of Prisoners of War, 1949.
- Geneva Convention relative to the Protection of Civilian Persons in Time of War, 1949.
- Protocol Additional to the Geneva Conventions of 12 August 1949, and relating to the Protection of Victims of International Armed Conflicts (Protocol I), 1977.
- Protocol Additional to the Geneva Conventions of 12 August 1949, and relating to the Protection of Victims of Non-International Armed Conflicts (Protocol II), 1977.
- Convention relating to the Status of Refugees, 1951.
- Protocol relating to the Status of Refugees, 1967.
- Guiding Principles on Internal Displacement, 1998.

III. International criminal law

- Rome Statute of the International Criminal Court, 2002.
- Amended Statute of the International Tribunal for the Prosecution of Persons Responsible for Serious Violations of International Humanitarian Law Committed in the Territory of the Former Yugoslavia since 1991, 1993 (as amended in 1998, 2000, 2002).
- Statute of the International Criminal Tribunal for Rwanda, 1994.
- Statute of the Special Court for Sierra Leone.

IV. Other relevant international principles, guidelines and normative instruments

- The Declaration on the Protection of Women and Children in Emergency and Armed Conflict, 1974.
- The Paris Commitments to Protect Children from Unlawful Recruitment or use by Armed Forces or Armed Groups adopted on 6 February 2007.
- The Paris Principles: Principles and Guidelines on Children Associated with Armed Forces or Armed Groups adopted on 6 February 2007.
- Report of the Special Representative of the Secretary-General for Children and Armed Conflict, Item 68(a) on the provisional agenda of the 2007 UN General Assembly (A/62/228).
- Enhancing the EU Response to Children Affected by Armed Conflict With Particular Reference to Development Policy, Study for the Slovenian EU Presidency prepared by Andrew Sherriff, December 2007.
- 'Will you listen?' Young Voices from Conflict Zones, prepared in 2007 by the OSRSG-CaAC, UNICEF, Global Youth Action Network, UN Population Fund, et al.
- The Convention against Torture and Other Cruel, Inhuman or Degrading Treatment or Punishment, 1987.
- The Convention on the Elimination of All Forms of Discrimination against Women 1979 (CEDAW) (also relates to children).
- The Convention on the Rights of Persons with Disabilities, 2008.

V. Regional instruments

- African Charter on the Rights and Welfare of the Child, 1990.
- The Arab Charter on Human Rights, 2004.
- The American Convention on Human Rights, 1978.

Bibliography

Abebe, Tatek and Anne Trine Kjørholt. 'Social Actors and Victims of Exploitation', *Childhood* 16(2) (May 2009).

Abiad, Nisrine and Farkhanda Zia Mansoor. 'Criminal Law and Rights of the Child in Afghanistan', in Nisrine Abiad and Farkhanda Zia Mansoor (eds.), *Criminal Law and the Rights of the Child in Muslim States: A Comparative and Analytical Perspective* (London: British Institute of International and Comparative Law, 2010) 85–100.

Achilihu, Stephen Nmeregini. *Do African Children Have Rights? A Comparative and Legal Analysis of the United Nations Convention on the Rights of the Child* (Florida: Universal Publishers, 2010).

Ackerly, Brooke. *Universal Human Rights in a World of Difference* (Cambridge: Cambridge University Press, 2008).

Afghanistan Independent Human Rights Commission. (AIHRC) 2008 report. 'AIHRC and UNICEF, Justice for Children: The Situation of Children in Conflict with the Law' (Kabul: AIHRC, 2008).

African Union Commission. *African Youth Charter* (African Union Commission, 2006) 11. Available at http://esaro.unfpa.org/webdav/site/africa/users/africa_admin/public/CHARTER_English.pdf.

Agamben, Giorgio (trans. Michael Rocke). 'We Refugees', *Symposium* 49(2) (1995) 114–19.

(trans. Daniel Heller-Roazen). *Homo Sacer: Sovereign Power and Bare Life* (Stanford: Stanford University Press, 1998).

(trans. Kevin Attell), *State of Exception* (Chicago, IL: University of Chicago Press, 2005).

Ahall, Linda, and Laura J. Shepherd (eds.). *Gender, Agency and Political Violence* (Basingstoke: Palgrave, 2012).

AIHRC and UNICEF. 'Justice for Children: The Situation of Children in Conflict with the Law' (Kabul: AIHRC, 2008).

Alanen, Leena. 'Review Essay: Visions of a Social Theory of Childhood', *Childhood* 7(4)(2000) 493–505.

Amnesty International. 'Sudan: Rape as a Weapon of War: Sexual Violence and its Consequences', September 2004. Available at

www.amnesty.org/en/library/asset/AFR54/076/2004/en/f86a52a0-d5
b4-11dd-bb24-1fb85fe8fa05/afr540762004en.html.

An-Na'im, Abdullahi Ahmed. 'Problems and Prospects of Universal Cultural
Legitimacy for Human Rights', in A. An-Na'im and F. Deng (eds.),
Human Rights in Africa: Cross-Cultural Perspectives (Washington
DC: Brookings Institution, 1990) 331–67.

Andvig, Jens Christopher, and Scott Gates. 'Recruiting Children for Armed
Conflict', in Scott Gates and Simon Reich (eds.), *Child Soldiers in the
Age of Fractured States* (Pittsburgh, PA: University of Pittsburgh Press,
2010) 77–92.

Appadurai, Arjun. 'Disjuncture and Difference in the Global Cultural
Economy', in M. Featherstone (ed.), *Global Culture: Nationalism,
Globalization and Modernity* (London: Sage, 1990) 295–310.

'The Capacity to Aspire: Culture and the Terms of Recognition', in
Vijayendra Rao and Michael Walton (eds.), *Culture and Public Action*
(Stanford, CA: Stanford University Press, 2004).

Appiah, Kwame Anthony. *In My Father's House: Africa in the Philosophy of
Culture* (New York, NY: Oxford University Press, 1992).

Aptel, Cécile. 'International Criminal Justice and Child Protection', in
Sharanjeet Parmar, Mindy Jane Roseman, Saudamini Siegrist and
Theo Sowa (eds.), *Children and Transitional Justice: Truth-Telling,
Accountability and Reconciliation* (Cambridge, MA: Harvard University
Press, 2010) 67–113.

Archard, David William. *Children, Family and the State* (Hampshire:
Ashgate, 2003).

Children: Rights and Childhood (2nd edn) (New York, NY: Routledge,
2004).

Archibald, Katherine. 'The Concept of Social Hierarchy in the Writings of St.
Thomas Aquinas', in John Dunn and Ian Harris (eds.),*Great Political
Thinkers Series*, Volume 4 (Cheltenham: Edward Elgar, 1997) 116–92;
originally published in *The Historian* 12 (1949), 28–54.

Arditti, Rita. *Searching for Life: The Grandmothers of the Plaza de Mayo
and the Disappeared Children of Argentina* (Berkeley, CA: University of
California Press, 1999).

Ariès, Philippe (trans. R. Baldick). *Centuries of Childhood* (London:
Jonathan Cape, 1962).

Arakan Project. 'Submission to the Committee on the Rights of the Child: For
the Examination of the Combined 3rd and 4th Periodic State Party
Reports' (January 2012). Available at www.crin.org/docs/Myanmar_AP_
CRC%20Report%20UPDATED.pdf.

Arts, Karin. 'General Introduction: A Child Rights-Based Approach
to International Criminal Accountability', in Karin Arts and

Vesselin Popovski (eds.), *International Criminal Accountability and the Rights of Children* (The Hague: Hague Academic Press, 2006) 3–16.

Ashbrook, Tom. 'U.S. Borders Swamped by Child Migrants', *Onpoint*, 9 June 2014. Available at http://onpoint.wbur.org/2014/06/09/child-migrants-border-patrol-mexico.

Ashley, Richard K. 'The Poverty of Neorealism', *International Organization* 38(2) (Spring 1984) 248–54.

Askin, Kelly. *War Crimes Against Women: Prosecution in International War Crimes Tribunals* (The Hague: Kluwer Law International, 1997).

Ausaid. 'East Timor Youth Status', *Focus*, June-September 2008. Available at www.ausaid.gov.au/publications/focus/june08/focus_June08_03.pdf.

Australian Human Rights and Equal Opportunity Commission. 'A Last Resort? National Inquiry into Children in Immigration Detention' (2004). Available at www.humanrights.gov.au/publications/last-resort-national-inquiry-children-immigration-detention.

Babo-Soares, Dionisio. 'NaheBiti: The Philosophy and Process of Grassroots Reconciliation (and Justice) in East Timor', *The Asia-Pacific Journal of Anthropology* 5(1) (2004) 15–33.

Backett-Milburn, Kathryn, Sarah Wilson, Angus Bancroft and Sarah Cunningham-Burley. 'Challenging Childhoods: Young People's Accounts of 'Getting By' in Families With Substance Use Problems', *Childhood* 15(4) (1 November 2008).

Badil Resource Center. 'Palestinian Refugee Children: International Protection and Durable Solutions', Information and Discussion Brief (January 2007). Available at www.childmigration.net/Badil_07.

Baines, Erin K. 'Complex Political Perpetrators: Reflections on Domini Ongwen', *The Journal of Modern African Studies* 47(2) (2009) 163–91.

Barkan, Elazar. *The Guilt of Nations: Restitution and Negotiating Historical Injustices* (Baltimore: Johns Hopkins University Press, 2000).

Barker, Anne. 'Drugs Fuelling East Timor Gangs, Youth Workers Say', *ABC The World Today*, 30 October 2006. Available at www.abc.net.au/worldtoday/content/2006/s1776961.htm.

Barstad, Kristin. 'Preventing the Recruitment of Child Soldiers: The IRCR Approach', *Refugee Survey Quarterly* 27 (2008) 142–9.

Bartholet, Elizabeth. 'Ratification by the United States of the Convention on the Rights of the Child: Pros and Cons from a Child's Rights Perspective', Annals, American Academy of Political and Social Sciences (1) (2011) 633–80.

Baudrillard, Jean. *The Gulf War Did Not Take Place* (Bloomington: Indiana University Press, 1995).

Bellamy, Alex J. *Responsibility to Protect* (Cambridge: Polity Press, 2009).

Bellamy, Alex J., and Paul D. Williams. *Understanding Peacekeeping* (2nd edn) (Cambridge: Polity, 2010).

Ben-Yehuda, Hemda, and Shmuel Sandler. *The Arab-Israeli Conflict Transformed* (New York, NY: State University of New York, 2002).

Beresford, Stuart. 'Child Witnesses and the International Criminal Justice System: Does the International Criminal Court Protect the Most Vulnerable?', *The Journal of International Criminal Justice* 3 (2005), 721–48.

Bergner, Daniel. *In the Land of Magic Soldiers: A Story of Black and White in West Africa* (New York, NY: Farrar, Strauss and Giroux, 2003).

Bessell, Sharon. 'Indonesian Children's Views and Experiences of Work and Poverty', *Social Policy and Society* 8(4) (2009).

Bhabha, Jacqueline. 'Arendt's Children: Do Today's Migrant Children Have a Right to Have Rights?', *Human Rights Quarterly* 31(2) (2009) 410–51.

Bhabha, Jacqueline, and Nadine Finch. 'Seeking Asylum Alone: Unaccompanied and Separated Children and Refugee Protection in the U.K.' (November 2006). Available at www.childmigration.net/files/SAA_UK.pdf.

Bhabha, Jacqueline, and Susan Schmidt. 'Seeking Asylum Alone: Unaccompanied and Separated Children and Refugee Protection in the U.S.', *Journal of the History of Childhood and Youth* 1(1) (Winter 2008) 127–38.

Bolzman, Lara. 'The Advent of Child Rights on the International Scene and the Role of the Save the Children International Union 1920–1945', *Refugee Survey Quarterly* 27(4) (2009).

Booth, Ken. 'Critical Explorations', in Ken Booth (ed.), *Critical Security Studies and World Politics* (Boulder, CO: Lynne Rienner, 2005).

Theory of World Security (Cambridge: Cambridge University Press, 2007).

Bowden, Tracey. 'Navy Chief Enters Asylum Seekers Debate, *ABC 7:30 Report*, 8 November 2001. Available at www.abc.net.au/7.30/content/2001/s412083.htm.

Boyden, Jo. *Families: Celebration and Hope in a World of Change* (Sydney: Doubleday, 1993).

'Childhood and the Policy Makers: A Comparative Perspective on the Globalization of Childhood', in Allison James and Alan Prout (eds.), *Constructing and Reconstructing Childhood: Contemporary Issues in the Sociological Study of Childhood* (2nd edn) (New York, NY: Routledge, 1997).

'Children, War and World Disorder in the 21st Century: A Review of the Theories and the Literature on Children's Contribution to Armed Violence', Working Paper No 138 (November 2006). Available at www3.qeh.ox.ac.uk/pdf/qehwp/qehwps138.pdf.

Boyden, Jo, and Joanna de Berry. *Children and Youth on the Front Line: Ethnography, Armed Conflict and Displacement* (New York, NY: Berghahn Books, 2004).

'Introduction', in Jo Boyden and Joanna Berry (eds.), *Children and Youth on the Front Line: Ethnography, Armed Conflict and Displacement* (New York, NY: Berghahn Books, 2004), xi–xxvii.

Braithwaite, John. 'Principles of Restorative Justice', in A. Von Hirsch, J. V. Roberts, A. E. Bottoms, K. Roach and M. Schiff (eds.), *Restorative Justice and Criminal Justice* (Portland: Hart Publishing, 2003).

Brenner, Marie. 'The Target', *Vanity Fair*, April 2013. Available at www.vanityfair.com/politics/2013/04/malala-yousafzai-pakistan-profile.

Brett, Rachel. 'Child Soldiering: Questions and Challenges for Health Professionals', *WHO Global Report on Violence* (May 2000).

Brett, Rachel, and Irma Specht. *Young Soldiers: Why They Choose to Fight* (Boulder, CO: Lynne Rienner, 2004).

Brighouse, Harry. 'What Rights (If Any) Do Children Have?', in David Archard and Colin Macleod (eds.), *The Moral and Political Status of Children* (Oxford: Oxford University Press, 2002).

Brocklehurst, Helen. *Who's Afraid of Children? Children, Conflict and International Relations* (Hampshire: Ashgate, 2006).

Burchill, Scott. 'Liberalism', in Scott Burchill, Andrew Linklater, Richard Devetak, Jack Donnelly, Terry Nardin, Matthew Paterson, Christian Reus-Smit and Jacqui True (eds.), *Theories of International Relations* (4th edn) (Hampshire: Palgrave, 2009).

Burke, Anthony. *Fear of Security: Australia's invasion anxiety* (Port Melbourne: Cambridge University Press, 2008).

Burman, Erica. 'Local, Global or Globalized?: Child Development and International Child', *Childhood* 3(1) (1996) 45–66.

Burr, Rachel. 'Global and Local Approaches to Children's Rights in Vietnam', *Childhood* 9(1) (February 2002) 49–61.

Butalia, Urvashi. *The Other Side of Silence: Voices from the Partition of India* (New Delhi: Penguin Books India, 1998).

Bynum, J. E., and W. E. Thompson. *Juvenile Delinquency: A Sociological Approach* (3rd edn)(Needham Heights, MA: Allyn and Bacon, 1996).

Cairns, Ed. *Children and Political Violence (Understanding Children's Worlds)* (Oxford: Blackwell, 1996).

Cameron, Sara. 'Children as Leaders: Lessons from Colombia's Children's Movement for Peace' *Peace News*, Issue 2444 (2001). Available at http://peacenews.info/node/3928/children-leaders-lessons-colombias-childrens-movement-peace.

Carpenter Charli, R. 'Surfacing Children: Limitations of Genocidal Rape Discourse', *Human Rights Quarterly* 22(2) (2000) 428–77.

'"Women, Children and Other Vulnerable Groups": Gender, Strategic Frames and the Protection of Civilians as a Transnational Issue', *International Studies Quarterly* 49 (2005) 295–334.

'Innocent Women and Children': Gender, Norms and the Protection of Civilians (Hampshire: Ashgate, 2006).

'Setting the Advocacy Agenda: Theorizing Issue Emergence and Non-emergence in Transnational Advocacy Networks', *International Studies Quarterly* 51(1)(2007) 99–120.

'"A Fresh Crop of Human Misery": Representations of Bosnian "War Babies" in the Global Print Media, 1991–2006', *Millennium – Journal of International Studies* 38(1) (2009) 25–54.

Forgetting Children Born of War: Setting the Human Rights Agenda in Bosnia and Beyond (New York, NY: Columbia University Press, 2010).

Cassidy, Barrie. 'Greens to Pursue Manus Island Inquiry', *Insiders*, Australian Broadcasting Corporation, 21 August 2011. Available at www.abc.net.au/insiders/content/2011/s3298357.htm.

Castells, Manuel. *The Information Age: Economy, Society, and Culture*, Volume III: End of Millennium (New York, NY: Wiley, 1998).

Center for Research on Globalisation. 'Iraqi Children: Deprived Rights, Stolen Future', Report published by the Center for Research on Globalisation (13 March 2013).

Chambers, Simone, and Kymlicka, Will (eds.). *Alternative Conceptions of Civil Society* (Princeton, NJ: Princeton University Press, 2002).

'Chega! Report of the Commission of Reception, Truth and Reconciliation in East Timor' (2004). Available at www.cavr-timorleste.org/en/chega Report.htm.

Cheney, Kristen E. '"Our Children Have Only Known War": Children's Experiences and the Uses of Childhood in Northern Uganda', *Children's Geographies* 3(1) (April 2005) 23–45.

Pillars of the Nation: Child Citizens and Ugandan National Development (Chicago: University of Chicago Press, 2008).

Chikuhwa, Tonderai W. 'The Evolution of the United Nations' Protection Agenda for Children', in Scott Gates and Simon Reich (eds.), *Child Soldiers in the Age of Fractured States* (Pittsburgh, PA: University of Pittsburgh Press, 2010) 37–55.

Child Rights International Network. 'Briefing from Global Initiative to End All Corporal Punishment of Children –Afghanistan' (n.d.). Available at www.crin.org/resources/infoDetail.asp?ID=23838&flag=legal.

'VIETNAM: Children's Rights References in the Universal Periodic Review', (8 May 2009). Available at www.crin.org/resources/infoDetail.asp?ID=21681.

Child Soldiers International. 'Who Are Child Soldiers?' (n.d.). Available at www.child-soldiers.org/about_the_issues.php.

'Report Priority to Protect Preventing Children's Association with Village Defence Militias in Southern Thailand', March 2011. Available at www.refworld.org/docid/4d79f35b2.html.

'Louder than Words: An agenda for Action to End State Use of Child Soldiers', (2012). Available at www.child-soldiers.org/global_report_reader.php?id=562.

'Children and Armed Conflict: Strategic Framework 2011–2013'. Available at https://childrenandarmedconflict.un.org/publications/StrategicFramework2011-2013.pdf.

Chinkin, Christine, and Hilary Charlesworth. 'Building Women into Peace: The International Legal Framework', *Third World Quarterly* 27(5) (2006) 937–57.

Clark, Christina. 'Juvenile Justice and Child Soldiering: Trends, Challenges, Dilemmas', in Charles W. Greenbaum, Philip Veerman and Naomi Bacon-Shnoor (eds.), *Protection of Children During Armed Political Conflict: A Multidisciplinary Perspective* (Oxford: Hart Publishing, 2006) 311–28.

Clark, Phil. *The Gacaca Courts, Post-Genocide Justice and Reconciliation in Rwanda* (Cambridge: Cambridge University Press, 2010).

Cohen, Cynthia Price. 'The Relevance of Theories of Natural Law and Legal Positivism', in Michael Freeman and Philip Veerman (eds.),*The Ideologies of Children's Rights* (Dordrecht: Martinus Nijhoff, 1992) 53–70.

'The United Nations Convention of the Rights of the Child: A Feminist Landmark', *William and Mary Journal of Women and the Law* 3(1) (1997).

Cole, Alison. 'International Criminal Law and Sexual Violence: An Overview', in Clare McGlynn and Vanessa E. Munro (eds.), *Rethinking Rape Law: International and Comparative Perspectives* (New York, NY: Routledge, 2010), 46–50.

Cook, Philip, and Cheryl Heykoop. 'Child Participation in the Sierra Leonean Truth and Reconciliation Commission', in Sharanjeet Parmar, Mindy Jane Roseman, Saudamini Siegrist and Theo Sowa (eds.), *Children and Transitional Justice: Truth-Telling, Accountability and Reconciliation* (Cambridge, MA: Harvard University Press, 2010) 159–91.

Corsaro, William. *The Sociology of Childhood* (3rd edn) (London: Sage, 2011).

Cowan, Jane K., Marie-Benedicte Dembour and Richard A. Wilson (eds.). *Culture and Rights: Anthropological Perspectives* (Cambridge: Cambridge University Press, 2001).

'Critical International Theory after 25 Years', *Review of International Studies* 33(1) (Special Edition, April 2007).

Cumming-Bruce, Nick. 'U.N. Panel Reports Increasing Brutality by Both Sides in Syria', *The New York Times*, 4 June 2013. Available at www.nytimes.com/2013/06/05/world/middleeast/un-panel-reports-incre asing-brutality-by-both-sides-in-syria.html?pagewanted=all&_r=0.

Curthoys, Anne. 'Whose Home? Expulsion, Exodus, and Exile in White Australian Historical Mythology', *Journal of Australian Studies* 61 (1999) 1–19.

D'Costa, Bina. *Nationbuilding, Gender and War Crimes in South Asia* (London: Routledge, 2011).

D'Costa, Bina, and Sara Hossain. 'Redress for Sexual Violence Before the International Crimes Tribunal in Bangladesh: Lessons from History and Hopes for the Future', *Criminal Law Forum* 21(2) (2010), 331–59.

D'Costa, Bina, and Katrina Lee-Koo (eds.). *Gender and Global Politics in the Asia-Pacific* (New York, NY: Palgrave, 2009).

Das, Veena. *Critical Events: An Anthropological Perspective on Contemporary India.* (Oxford: Oxford University Press, 1995).

de Certeau, Michel (trans. Steven Rendall). *The Practice of Everyday Life* (1st edn) (Berkeley, CA: University of California Press, 1984).

de Tréglodé, Benoît (trans Claire Duiker). *Heroes and Revolution in Vietnam* (Singapore: NUS Press, 2012).

Del Felice, Celina, and Andria Wisler. 'The Unexplored Power and Potential of Youth as Peace-builders', *Journal of Peace, Conflict and Development* 11 (November 2007) 1–29.

Der Derian, James. *Virtuous War: Mapping the Military-Industrial-Media-Entertainment Network* (2nd edn) (London: Routledge, 2009).

Devetak, Richard. 'Critical Theory', in Scott Burchill, Andrew Linklater, Richard Devetak, Jack Donnelly, Terry Nardin, Matthew Paterson, Christian Reus-Smit and Jacqui True (eds.), *Theories of International Relations* (4th edn) (Hampshire: Palgrave, 2009).

Diamond, Jared. *The World Until Yesterday: What Can We Learn from Traditional Societies?* (New York, NY: Viking, 2012).

Dickinson, Edward R. *The Politics of German Child Welfare from the Empire to the Federal Republic* (Cambridge, MA: Harvard University Press, 1996).

Doná, Giorgia, and Angela Veale. 'Divergent Discourses, Children and Forced Migration', *Journal of Ethnic and Migration Studies* 37(8) (2011) 1273–89.

Donnelly, Jack. 'The Social Construction of International Human Rights', in Tim Dunne and Nicholas J. Wheeler (eds.), *Human Rights in Global Politics* (Cambridge: Cambridge University Press, 1999) 82–3.

Universal Human Rights: In Theory and Practice (Ithaca, NY: Cornell University Press, 2003).

Dougherty, Beth K. 'Searching for Answers: Sierra Leone's Truth and Reconciliation Commission', *African Studies Quarterly* 8(1) (2004), 40–56.

Doyle, Michael. 'Liberalism and World Politics', *American Political Science Review* 80 (December 1986) 1151–69.

Driscoll, Catherine. 'The Moving Ground: Locating Everyday Life', *The South Atlantic Quarterly* 100(2) (2001).

Duffield, Mark. *Global Governance and the New Wars: The Merging of Development and Security* (London: Zed Books, 2001).

Dunne, Tim, and Brian C. Schmidt. 'Realism', in John Baylis and Steve Smith (eds.), *The Globalization of World Politics: An Introduction to International Relations* (3rd edn) (Oxford: Oxford University Press, 2005).

Eastmond, Marita, and Henry Ascher. 'In the Best Interest of the Child? The Politics of Vulnerability and Negotiations for Asylum in Sweden', *Journal of Ethnic and Migration Studies* 37(8) (2011) 1185–1200.

Eder, Klaus. 'Europe's Borders: The Narrative Construction of the Boundaries of Europe', *European Journal of Social Theory* 9 (May 2006) 255–71.

Eggers, David. *What is the What: The Autobiography of Valentine Achak Deng (a novel)* (New York, NY: Penguin, 2007).

Emerson, Craig. 'Refugee Politics with Kim Huynh', *Emmo Forum*, Episode 14, 19 January 2014. Available at http://craigemersoneconomics.com/blog/2014/1/19/emmo-forum-ep-14-refugee-politics-w-kim-huynh.

Elbe, Stefan. *Strategic Implications of HIV/AIDS* (Oxford: Oxford University Press, 2003).

Elshtain, Jean Bethke. *The Family in Political Thought* (Amhurst, MA: University of Massachusetts Press, 1982).

Enloe, Cynthia. 'Women and Children: Making Feminist Sense of the Persian Gulf War', *The Village Voice* 25 (September 1990).

The Curious Feminist: Searching for Women in a New Age of Empire (California, CA: University of California Press, 2004).

Ensalaco, Mark. 'The Right of the Child to Development', in Mark Ensalaco and Linda C. Majka (eds.), *Children's Human Rights: Progress and Challenges for Children Worldwide* (Oxford: Rowman and Littlefield, 2005) 9–30.

Estrada, Felipe. 'Juvenile Crime Trends in Post-War Europe', *European Journal on Criminal Policy and Research* 7(1) (1999) 23–42.

Everitt, Jacquie. *The Bitter Shore: An Iranian Family's Escape to Australia and the Hell They Found at the Border of Paradise* (Sydney: Macmillan, 2008).

Farson, Richard. *Birthrights* (New York, NY: Penguin, 1978).

Fass, Paula S. 'Children in Global Migrations', *Journal of Social History* 38(4) (July 2005) 937–53.

Fassin, Didier. 'The Biologics of Otherness: Undocumented Foreigners and Racial Discrimination in French Public Debate', *Anthropology Today* 17(1) (2001) 3–7.

Humanitarian Reason: A Moral History of the Present (Berkeley, CA: University of California Press, 2011).

Fassin, Didier, and Estelle d'Halluin. 'Critical Evidence: The Politics of Trauma in French Asylum Policies', *ETHOS* 35(3) (2007) 300–29.

Feinstein, Clare, Annette Giertsen and Claire O'Kane. 'Children's Participation in Armed Conflict and Post-Conflict Peacebuilding', in Barry Percy-Smith and Nigel Thomas (eds.), *A Handbook of Children and Young People's Participation: Perspectives from Theory and Practice* (Abingdon: Routledge, 2010) 53–62.

Fierke, K. M. *Critical Approaches to International Security* (Cambridge: Polity Press, 2007).

Fisher, Nigel. 'Leadership and Impunity: The Politics Behind the Traumatization of Children during Armed Conflicts', *Traumatology* 8(3) (2002) 146–59.

Fortin, Jane. *Children's Rights and the Developing Law* (Cambridge: Cambridge University Press, 2003).

Fox, Mary-Jane. 'Girl Soldiers: Human Security and Gendered Insecurity', *Security Dialogue* 35(4) (2004) 465–79.

Frank, Anne. *Anne Frank: The Diary of a Young Girl* (First Published January 1 1947) (Ealing: Bantam, 1993).

Franklin, Bob. *The New Handbook of Children's Rights: Comparative Policy and Practice* (New York, NY: Taylor & Francis, 2001).

Freeman, Michael D. *The Rights and Wrongs of Children.* (London: Frances Pinter, 1983).

'The Limits of Children's Rights', in Michael Freeman and Philip Veerman (eds.),*The Ideologies of Children's Rights* (Dordrecht: Martinus Nijhoff, 1992).

'Children as Persons', in Michael Freeman (ed.), *Children's Rights: A Comparative Perspective* (Aldershot: Dartmouth, 1993).

Frey, Rebecca Joyce. *Genocide and International Justice* (New York, NY: Infobase Publishing, 2009).

Galtung, Johan. *After Violence: 3R, Reconstruction, Reconciliation, Resolution; Coping with Visible and Invisible Effects of War and Violence* (New York, NY: Transcend, 1998).

Peace by Peaceful Means, Peace and Conflict, Development and Civilization (London: Sage, 1996).

Galway, Elizabeth A. 'Competing Representations of Boy Soldiers in WWI Children's Literature', *Peace Review* 24 (2012) 298–304.

Gates, Scott. 'Why Do Children Fight? Motivations and the Mode of Recruitment', in Alpaslan Özerdem and Sukanya Podder (eds.), *Child Soldiers: From Recruitment to Reintegration* (Houndmills: Palgrave Macmillan, 2011) 29–49.

Gates, Scott, and Simon Reich. *Child Soldiers in the Age of Fractured States* (Pittsburgh, PA: University of Pittsburgh Press, 2010).

'Conclusion', in Scott Gates and Simon Reich (eds.), *Child Soldiers in the Age of Fractured States* (Pittsburgh, PA: University of Pittsburgh Press, 2010) 247–54.

'Introduction', in Scott Gates and Simon Reich (eds.), *Child Soldiers in the Age of Fractured States* (Pittsburgh, PA: University of Pittsburgh Press, 2010) 3–13.

Gellately, Robert, and Ben Kiernan (eds.). *The Specter of Genocide: Mass Murder in Historical Perspective* (Cambridge: Cambridge University Press, 2003).

George, Jim. *Discourses of Global Politics: A Critical (re)Introduction to International Relations* (Boulder, CO: Lynne Rienner, 1994).

Georgiou, Petro. 'Petro Georgiou: It's War Without Blood', speech to Cranala in Melbourne, 14 April 2010. Available at www.culturaldiversity.net.au/ index.php?option=com_content&view=article&id=551:petro-georgiou-its-war-without-blood&catid=14:human-rights-articles&Itemid=24.

Gibbs, Nancy. 'The Growing Backlash Against Overparenting', *Time*, 20 November 2009. Available at http://content.time.com/time/magazine/article/0,9171,1940697,00.html.

Gillard, Steve. 'Winning the Peace: Youth, Identity and Peacebuilding in Bosnia and Herzegovina', *International Peacekeeping* 8(1) (2001) 77–98.

Glen Johnson, M. 'Human Rights in Divergent Conceptual Settings – How Do Ideas Influence Policy Choices?', in David Louis Cingranelli (ed.), *Human Rights Theory and Measurement* (London: Macmillan Press, 1988).

Goodwin-Gill, Guy S. 'Protecting the Human Rights of Refugee Children: Some Legal and Institutional Possibilities', in Jaap Doek, Hans van Loon and Paul Vlaardingerbroek (eds.), *Children on the Move: How to Implement their Right to Family Life* (The Hague: Martinus Nijhoff Publishers, 1996) 97–111.

Goodrich, Frances. *Anne Frank: The Diary of Anne Frank*, (Boston, MA: Houghton Mifflin, 1989).

Gopnik, Alison. *The Philosophical Baby: What Children's Minds Tell Us about Truth, Love, and the Meaning of Life* (New York, NY: Farrar, Straus and Giroux, 2009).

Gopnik, Alison, and Henry M. Wellman. 'The Theory Theory', in L. Hirschfield and S. Gelman (eds.), *Mapping the Mind: Domain Specificity in Cognition and Culture* (New York, NY: Cambridge University Press, 1994) 257–93.

Gopnik, Alison, Andrew N. Meltzoff and Patricia K. Kuhl. *The Scientist in the Crib: Minds, Brains and How Children Learn* (New York, NY: HarperCollins, 2000).

Gorbachev, Mikhail. 'Nobel Speech', *Nobelprize.org*, 5 June 1991. Available at www.nobelprize.org/nobel_prizes/peace/laureates/1990/gorbachev-lecture.html.

Goscha, Christopher. 'A "Total War" of Decolonization? Social Mobilization and State-Building in Communist Vietnam (1949–54)', *War & Society* 31(2) (August 2012) 136–62.

Gramsci, Antonio (edited by Quentin Hoare and Geoffrey Nowell Smith). *Prison Note: Selections* (London: International Publishers Company, 1971).

Grover, Sonja C. *Child Soldier Victims of Genocidal Forcible Transfer: Exonerating Child Soldiers Charged with Grave Conflict-related International Crimes* (Springer: Heidelberg, 2012).

Guillemot, François. 'Death and Suffering at First Hand: Youth Shock Brigades During the Vietnam War (1950–1975)', *Journal of Vietnamese Studies* 4(3) (1 October 2009) 17–60.

Gumbel, Andrew. 'Colombian Kidnappers "Targeting Children"', *The Independent*, 1 February 2003.

Ha, Nguyet, '"Doi Vien Tinh Bao Bat Sat": Huyen Thoai Giua Doi Thuong ("The Bat Sat Intelligence Squad": Common life legends)', *cand.com.vn*, 2 April 2013. Available at http://vnca.cand.com.vn/vi-vn/truyenthong/2013/3/57912.cand.

Hamlin, J. Kiley. 'A Developmental Perspective on the Moral Dyad', *Psychological Inquiry* 23(2) (2012).

Hampson, Françoise J. 'Legal Protection Afforded to Children Under International Humanitarian Law', Report for the Study on the Impact of Armed Conflict on Children (1996). Available at www.essex.ac.uk/armedcon/story_id/000578.html.

Hanh, Thich Nhat. 'The Magical Warrior', in Thich Nhat Hanh, *The Dragon Prince: Stories and legends from Vietnam* (Berkeley, CA: Paralax Press, 2007) 115–22.

Hannerz, Ulf. *Transnational Connections: Culture, People, Places* (London: Routledge, 1996).

Happold, Matthew. 'The Optional Protocol to the Convention on the Rights of the Child on the Involvement of Children in Armed Conflict', *Yearbook of International Humanitarian Law* 3 (2000) 226–44.

Child Soldiers in International Law, (Manchester: Manchester University Press, 2005).

'The Age of Criminal Responsibility for International Crimes under International Law', in Karin Arts and Vesselin Popovski (eds.), *International Criminal Accountability and the Rights of Children* (The Hague: Hague Academic Press, 2006) 69–84.

Hart, Jason and Tyrer Bex, 'Research with Children Living in Situations of Armed Conflict: Concepts, Ethics and Methods', Refugees Studies Centre Working Paper No. 30 (May 2006).

Hauge, Wenche. 'Girl Soldiers in Guatemala', in Alpaslan Özerdem and Sukanya Podder (eds.), *Child Soldiers: From Recruitment to Reintegration* (Houndmills: Palgrave Macmillan, 2011) 91–103.

Hayner, Priscilla. *Unspeakable Truths: Confronting State Terror and Atrocity* (New York, NY: Routledge, 2001).

Heidelberg Institute for International Conflict Research. *Conflict Barometer 2010*. Available at www.hiik.de/en/konfliktbarometer/pdf/ConflictBaro meter_2010.pdf.

Hendrick, Harry. 'Constructions and Reconstructions of British Childhood', in Allison James and Alan Prout (eds.), *Constructing and Reconstructing Childhood: Contemporary Issues in the Sociological Study of Childhood* (New York, NY: Routledge, 1997).

Herd, Andrew. 'Amplifying Outrage over Children Overboard', Social Alternatives 25(2) (2006) 59–63. Available at www.uow.edu.au/arts/ sts/bmartin/pubs/bf/06saHerd.html (accessed 14 June 2011).

Hess, Julia Meredith and Dianna Shandy. 'Kids at the Crossroads: Global Childhood and the State', *Anthropological Quarterly* 81(4)(October 2008) 765–76.

Highmore, Ben. *Everyday Life and Cultural Theory: An Introduction* (1st edn) (New York, NY: Routledge, 2001).

Hilker, Lyndsay McLean and Erika Fraser. 'Youth, Exclusion, Violence, Conflict and Fragile States: Report prepared for DFID's Equity and Rights Team', 30 April 2009. Available at www.gsdrc.org/docs/open/ CON66.pdf.

Hinsliff, Gaby. 'Can We Be Sure Afghan Child Suicide Bomber Knew What He Was Doing?', *Guardian.co.uk*, 14 December 2008. Available at www.guardian.co.uk/world/blog/2008/dec/14/afghanistan-military.

Hobbes, Thomas (edited by M. Oakeshott). *Leviathan* (New York, NY: Collier, 1962, orig. 1651).

Hodgson, D. 'The Historical Development and Internationalisation of the Children's Rights Movement', *The Australian Journal of Family Law* 6 (1992) 252–78.

Holt, John. *Escape from Childhood* (Boston, MA: E. P. Dutton, 1974).

Holzscheiter, Anna. *Children's Rights in International Politics: The Transformative Power of Discourse* (New York, NY: Palgrave Macmillian Press, 2010).

Honwana, Alcinda. 'Negotiating Postwar Identities: Child Soldiers in Mozambique and Angola', in George Bond and Nigel Gibson (eds.), *Contested Terrains and Constructed Categories* (Boulder, CO: Westview Press, 2002) 277–98.

'Innocent and Guilty: Child-Soldiers as Interstitial and Tactical Agents', in Alcinda Honwana and Filip de Boeck (eds.), *Makers and Breakers: Children and Youth in Postcolonial Africa* (Oxford: James Currey, 2005).

Hough, Peter. *Understanding Global Security* (London: Routledge, 2004).

Howard, Michael. 'Children of War: The Generation Traumatised by Violence in Iraq', *Guardian Weekly*, 6 February 2007. Available at www.guardian.co.uk/world/2007/feb/06/iraq.topstories3.

Huijsman, Roy. 'Child Migration and Questions of Agency', *Development and Change* 42 (5) (2011) 1307–21.

Human Rights Watch. 'Lasting Wounds: Consequences of Genocide and War for Rwanda's Children', (March 2003). Available at www.hrw.org/en/reports/2003/04/03/lasting-wounds.

Huntington, Samuel P. *The Clash of Civilisations and the Remaking of World Order* (New York, NY: Simon & Schuster, 1996).

Huynh, Kim. *Where the Sea Takes Us: A Vietnamese-Australian Story* (Sydney: Harper Perennial, 2008).

'One Woman's Everyday Resistance: An Empowering Yet Cautionary Tale from Vietnam', in Bina D'Costa and Katrina Lee-Koo (eds.), *Gender and Global Politics in the Asia-Pacific* (New York, NY: Palgrave, 2009), 129–42.

Ibrahim, Nalima. *Ami Birangona Bolchi* (Dhaka: Jagriti Prokashoni, 1998).

ICRC. *Children in War* (Geneva: ICRC, November 2009).

Workshop report, 'Children Affected by Armed Conflict and other Situations of Violence' (March 2011). Available at www.icrc.org/eng/resources/documents/publication/p4082.htm.

Igreja, Victor. 'Cultural Disruption and the Care of Infants in Post-War Mozambique', in Jo Boyden and Joanna Berry (eds.), *Children and Youth on the Front Line: Ethnography, Armed Conflict and Displacement* (New York, NY: Berghahn Books, 2004) 23–44.

International Bureau for Children's Rights. *Children and Armed Conflict* (Montreal: Quebec, 2010).

International Institute for Strategic Studies. Armed Conflict Database. Available at http://acd.iiss.org.virtual.anu.edu.au/armedconflict/Main Pages/dsp_Page.asp?PageID=2.

International Rescue Committee. Mortality in the Democratic Republic of Congo: An Ongoing Crisis (2008). Available at www.rescue.org/sites/default/files/migrated/resources/2007/2006-7_congomortality survey.pdf.

Isacson, Adam, and Jorge Rojas Rodríguez. 'Origins, Evolution, Lessons of the Colombian Peace Movement', in Virginia M. Bouvier (ed.), *Colombia: Building Peace in a Time of War* (Washington, DC: United States Institute of Peace, 2009) 19–38.

Jackson, Richard, Marie Breen Smyth and Jeroen Gunning (eds.). *Critical Terrorism Studies* (London: Routledge, 2009).

Jacob, Cecilia. *The Politics of Protecting Children Affected by Political Violence* (London: Routledge, 2013).

Child Security in Asia: The Impact of Armed Conflict in Cambodia and Myanmar (London: Routledge, 2014).

Jal, Emmanuel, and Megan Lloyd Davies. *War Child: A Child Soldier's Story*, 1st edn (New York, NY: St. Martin's Griffin, 2010).

James, Adrian L. 'Competition or Integration? The Next Step in Childhood Studies?', *Childhood* 17(4) (November 2010).

James, Adrian L., and Allison James. 'Childhood: Toward a Theory of Continuity and Change', *Annals of the American Academy of Political and Social Science* 575(1) (2001) 25–37.

James, Allison. 'Giving Voice to Children's Voices: Practices and Problems, Pitfalls and Potentials', *American Anthropologist* 109(2)(2007) 261–72.

James, Allison, and Adrian James. *Constructing Childhood: Theory, Policy and Social Practice* (New York, NY: Palgrave Macmillan, 2004).

James, Allison and Alan Prout (eds). *Constructing and Reconstructing Childhood: Contemporary Issues in the Sociological Study of Childhood* (2nd edn) (New York, NY: Routledge, 1997).

Johnson, David. 'Cultural and Regional Pluralism in the Drafting of the UN Convention on the Rights of the Child', in Michael Freeman and Philip Veerman (eds.),*The Ideologies of Children's Rights* (Dordrecht: Martinus Nijhoff, 1992).

Jones, Adele. 'Child Asylum Seekers and Refugees: Rights and Responsibilities', *Journal of Social Work* 1(3) (December 2001) 253–71.

Jones, Gemma. 'Save Boat Babies', *The Herald Sun*, 9 June 2013, 1, 4.

Joseph, Rita. *Human Rights and the Unborn Child* (Leiden: Martinus Nijhoff Publishers, 2009).

Junne, Gerd, and Willemijn Verkoren. 'The Challenges of Postconflict Development', in Junne Gerd and Willemijn Verkoren (eds.), *Postconflict Development: Meeting New Challenges* (Boulder, CO: Lynne Rienner Publishers, 2005) 1–18.

Kaldor, Mary. *Global Civil Society: An Answer to War* (Cambridge: Polity, 2003).

New and Old Wars: Organised Violence in a Global Era (2nd edn) (Oxford: Polity Press, 2006).

Kaplan, Robert D. 'The Coming Anarchy', *Atlantic Monthly*, 1 February 1994. Available at www.theatlantic.com/magazine/archive/1994/02/the-coming-anarchy/304670/.

Kaviraj, Sudipta, and Sunil Khilnani (eds.). *Civil Society: History and Possibilities* (Cambridge: Cambridge University Press, 2001).

Keairns, Yvonne. 'The Voices of Girl Child Soldiers: Summary' (Quaker United Nations Office and Coalition to Stop the Use of Child Soldiers, 2002). Available at www.quno.org/sites/default/files/resources/The%20 voices%20of%20girl%20child%20soldiers_PHILIPPINES.pdf.

Keane, John. 'Children and Civil Society', Presentation for *Neglecting Children and Youth: Democracies at Risk*, a seminar held at The University of Sydney, 5 November 2008.

Keck, Margaret E., and Kathryn Sikkink. *Activists Beyond Borders: Advocacy Networks in International Politics* (New York, NY: Cornell University Press, 1998).

Keen, David. *Complex Emergencies* (Oxford: Polity Press, 2007).

Kertzer, Adrienne. 'What Good are the Words?': Child Memoirs and Holocaust Fiction', in Daniel Thomas Cook and John Wall (eds.), *Children and Armed Conflict: Cross Disciplinary Investigations* (Basingstoke: Palgrave Macmillan, 2001) 22–38.

Kesby, M., F. Gwanzura-Ottemoller and M. Chizororo. 'Theorising Other, Other Childhoods: Issues Emerging from Work on HIV in Urban and Rural Zimbabwe', *Children's Geographies* 4(2) (2006) 185–202.

King, Michael. 'The Sociology of Childhood as Scientific Communication: Observations from a Social Systems Perspective', *Childhood* 14(2) (May 2007).

Kingston, Jeffrey. 'Balancing Justice and Reconciliation in East Timor', *Critical Asian Studies* 38(3) (2006) 271–302.

Kirby, R. G., and A. E. Musson. *The Voices of the People: John Doherty, 1798–1854, Trade Unionist, Radical and Factory Reformer* (Manchester: Manchester University Press, 1975).

Kitzinger, Jenny. 'Who are you Kidding? Children, Power, and the Struggle Against Sexual Abuse', in Allison James and Alan Prout (eds.), *Constructing and Reconstructing Childhood: Contemporary Issues in the Sociological Study Of Childhood* (New York, NY: Routledge, 1997).

Kjørholt, A. T. *Childhood as a Social and Symbolic Space: Discourses on Children as Social Participants in Society* (Trondheim: Norwegian Centre for Child Research, 2004).

Klare, Michael. *Resource Wars: The New Landscape of Global Conflict* (New York, NY: Henry Holt and Company, 2002).

Koser, Khalid. 'Why Take the Risk? Explaining Migrant Smuggling', in Tariq Modood and John Salt (eds.), *Global Migration, Ethnicity and Britishness* (Basingstoke, Hampshire (UK): Palgrave Macmillan, 2011).

Kostelny, Kathleen and James Garbarino. 'Coping with the Consequences of Living in Danger: The Case of Palestinian Children and Youth', *International Journal of Behavioral Development* 17(4) (December 1994) 595–611.

Krishna, Sankaran. *Globalisation and Postcolonialism: Hegemony and Resistance in the Twenty-first Century* (Lanham, MD: Rowman and Littlefield, 2009).

Kumin, Judith. 'Orderly Departure from Vietnam: Cold War Anomaly or Humanitarian Innovation?', *Refugee Survey Quarterly* 27(1) (1 January 2008).

Kuper, Jenny. *International Law Concerning Child Civilians in Armed Conflict* (Oxford: Clarendon Press, 1997).

Lambourne, Wendy. 'Justice and Reconciliation: Postconflict Peacebuilding in Cambodia and Rwanda', in Mohammed Abu-Nimer (ed.), *Reconciliation, Justice and Coexistence: Theory and Practice* (Lanham, MD: Lexington Books, 2001) 311–37.

Lane, Sabra. 'Foreign Spending Boosted and Aid Money Capped for Onshore Asylum Costs', *AM*, ABC Radio National, 13 May 2013. Available at www.abc.net.au/news/2013–05–13/foreign-spending-boosted-and-aid-money-capped-for/4685104?section=business.

Leatherman, Janie L. *Sexual Violence and Armed Conflict* (Cambridge: Polity, 2011).

Lee, Ah-Jung. 'Understanding and Addressing the Phenomenon of 'Child Soldiers: The Gap between the Global Humanitarian Discourse and the Local Understandings and Experiences of Young People's Military Recruitment', Working paper 52, Refugee Studies Centre (January 2009). Available at www.rsc.ox.ac.uk/publications/working-papers-folder_contents/RSCworkingpaper52.pdf.

Lee Koo, Katrina. 'Security as Enslavement, Security as Emancipation: Gendered Legacies and Feminist Futures in the Asia-Pacific', in Anthony Burke and Matt McDonald (eds.), *Critical Security in the Asia-Pacific* (Manchester: Manchester University Press, 2007).

'Horror and Hope: (Re)presenting Militarised Children in Global North-South Relations', *Third World Quarterly* 32(4) (2011) 725–42.

'Not Suitable for Children: The Politicisation of Conflict-Affected Children in Post-2001 Afghanistan', *Australian Journal of International Affairs* 67(4) (August 2013) 475–90.

Levi, Primo (trans. Stuart Woolf). *If This is a Man and The Truce* (New York, NY: Abacus, 1988).

(trans. Raymond Rosenthal), *Other People's Trades* (London: Michael Joseph, 1989).

Levy, Allan. 'Children in Court', in Julie Fionda (ed.), *The Legal Concept of Childhood* (Oxford: Hart Publishing, 2001) 99–110.

Linton, Suzannah. 'Cambodia, East Timor and Sierra Leone: Experiments in International Justice', *Criminal Law Forum* 12(2001) 185–246.

Lundman, R. J. *Prevention and Control of Delinquency* (2nd edn) (New York, NY: Oxford University Press, 1993).

Lynn-Jones, Sean M. 'Realism and Security Studies', in Craig A. Snyder (ed.), *Contemporary Security and Strategy* (New York, NY: Palgrave, 2008).

M'Jid, Najat. 'The Situation of Unaccompanied Minors in Morocco', 10. Paper presented at the 'Migration of Unaccompanied Minors: Acting in the Best Interests of the Child' Conference, 27–28 October 2005. Available at www.coe.int/t/dg3/migration/archives/Source/Malaga RegConf/MG-RCONF_2005_3_Report_Morocco_en.pdf.

MacGinty, Roger. 'Hybrid Peace: The Interactions between Top-Down and Bottom-Up Peace', *Security Dialogue* 41(4) (2010) 391–412.

Machel, Graça. 'Impact of Armed Conflict on Children', Report of the expert of the Secretary-General, (1996). Available at www.unicef.org/graca.

Machel, Graça, 'The Impact of Armed Conflict on Children: A Critical Review of Progress Made and Obstacles Encountered in Increasing Protection for War-Affected Children', presented at The International Conference on War-affected Children Winnipeg, Canada (September 2000). Available at http://rsx23.justhost.com/~victimas/recursos_user/documentos/kb5736.pdf.

Mack, Andrew. 'Ending the Scourge of Child Soldiering: An indirect approach', in Scott Gates and Simon Reich (eds.), *Child Soldiers in the Age of Fractured States* (Pittsburgh, PA: University of Pittsburgh Press, 2010) 242–46.

Macmillan, Lorraine. 'The Child Soldier in North-South Relations', *International Political Sociology* 3(1) (2009) 36–52.

Malkki, Liisa H. 'Speechless Emissaries: Refugees, Humanitarianism and Dehistoricization', *Cultural Anthropology* 11(3) (1996), 383.

Manara Network for Child Rights. 'Mapping Child Protection Systems in Place for Palestinian Refugee Children in the Middle East', (August

2011), 21. Available at http://mena.savethechildren.se/pageFiles/2131/ Mapping%20Protection%20Systems%20August%202011.pdf.

Marchetti, Raffaele, and Nathalie Tocci. 'Conflict Society: Understanding the Role of Civil Society in Conflict', *Global Change, Peace and Security* 21(2) (2009) 201–17.

Marr, David. 'Truth Overboard – The Story That Won't Go Away', *The Sydney Morning Herald*, 28 February 2006. Available at www.smh.com. au/news/national/truth-overboard–the-story-that-wont-go-away/2006/02/27/1141020023654.html.

Mathews, Gordon. *Global Culture/Individual Identity: Searching for Home in the Cultural Supermarket* (New York, NY: Routledge, 2000).

Mathews, Jessica Tuchman. 'Redefining Security', *Foreign Affairs* 68(2) (Spring 1989) 162–77.

Mayall, Berry. *Towards a Sociology for Childhood* (1st edn) (Buckingham: Open University Press, 2002).

Mazurana, Dyan, and Khristopher Carlson. 'Reparations as a Means for Recognising and Addressing Crimes and Grave Rights Violations against Girls and Boys during Situations of Armed Conflict and Under Authoritarian and Dictatorial Regimes', in Ruth Rubio-Marín (ed.), *The Gender Reparations: Unsettling Sexual Hierarchies While Redressing Human Rights Violations* (New York, NY: Cambridge University Press, 2009) 162–214.

McClure, Maureen W., and Gonzalo Retamal. 'Wise Investments in Future Neighbours: Recruitment Deterrence, Human Agency, and Education', in Scott Gates and Simon Reich (eds.), *Child Soldiers in the Age of Fractured States* (Pittsburgh, PA: University of Pittsburgh Press, 2010) 223–41.

McEvoy-Levy, Siobhan. 'Youth as Social and Political Agents: Issues in post-Settlement Peace Building', Kroc Institute Occasional Paper 21, (December 2001).

'Youth, Violence and Conflict Transformation', *Peace Review: A Journal of Social Justice* 13(1)(2001) 89–96.

'Introduction: Youth and the Post-Accord Environment', in Siobhan McEvoy-Levy (ed.), *Trouble Makers or Peace Makers? Youth and post-Accord Peace Building* (Notre Dame, IN: University of Notre Dame Press, 2006) 1–26.

(ed.). *Trouble Makers or Peace Makers? Youth and post-Accord Peacebuilding* (Notre Dame, IN: University of Notre Dame Press, 2006).

McGlynn, Clare. 'Feminist Activism and Rape Law Reform in England and Wales: A Sisyphean Struggle?', in Clare McGlynn and Vanessa E. Munro (eds.), *Rethinking Rape Law: International and Comparative Perspectives* (New York, NY: Routledge, 2010) 139–53.

McGlynn, Clare, and Vanessa E. Munro (eds.). *Rethinking Rape Law: International and Comparative Perspectives* (New York, NY: Routledge, 2010).

McKay, Susan, and Dyan Mazurana. *Where Are the Girls? Girls in Fighting Forces in Northern Uganda, Sierra Leone and Mozambique: Their Lives During and After War* (Montreal: International Center for Human Rights and Democratic Development, 2004).

McMaster, Don. 'Asylum-seekers and the Insecurity of a Nation', *Australian Journal of International Affairs* 56(2) (July 2002), 279–90.

McNevin, Anne. 'The Liberal Paradox and the Politics of Asylum in Australia', *Australian Journal of Political Science* 42(4) (December 2007) 611–30.

'Ambivalence and Citizenship: Theorising the Political Claims of Irregular Migrants', *Millennium – Journal of International Studies* 41(2) (January 2013) 182–200.

Mearsheimer, John J. *The Tragedy of Great Power Politics* (New York, NY: Norton, 2001).

Medecins Sans Frontieres, 'The Crushing Burden of Rape: Sexual Violence in Darfur', March 2005. Available at www.doctorswithoutborders.org/publications/reports/2005/sudan03.pdf.

Mello, Patrick A. 'In Search of New Wars: The Debate about a Transformation of War', *European Journal of International Relations* 16(2) (2010) 297–309.

Menon, Ritu, and Kamla Bhasin. *Borders and Boundaries: Women in India's Partition.* (New Delhi: Kali for Women, 1998).

Merry, Sally Engle. 'Measuring the World: Indicators, Human Rights, and Global Governance', *Current Anthropology* 52 (3) (April 2011).

Messer, Ellen. 'Pluralist Approaches to Human Rights', *The Journal of Anthropological Research* 53(3) (1997) 293–317.

Michels, Ann. '"As If It Was Happening Again": Supporting Especially Vulnerable Witnesses, In Particular Women and Children, at the Special Court for Sierra Leone', in Karin Arts and Vesselin Popovski (eds.), *International Criminal Accountability and the Rights of Children* (The Hague: Hague Academic Press, 2006) 133–45.

Ministry of Justice, Afghanistan. International Juvenile Justice Observatory, 'Afghanistan: Child Justice Brief', (June, 2012). Available at www.ipjj.org/fileadmin/data/documents/reports_monitoring_evaluation/Justice Studio_AfghanistanChildJusticeBrief_2012_EN.pdf.

Mitchell, Neil. 'Above the Law in the Suburbs', *Herald Sun*, 4 October 2007. Available at www.heraldsun.com.au/news/above-the-law-in-the-suburbs/story-e6frfigo-1111114562102.

Montgomery, Nancy. 'Reports of Family Violence, Abuse, Within Military Rise', *Stars and Stripes*, 10 July 2011. Available at www.stripes.com/ reports-of-family-violence-abuse-within-military-rise-1.148815.

Morgenthau, Hans J. *Politics Among Nations: The Struggle for Peace and Power* (4th edn) (New York, NY: Alfred A Knopf, 1967).

Morris, Claire. 'Developing a Juvenile Justice System in Bosnia and Herzegovina: Rights, Diversion and Alternatives', *Youth Justice* 8(3) (2008) 197–213.

Motley, K. M. An Assessment of Juvenile Justice in Afghanistan, Report published by Terre des homes, 2010. Available at http://www.crin.org/ docs/Tdh_Juvenile_justice_web.pdf.

Mower, Alfred Glenn. *The Convention on the Rights of the Child: International Law Support for Children* (Westport, CT: Greenwood Publishing Group, 1997).

Myers-Verhage, Shelby. 'Postmarked from Amsterdam – Anne Frank and Her Iowa Pen Pal', in Harold Bloom (ed.),*The Diary of Anne Frank* (New York, NY: Infobase Publishing, 2010) 37–44.

Naftali, Orna. 'Recovering Childhood: Play, Pedagogy, and the Rise of Psychological Knowledge in Contemporary Urban China', *Modern China* 36(6) (2010) 589–617.

Nandy, Ashis. *The Intimate Enemy: Loss and Recovery of Self Under Colonialism* (Delhi: Oxford University Press, 1983).

National Coalition for Children as Zones of Peace and Child Protection. 'Coalition's Visions', 2012. Available at http://resourcecentre.savethe children.se/library/national-coalition-children-zones-peace-national-campaign-protect-children-armed-conflict.

Nazario, Sonia. *Enrique's Journey* (Melbourne: Scribe, 2006).

Nelson, Dean and Emal Khan. 'Taliban Underlines Its Growing Power With Killing of 'Dancing Girl' In Pakistan', *The Telegraph* (11 January 2009). Available at www.telegraph.co.uk/news/worldnews/asia/pakistan/421 7690/Taliban-underlines-its-growing-power-with-killing-of-dancing-girl-in-Pakistan.html.

Neufeld, Mark. 'Pitfalls of Emancipation and Discourses of Security: Reflections on Canada's "Security with a Human Face"', *International Relations* 18(1) (2004) 109–23.

Neumann, Klaus. 'The Politics of Compassion', *Inside Story*, 1 March 2012. Available at http://inside.org.au/the-politics-of-compassion/.

Newman, Edward. '"Liberal" Peace building Debates' in Edward Newman, Roland Paris and Oliver P. Richmond (eds.), *New Perspectives on Liberal Peacebuilding* (Tokyo: United Nations University Press, 2009) 26–53.

Newman, Edward, Roland Paris and Oliver P. Richmond. 'Introduction', in Edward Newman, Roland Paris and Oliver P. Richmond (eds.), *New Perspectives on Liberal Peacebuilding* (Tokyo: United Nations University Press, 2009) 3–25.

Nieuwenhuys, Olga. 'Keep Asking: Why Childhood? Why Children? Why Global?', *Childhood* 17 (3) (2010) 291–96.

Norrie, Ross. 'Two Jailed Over 'Brutal and Unprovoked' Killing of Sudanese Refugee Liepgony in Noble Park', *heraldsun.com.au*, 18 December 2009. Available at www.heraldsun.com.au/news/two-jailed-over-brutal-and-unprovoked-killing-of-sudanese-refugee-liep-gony-in-noble-park/story-e6frf7jo-1225811762854.

Nura, Taefi. 'The Synthesis of Age and Gender: Intersectionality, International Human Rights Law and the Marginalisation of the Girl-Child', *The International Journal of Children's Rights* 17(3) (2009) 345–76.

Nye, Joseph S. *Peace in Parts: Integration and Conflict in Regional Organization* (Boston, MA: Little Brown and Company, 1971).

'Obama and Chinese President Hu Jintao exchange toasts at state dinner'. *The Washington Post*, 19 January 2011. Available at http://blogs.wsj. com/chinarealtime/2011/01/20/hus-white-house-dinner-the-toasts/.

O'Kane, Claire, Clare Feinstein and Annette Giertsen. 'Children and Young People in Post-Conflict Peacebuilding', in David Nosworthy (ed.), *Seen, But Not Heard: Placing Children and Youth on the Security Governance Agenda* (New Brunswick, NJ: Transaction Publishers, 2009) 259–84.

O'Neill, Margot. *Blind Conscience* (Sydney: UNSW Press, 2009).

Office of the Special Representative of the Secretary-General for Children and Armed Conflict(OSRSG-CaAC). 'The Six Grave Violations Against Children During Armed Conflict: The Legal Foundation', Working Paper No. 1, October 2009. Available at www.un.org/children/con flict/english/legalfoundation.htm.

'Mission Report: Visit of the Special Representative for Children and Armed Conflict to Afghanistan', 20–26 February 2010, 10. Available at http://unama.unmissions.org/Portals/UNAMA/Publication/may22010_ PublicationSRSG_CAAC_Afghanistan_mission_report.pdf.

'Sexual Violence', 2013. Available at http://childrenandarmedconflict.un. org/effects-of-conflict/the-most-grave-violations/sexual-violence/.

'Protect Schools and Hospitals: Guidance Note on Security Council Resolution 1998' (New York: United Nations, May 2014). Available at https://childrenandarmedconflict.un.org/publications/AttacksonSchools Hospitals.pdf.

Otunnu, Olara, 'Protection of Children Affected by Armed Conflict', Report of the Special Representative of the Secretary–General for Children and

Armed Conflict, UNGA, Fifty-fifth session, agenda item 110, 3 (October 2000).

Olsen, Frances. 'Children's Rights: Some Feminist Approaches to the United Nations Convention on the Rights of the Child', in Philip Alston, Stephen Parker and John Seymour (eds.), *Children, Rights and the Law* (Oxford: Oxford University Press, 1992, reprinted 1995) 192–220.

Oviedo, Sheila. 'Jackie Chan takes on Timor's Karate Kids', *Asia Times*, 18 September 2008. Available at www.atimes.com/atimes/Southeast_Asia/JI18Ae01.html.

Ozdowski, Sev. 'An Absence of Human Rights: Children in Detention', Human Rights Law and Policy Conference, Melbourne, 17 June 2008. Available at www.uws.edu.au/equity_diversity/equity_and_diversity/tools_and_resources/speeches_-and-_articles_by_dr_sev_ozdowski/an_absence_of_human_rights_children_in_detention.

Özerdem, Alpaslan, and Sukanya Podder. 'How Voluntary? The Role of Community in Youth Participation in Muslim Mindanao', in Alpaslan Özerdem and Sukanya Podder (eds.), *Child Soldiers: From Recruitment to Reintegration* (Houndmills: Palgrave Macmillan, 2011) 3–28.

Palestinian Centre for Human Rights. Submission to the 62–63rd Session of the Committee on the Rights of the Child: Report of Israel under the Convention on the Rights of the Child, 15 July 2012. Available at www.bettercarenetwork.org/resources/infodetail.asp?id=29707.

Park, Augustine S. J. '"Other Inhumane Acts": Forced Marriage, Girl Soldiers and the Special Court for Sierra Leone', *Social and Legal Studies* 15(3) (2006) 315–37.

Partnerships for Protecting Children in Armed Conflict. 'The Monitoring and Reporting Mechanism on Grave Violations against Children in Armed Conflict in Nepal, 2005–2012: A Civil Society Perspective', September, 2012. Available at http://watchlist.org/wordpress/wp-content/uploads/PPCC-Nepal-MRM-Study-FINAL-16p.pdf.

Peoples, Columba. 'Security after Emancipation? Critical Theory, Violence and Resistance', *Review of International Studies* 37(3)(2011) 1113–35.

Peters, Krijn. 'Group Cohesion and Coercive Recruitment: Young Combatants and the Revolutionary United Front of Sierra Leone', in Alpaslan Özerdem and Sukanya Podder (eds.), *Child Soldiers: From Recruitment to Reintegration* (Houndmills: Palgrave Macmillan, 2011) 76–90.

Peterson, V. Spike, and Anne S. Runyan. *Global Gender Issues* (Boulder, CO: Westview Press, 1993).

Pettman, Jan Jindy. *Worlding Women* (St. Leonards: Allen and Unwin, 1996).

'The Philosophical Baby – Alison Gopnik'. *The Philosopher's Zone*, 29 January 2011. Available at www.abc.net.au/rn/philosopherszone/stories/2011/3121263.htm.

Physicians for Human Rights. 'The Use of Rape as a Weapon of War in Darfur, Sudan', October, 2004. Available at http://physiciansforhuman rights.org/library/reports/darfur-use-of-rape-as-weapon-2004.html.

Piaget, Jean (trans. Joan Tomlinson and Andrew Tomlinson). *The Child's Conception of the World* (London: Routledge & Kegan Paul, 1929).

    (trans. Marjorie Gabain). *The Language and Thought of the Child* (London: Routledge & Kegan Paul, 1932).

Pillay, Navanethem. 'Foreword', in Clare McGlynn and Vanessa E. Munro (eds.), *Rethinking Rape Law: International and Comparative Perspectives* (New York, NY: Routledge, 2011) xiv-xv.

Polanski, Roman. *Roman* (London: Heinemann, 1984).

Poretti, Michele. 'Preventing Children from Joining Armed Groups', *Refugee Survey Quarterly* 27(4) (2009) 123–41.

Poulatova, Chaditsa. *Children and Armed Conflict* (Newcastle: Cambridge Scholars Publishing, 2013).

Poullard, Alex. 'Press-ganged Children', in 'Democratic Republic of Congo: Past, Present, Future?', *Forced Migration Review* 36 (November 2010) 24–5.

Project Ploughshares. 'Defining Armed Conflict' (n.d.). Available at http://ploughshares.ca/programs/armed-conflict/defining-armed-conflict/.

Prout, Alan. 'Researching Children as Social Actors: An Introduction to the Children 5–16 Programme', *Children and Society* 16(2) (2002).

Prout, Alan, and Allison James. 'A New Paradigm for the Sociology of Childhood? Provenance, Promise and Problems', in Allison James and Alan Prout (eds.), *Constructing and Reconstructing Childhood: Contemporary Issues in the Sociological Study of Childhood* (2nd edn) (New York, NY: Routledge, 1997).

Pruitt, Lesley J. *Youth Peacebuilding: Music, Gender and Change* (New York, NY: SUNY Press, 2013).

Punamaki, Raija-Leena. 'Can Ideological Commitment Protect Children's Psychosocial Well-Being in Situations of Political Violence?', *Child Development* 67(1) (1996).

Pupavac, Vanessa. 'Misanthropy without Borders: The International Children's Rights Regime', *Disasters* 25(2) (2001).

    'The International Children's Rights Regime', in David Chandler (ed.), *Rethinking Human Rights: Critical Approaches to International Politics* (Basingstoke: Palgrave, 2002) 57–75.

Quan, Phung. *Tuoi Tho Duoi Doi (A Fierce Childhood)* (NXB Văn Học, 2011).

Qvortrup, Jens., Bardy Marjatta, Giovanni Sgritta and Helmet Wintersberger (eds.), *Childhood Matters: Social Theory, Practice and Politics* (Aldershot: Avebury, 1994).

Radačić, Ivana and Ksenija Turković. 'Rethinking Croatian Rape Laws: Force, Consent and the Contribution of the Victim', in Clare McGlynn and Vanessa E. Munro (eds.), *Rethinking Rape Law: International and Comparative Perspectives* (New York, NY: Routledge, 2010) 168–82.

Rakisits, Claude. 'Child Soldiers in the East of the Democratic Republic of Congo', *Refugee Survey Quarterly* 27 (4) (2009) 109–22.

Ramsbotham, Oliver, Tom Woodhouse and Hugh Miall. *Contemporary Conflict Resolution* (3rd edn) (London: Polity, 2011).

Reus-Smit, Christian. 'Constructivism', in Scott Burchill, Andrew Linklater, Richard Devetak, Jack Donnelly, Terry Nardin, Matthew Paterson, Christian Reus-Smit and Jacqui True (eds.), *Theories of International Relations* (4th edn) (Hampshire: Palgrave, 2009).

Reuters, 'Timorese Pray for Peace as Youth Gangs Rampage', *The Epoch Times*, 28 May 2006. Available at www.theepochtimes.com/news/6-5-28/42043.html.

Reynolds, Kimberley. 'Words about War for Boys: Representations of Soldiers and Conflict in Writing for Children before World War I', *Children's Literature Association Quarterly* 34(2) (2009), 255–71.

Richmond, Oliver P. 'Becoming Liberal, Unbecoming Liberalism: Liberal-Local Hybridity Via the Everyday as a Response to the Paradoxes of Liberal Peacebuilding', *Journal of Intervention and Statebuilding* 3(3) (2009) 324–44.

'A Post-liberal Peace: Eirenism and the Everyday', *Review of International Studies* 35(3) (2009) 557–8.

'Resistance and the post-Liberal Peace', *Millennium: Journal of International Studies* 38 (3) (2010) 665–92.

'Rival Youth Gangs Clash in East Timor', ABC Radio Australia, 16 November 2006. Available at www.radioaustralia.net.au/international/2006-11-16/rival-youth-gangs-clash-in-east-timor/730128.

Rosen, David M. *Armies of the Young: Child Soldiers in War and Terrorism* (New Brunswick, NJ: Rutgers University Press, 2005).

'Child Soldiers, International Humanitarian Law, and the Globalization of Childhood', *American Anthropologist* 109(2) (June 2007).

Rosen, Sarah Maya and David M. Rosen. 'Representing Child Soldiers in Fiction and Film', *Peace Review* 24 (2012) 305–12.

Rotberg, Robert I. and Dennis Thompson (eds.). *Truth v. justice: The Morality of Truth Commissions*, (Princeton, NJ: Princeton University Press, 2000).

Rousseau, Jean-Jacques (trans. Donald A. Cress). *Basic Political Writings* (Indianapolis, IN: Hackett, 1987).

Rush, Emma, and Andrea La Nauze. 'Corporate Paedophilia Sexualisation of Children in Australia', *The Australia Institute*, Discussion Paper 90 (October 2006).

Samaddar, Ranabir, and Helmut Reifeld (eds.). *Peace as Process: Reconciliation and Conflict Resolution in South Asia* (New Delhi: Manohar, 2001).

Save the Children. 'Child Soldiers: Care and Protection of Children in Emergencies: A field guide' (2001). Available at http://resourcecentre.savethechildren.se/library/child-soldiers-care-protection-children-emergencies-field-guide.pdf.

——— 'Adult's War and Young Generation's Peace: Children's Participation in Armed Conflict, Post Conflict and *Peacebuilding*' (2008). Available at http://resourcecentre.savethechildren.se/library/global-report-adults-war-and-young-generations-peace-childrens-participation-armed-conflict.

——— 'No One to Turn To: The Under-reporting of Child Sexual Exploitation and Abuse by Aid Workers and Peacekeepers' (2008). Available at www.un.org/en/pseataskforce/docs/no_one_to_turn_under_reporting_of_child_sea_by_aid_workers.pdf.

——— 'Childhood Under Fire: The Impact of Two Years Conflict in Syria' (2013). Available at www.savethechildren.org.uk/resources/online-library/childhood-under-fire.

Schabas, William A. 'The Rights of the Child, Law of Armed Conflict and Customary International Law: A Tale of Two Cases', in Karin Arts and Vesselin Popovski (eds.), *International Criminal Accountability and the Rights of Children* (The Hague: Hague Academic Press, 2006) 19–35.

Schaller, Dominik K. 'Raphael Lemkin's View of European Colonial Rule in Africa: Between Condemnation and Admiration', *Journal of Genocide Research* 7(4) (2005) 531–8.

Schapiro, Tamar. 'What is a Child?', *Ethics* 109(4) (July 1999).

Scheper-Hughes, Nancy. *Child Survival: Anthropological Perspectives on the Treatment and Maltreatment of Children* (Dordrecht: D. Reidel, 1987).

Schmitt, Carl. *The Concept of the Political* (Chicago, IL: University of Chicago Press, 1996).

Schwartz, Stephanie. *Youth in Post-Conflict Reconstruction: Agents of Change* (Washington, DC: United States Institute of Peace Press, 2010).

Scott, James C. *Domination and the Arts of Resistance: Hidden Transcripts* (New Haven, CT: Yale University Press, 1990).

Seth, Sanjay (ed.). *Postcolonial Theory and International Relations: A Critical Introduction* (London: Routledge, 2013).

Seto, Donna. *No Place for a War Baby: The Global Politics of Children Born of Wartime Sexual Violence* (London: Ashgate, 2013).

Shandy, Dianna J. 'Irish Babies, African Mothers: Rites of Passage and Rights in Citizenship in Post-Millennial Ireland', *Anthropological Quarterly* 81(4) (October 2008) 803–31.

Shepler, Susan. 'Conflicted Childhoods: Fighting Over Child Soldiers in Sierra Leone', Thesis (Ph.D.), (Department of Social and Cultural Studies in Education, University of California Berkeley, 2005).

'The Rites of the Child: Global Discourses of Youth and Reintegrating Child Soldiers in Sierra Leone', *Journal of Human Rights* 4(2005) 197–211.

Sharkey, Donna. 'Picture the Child Soldier', *Peace Review* 24 (2012) 262–7.

Shaw, Rosalind. 'Rethinking Truth and Reconciliation Commissions: Lessons from Sierra Leone', Special Report 130 (Washington, DC: United States Institute of Peace (USIP), 2005).

'Memory Frictions: Localizing the Truth and Reconciliation Commission in Sierra Leone', *The International Journal of Transitional Justice* 1 (2007) 183–207.

Shriver, Lionel. *We Need to Talk About Kevin* (Melbourne: Text Publishing, 2003).

Singer, Peter W. *Children at War* (Berkeley, CA: University of California Press, 2006).

'The Enablers of War: Causal Factors Behind the Child Soldier Phenomenon', in Scott Gates and Simon Reich (eds.), *Child Soldiers in the Age of Fractured States* (Pittsburgh, PA: University of Pittsburgh Press, 2010) 93–107.

Skenazy, Lenore. 'Why I Let My 9-Year-Old Ride the Subway Alone', *The New York Sun*, 1 April 2008. Available at www.nysun.com/opinion/why-i-let-my-9-year-old-ride-the-subway-alone/73976/.

Free-Range Kids: Giving our Children the Freedom We Had Without Going Nuts With Worry (San Francisco, CA: Jossey-Bass, 2009).

Smith, Alison. 'Basic Assumptions of Transitional Justice and Children', in Sharanjeet Parmar, Mindy Jane Roseman, Saudamini Siegrist and Theo Sowa (eds.), *Children and Transitional Justice: Truth-Telling, Accountability and Reconciliation* (Cambridge, MA: Harvard University Press, 2010) 31–65.

'Speaking the Language of Exile: Dissidence in International Studies', *International Studies Quarterly* 34(3) (Special Edition, September 1990).

Sporton, Deborah, Gill Valentine and Katrine Bang Nielsen. 'Post-Conflict Identities: Affiliations and Practices of Somali Asylum Seeker Children', *Children's Geographies* 4(2) (2006) 203–17.

Stargardt, Nicholas. *Witnesses of War: Children's Lives under the Nazis* (New York, NY: Alfred A. Knopf, 2006).

Stephens, Sharon (ed.). *Children and the Politics of Culture* (Princeton, NJ: Princeton University Press, 1995).

Stohl, Rachel. 'Targeting Children: Small Arms and Children in Conflict', *The Brown Journal of World Affairs* 4(1) (2002) 281–92.

Streib, Victor. 'The Juvenile Death Penalty Today: Death Sentences and Executions for Juvenile Crimes, January 1, 1973–February 28, 2005'. Periodic Report on Death Penalty Information (2005). Available at www.deathpenaltyinfo.org/juveniles-and-death-penalty.

'Study: Gulf War Vets' Children Have Higher Birth Defect Rates'. *USA Today*, 3 June 2003. Available at www.usatoday.com/news/health/2003-06-03-vets-birth-defects_x.htm.

Taylor, Rob. 'Timor Gangs Promise Mayhem on East Timor's Streets', *Reuters*, 6 March 2007. Available at www.reuters.com/article/2007/03/06/us-timor-australia-gangs-idUSSYD9080920070306.

Teeple, Gary. *The Riddle of Human Rights* (Toronto: University of Toronto Press, 2004).

Thang, Pham. *Doi Tinh Bao Thieu Nien (The Youth Intelligence Squad)*, (2nd edn)(Hanoi: So Van Hoa, 1972).

Thompson, Geoff. 'Asylum Seekers Issue Personal Plea to PM' *AM, ABC Radio National*, 15 October 2009. Available at www.abc.net.au/am/content/2009/s2714594.htm.

Tickner, J. Ann. *Gender in International Relations: Feminist Perspectives on Achieving Global Security* (New York, NY: Columbia University Press, 1992).

Tillett, Andrew. 'Asylum Seekers "Lie About Age"', *The West Australian*, 7 January 2011. Available at http://au.news.yahoo.com/thewest/a/-/break ing/8607237/asylum-seekers-lie-about-age/.

Twining, William. *Human Rights, Southern Voices*, (Cambridge: Cambridge University Press, 2009).

Uehling, Greta Lynn. 'The International Smuggling of Children: Coyotes, Snakeheads, and the Politics of Compassion', *Anthropological Quarterly* 81(4) (October 2008) 833–71.

UNAMA. 'Understanding and Combating Arbitrary Detention Practices in Afghanistan: A Call for Action, Vol. II'. Report published by the United Nations Assistance Mission in Afghanistan (UNAMA), Human Rights, Kabul (2009). Available at www.unama.unmissions.org/Default.aspx?ctl=Details&tabid=12254&mid=15756&ItemID=31488.

'Afghanistan Mid-Year Report 2010 Protection of Civilians in Armed Conflict' UN Kabul, 2010. Available at http://unama.unmissions.org/Portals/UNAMA/Publication/August102010_MID-YEAR%20REPORT%202010_Protection%20of%20Civilians%20in%20Armed%20Conflict.pdf.

'Treatment of Conflict-Related Detainees in Afghan Custody' (Kabul: UN OHCHR, October 2011).

'Afghanistan Annual Report: Protection of Civilians in Armed Conflict', UN Kabul (2013), 54. Available at http://unama.unmissions.org/Por tals/UNAMA/human%20rights/Feb_8_2014_PoC-report_2013-Full-report-ENG.pdf.

UNESCO. 'What Do We Mean by Youth?'. Available at www.unesco.org/ new/en/social-and-human-sciences/themes/youth/youth-definition/.

UNHCR. 'Global Trends 2012: Displacement: The New 21st Century Global Challenge'. Available at http://unhcr.org/globaltrendsjune2013/. 'Global Trends 2013: War's Human Cost'. Available at http://unhcr.org/ trends2013/.

UNICEF. Cape Town Principles and Best Practices, April 1997, adopted at the Symposium of Recruitment of Children into the Armed Forces and on Demobilisation and Social Reintegration of Child Soldiers in Africa. Available at www.unicef.org/emergencies/files/Cape_Town_ Principles(1).pdf.

'The Prosecutor against Sam Hinga Norman. Amicus Curiae of the United Nations Children's Fund (UNICEF)', 21 January 2004. Available at www.refworld.org/docid/49aba9462.html.

'The Paris Principles: Principles and Guidelines on Children Associated with Armed Forces or Armed Groups' (February 2007). Available at www.unicef.org/emergencies/files/ParisPrinciples310107English.pdf.

Machel Study 10-year Strategic Review: Children and Conflict in a Changing World: (New York, NY: UNICEF, 2009). Available at www.unicef.org/publications/files/Machel_Study_10_Year_Strategic_ Review_EN_030909.pdf (accessed 23 August 2014).

'Conflict Creating Unprecedented Threats to Children's Lives' (12 June 2011). Available at www.unicef.org/media/media_69614.html.

UNICEF Innocenti Research Centre. 'Children and Truth Commissions' (2010). Available at www.unicef-irc.org/publications/pdf/truth_ commissions_eng.pdf.

United Nations. 'Fact Sheet on Youth and Juvenile Justice' (n.d.). Available at www.un.org/esa/socdev/unyin/documents/wyr11/FactSheetonYouth andJuvenileJustice.pdf.

United Nations Standard Minimum Rules for the Administration of Juvenile Justice ("The Beijing Rules"), 29 November 1985, A/RES/ 40/33. Available from http://www2.ohchr.org/english/law/pdf/beijin grules.pdf.

'Millennium Development Goals', 2000. Available at www.un.org/millen niumgoals/education.shtml.

'Building a Culture of Peace for the Children of the World', 2001. Available at www.un.org/events/UNART/panel_culture_of_peace04.pdf.

The Millennium Development Goals Report, 2010. Available at www.un. org/millenniumgoals/pdf/MDG%20Report%202010%20En%20r15 %20-low%20res%2020100615%20-.pdf#page=18.

UN Peacebuilding Commission. 'Mandate of the Peacebuilding Commission' (n.d.). Available at www.un.org/en/peacebuilding/mandate.shtml.

'UN Peacebuilding: an Orientation', September 2010, 49. Available at www.un.org/en/peacebuilding/pbso/pdf/peacebuilding_orientation.pdf.

UN Security Council. 'Rule of Law and Transitional Justice in Conflict and Post-Conflict Societies', Report of the Secretary-General, UN Doc S/2004/616, 23(2)(August 2004).

'Report of the Secretary-General on Children and Armed Conflict in the Sudan', Document No. S/2007/520, 29 August 2007.

'Report of the Secretary-General on Children and Armed Conflict in the Democratic Republic of the Congo', Document No. S/2010/369, 9 July 2010.

'Report of the Secretary-General on Children and Armed Conflict in Somalia', Document No. S/2010/577, 9 November 2010.

'Report of the Secretary-General on children and armed conflict in Afghanistan', Document No. S/2011/55, 3 February 2011.

Urdal, Henrik. 'The Devil in the Demographics: The Effect of Youth Bulges on Domestic Armed Conflict, 1950–2000', Social Development Papers: Conflict Prevention and Reconstruction, The World Bank, Paper No. 14, July 2004. Available at www-wds.worldbank.org/servlet/WDSCon tentServer/WDSP/IB/2004/07/28/000012009_20040728162225/Rend ered/PDF/29740.pdf.

Utas, Mats. 'West-African Warscapes: Victimcy, Girlfriending, Soldiering: Tactic Agency in a Young Woman's Social Navigation of the Liberian War Zone', *Anthropological Quarterly* 78(2) (Spring 2005) 403–30.

'Victimcy as Social Navigation: From the Toolbox of Liberian Child Soldiers', in Alpaslan Özerdem and Sukanya Podder (eds.), *Child Soldiers: From Recruitment to Reintegration* (Houndmills: Palgrave Macmillan, 2011) 213–28.

Vanderbeck, Robert M. 'Reaching Critical Mass? Theory, Politics, and the Culture of Debate in Children's Geographies', *Area* 40(3) (2008).

van Bueren, Geraldine. *The International Law on the Rights of the Child* (The Hague: Martinus Nijhoff Publishers, 1998).

Van Emden, Richard. *Boy Soldiers of the Great War* (London: Headline Book Publishing, 2005).

van Klinken, Helene. *Making them Indonesians: Child Transfers out of East Timor* (Clayton: Monash University Publishing, 2012).

van Krieken, Peter. 'Rwanda: Children in Conflict with the Law', Report published by UNICEF Rwanda (2000).

Vautravers, Alexandre J. 'Why Child Soldiers Are Such a Complex Issue', *Refugee Survey Quarterly* 27(4) (2009) 96–107.

Velicaria, Aimyleen, and Maria Cecil Laguardia. 'Building Bridges of Peace for Mindanao: A Role for Children', in World Vision, *Children and Peacebuilding: Experiences and Perspectives, September 2012* (London: World Vision, 2012).

Vittachi, Virandra Tarzie. *Between the Guns – Children as a Zone of Peace* (London: Hodder and Stoughton, 1993).

Wagnsson, Charlotte, Maria Hellman and Arita Holmberg. 'The Centrality of Non-traditional Groups for Security in the Globalized Era: The Case of Children', *International Political Sociology* 4(1) (2010) 1–14.

Wallensteen, Peter and Margareta Sollenberg. 'Armed Conflict 1989–2000', *Journal of Peace Research* 38(5) (2003) 629–44.

Walsh, Annelotte. 'International Criminal Justice and the Girl Child', in Lisa Yarwood (ed.), *Women and Transitional Justice: The Experience of Women as Participants* (London: Routledge, 2013) 54–74.

Waltz, Kenneth. *Man, the State and War* (New York, NY: Columbia University Press, 1954).

Theory of International Politics (New York, NY: McGraw Hill, 1979).

Ward, Lee. *John Locke and Modern Life* (Cambridge: Cambridge University Press, 2010).

Watchlist on Children and Armed Conflict. 'Setting the Right Priorities: Protecting Children Affected by Armed Conflict in Afghanistan', June 2001.

'Colombia's War on Children', February 2004, 20. Downloaded from Watchlist on Children and Armed Conflict, 'No More Denial: Children Affected by Armed Conflict in Myanmar (Burma)', May 2009. Available at www.watchlist.org/reports/pdf/myanmar/myanmar_english_full.pdf.

'Sudan's Children at a Crossroads: An Urgent Need for Protection', April 2007. Available at www.watchlist.org/reports/pdf/sudan_07_final.pdf.

Watkins, John. *The Juvenile Justice Century: A Sociological Commentary on American Juvenile Courts* (Durham, NC: Carolina Academic, 1998).

Watson, Alison. 'Children and International Relations: A New Site of Knowledge?', *Review of International Studies* 32(2) (2006) 237–50.

'Can There Be a "Kindered" Peace?', *Ethics and International Affairs* 22(1) (2008) 35–42.

'Children's Rights and the Politics of Childhood', in Patrick Hayden (ed.), *The Ashgate Research Companion to Ethics and International Relations* (Farnham: Ashgate, 2009).

Watters, Charles. *Refugee Children: Towards the Next Horizon* (New York, NY: Routledge, 2000).

Webster, Timothy. 'Babes with Arms: International Law and Child Soldiers', *The George Washington International Law Review* 39(2) (2007) 227–54.

Weinstein, Jeremy M. 'Resources and the Information Problem in Rebel Recruitment', *Journal of Conflict Resolution* 49(4) (2005) 598–624.

Weissbrodt, David, Joseph C. Hansen and Nathaniel H. Nesbitt. 'The Role of the Committee on the Rights of the Child in Interpreting and Developing International Humanitarian Law', *Harvard Human Rights Journal* 24 (1) (2011) 115–53.

Wells, Karen. *Childhood in a Global Perspective* (Cambridge: Polity, 2009). 'The Politics of Life: Governing Childhood', *Global Studies of Childhood* 1 (1) (2011) 15–25.

Wessells, Michael. 'Children, Armed Conflict, and Peace', *Journal of Peace Research* 35(5) (1998) 635–46.

Child Soldiers: From Violence to Protection (Cambridge, MA: Harvard University Press, 2006).

Whitmont, Debbie. 'The Inside Story', *4 Corners*, 13 August 2001. Available at www.abc.net.au/4corners/stories/2011/08/08/3288532.htm.

Whitmont, Debbie, and Janine Cohen. 'No Advantage', *4Corners*, 29 April 2013. Available at www.abc.net.au/4corners/stories/2013/04/29/3745 276.htm.

Wilson, Janet. *One Peace: True Stories of Young Activists* (Victoria: Orca Book Publishers, 2008).

Wolf, Diana L. *Beyond Anne Frank: Hidden Children and Postwar Families in Holland* (Berkeley, CA: University of California Press, 2007).

Woodside, Alexander B. *Community and Revolution in Modern Vietnam* (Boston, MA: Houghton Mifflin Company, 1976).

World Bank. 'Data: Population Ages 0–14 (% of total)' (n.d.). Available at http://data.worldbank.org/indicator/SP.POP.0014.TO.ZS.

'Crisis Impact: Fragile and Conflict-affected Countries Face Greater Risks', 2 October 2009. Available at http://web.worldbank.org/WBSITE/EXTER NAL/NEWS/0,contentMDK:22337380~pagePK:64257043~piP K:437376~theSitePK:4607,00.html.

World Vision. 'Children and Peacebuilding: Experiences and Perspectives', September 2012 (London: World Vision, 2012).

'Untying the Knot: Exploring Early Marriage in Fragile States', March 2013. Available at www.worldvision.org/resources.nsf/main/press-reports/$file/Untying-the-Knot_report.

Wright, Anne. 'Asylum Seekers Pretending To Be Teenagers for Faster Processing', *The Herald Sun*, 16 May 2011. Available at

www.heraldsun.com.au/news/asylum-seekers-pretending-to-be-teen
agers-for-faster-processing/story-e6frf7jo-1226056354628.

Wyness, Michael, Lisa Harrison and Ian Buchanan. 'Childhood, Politics and
Ambiguity: Towards an Agenda for Children's Political Inclusion',
Sociology 38(1) (2004).

Xanthaki, Alexandra. *Indigenous Rights and United Nations Standards:
Self-Determination, Culture and Land* (Cambridge: Cambridge
University Press, 2004).

Yew, Lee Kuan. 'Warning Bell for Developed Countries: Declining Birth
Rates', *Forbes.com*, 16 October 2012. Available at www.forbes.com/
sites/currentevents/2012/10/16/warning-bell-for-developed-countries-
declining-birth-rates/.

York, Geoffrey, and Hayley Mick. '"Last Ghost" of the Vietnam War', *The
Global and Mail*, 31 March 2009.

Yousafzai, Malala. '"Saturday 03 January: I am Afraid" – Diary of a Pakistani
Girl', *BBC News*, 19 January 2009. Available at http://news.bbc.co.uk/2/
hi/south_asia/7834402.stm.

Zandvliet, Luc and Orion Kriegman. 'Reflecting on Peace Practice Project',
Report (Life and Peace Institute, Uppsala, 2001).

Zerrougui, Leila. 'Syria Has Become One of the Most Dangerous Places to be
a Child', OSRSG-CaAC (12 March 2014). Available at http://children
andarmedconflict.un.org/statement/syria-has-become-one-of-the-most-
dangerous-places-to-be-a-child/.

Zusak, Marcus. *The Book Thief* (New York, NY: Alfred A. Knopf Books,
2006).

Index

abduction, 21, 27, 33, 49, 71, 207, 274–275, 276
abilities, 14, 15, 20–21, 30, 40–41, 58, 62, 197, 206
abuse, 18, 27, 29, 32, 82, 85, 239, 241, 250
  domestic, 30, 234
  sexual, 235
accountability, 76, 214, 226, 227, 255
Achak Deng, Valentino, 124
Achilihu, S. N., 98
active participation, 115, 209
activism, 7, 51, 102, 185, 187, 249–252, 255, 278–279
  children as activists, 268–272
  political, 22, 71
actors, 62, 65, 85, 88, 91, 192, 250, 252, 254–255
  local, 192–194
  non-state, 70, 130, 256
  non-traditional, 81–82, 169
  social, 36, 56, 202, 271
  strategic, 57
Additional Protocols, 27, 112, 113, 130
adolescents, 13, 133, 213, 280
adoption, 112, 113, 249, 273, 277
adult asylum seekers, 175
adult worlds, 46, 49, 69
adulthood, 10–14, 35, 37, 44–45, 50, 134, 150, 155
adults, 2, 14–15, 37–38, 40–42, 46–52, 55–57, 202–204, 216–217, 264–265
  young, 215, 217, 270
advocacy, 2, 7, 189, 195, 249–250, 255, 258, 262, 277–279
  movements, 254
  networks, 102, 279

strategies, 114, 254, 258, 262, 267–268, 278
transformative politics of, 255–268
Afghan children, 78, 85
Afghanistan, 23–25, 76, 78–79, 85, 161, 192, 195, 199, 221–223
  government, 75, 258
  ISAF (International Security Assistance Forces), 23
Afghans, 159, 161, 166
Africa, 13, 28, 100, 103, 136, 159, 232, 239, 280
  sub-Saharan, 45, 127
  West, 111, 196
African Charter on the Rights and Welfare of the Child, 119, 228
African Youth Charter, 13
Agamben, G., 160, 162–164, 176, 178, 183
age, 10–16, 45–46, 112, 115–118, 154–155, 196–197, 215, 219–225, 228–230
age, minimum, 100, 118–119, 130, 226
Age of Forced Migration, 160–172
  and children, 165–172
agency, 39–40, 42–43, 49, 60–61, 86, 182, 187, 201–202, 263
  of children, 33, 175
  political, 182, 196, 209, 227
  rights, 42, 52
  tactical, 61, 64
agenda, realist, 72–73
agents, 3, 29, 50, 73, 82, 88, 131
  of peace, 195, 201
aggression, 20, 244
Alternative Places of Detention (APODs), 184
aluminum, 260
ambivalence, 159, 165, 184